State Tax Liability and Compliance Manual

State Tax Liability and Compliance Manual

LLOYD S. HALE

RUTH KRAMER

A RONALD PRESS PUBLICATION

JOHN WILEY & SONS　　New York　·　Chichester　·　Brisbane　·　Toronto

Library of Congress Cataloging in Publication Data:

Hale, Lloyd S. 1931-
  State tax liability and compliance manual.

  "A Ronald Press publication."
  Includes index.
    1. Corporations;—Taxation;—United States;—
States. 2. Taxation, State. I. Kramer, Ruth,
1954-   joint author. II. Title.

KF6755.H34   343.7306'7   80-21616
ISBN 0-471-08488-3

Printed in the United States of America

10 9 8 7 6 5 4 3 2 1

FOR TOBY

Preface

The State Tax Liability and Compliance Manual was compiled to provide an overview to state taxation necessary for the minimization and/or avoidance as well as the compliance with the state tax structures facing the interstate taxpayer. This overview is essential for those who need a quick indoctrination into state taxation and will be useful to the more experienced tax person. A detailed analysis of a specific tax or of the tax structure of a particular state was not attempted, this being far beyond the scope of the book and also because such detailed analyses are presently published by Commerce Clearing House and Prentice-Hall.

The book is organized by type of tax, covering the following classes:

Income based.
Capital based.
Sales and use.
Gross receipts.
Value added.

There is also a chapter dealing with the Multistate Tax Compact which is designed to reveal the impact that this organization has on state taxation.

Each type of tax is, if appropriate, first observed from a jurisdictional viewpoint, since jurisdiction is the threshold issue for any taxpayer. Jurisdiction is the determinant factor about whether a tax or collection of a tax is necessary. A thorough understanding of the principles will provide the input for a decision on compliance or of avoidance: the former accepting jurisdiction and the latter denying it to the state through the planning of methods of doing business. The jurisdictional question is approached primarily by an examination of the leading U.S. Supreme Court decisions. The law in this area is principally case law, since the defenses of interstate taxpayers against state attempts to impose tax burdens are the Due Process and Commerce clauses of the U.S. Constitution.

Computational matters have been avoided in the book, because once the tax concepts are understood, the mathematical process is basic. Thus it was felt that examples of returns and computations of tax liabilities would be unnecessary. This is not to say that the preparation and filing of returns is not a difficult and time-consuming chore. The proper computation of tax liabilities is a very important function and should receive complete professional attention. In practice, the variety of forms, instructions, and computational methods is astounding, even with a lengthy trend toward uniformity. This, coupled with forms that are in many cases poorly designed and contain minimum instructions, easily enables the inexperienced preparer to be distracted.

The exception to the lack of computational processes is the exercise dealing with combined reporting. Since this is a relatively new approach to computing a state tax liability and because the technique is being adopted by a growing number of states, it was felt that the method ought to be illustrated in some depth. It was also important in order to emphasize that the concept is applicable to each taxpayer.

In some instances it was necessary to repeat some of the material. This duplication will be recognized when the book is read in its entirety. The purpose of this duplication is to insure that the pertinent material will be seen by a reader who is interested in only a particular chapter.

State taxation has become increasingly important to the multistate company for two basic reasons. First, the natural growth of a business brings it increasingly into the grasp of additional states, thereby multiplying state tax compliance problems and tax costs. Second, the states have successfully brought the interstate company into their jurisdiction through favorable court decisions. In the past 25 to 30 years the interstate company has moved from somewhat of a "free trade" atmosphere of doing business to a very restrictive "pay your way" philosophy. Avoidance of state jurisdiction is presently a difficult maneuver that must be carefully planned in the light of Federal law to be successful. Further, whereas each state previously was concerned with its own tax administration, presently, the impact of the Multistate Tax Compact is apparent. The 19 members and 13 associate members of this organization provide a forum for exchange of information that did not previously exist.

Tax practitioners, employees of taxpayers engaged in interstate as well as intrastate enterprises, state tax administrators, and students of taxation all have a need for a sound background in state taxation. Although the main emphasis in the field of corporate taxation is the Federal income tax, there are compelling reasons why the importance of state taxation should be recognized.

1   The state tax cost may be of great significance for many companies, perhaps more than the Federal income tax. For example, in a particular

year, some taxpayers may incur no Federal income tax liability, whereas significant state taxes that have no relation to income may continue. As a further example, exposure to back liabilities for state taxes where the taxpayer has failed in its compliance requirements may be very substantial. This could occur through nonrecognition of the duty to collect sales tax or nonrecognition of the duty to pay income tax.

2 Normally, the tax function within an enterprise encompasses Federal and state taxation. Familiarity with Federal taxation is paramount, but proficiency in state tax problems facing the enterprise must also be attained if professional tax management is to be achieved. The clients of practitioners and the management of an enterprise both expect that they will have state as well as Federal taxes handled in a professional manner. Failure to give proper advice on state tax matters would be a serious oversight.

3 If not now confronted with sizable state tax problems, the importance of state taxes should be thoroughly understood to permit complete planning for the future. It can be expected that state taxation will become increasingly significant.

The *State Tax Liability and Compliance Manual* provides a thorough understanding of state taxes through detailed information concerning the underlying concepts and the manner in which state tax liabilities are incurred. The book does not include "local" taxes, that is, taxes imposed by counties, municipalities, and other taxing jurisdictions. These taxes, while extremely significant, consist primarily of ad valorem taxes and are beyond the scope of this book. Also, only state tax impact on corporate taxpayers is considered, primarily because this is the type of enterprise that will be facing interstate taxing jurisdictions.

The major difficulty in undertaking the task of compiling a book dealing with state taxation is determining the proper cutoff regarding the depth of the material to be presented. Too great a depth into specific areas would result in a cumbersome mass with limited usefulness. Thus it was concluded that a compromise was necessary concerning the volume of material. It was intended that this reference book encompass all the general needs of the interstate taxpayer. As such it should provide the basic tools for experienced state tax personnel and also reveal a basic understanding of state tax concepts to the individuals just becoming familiar with the field.

LLOYD S. HALE
RUTH KRAMER

Chicago, Illinois
October 1980

Contents

CHAPTER 4

THE MULTISTATE COMPACT

CHAPTER 6

MICHIGAN SINGLE BUSINESS TAX (VALUE ADDED)

CHAPTER 8

GROSS RECEIPTS TAXES

CHAPTER ONE

Jurisdiction—Taxes Based on Income

JURISDICTION IN GENERAL

Taxes imposed by state governments must be within the framework of Federal statutes and the U.S. Constitution. The enterprise engaged in interstate activities should be very much concerned with this protection. If, under the Constitution, or Federal statute, certain activities do not subject the enterprise to state tax, then the amount, computation, and other compliance problems that would arise are not relevant. As an example, assume a seller must ship all of his merchandise through Iowa, Illinois, and Indiana from his place of business in Nebraska in order to make delivery to his customer in Ohio. This movement in interstate commerce of this seller's product would not create a state tax liability to those states. Therefore, the income taxes of Iowa, Illinois, and Indiana are of no concern to this seller once this fact is recognized.

While the preceding example was easily recognizable as an interstate activity, not all situations are so easily determinable. As the contact with a state increases, the determination of when exemption exists and when it doesn't becomes more complex. Initially, a seller gains customers in another state and makes deliveries to those customers. This in-state activity may eventually be expanded to include one or more of (1) sales solicitation by employees, (2) customer product service, (3) creation of a sales office, (4) establishment of a stock of goods, or (5) the establishment of a complete place of business. As the seller moves along a continuum from strictly interstate activity to a complete business establishment, state income taxes will come into play. Further, as brought out subsequently in this chapter, the seller does not have to move very far along this continuum before it is certain that the jurisdictional boundary has been crossed.

TERMS COMMON TO STATE TAXATION

Before going into a discussion of jurisdictional standards, certain definitions of terms used in this chapter and throughout the book are useful.

1

Incorporation

Incorporation refers to the initial creation of the legal entity. Incorporation is accomplished by making application under the corporate law of the particular state. Having met all legal requirements and having paid initial fees to the state, a taxpayer is granted its "charter." The *charter* is a document issued by the state recognizing a taxpayer as a legal entity and authorizing it to engage in the business activity specified in its corporate application. The taxpayer thus can carry out its functions, subject to state corporation law.

Domestic and Foreign Corporations

Assume that a taxpayer has thus obtained a charter in the state of Delaware. This company is a "domestic corporation" from the viewpoint of Delaware. To all other states, it is a "foreign corporation." The term "foreign corporation" identifies those corporations that may (or may not) have legal existence in-state but have received a charter from another state. The terms domestic corporation and foreign corporation are routinely referred to in state income tax statutes and state tax cases.

Qualification

Closely related to incorporation is the term "qualification" or sometimes referred to as "authority to do business." Qualification also provides legal recognition of the corporate entity. Qualification permits a corporation to engage in business activity in several states as the same corporate entity, thus obviating the need to obtain a corporate charter in each state. Qualification is accomplished by filing a legal request with the state and paying all initial fees. The state, if all requirements are met, will then issue a "certificate of authority." The certificate of authority is similar to the charter received in the state of incorporation. Both grant the corporation certain legal rights within the state. Both impose legal obligations on the part of the recipient. As interstate taxpayer will be incorporated in one state and will be qualified in others, or perhaps all, of the remaining states.

Doing Business

The term *doing business* refers to activities sufficient to require qualification. The formal act of qualification is not strictly at the option of the corporation. The state will require qualification if business activity is at a level sufficient to trigger the law of that state. In practice, the term "doing business" describes a state where qualification has been accomplished. For example, a taxpayer is "doing business" (qualified) in Illinois but not Iowa. The term is also used to describe the level of business activity in a state where the corporation is not qualified but ought to be. For example, it might be said that a taxpayer is "doing business" in New York if it engages in a series of activities that would lead to qualifications being required.

Nexus

Nexus is some definite link, some minimum connection, between a state and the person, property, or transaction it seeks to tax. If nexus exists, state taxation will be imposed. If nexus can be avoided, state taxation is circumvented. Numerous state tax decisions have focused on nexus, and the leading decisions are discussed with each type of tax.

U.S. CONSTITUTIONAL PROTECTION

Commerce Clause

> The Congress shall have power . . . To regulate commerce with foreign nations and among the several states and with the Indian tribes . . . *U.S. Constitution,* Article 1, Section 8, Clause 3.

Due Process Clause

> No person shall . . . be deprived of life, liberty, or property, without due process of law; . . . *U.S. Constitution,* Amendment V.

> No state shall . . . nor shall any state deprive any person of life, liberty, or property, without due process of law; . . . *U.S. Constitution,* Amendment XIV, Section 1.

The Due Process and Commerce clauses are the important clauses of the Constitution with respect to state taxation. They are the principal sources of remedies sought by taxpayers in appeals to the U.S. Supreme Court.

What protection do the Commerce and Due Process clauses afford the interstate seller?

The Commerce Clause basically prevents state interference with interstate commerce. The U.S. Constitution was designed with the clear intention that there should exist an atmosphere of free trade between the states. Such an atmosphere could exist only if the power to regulate interstate commerce was vested in the Federal government.

The protection offered by the Commerce Clause extends to state taxes. If the state tax as imposed has the effect of interfering with or being a burden on free trade, then it is in violation of the Commerce Clause and will not be upheld. On the other hand, if the state tax as imposed merely causes the interstate seller to bear his just share of the state tax burden and this is coupled with nexus, then the tax will not be in violation of the Commerce Clause. The distinction about when the Commerce Clause has been violated and when it hasn't has been an issue in most of the state income tax cases coming before the U.S. Supreme Court.

The Due Process language appears in the Fifth and the Fourteenth amendments. The Fifth Amendment grants protection to the individual with respect to actions taken by the Federal government. The Fourteenth imposes the same restrictions with respect to actions by the states.

The Due Process Clause, as it pertains to state taxation, can be thought of in the context of whether the tax is fair and reasonable or whether it is arbitrary or an unreasonable or unnecessary interference with the basic right of the seller. Due Process also refers to procedural activities, but it is the former, more substantive issue that comes into play in state tax cases. Again, there have been numerous state tax cases decided by the U.S. Supreme Court where protection under the Due Process Clause has been raised. It is common to see both the Commerce and Due Process clauses raised as protective remedies in state tax cases.

VALIDITY OF APPORTIONMENT

Several early court decisions established the legality of a state to devise an apportionment formula to determine the income of an interstate taxpayer.

Underwood Typewriter Company v. Chamberlain 254 U.S. 113 (1920)

The decision reached by the Connecticut courts in this case was affirmed by the U.S. Supreme Court. The case involved the U.S. constitutional questions of whether the Due Process or Interstate Commerce clauses prevented Connecticut from imposing its income tax. The Commerce Clause defense was that an income tax in effect compelled the company to pay for the privilege of engaging in interstate commerce. The Due Process Clause defense centered on apportionment of income.[1]

Underwood, a Delaware corporation, manufactured its products in Connecticut. It had its main office in New York City. Branch offices were maintained in other states. The branch office functions were the sale, lease, and repair of machines and the sale of supplies. The products manufactured by Underwood were stored in Connecticut and shipped from there direct to the branch offices or directly to purchasers and lessees.

Connecticut imposed a tax of 2 percent on the net income of manufacturing corporations. In the case of an interstate company, the Connecticut taxable income was to be determined by an apportionment formula as follows:

---

[1]*Underwood Typewriter Company* v. *Chamberlain* 254 U.S. 113 (1920).

$$\frac{\text{Fair cash value of real and tangible personal property in Connecticut}}{\text{Fair cash value of real and tangible personal property everywhere}} \times \text{total net income}$$

Application of the formula to Underwood for the year in question resulted in Connecticut taxable income of $629,668.50, which was approximately 47 percent of the total net income of $1,293,643.95 of Underwood. The company paid the tax under protest and brought action to recover the amount paid. Underwood contended that the correct amount of income earned in Connecticut, as evidenced by its records, was $42,942.18.

In regard to the Commerce Clause, the Court found that the Connecticut statute did not compel the company to pay for the privilege of engaging in interstate commerce, since the payment of the tax was not a condition precedent to the right of the corporation to carry on business, including interstate business.

On the Due Process question, it was contended by the taxpayer that the tax was directly or indirectly imposed on income arising from business conducted beyond the boundaries of Connecticut, taxing extraterritorial values. The basis for this argument was the separate accounting income amount computed by the taxpayer. If the records of the company revealed the exact earnings in Connecticut, then the higher amount calculated by formula must be the taxing amount earned outside the state. In rejecting this argument, the Court stated that the taxpayer had the burden of showing that the apportionment produced an unreasonable result and that it had failed to do so. In essence, the Court approved an apportionment formula in the computation of taxable income as opposed to separately computing income and expenses within the state's boundaries.

Two important features are recognizable in the Underwood decision: (1) the taxpayer has the burden of showing that an apportionment formula devised by state law produces an unreasonable result, and (2) a showing of separate accounting results will not overcome a state's formula approach.

Bass Ratcliff and Gretton, Limited v. State Tax Commissioner 266 U.S. 271 (1924)

A case very similar to *Underwood* was that of *Bass Ratcliff*.[2] The principal difference between the two cases is that *Bass Ratcliff* involved a privilege tax rather than an income tax. (See Chapter 3 for a discussion of the facts and decision in the case.) The important features are, first, that the classification of the tax as a privilege tax measured by net income would not, as in the case of Underwood, violate the Commerce Clause. Second, the formula for apportionment of net income used by New York did not

---

[2]*Bass Ratcliff and Gretton, Limited* v. *State Tax Commission* 266 U.S. 271 (1924).

violate Due Process in the absence of a showing by the taxpayer of an unreasonable result. *Bass Ratcliff* had attempted to show the unreasonableness of apportioned income by introducing computations of net income based on separate accounting. This failed for the same reason as *Underwood* had failed.

Separate accounting failed for both taxpayers because the courts concluded that it was not possible to precisely identify the profits within the taxing state. Each taxpayer earned its profits by a series of transactions, beginning with the manufacture of a product at one location and the ultimate sale in other states. The taxing states adopted methods of apportionment to reach the profits earned within the state, and while it is recognized that no apportionment formula will be precise, it will be the burden of the taxpayer to show the unreasonableness of the result. This concept is the unitary theory that carries forward today as the basis for combined reporting.

Other court decisions where the apportionment formula was upheld as opposed to separate accounting include *Butler Brothers*[3] (see Chapter 3) and *Ford Motor Company*[4] (see Chapter 5). The circumstances in *Butler Brothers* are the same as in the preceding cases of *Underwood* and *Bass Ratcliff*. In the *Ford* case, however, the tax involved was a privilege tax (Texas franchise), and the measure of the tax was the value of capital rather than net income.

The taxpayers in these cases attempted to prove the unreasonableness of the apportionment by showing the actual earnings or value of property in the state. In essence, separate accounting versus apportionment. The court again looked at the unitary nature of these enterprises and upheld apportionment.

Hans Rees' Sons, Incorporated v. North Carolina 283 U.S. 123 (1931)

An instance where the apportionment formula used by the state was shown to be unreasonable was in the case of *Hans Rees' Sons, Incorporated*.[5] In most respects, this taxpayer appeared identical to *Underwood* and *Bass Ratcliff*. It was engaged in a unitary business of manufacturing leather products and selling these products at wholesale and at retail. The North Carolina Supreme Court had little difficulty then in sustaining income tax assessments for a four-year period that reached from 66 to 85 percent of the total profits of the company.

The taxpayer on the other hand submitted evidence that the percentage of income attributable to North Carolina for any of the years in question did not exceed 21.7 percent. The method used to arrive at this percentage

---

[3]*Butler Brothers* v. *McColgan* 315 U.S. 501 (1941).
[4]*Ford Motor Company* v. *Beauchamp* 308 U.S. 331 (1939).
[5]*Hans Rees' Sons, Incorporated* v. *North Carolina* 283 U.S. 123, (1931).

was to show that the income of the business was derived from three sources—buying profit, manufacturing profit, and selling profit. Each part was then analyzed to reflect its relationship to North Carolina. The evidence submitted was sufficient to convince the U.S. Supreme Court that the apportionment formula used by the state operated unreasonably and arbitrarily and attributed to North Carolina income out of all appropriate proportion to the actual income earned in the state.

NEXUS

The Due Process Clause requires some definite link, some minimum connection, between a state and the person, property, or transaction it seeks to tax.[6] Nexus must be present in order for any state to have jurisdiction to impose any tax or tax collection requirement. However, since the nexus requirements are different, depending on the type of tax involved, the following discussion is limited to the requirements for taxes based on income. Nexus applicable to gross receipts, sales and use, or taxes based on capital are reserved for the chapters dealing with those taxes.

West Publishing Company v. McColgan 166 P.2d 861 (1946) California S.Ct.

The *West Publishing Company*[7] case was affirmed by the U.S. Supreme Court in a per curiam decision. The decision by the California Supreme Court[8] had held that West was subject to the California Franchise Tax, a tax measured by apportioned net income. The case involved the validity of California's tax on the apportioned net income of the company where the business being conducted was exclusively interstate. A study of the case is useful as a backdrop to the more landmark decisions in Northwestern and Stockham Values, which follow. From the opinion of the California Supreme Court:[9]

> Plaintiff contends that the tax violates the Due Process Clause of the Fourteenth Amendment of the Constitution of the United States on the grounds that the state is without jurisdiction of the person, property, or business of the plaintiff and that it gives plaintiff no protection, opportunities, or benefits that would justify a tax. The record shows without conflict that plaintiff engages in substantial income producing activities in California. It has local offices here

---

[6]*Miller Brothers Company* v. *Maryland* 347 U.S. 340, citing *Maguire* v. *Trefry* 253 U.S. 12; *Lawrence* v. *State Tax Commission* 286 U.S. 276; *New York ex rel. Cohn* v. *Graves* 300 U.S. 308; *Guaranty Trust Company* v. *Virginia* 305 U.S. 19.

[7]*West Publishing Company* v. *McColgan* 328 U.S. 823.

[8]*West Publishing Company* v. *McColgan* 166 P.2d 861, (1946).

[9]*West Publishing Company* v. *McColgan* 166 P.2d 861, 866 (1946).

as well as employees who devote their entire time to soliciting orders, receiving payments, adjusting complaints, collecting delinquent accounts, and performing other services for plaintiff. This state provides a market in which plaintiff operates in competition with local law book publishers. Plaintiff's agents receive the same protection and other benefits from the state as agents carrying on business activities for a principal engaged in intrastate business.

By virtue of these activities, it was found that West was present in the state and subject to the jurisdiction of the state's courts. The California Supreme Court compared West's activities to that of *International Shoe Company*.[10] This company's activities in Washington were considered by the court to be less extensive than West's in California. Yet *International Shoe's* Due Process defense was defeated, thus establishing the doctrine that a company engaged exclusively in interstate commerce can be subject to state tax without violating the Due Process Clause.

Spector Motor Service, Incorporated v. O'Connor, Tax Commissioner 340 U.S. 602 (1951)

In *Spector Motor*[11] a precedent was established that caused considerable confusion about jurisdictional standards from 1951 until the decision was overruled in *Complete Auto Transit*[12] in 1977. The taxing state in *Spector*, Connecticut, imposed "a tax or excise upon its franchise for the privilege of carrying on or doing business within the state" upon every corporation carrying on business in Connecticut. The tax was declared invalid because it was characterized as a levy on the "privilege" of doing business within the state. Thus the wording of the levy became paramount in determining whether the Commerce Clause was violated.

In a dissenting opinion by Mr. Justice Clark, with whom Mr. Justice Black and Mr. Justice Douglas joined, it was pointed out that the tax was nondiscriminatory, fairly apportioned, and not an undue burden on interstate commerce. Also, that *Spector* had considerable activity within the state, maintaining terminals, operating light pickup trucks, employing some 27 full-time workers, and operating heavy trucks on the highway. Thus all the elements were present that should have justified a tax, save the wording of the statute.

An indication of the force of the *Spector* rule can be seen in at least two other court decisions on the issue. In the *Colonial*[13] decision, the U.S. Supreme Court sustained a privilege tax imposed by the state of Louisiana, but only after an amendment to the Louisiana statute had removed the constitutional flaw previously perceived by the Louisiana Supreme Court.

---

[10]*International Shoe Company* v. *Washington* 66 S. Ct. 154.
[11]*Spector Motor Service, Incorporated* v. *O'Connor, Tax Commissioner* 340 U.S. 602, (1951).
[12]*Complete Auto Transit, Incorporated* v. *Charles R. Brady, Jr.* 430 U.S. 274.
[13]*Colonial Pipeline Company* v. *Traigle* 421 U.S. 100.

Similarly, in *Railway Express*,[14] Virginia's "annual license tax" imposed on express companies expressly "for the privilege of doing business" was found to have a fatal constitutional flaw.

In a concurring opinion in *Colonial*, Mr. Justice Blackman aptly forecast the demise of the *Spector* rule[15] when he wrote, "Spector, it seems to me, is a derelict and an aberration, and I would discard it."

Northwestern States Portland Cement Company v. Minnesota; T.V. Williams, Commissioner v. Stockham Valves and Fittings, Incorporated 358 U.S. 450

The *Northwestern States*[16] and *Stockham Valves*[17] decisions were handed down by the U.S. Supreme Court in 1959. These two cases were reviewed simultaneously by the U.S. Supreme Court and became landmark jurisdictional decisions. The principal issues were whether the Commerce and Due Process clauses took precedence over the right of Georgia and Minnesota to impose income taxes on companies engaged exclusively in interstate commerce.

The Court's opinion stated: "We conclude that net income from the interstate operations of a foreign corporation may be subjected to state taxation provided the levy is not discriminatory and is properly apportioned to local activities within the taxing state forming sufficient nexus to support the same."[18]

Nexus, as determined by the *Northwestern* and *Stockham Valves* decisions and modified by Public Law (P.L.) 86-272, discussed later in this chapter, is basic to the understanding of jurisdictional standards for state income taxes. A more detailed study of the facts of these two cases is useful to the understanding of P.L. 86-272 that ensued from these decisions. (See Exhibit 1.1.)

Exhibit 1.1

		Northwestern	Stockham Valves
(a)	State Supreme Court opinion	Tax upheld (Minnesota)	Tax in violation of Commerce and Due Process (Georgia)
(b)	Home office	Mason City, Iowa	Birmingham, Alabama
(c)	State of incorporation	Iowa	Delaware
(d)	Qualified in taxing state	No	No

[14]*Railway Express Agency* v. *Virginia (Railway Agency I)* 347 U.S. 359.

[15]*Railway Express Agency* v. *Virginia (Railway Agency I)*, p. 115.

[16],[17]*Northwestern States Portland Cement Company* v. *Minnesota; T. V. Williams, Commissioner* v. *Stockham Valves and Fittings, Incorporated* 358 U.S. 450.

[18]*Northwestern States Portland Cement Company* v. *Minnesota*, p. 452.

Exhibit 1.1 (continued)

		Northwestern	Stockham Valves
(e)	Manufacturing facilities	Mason City, Iowa	Birmingham, Alabama
(f)	Sales office in state	Yes—Minneapolis	Yes—Atlanta
(g)	Number of employees	2 salesmen, manager, and secretary	1 salesman, secretary
(h)	Bank account	No	No
(i)	Inventory in state	No	No
(j)	Real estate owned in state	No	No
(k)	Function of salesmen	Solicit orders from customers and forward to home office for acceptance	Same
(l)	Place from where shipments made	Mason City, Iowa	Birmingham, Alabama

Both Minnesota and Georgia used methods of apportionment that were not challenged in regard to the reasonableness of the result.

Excerpts from the Opinions and Dissents

The opinion of the Court was written by Mr. Justice Clark. Mr. Justice Harlan wrote a separate concurring opinion. Mr. Justice Frankfurter and Mr. Justice Whittaker wrote dissenting opinions. The decision was 6 to 3. The pertinent arguments raised by the opinions and dissenting opinions are worthy of review, since they reveal the reasoning of the Supreme Court justices.

JUSTICE CLARK

a. Prior decisions, some three hundred full-dress opinions, dealing with the Commerce and Due Process Clauses have not always been clear, consistent, and reconcilable.[19]

b. It is clear that Congress has the power to regulate interstate commerce. Thus, a state may not impose a tax on a transient nor lay a tax on the "Privilege" of interstate commerce.[20]

c. A state may not impose a tax which discriminates against interstate commerce such as providing a commercial advantage to local business.[21]

[19]*Northwestern States Portland Cement Company v. Minnesota*, pp. 457, 458.
[20]*Northwestern States Portland Cement Company v. Minnesota*, p. 458.
[21]*Northwestern States Portland Cement Company v. Minnesota*, p. 458.

d. The doctrine that the entire net income of a corporation may be apportioned by formula has been clearly established by prior decision. (*Bass, Ratcliff, and Gretton, Limited* v. *State Tax Commission 266 U.S. 271 (1924), and Norfolk and Western Railway Company* v. *North Carolina 297 U.S. 682 (1936).*)[22]

e. *West Publishing Company* v. *McColgan 166 P.2d 861 (1946)* dispels any doubt of the validity of this decision since the decision there specifically related to interstate activities.[23]

f. We believe that the rationale of these cases involving income levies by state controls the issues here. The taxes are not regulations in any sense of that term. Admittedly, they do not discriminate against nor subject either corporation to an undue burden. While it is true that a state may not erect a wall around its borders preventing commerce an entry, it is axiomatic that the founders did not intend to immunize such commerce from carrying its fair share of the costs of the state government in return for the benefits it derives from within the state.[24]

g. The taxes do not contravene the Due Process Clause because the very substantial contact with the respective states provide sufficient "nexus," and the taxes are imposed only on the portion of net income which arises from activities within the taxing state.[25]

h. The controlling question is whether the state has given anything for which it can ask in return. The facts reveal that the taxing power has been exerted in relation to opportunities given, protection afforded to benefits conferred.[26]

JUSTICE HARLAN

a. *West Publishing Company* v. *McColgan* squarely governs the two cases. (The U.S. Supreme Court unanimously confirmed, per curiam, the California Supreme Court decision.)[27]

b. The taxes are not hostile discrimination against interstate commerce but rather a seeking of some compensation for facilities and benefits afforded by the taxing states to income producing activities therein. This is consistent with the Commerce Clause as established in past decisions.[28]

---

[22]*Northwestern States Portland Cement Company v. Minnesota*, pp. 459, 460.
[23]*Northwestern States Portland Cement Company v. Minnesota*, p. 460.
[24]*Northwestern States Portland Cement Company v. Minnesota*, pp. 460, 461.
[25]*Northwestern States Portland Cement Company v. Minnesota*, p. 460.
[26]*Northwestern States Portland Cement Company v. Minnesota*, p. 465.
[27]*Northwestern States Portland Cement Company v. Minnesota*, p. 468.
[28]*Northwestern States Portland Cement Company v. Minnesota*, p. 469.

JUSTICE FRANKFURTER (DISSENTING)

a.   *West Publishing Company* v. *McColgan* is distinguished from the present situation by the extent of its in-state activity. Those activities were more than an essential part of interstate commerce; they were activities constituting intrastate business. All other cases hinged on such intrastate business.[29]

b.   The decision constitutes the breaking of new ground since it is not established by precedent. If new ground is to be broken, it must be justified and not treated as though it were old ground.[30]

c.   The decision will compel other states to devise taxes based on apportionment, and interstate commerce will be burdened by these taxes contrary to the policy underlying the Commerce Clause. Burdens on interstate commerce will be for two reasons: (1) cost of compliance by interstate companies, and (2) litigation resulting from the natural temptation of the states to absorb more than their fair share of interstate revenue.[31]

d.   The problem calls for solution by devising a congressional policy. Congress alone can provide for a full and thorough canvassing of the taxing practices of the states.[32]

JUSTICE WHITTAKER (DISSENTING)

a.   The Commerce Clause precludes the imposition of the taxes under the circumstances of the cases. The facts clearly show (1) the statutes of the taxing states purport to tax income derived exclusively from interstate commerce, (2) the state courts in both cases held that the income involved was derived exclusively from interstate commerce, and (3) the taxes were laid directly on that interstate commerce.[33]

b.   The principles stated in *Spector Motor* v. *O'Connor 340 U.S. 602 (1951)* should be followed which are consistent with other prior decisions.[34]

c.   In *West Publishing,* the court did not sustain a tax on interstate commerce, only on intrastate activities.[35]

A summary of major points would include the following:

a.   A foreign corporation engaged solely in interstate commerce within a state is not immune from that state's income tax, provided sufficient nexus exists.

[29]*Northwestern States Portland Cement Company v. Minnesota*, pp. 471, 472.
[30]*Northwestern States Portland Cement Company v. Minnesota*, p. 473.
[31]*Northwestern States Portland Cement Company v. Minnesota*, pp. 474, 475.
[32]*Northwestern States Portland Cement Company v. Minnesota*, p. 477.
[33]*Northwestern States Portland Cement Company v. Minnesota*, pp. 482, 483.
[34]*Northwestern States Portland Cement Company v. Minnesota*, p. 486.
[35]*Northwestern States Portland Cement Company v. Minnesota*, p. 494.

b. A commercial domicile in the taxing state is not a controlling factor in determining the validity of the tax.

c. Taxes imposed only on that portion of the taxpayers net income which arose from intrastate activity are not contrary to the Due Process Clause.

d. A tax on the "privilege" of engaging in interstate commerce is in violation of the Commerce Clause.

The dissenting justices of the U.S. Supreme Court and the Georgia Supreme Court were of the opinion that a tax could not be levied on a company whose activities were exclusively interstate. The Court's opinion sustaining the Minnesota Supreme Court ruled that interstate activities could be subjected to state taxation given sufficient nexus and that this approach was consistent with prior decisions, particularly *West Publishing*. The dissenters felt that *West Publishing* was distinguished from the present cases by its intrastate functions.

P.L. 86-272

The *Northwestern* and *Stockham Valves* decisions were not well received by interstate taxpayers. In fact, they led to very substantial pressures being exerted by businessmen and probusiness groups on Congress. The Congress responded with astonishingly quick action with the passage of the much-publicized Public Law 86-272. This statute was not intended to be a solution to the interstate tax problem. The statute's purpose was to act as a stopgap until such time as the ultimate solution could be achieved. The provisions are reproduced next.[36]

Title I

Section 101

(a) No state, or political subdivision thereof, shall have power to impose, for any taxable year ending after the date of enactment of this Act, a net income tax on the income derived within such State by any person from interstate commerce if the only business activities within such State by or on behalf of such person during such taxable year are either, or both, of the following:

   (1) The solicitation of orders by such person, or his representative, in such State for sales of tangible personal property, which orders are sent outside the State for approval or rejection, and, if approved, are filled by shipment or delivery from a point outside the State: and

---

[36]P.L. 86-272 is Codified at 15 U.S.C. 381.

(2) The solicitation of orders by such person, or his representative, in such State in the name of or for the benefit of a prospective customer of such person, if orders by such customer to such person to enable such customer to fill orders resulting from such solicitation are orders described in paragraph (1).

(b) The provisions of subsection (a) shall not apply to the imposition of a net income tax by any State, or political subdivision thereof, with respect to:

(1) any corporation which is incorporated under the laws of such State; or

(2) any individual who, under the laws of such State, is domiciled in, or a resident of, such State.

(c) For purposes of subsection (a), a person shall not be considered to have engaged in business activities within a State during any taxable year merely by reason of sales in such State, or the solicitation of orders for sales in such State, of tangible personal property on behalf of such person by one or more independent contractors, or by reason of the maintenance of an office in such State by one or more independent contractors whose activities on behalf of such person in such State consists solely of making sales, or soliciting orders for sales, of tangible personal property.

(d) For purposes of this section:

(1) The term "independent contractor" means a commission agent, broker, or other independent contractor who is engaged in selling, or soliciting orders for the sale of, tangible personal property for more than one principal and who holds himself out as such in the regular course of his business activities; and

(2) The term "representative" does not include an independent contractor.

Section 102

(a) No State, or political subdivision thereof, shall have power to assess, after the date of the enactment of this Act, any net income tax which was imposed by such State or political subdivision, as the case may be, for any taxable year ending on or before such date, on the income derived within such State by any person from interstate commerce, if the imposition of such tax for a taxable year ending after such date is prohibited by Section 101.

(b) The provisions of subsection (a) shall not be construed:

(1) to invalidate the collection, on or before the date of the enactment of this Act, of any net income tax imposed for a taxable year ending on or before such date, or

(2) to prohibit the collection, after the date of the enactment of this Act, of any net income tax which was assessed on or before such date for a taxable year ending on or before such date.

Section 103

For purposes of this title, the term "net income tax" means any tax imposed on, or measured by, net income.

Section 104

If any provision of this title or the application of such provision to any person or circumstance is held invalid, the remainder of this title or the application of such provision to persons or circumstances other than those to which it is held invalid, shall not be affected thereby.

Title II

Section 201

The Committee on the Judiciary of the House of Representatives and the Committee on Finance of the United States Senate, acting, separately or jointly, or both, or any duly authorized subcommittees thereof, shall make full and complete studies of all matters pertaining to the taxation of interstate commerce by the States, territories, and possessions of the United States, the District of Columbia, and Commonwealth of Puerto Rico, or any political or taxing subdivision of the foregoing.

Section 202

The Committees shall report to their respective House the results of such studies together with their proposals for legislation or or before June 30, 1965

Significant Aspects

The more significant protection aspects of P.L. 86-272 include the following:

1 The application of the law is only to taxes based on income.
2 The protection is not afforded to domestic corporations.
3 The protection given to interstate activity is narrow, applying only in circumstances where the following exist:
   (a) Sales solicitation for tangible personal property is the only activity.
   (b) Orders received are forwarded out of state for acceptance.
   (c) Shipment of the tangible property is made from out of state.

Interpretation of P.L. 86-272

If the business community were expecting a law that would immunize an interstate enterprise from income tax under business activities, such as those being conducted by *Northwestern Portland Cement Company* and *Stockham Valves, Incorporated*, it must have been sorely disappointed. P.L. 86-272 falls far short of that. On the other hand, it does provide some standard of predictability so as to remove much of the uncertainties about jurisdiction.

The ambiguity of the law is created by the term "solicitation." Several state court cases have attempted to resolve the meaning of the term.

Indiana Department of Revenue v. Kimberly-Clark Corporation 375 N.E. 2d 1146 (1978) Indiana Ct. of App.

Activity in excess of solicitation was tested in the *Kimberly-Clark*[37] case concerning jurisdiction by Indiana. Kimberly-Clark's sales activities in Indiana were conducted by some 16 salaried salesmen. The salesmen each were provided with an automobile, and some had equipment such as portable typewriters, staple guns, case cutters, and selling cases. They had the usual brochure material and samples. The company maintained no business telephone listing, no inventory, no bank account, no offices, and no rented buildings or real estate. Purchase orders were forwarded out of state for acceptance.

The salesmen had contact with direct customers, that is, customers who bought directly from Kimberly-Clark, and with indirect customers such as retailers, hotels, and beauty shops, who purchased Kimberly-Clark products from the direct customers. The sales effort focused toward the direct customer consisted of the normal sales activity of discussing ways to increase sales with a view of inducing the customer to make purchases. The effort toward indirect customers was in the nature of "missionary work" to induce these customers to buy from the direct customers, thereby increasing sales to the direct customers. The court recognized seven such activities:

a. Checking inventories.
b. Checking shelf facings.
c. Pricing products and putting them on shelves when requested to do so by the customer.
d. Setting up displays when requested to do so by the customer.
e. Conveying information on out-of-stock conditions or delays in shipment.
f. Verifying destruction of damaged goods when requested to do so by the customer.
g. Coordinating deliveries.

[37]*Indiana Department of Revenue* v. *Kimberly-Clark Corporation* 375 NE2d 1146 (1978) Indiana Ct. of App.

The first four activities were found to be associated with the placing of orders and within the definition of solicitation. The latter three were found to be beyond solicitation and thus beyond the protection of P.L. 86-272. Thus the taxpayer was within Indiana's jurisdiction.

United States Tobacco[38] *Company v. Commonwealth of Pennsylvania 386 A.2d 471 (1978) Pennsylvania S. Ct.*

In a similar Pennsylvania Supreme Court case, the taxpayer engaged 10 "missionary representatives." These representatives also had automobiles provided by the employer, but the company had no offices, no inventory, and no bank account in the state.

The representatives visited wholesalers to inform them of company activities and promotions and sometimes took orders to be forwarded out of state for acceptance. They also visited retail outlets (i.e., indirect customers) where they could do the following:

(a) Carry samples purchased from wholesalers at the wholesale price. These samples would be resold at that price to the retailers if requested.

(b) Check inventory to determine freshness and attractiveness of displays.

(c) Set up counter displays and give free samples in exchange for more extensive counter space.

The court held that "solicitation" was not to be narrowly construed. Sundry activities incidental to initial contact between buyer and seller, such as the foregoing, are within the meaning of the term, inasmuch as they are closely related to the eventual sale of the product.

The opinion contains a review of various other court decisions that have construed the Federal law.[39] These cases are summarized in Exhibit 1.2.

Gillette Company[40] *v. State Tax Commissioner 45 N.Y. 2d 846 (1978) Ct. of App.*

The taxpayer in this case had no place of business in the state, had no inventory, except the samples carried by salesmen, and all orders were

---

[38]*United States Tobacco Company* v. *Commonwealth of Pennsylvania* 386 A.2d 471 (1978).

[39]The U.S. Supreme Court has never ruled on the interpretation of "solicitation," the closest brush being in *Neublein* v. *South Carolina Tax Commission* 409 U.S. 275. Here the court found the taxpayer to be outside the immunity of P.L. 86-272 for other reasons and did not have to face up to the "solicitation" issue.

[40]*Gillette Company* v. *State Tax Commission* 45 N.Y.2d 846 (1978) (Ct. of App.).

sent out of state for acceptance. Gillette sold to wholesalers who in turn sold to retailers. Gillette's representatives did the following:

(a) Informed the retailer of changes in products and of new promotions to induce the retailer to make purchases from the wholesaler.

(b) Reviewed retailer displays of Gillette products for attractive arrangement and salable condition. (The Tax Commission characterized this as "merchandising," an activity beyond solicitation.)

The New York trial court stated:[41]

> Although it is not possible to state a general rule demarcating solicitation from merchandising, certainly where, as here the complaining taxpayer owns no real or personal property (except salesmen's samples) in the state and makes no repairs on its goods after sale, the purpose of P.L. 86-272 would be frustrated by permitting the tax. Advice to retailers on the act of displaying goods to the public can hardly be more thoroughly solicitation, i.e., in this context, an effort to induce purchase of Gillette products. Making the evanescent distinctions which would be necessary to justify the imposition of the tax upon petitioner herein would, if indulged in by the several states, tend to "Balkanize the American economy," a result which it was Congress' purpose to prevent.

State Interpretations—Wisconsin

Some states have issued announcements about their own interpretation of the protection offered by P.L. 86-272. An example is that of Wisconsin, reproduced next.

Nexus

State of Wisconsin

(1) DEFINITIONS. In this rule: (a) "Representative" does not include an independent contractor. A person may be considered a representative even though he or she may not be considered an employee for other purposes such as the withholding of income tax from commissions. If a person is subject to the direct control of the foreign corporation, he or she may *not* qualify as an independent contractor under P.L. 86-272. (*Herff Jones Company* v. *State Tax Commission,* Oregon Supreme Court, August 23, 1967, 430 P. 2d 998.)

(b) "Business location" includes a repair shop, parts department, purchasing office, employment office, warehouse, meeting place for directors, sales office, permanent sample or display room, research facility for

---

[41]*Gillette Company* v. *State Tax Commissioner* 393 N.Y.S.2d 186 (1977) at 191.

use of employees or customers. A residence of an employee or representative is not ordinarily considered a business location of the employer unless the facts indicate otherwise. It could be considered a business location under one or more of the following conditions: a portion of the residence is used exclusively for the business of the employer, the employee is reimbursed or paid a flat fee for the use of this space by the employer; the employee's phone is listed in the yellow pages under the name of the employer; the employee uses supplies, equipment or samples furnished by the employer; or the space is used by the employee to interview prospective employees, hold sales meetings, or discuss business with customers.

(2) BACKGROUND. (a) Every domestic corporation (one incorporated under Wisconsin's laws), except those exempt under s. 71.01 (3) Stats., and every "licensed" foreign corporation (one not incorporated in Wisconsin) is required to file a complete corporation franchise/income tax return (Form 4 or 5) regardless of whether or not business was transacted.

(b) A foreign corporation is "licensed" if it has obtained a Certificate of Authority from the Wisconsin secretary of state to transact business in this state pursuant to s. 180.801, Wis. Stats. A "licensed" foreign corporation is presumed to be subject to Wisconsin franchise/income taxes.

(c) An unlicensed foreign corporation is subject to Wisconsin franchise/income taxes if it has "nexus" with Wisconsin. The purpose of this rule is to provide guidelines for determining what constitutes "nexus," that is, what business activities are needed for a foreign corporation to be subject to Wisconsin franchise/income taxes.

(3) FEDERAL LIMITATIONS ON TAXATION OF FOREIGN CORPORATIONS. (a) *Federal constitutional provisions.* 1. Article I, Section 8 of the U.S. Constitution grants Congress the power to regulate commerce with foreign nations and among the several states. States are prohibited from levying a tax which imposes a burden on interstate or foreign commerce. However, this does not mean states may not impose any tax on interstate commerce. A state tax on net income from interstate commerce which is fairly attributable to the state is constitutional. (*Northwestern States Portland Cement Co.* v. *Minnesota; Williams* v. *Stockham Valves & Fittings, Inc.,* 358 U.S. 450, 79 S.Ct. 357.)

2. Section I of the 14th Amendment protects taxpayers within any class against discrimination and guarantees a remedy against illegal taxation.

(b) Federal Public Law 86-272. 1. Under Public Law 86-272, a state may not impose its franchise/income tax on a business selling tangible personal property, if the *only* activity of that business is the solicitation of orders by its salesman or representative which orders are sent outside the state for approval or rejection, and are filled by delivery from a point outside the state. The activity must be *limited* to solicitation. If there is any activity which exceeds solicitation, the immunity from taxation under Public Law 86-272 is lost.

2.   This law, enacted by Congress in 1959, does not extend to:

a.   Those businesses which sell services, real estate or intangibles in more than one state; b. Domestic corporations; or c. Foreign nation corporations, i.e., those not incorporated in the United States.

3.   If the *only* activities in Wisconsin of a foreign corporation selling tangible personal property are those described below (a and b) such corporation is not subject to Wisconsin franchise/income taxes under P.L. 86-272: a. Usual or frequent activity in Wisconsin by employees or representatives soliciting orders for tangible personal property which orders are sent outside this state for approval or rejection. b. Solicitation activity by non-employee independent contractors, conducted through their own office or business location in Wisconsin.

(4)   WHAT CONSTITUTES "NEXUS." (a) *Factors.* If a foreign corporation has one or more of the following activities in Wisconsin, it is considered to have "nexus" and shall be subject to Wisconsin franchise/income taxes:

1.   Maintenance of any business location in Wisconsin, including any kind of office.
2.   Ownership of real estate in Wisconsin.
3.   Ownership of a stock of goods in a public warehouse or on consignment in Wisconsin.
4.   Ownership of a stock of goods in the hands of a distributor or other non-employee representative in Wisconsin, if used to fill orders for the owner's account.
5.   Usual or frequent activity in Wisconsin by employees or representatives soliciting orders with authority to accept them.
6.   Usual or frequent activity in Wisconsin by employees or representatives engaged in a purchasing activity or in the performance of services (including construction, installation, assembly, repair of equipment).
7.   Operation of mobile stores in Wisconsin (such as trucks with driver-salespersons), regardless of frequency.
8.   Miscellaneous other activities by employees or representatives in Wisconsin such as credit investigations, collection of delinquent accounts, conducting training classes or seminars for customer personnel in the operation, repair and maintenance of the taxpayer's products.
9.   Leasing of tangible property and licensing of intangible rights for use in Wisconsin.
10.   The sale of other than tangible personal property such as real estate, services and intangibles in Wisconsin.
11.   The performance of construction contracts and personal services contracts in Wisconsin.

(b)   *How to obtain ruling.* The guidelines in par. (a) as to what activities constitute "nexus" should not be considered all-inclusive. A ruling may be requested about a particular foreign corporation as to whether it is subject to Wisconsin franchise/income taxes by writing to the Wisconsin Department of Revenue, Audit Technical Services Section, P.O. Box 8906, Madison, Wisconsin 53708.

Planning within P.L. 86-272

It must be remembered that immunity claimed under P.L. 86-272 can have various results. The first and most frequently discussed feature is that an interstate company can avoid the income tax of a state, provided it operates within the nexus rules established by that law. It must be noted, however, that if a company is not subject to tax in at least one other state, then the allocation and apportionment rules of some states would not apply and 100 percent of the income would be taxable by the state of commercial domicile.

Specifically, those states that have adopted the Multistate Tax Commission (MTC) regulations to the Uniform Division of Income for Tax Purposes Act (UDITPA) would take this view.[42] Eighteen states have adopted these regulations.[43] Similarly, those states that apply the "throw-back" rule to the sales factor of the apportionment formula would attribute sales having a destination to an 86-272 state to the state from which the shipment originated. The states that would make this adjustment would include those which have substantially adopted UDITPA. Some 24 states have adopted UDITPA without substantial change.[44]

An interstate company then must plan the most effective utilization of P.L. 86-272.

Example 1

A company with its commercial domicile in Illinois makes shipments of tangible personal property to Wyoming.

Since Wyoming has no income tax, the taxpayer here should not attempt to establish immunity under P.L. 86-272 for Wyoming. To do so would mean that the sales going into Wyoming from Illinois would be attributed to Illinois under the throw-back rule, thereby increasing the Illinois tax. To avoid 86-272 application to the sales into Wyoming the taxpayer could establish activities beyond mere solicitation.

Example 2

This poses the same situation as in Example 1, except that the sales are destined for a state having an income tax but where the tax rate is lower than Illinois. The taxpayer should again avoid the immunity of 86-272.

Example 3

Assume a taxpayer has its commercial domicile and principal operations in North Dakota. The taxpayer makes shipments of most of its products to

---

[42]Reg. IV.3.(a) MTC UDITPA Regulations.
[43]State of Indiana, "Survey on the Uniformity of State Tax Laws," February 1977. (See Exhibit 1.3.)
[44]State of Indiana, "Survey on the Uniformity of State Tax Laws."

out-of-state destinations and allocates and apportions its net income to
North Dakota under UDITPA. Unless it establishes nexus in another state
(such that it would not be immune under 86-272), it will not be subject to
allocation and apportionment in North Dakota. Thus that state could tax
100 percent of the income.

Coors Porcelain Company[45] involved a taxpayer that lost its advantage to
apportion income for Colorado income tax purposes when the Supreme
Court of that state used P.L. 86-272 as a guide in determining whether
Coors was subject to the income tax of other states where it had sales and
related activities. The out-of-state activities were held to consist of "solicitation" only, and under Colorado law, 100 percent of the income of the
taxpayer became subject to Colorado income tax.

   Coors maintained some 10 employees outside Colorado. Each salesper-
son maintained a sales office. The sales personnel functioned to do the
following:

1   Demonstrate the advantage of Coors products.
2   Design parts to fit the needs of customers.
3   Discuss engineering problems and recommend Coors-designed prod-
    ucts to solve these problems.
4   Present price quotations and negotiate such prices.
5   Follow up on contact.
6   Develop new applications of Coors products.
7   Develop and maintain good relations with customers' technical and
    purchasing employees.
8   Maintain field records on orders and deliveries.
9   Discuss complaints or problems with products purchased from Coors
    with customers.
10 Demonstrate the operation of Coors products.

   Orders were forwarded to Colorado for acceptance and shipment,
although some of the representatives bought the products themselves and
resold them to the customer. Each representative was supplied with an
automobile and samples. A business telephone listing was present for each
sales office. The company had no inventory in the states, but occasionally
the representatives temporarily possessed products for shipment to customers or products that had been rejected by the customer.

   The taxpayer never contended that it was subject to the income tax of
another state. The taxpayer's defense was that the Federal statute relates
"only to standards applicable to a foreign corporation and that the corol-
lary cannot be used as standards for taxable income by the state in which

---

[45]*Coors Porcelain Company* v. *State of Colorado* 517 P.2d 838 (1973).

the corporation is a domestic." This argument was rejected by the court, which then proceeded to examine and to draw its conclusion about the term solicitation.

The Coors decision appears to be a very broad interpretation of solicitation. A foreign corporation would thus have considerable leeway in planning its Colorado activities if its goal was to seek immunity under P.L. 86-272 for its Colorado operations.

ADDITIONAL JURISDICTIONAL STANDARDS— JAPAN LINE, LIMITED

In *Complete Auto Transit*[46] the jurisdictional standards established in the decisions discussed in this chapter were repeated. That is, to avoid being a burden on interstate commerce, the tax must be *fairly apportioned,* must not *discriminate against interstate commerce,* must be *fairly related to the services provided by the state,* and *nexus* must be present.

In addition to the forementioned, two new criteria were injected with the U.S. Supreme Court decision in the *Japan Line, Limited,* case.[47] These being, first, whether the tax creates a *substantial risk of international multiple taxation* and, second, whether the tax *prevents the Federal government from speaking with one voice when regulating commercial relations with foreign governments.* While this case involved California property tax assessments, the additional elements necessary to avoid conflict with the Commerce Clause could have ramifications in state income taxation. In *Japan Line, Limited,* multiple taxation was in fact present. Generally, the argument of possible multiple taxation in state income taxes will not prevail. For example, see *Moorman Manufacturing.*[48] However, where international aspects are involved, such as appears in "combined reporting," these criteria may have some future impact.

The second criterion, that is, the concern that "the Federal government must speak with one voice when regulating commercial relations with foreign governments," has not heretofore appeared in state income taxation, although recognized in the *Michelin Tire Corporation*[49] case in the context of the Import-Export Clause of the Constitution. This too may have significance in "combined reporting" techniques. For example, a state could possibly be in conflict with the Commerce Clause if it attempted to apply combined reporting to foreign corporations and their affiliates or to include foreign subsidiaries in the combined report computation of a U.S. company.

[46]*Complete Auto Transit, Incorporated* v. *Charles R. Brady, Jr.* 430 U.S. 274.
[47]*Japan Line, Limited, et al.* v. *County of Los Angeles et al.* 60 L Ed 2d 336 (1959).
[48]*Moorman Manufacturing Company* v. *G. D. Bair* 437 U.S. 267.
[49]*Michelin Tire Corporation* v. *W. L. Wages, Tax Commissioner et al.* 423 U.S. 276.

P.L. 86-272—DIRECTIVE TO CONGRESS

Another aspect of P.L. 86-272 (Section 201) was the directive to the House and Senate to make a study of "all matters pertaining to the taxation of interstate commerce . . ." This directive led to the establishment of the subcommittees on State Taxation of Interstate Commerce of the House Committee on the Judiciary. Four years of in-depth investigation was necessary before the subcommittee published the two-volume results of its work on income taxes (June 15, 1964). A third volume was published one year later (June 30, 1965), disclosing the work done on sales and use, capital stock, and gross receipts taxes. Volume 4, published September 2, 1965, contained the recommendations of the subcommittee on all taxes.

The following is a summary of recommendations with respect to taxes based on income.[50]

Division of Income

All income is apportioned by a two-factor formula based on property and payroll.

The property factor includes all tangible property except: (1) inventory, (2) personalty leased out for more than one year, and (3) property outside the United States. Property is valued at its original cost. For purposes of the property factor numerator, moving property is attributed to a state if: (1) it is operated entirely within that state, or (2) if it is operated partly within the state and its base of operations is in the state. Moving property is eliminated from both the numerator and denominator if its operation is not entirely within a state and it has no base of operations in any state.

The payroll factor includes wages paid to employees except retirement pay and the amount of wages in excess of $40,000.00 per annum paid to any one employee. For purposes of the payroll factor numerator, the two primary tests used by all the states for unemployment compensation are adopted. Wages are attributed to a state if: (1) the employee's service is entirely within the state, or (2) the employee's service is partly within the state and his base of operations is in the state. Wages are eliminated from both the numerator and denominator if the service is not entirely within one state and the employee has no base of operations in any state.

Jurisdiction

Jurisdiction is congruent with the apportionment of income. A corporation is taxable if it: (1) owns or leases realty in the state, or (2) has an employee whose services are performed entirely in the state. If a corporation has personalty in a state but has neither realty nor an employee in that state, the

[50]State Taxation of Interstate Commerce. Report of the Special Subcommittee on State Taxation of Interstate Commerce Volume 4, p. 1135.

personalty is eliminated from the denominator of the property factor for all states. Any state may tax the income attributed to it by the uniform formula regardless of whether the state tax is imposed in the form of a franchise tax or a direct tax. Liability is barred for unassessed taxes from prior years in which the corporation had neither realty nor an employee in the state.

Tax Base

Federal taxable income must be used as the starting point for the computation of state tax bases. Each state may require its own adjustments to federal taxable income except that no adjustments are permitted which favor local taxpayers or which involve depreciation, amortization, or the time for reporting items of income or expense.

Consolidation of Returns

Consolidation can be required by a state and nust be permitted in any case of affiliation by common ties of more than 50 per cent of stock ownership. Consolidation is prohibited with respect to any income which is exempt from Federal taxation because considered to be derived from sources outside the United States.

Uniform Regulations and Forms

The Treasury Department[51] is to issue rules and regulations for the operation of the uniform apportionment formula and to devise a uniform return form for the filing of apportionment data. Periodic conferences are to be held with state administrators, and procedures are provided whereby state administrators can contribute their knowledge and experience to the operation and development of the uniform apportionment program.

Modification

The Secretary of the Treasury or his delegate is authorized to prescribe a modified apportionment formula or separate accounting for particular taxpayers. This power is to be sparingly exercised, only as necessary to effectuate the policies of the recommendations, and upon notice to the taxpayer and all affected states. Any modification made and the supporting findings shall be published.

Resolution of Multistate Conflicts

Procedures are established for the resolution of multistate tax disputes by the Treasury Department whenever the interested states do not agree to be bound

---

[51]All references to the Treasury Department or to the Secretary or his delegate are intended to mean that division of the Treasury Department, such as the Internal Revenue Service (IRS), to which the relevant duties would be assigned.

by the findings of a single state. The determinations by the Treasury are subject to review by the Tax Court.

Local Income Taxes

Subdivision of states are subject to the same rules that apply to states.

Attempts by Congress to legislate in the state tax area are discussed in Chapter 4.

Exhibit 1.2   State Interpretations of P.L. 86-272

Case	Activity	Immunity Granted
Accord *CIBA Pharmaceutical Products, Incorporated* v. *State Tax Commissioner* 382 S.W. 2d 645 (Missouri, 1964)	Representative explained products, left literature and samples to persuade doctors to write prescriptions for sellers' products	Yes
Coors Porcelain Company v. *State* 517 P.2d 838 (Colorado, 1973)	Representative demonstrated products, negotiated prices, had company automobile	Yes
Clairol, Incorporated v. *Kingsley* 262 A.2d 213, Aff'd. 270 A.2d 702 (1970), dismissed for want of a substantial federal question, 402 U.S. 902 (1971)	Representatives visited retail druggists, reviewing displays, arranging promotion, and suggesting ways to merchandise Clairol products. Also took inventory and suggested orders. Technicians in state to instruct customers in how to use Clairol's products	No
Miles Laboratories, Incorporated v. *Department of Revenue* 546 P.2d 1081 (Oregon, 1976)	Salespeople maintenance stock to replace damaged merchandise, service accounts, and arrange advertising displays	No
Hervey v. *AMF Beaird, Incorporated* 464 S.W. 2d 557 (Arkansas, 1971)	Representatives make regular checks of customers' inventories of company's equipment	No
Olympia Brewing Company v. *Department of Revenue* 511 P.2d 837 (Oregon, 1973)	Presence of beer kegs prevented immunity; no opinion concerning regular inspections of supply to check for shortages and efforts to induce attractive displays	No

Exhibit 1.3

States	Substantially Adopted UDITPA[a]	Adopted MTC to UDITPA[a]	Multistate Compact Members as of January 1, 1980
Alabama	X	X	
Alaska	X	X	X
Arkansas	X	X	X
California	X	X	X
Colorado	X	X	X
Hawaii	X		X
Idaho	X	X	X
Illinois	X		
Indiana	X	X	
Kansas	X	X	X
Kentucky	X	X	
Maine	X	X	
Michigan	(1)	(1)	X
Missouri	X	X	X
Montana	X	X	X
Nebraska	X	X	X
Nevada	(1)	(1)	X
New Mexico	X	X	X
North Carolina	X	X	
North Dakota	X	X	X
Oregon	X	X	X
Pennsylvania	X		
South Carolina	X		
South Dakota	(1)	(1)	X
Tennessee	X		
Texas	(1)	(1)	X
Utah	X	X	X
Virginia	X		
Washington	(1)	(1)	X

[a]Survey on the uniformity of state tax laws, state of Indiana (February 1977).

(1) State does not have an income tax.

CHAPTER TWO

Determination of State Taxable Income

TOTAL TAXABLE INCOME

If each state having taxing jurisdiction over the interstate enterprise were to impose a tax on the entire income of the company, the taxpayer would be quickly taxed out of existence. Therefore, each state is permitted to tax only in relation to the activity in that state (properly apportioned). The measure of activity and thus the measure of taxable income must be reasonable, although not necessarily precise.

In the discussion of the *Underwood*[1] case in Chapter 1, it was noted that the state had applied an apportionment formula based on tangible property to derive the Connecticut tax base. The taxpayer, on the other hand, contended that its records reflected a more precise determination of the Connecticut tax base. The method used by Connecticut is called, appropriately, the "apportionment method," and that proposed by the taxpayer is generally known as "separate accounting." These methods are further discussed later in this chapter. For the present, we are concerned with what constitutes the total income of the firm. This total income is partially taxed by the states having jurisdiction, depending on the various rules enumerated in the statutes of those taxing states.

Reference to Internal Revenue Code (IRC)

A convenient and widely used computational starting point is to make reference to the Internal Revenue Code. This is accomplished merely by defining such as the starting point in the state income tax statute. For example, for the interstate corporation, this tie-in might be Federal taxable income. The tie-in may be permanent that is, Federal taxable income as defined in the Internal Revenue Code of 1954 as amended, or it may be qualified or limited for example, Federal taxable income as defined in the Internal Revenue Code of 1954 as amended through December 31, 1971.

---

[1] *Underwood Typewriter Company* v. *Chamberlain* 254 U.S. 113 (1920).

The latter permits the state to analyze the impact of Federal changes on its tax revenue before it becomes part of the state tax structure. This has an advantage over a complete tie-in to the IRC but is disruptive to the compliance effort by interstate taxpayers. A complete tie-in to the IRC simplifies the administration but may at times cause some loss of revenue due to Federal increased or liberalized deductions.

Some states only remotely resemble the IRC in their taxable income definitions. From a compliance viewpoint, these states are the most difficult, since major differences may be present that require the maintenance of special records. Examples observed include depreciation deductions, where the Federal may be more liberal, and in bad debt deductions, where the Federal allows a reserve method, and the state recognizes the specific charge-off method only. In practice, the variance from Federal taxable income for the corporate taxpayer is not usually a major problem. Even though a particular state may not be technically tied to the IRC, in practice, Federal taxable income is still the reference point for determination of the starting point.

State Modifications to Federal Taxable Income

Federal taxable income is never the exact starting point for the apportionment of taxable income to the taxing state. All taxing states require adjustments to arrive at the total income to be apportioned. The following is a list of state modifications commonly encountered. These are given as illustrations only and are not intended to be inclusive.

Additions to Federal Taxable Income

1 Interest income on certain state or municipal obligations (increases Federal taxable income that has been excluded as exempt for Federal income tax purposes).
2 State income tax deducted (taxing state only).
3 Taxes based on income (all states).
4 Net operating loss deductions allowable for Federal income tax purposes but not for state tax purposes.

Deduction from Federal Taxable Income

1 Interest on federal obligations (This is to allow an exemption for interest earned on Federal obligations that would be includable in Federal taxable income).
2 Foreign dividend gross-up.
3 State net operating loss.

STATE TAXABLE INCOME

Having determined the total taxable income of an enterprise, the next significant step is to determine under state law the portion that is taxable.

Separate Accounting

Separate accounting, as the name implies, is the determination of income within the geographical boundaries of a particular state. Examples of separate accounting are observed in the *Underwood*[2] case described in chapters 1 and 3 and in *Butler Brothers*[3] as outlined in Chapter 3.

Normally, separate accounting would be computed from the books and records in somewhat the following manner.

Sales of products or services in-state (Specific identification of revenue received from customers within the taxing state)	$ XXX
Cost of products or services (Specific accounting for the costs related to the above revenue)	XXX
Gross income	$ XXX
Marketing expense (Specific association or apportionment on some reasonable basis)	XXX
General office overhead (Usually allocated on some reasonable basis)	XXX
State taxable income	$ XXX

This is an acceptable method of computing state taxable income in some states. The problems associated with it are more fully described in Chapter 3. From an administrative viewpoint, this method obviously presents difficulties. For example, some of the difficulties are these: (1) How would gross income be defined? Would it include sales originating in the taxing state and terminating in other states, or would it be measured with reference to a sales office or warehouse? (2) How is the cost of products to be determined? (3) What methods will be specified for apportionment of general office costs. The answers to these questions and many others would need to be provided by tax administrators. This causes considerable difficulty when it involves the complex operations of a large interstate enterprise. Attempts aimed at solving the difficulties of administration are

[2]*Underwood Typewriter Company* v. *Chamberlain* 254 U.S. 113 (1920).
[3]*Butler Brothers* v. *McColgan* 315 U.S. 501 (1941).

likely to fall short of being comprehensive, which leaves it to the taxpayer to devise the computations. This, in turn, is likely to lead to many computational controversies.

As alluded to in Chapter 3, taxpayers are motivated to minimize state income tax while the adversary, the tax administrator, has the opposite goal. The difficulty of defining separate accounting income has indirectly been recognized by the courts. While not specifically prohibiting separate accounting, formula apportionment methods devised by the states have been upheld, with a heavy burden placed on the taxpayer to demonstrate that the formula produces an unreasonable result. This doctrine was established in the *Underwood* case and reinforced by many other court decisions.[4] However, in Hans Rees' Sons, Incorporated,[5] separate accounting was apparently used to show that apportionment produced an unreasonable result.

The opinion in Underwood[6] stated that "the taxpayer carries the burden of showing that 47 per cent of its net income is not reasonably attributable, for purposes of taxation, to the manufacture of products from the sale of which 80 per cent of its gross earnings was derived after paying manufacturing costs. Further, the corporation has not even attempted to show this; and for aught that appears the percentage of net profits earned in Connecticut may have been larger than 47 per cent. There is, consequently, nothing in this record to show that the method of apportionment adopted by the state was inherently arbitrary, or that its application to this corporation produced an unreasonable result."

Also, the opinion in *Butler Brothers*[7] stated that "we cannot say that property, payroll, and sales are inappropriate ingredients of an apportionment formula. We agree with the Supreme Court of California that these factors may properly be deemed to reflect 'the relative contribution of the activities in the various states to the production of the total unitary income,' so as to allocate to California its just proportion of the profits earned by appellant from this unitary business."

Allocation and Apportionment of Total Taxable Income

Apportionment formulas devised by the states will, therefore, not generally be overturned by the courts. Various formulas have evolved. Traditionally, two types of income have been recognized by the states: business and nonbusiness.[8]

[4]*Bass Ratcliff and Gretton, Limited* v. *State Tax Commission* 266 U.S. 271 (1924); *Butler Brothers* (prev. cited); *Edison California Stores, Incorporated* v. *McColgan*, 183 P.2d 16; *Ford Motor Company* v. *Beauchamp* 308 U.S. 331 (1939).
[5]*Hans Rees' Sons, Incorporated* v. *North Carolina* 283 U.S. 123 (see Chapter 1).
[6]*Underwood Typewriter Company* v. *Chamberlain* 254 U.S. 113 (1920) P.121.
[7]*Butler Brothers* v. *McColgan* 315 U.S. 501 (1941) p.509.
[8]For a detailed analysis of this topic see James H. Peters, "The Distinction between Business Income and Nonbusiness Income," *Law Center Institute*, 25th Tax Institute, University of

Nonbusiness Income

The first type of income is known as "nonbusiness income." Frequently, it is called "allocable income." The terms are used synonymously.

Classification of income as nonbusiness is an attempt to segregate certain types of income that could clearly be assigned in total to a certain state. In other words, separate accounting would apply to this type of income. Examples of income that has traditionally been classified as nonbusiness income by many states include rents, interest, dividends, royalties, and gains and losses from the sale of property.

The significance of a nonbusiness classification from the taxing states' view is that one and only one state is permitted to impose a tax on it. It doesn't matter whether the state entitled to tax this income does, in fact, impose a tax. The classification prevents all other states that recognize the classification from imposing a tax. Double taxation of this income arises when one taxing state views a class of income as nonbusiness and another taxing state does not. The first state may then be entitled to tax the income at 100 percent, and the second state may be entitled to tax the same income based on some apportionment method.

The situation just described was the issue in *Mobil Oil Corporation* v. *Commissioner of Taxes* 394A.2d N47 (1978). In this case, the state of Vermont sought to apportion the dividend and interest income of Mobil received from affiliated and nonaffiliated companies to Vermont. In short, Vermont maintained that this income was business income. The taxpayer contended that the income was nontaxable by Vermont for the following reasons:

1 The dividend income had insufficient nexus with Vermont.
2 The benefits conferred by Vermont cannot be related to the income being taxed.
3 A possibility of double taxation exists, since the state of New York can tax the same income entirely.

This Vermont Supreme Court held for the state of Vermont, and this decision was affirmed by the U.S. Supreme Court. See Chapter 4 for a more detailed account of this litigation.

Business Income

The second type of income traditionally recognized is known as "business income," or "apportionable income." This class of income was acknowledged to be income that would be divided between the states on a formula

California Law Center, Vol. 25, p. 251. Also, Gary J. Hansen, "Business v. Nonbusiness Income of Large Multinational Corporations under UDITPA. *Taxes,* Vol. 57, No. 6, p. 366. June 1979.

method. In theory, this was income that related to activities among all the states, and although separate accounting would be possible, it appeared more reasonable to relate the entire class to the various states by formula. For example, a manufacturing enterprise selling in several states would admittedly have income attributable to many of those states. An apportionment of this income would be reportable to each state by means of a formula.

Commonly, a state would recognize various categories of nonbusiness income with the residual income being business income. The classes of nonbusiness income would then typically be attributable to a particular state in the following manner:

Rents and royalties—real property	States where property located
Rents and royalties—tangible personal property	States where property utilized
Gains and losses from the sale of real property on tangible personal property	States where property located
Interest and dividends	State of commercial domicile
Patent on copyright royalties	States where the patent or copyright is utilized

The residual or business income was apportioned by formula. Although many variations existed, this was the general pattern.

Difference between the Traditional View and the MTC's View in Distinguishing Business Income and Nonbusiness Income

The MTC is discussed in Chapter 4. However, the conflict in the traditional approach with the MTC approach should be mentioned at this time.

In the regulations to UDITPA[9] adopted by the MTC on February 21, 1973, the distinction between business and nonbusiness income was deemphasized if not entirely extinguished. Nonbusiness income is barely recognized.

In contrast to the traditional view that nonbusiness income represents a class of income to which separate accounting could be applied, Reg. IV. 1(a) defines *nonbusiness income* as that income which is not business income. This very unhelpful definition is explained to mean that nonbusi-

---

[9]UDITPA was submitted by the National Conference of Commissioners on Uniform State Laws to the American Bar Association and approved by that body in 1957. UDITPA is embodied in the Multistate Tax Compact and is therefore applicable to the MTC members. Additionally, other states have substantially adopted UDITPA in their income tax laws.

ness income is income which is not income arising from transactions and activity in the regular course of the taxpayer's trade or business. The burden is placed on the taxpayer to show that some income is outside the regular course of business. Specifically, all income from tangible and intangible property is business income if the acquisition, management, and disposition of the property constitute integral parts of the taxpayer's regular trade or business operations. Further, the classification of income by labels such as interest, dividends, rents, royalties, and gains and losses have nothing to do with the classification as nonbusiness. The concept of being an integral part of the taxpayer's regular trade or business governs.[10]

The regulations then give examples indicating what certain types of income would be business income and when they would constitute nonbusiness income.

Exhibit 2.1

States	Substantially Adopted UDITPA[a]	Adopted the MTC Proposed UDITPA Regulations[a]	Members of the Multistate Tax Compact (1/1/79)
Alabama	X	X	
Alaska	X	X	X
Arkansas	X	X	X
California	X	X	X
Colorado	X	X	X
Hawaii	X		X
Idaho	X	X	X
Illinois	X		
Indiana	X	X	
Kansas	X	X	X
Kentucky	X	X	
Maine	X	X	
Michigan	X		X
Missouri	X	X	X
Montana	X	X	X
Nebraska	X	X	X
Nevada	X		X
New Mexico	X	X	X
North Carolina	X	X	
North Dakota	X	X	X
Oregon	X	X	X
Pennsylvania	X		

[10]The regulations dealing with the allocation and apportionment provisions of UDITPA were adopted by the MTC, which is the administrative arm of the Multistate Tax Compact. The regulations are subject to adoption by each compact member state in accordance with its own laws and procedures. Virtually all the member states that have an income tax have adopted the regulations (see State of Indiana, "Survey on the Uniformity of State Tax Laws" February 1977). See Exhibit 2.1.

Exhibit 2.1 (continued)

States	Substantially Adopted UDITPA[a]	Adopted the MTC Proposed UDITPA Regulations[a]	Members of the Multistate Tax Compact (1/1/79)
South Carolina	X		X
South Dakota	X		
Tennessee	X		
Texas	X		X
Utah	X	X	X
Virginia	X		
Washington	X		X

[a]State of Indiana, "Survey on the Uniformity of State Tax Laws," February 1977.

	Examples of Business Income	Examples of Nonbusiness Income
Rents from real and tangible personal property	4	3
Gains or losses from sales of assets	4	2
Interest income	5	1
Dividends	5	1
Patent and copyright royalties	2	1

The weight given to the number of examples classifying income as business income does not necessarily reflect bias on the part of the MTC. However, it has never been a disguised fact that the aim of the MTC is to severely restrict classifications of nonbusiness income. The underlying motivation for this might be that the members of the MTC are not generally those states which have a preponderance of corporate headquarters or manufacturing facilities. These two elements for the most part result in nonbusiness income being attributed to a state. Thus the member states would have a smaller amount of apportionable income under the traditional classification than they would by maximizing business income classification. Consider this example in which a company has the following income subject to taxation by states A and B and the percentage of business income apportionable to each state is 50 percent.

Nonbusiness income (allocable to B)	100,000
Business income	300,000
	400,000

If it is maintained that all income is business income

State A would tax 0.50 (400,000) =	200,000
State B would tax 0.50 (400,000) =	200,000
	400,000

If it is maintained that only 300,000 is business income

State A would tax 0.50 (300,000)	150,000
State B, on the other hand, would tax	
Nonbusiness income	100,000
Business income 0.50 (300,000)	150,000
	400,000

UDITPA was drafted by William J. Pierce, professor of law, University of Michigan Law School. Professor Pierce clearly must have felt that the traditional distinctions between business and nonbusiness income were to be retained in UDITPA. Writing in *Taxes*[11] he stated:

> *Allocation of nonbusiness income.* Sections 4 through 8 of the act provide for the allocation of four types of nonbusiness income to specific states, rather than apportioning on the basis of a formula. The reason for this treatment, *which is representative of the existing patterns of legislation, is that these items of income can appropriately be attributed to a specific state* (emphasis added).

The only change with respect to nonbusiness income treatment from the generally prevailing rules was the feature of allocation to the commercial domicile when the taxpayer was not taxable in the particular state to which the specific item of income would otherwise be allocated. Professor Pierce felt this was necessary in order that the income not escape state taxation.

Thus the MTC's view[12] that all income of the corporation is business income is not founded in the prevailing rules prior to UDITPA, nor in the intent of UDITPA itself. However, in *Mobil Oil Corporation* v. *Commissioner of Taxes in Vermont* (U.S. Supreme Court Docket No. 78–1201) the Supreme Court found no preference for allocation of income to a single situs. See Chapter 4 for more details of this case.

Apportionment of Income Based on a Three-Factor Formula

It was previously mentioned that many different apportionment formulas have been devised by the states. Without going into the history of the formula, the one known as the "Massachusetts formula" has had the most

---

[11]William J. Pierce, "The Uniform Division of Income for State Tax Purposes." *Taxes*, CCH, October 1957, Vol. 35, No. 10, p. 747.

[12]W. D. Dexter, "The Business v. Nonbusiness Distinction Under UDITPA," 10 *Urban Lawyer* 2 (Spring 1978). (Dexter is General Counsel, MTC.)

acceptance. This formula has been upheld by various courts and basically is the formula used in UDITPA. Because of its wide acceptance, by MTC members and others, this is the formula being reviewed in this chapter. Specifically, the previously mentioned MTC regulations to UDITPA are examined.[13] The apportionment formula develops a percentage that is then applied to total business income to arrive at the amount of business income taxable by the state. The simple formula is shown here:

$$\frac{In\text{-}state\ property}{Everywhere\ property} \qquad \%$$

$$\frac{In\text{-}state\ payroll}{Everywhere\ payroll} \qquad \%$$

$$\frac{In\text{-}state\ receipts}{Everywhere\ receipts} \qquad \%$$

Sum of above ratios $\qquad \%$

Sum divided by 3 = $\qquad \%$ applied to total business income

In some cases, a taxpayer may not have elements of all these factors. If the taxpayer has the element present concerning the denominator, it is included in the computation even though the numerator may be zero. If the element is not present even in the denominator, then this factor is eliminated from the formula, leaving only the remaining two factors. The sum of the other two factors would then be divided by two rather than three.

PROPERTY FACTOR

Regulation IV. 10 MTC defines property for purposes of that factor as all real and tangible personal property owned or rented and used during the year by the taxpayer in the regular course of his trade or business. The concept of business versus nonbusiness income is reflected in the apportionment factors in that only property, payroll, and receipts that are related to business income are used in the factors.

The principal features to be considered in working with the property factor are these:

1 The definition of real and tangible personal property includes land, depreciable or depletable property, inventory, and other tangible assets. Intangible assets such as patents or goodwill are not to be included.
2 The assets must be in use. Incomplete construction, since it is not in use, would be excluded. All inventories, whether raw materials, materials and supplies, work in process, or finished goods are considered in

[13]These regulations are reproduced in Appendix A.

use. Property temporarily withdrawn from use is considered in use until some identifiable event occurs that marks its permanent withdrawal from use.

3 The value of property in the factors is to be at original cost, which, in turn, is deemed to be the unadjusted basis for Federal income tax purposes.

4 The property factor is an average of beginning year and end-of-year values, unless distortions are present that would require monthly averaging. The tax administrator of a state may require or allow averaging by monthly values if such a method of averaging more properly reflects the average value of property.

5 Rent expense for real and tangible property is considered in the property factor by multiplying the gross rents by eight. The purpose of this is to equate taxpayers who lease property with those who own it. As to rent, the averaging of the value is not used, since it is considered to have been achieved automatically through the mechanism of estimation of value that is, multiplying by eight. The distinction between business and nonbusiness rent expense is stressed. Only rent expense associated with the production of business income enters into the property factor.

6 Mobile equipment such as rail cars or other transportation equipment is assigned to the different states based on the time used in each state. Automobiles assigned to traveling employees follow the payroll for that salesman, or, alternatively, that of the state where the automobile is licensed.

7 Property in transit, for example, inventory, is attributed to the state of destination.

PAYROLL FACTOR

The payroll factor closely follows IRC definitions of compensation. The amounts to be used depend on the method of accounting used by the taxpayer, but at the taxpayer's election, a cash method may be used. This election allows a taxpayer to tie in its payroll amounts to state unemployment compensation reports. Other features of the payroll factor are these:

1 Payroll applicable to the production of nonbusiness income is not used in the payroll factor.

2 Determination of the state in which services are performed is derived from the Model Unemployment Compensation Act. Variations from the amount reported to a state for unemployment purposes and that used for the payroll factor must be explained.

3 The payroll factor is derived from all employees of the taxpayer. Generally, a person will be considered to be an employee if he is included by the taxpayer as an employee for purposes of the payroll taxes imposed by the Federal Insurance Contributions Act.

SALES FACTOR

Regulation IV. 15 MTC defines "sales" to mean all gross receipts derived from transactions and activity in the regular course of business. Thus the term includes all business receipts falling into the category of business income. Interest, royalties, fees, commissions, net sales from the sale of tangible property, proceeds from the sale of equipment used in the business, and rents would all be considered in the sales factor if the income is classified as business income. Receipts classified as nonbusiness income would not be included in the sales factor. Other features are as follows:

1 Federal and state excise taxes are included in the receipts factor to the extent passed on to the buyer or included as part of the selling price of the product.
2 The general rule is that sales of tangible personal property are attributed to the state of destination. The intent is that the sale is to be attributed to the state where the ultimate consumer is located. There are two major exceptions to this general rule.
   (a) Shipments going to states where the taxpayer is not subject to state corporate taxes or would not be subject to state tax, for example, by reason of P.L. 86–272, are attributed to the state where the shipment originated. This exception is commonly known as the "throw-back rule."
   (b) Sales made to the U.S. government pursuant to the terms of a contract are attributed to the state of origin.
3 The general rule on receipts from activities other than the sale of tangible personal property is that such receipts are attributed to the state where the income-producing activity which gave rise to the income is performed. Business rental from real estate is attributable to the state where the property is located. Rentals from other tangible property is the same, but where more than one state is involved, the rental income is attributed to the various states in the ratio of time used in each state. These rules are the same as for owned property.

SPECIAL RULE

The UDITPA and the MTC regulations contain a controversial special rule that is also common to various states which have not adopted UDITPA.

Regulation IV.18 provides that if the allocation and apportionment provisions of Article IV of UDITPA do not fairly represent the extent of the taxpayer's business activity in a state, the taxpayer may petition for, or the tax administrator may require, in respect to all or any part of the taxpayer's business activity, if reasonable, the following:

1 Separate accounting.
2 The exclusion of any one or more of the factors.

3   The inclusion of one or more additional factors that will fairly represent the taxpayer's business activity in this state.

4   The employment of any other method to effectuate an equitable allocation and apportionment of the taxpayer's income.

This provision permits a departure from the allocation and apportionment provisions of Article IV. It was intended to be invoked only in specific cases where unusual fact situations (that ordinarily would be unique and nonrecurring) produce incongruous results under the apportionment and allocation provisions contained in Article IV.

The three-factor formula is perhaps the fairest and most reasonable formula ever developed for the apportionment of income to the states. It is universally conceded that a precise formula will never be devised. However, there are instances where the strict adherence to mechanical steps would produce distorted results. For this reason, most tax administrators feel that they should be empowered to make adjustments to the formula to protect the revenue of their state. Taxpayers may view this as a one-way street. If the taxpayer petitions for relief under this provision, it is safe to assume that it will ordinarily not be allowed by the tax administrator because it would decrease state revenue. On the other hand, since the tax administrator may require the modification, the taxpayer is forced to accept it or seek a remedy to the situation through litigation.

Examples of the employment of Rule 18 of UDITPA are seen in the *GTE*[14] and *Kennecott Copper*[15] cases.

In *GTE* the issue was the proper treatment of "drop shipment" sales for purposes of the sales factor of the Illinois income tax apportionment formula. (The allocation and apportionment of income in the Illinois Income Tax Act is substantially the same as in UDITPA.) The sales in question were those shipped directly from suppliers to customers of GTE located in states where GTE was not taxable. Some of the shipments originated in Illinois, and others originated in states where GTE was not taxable.

With regard to the shipments originating in Illinois and terminating in states where the taxpayer was not taxable these were found by the court to be includable in the Illinois numerator in accordance with the statute (throw-back rule). However the Illinois Income Tax Act does not specify the treatment for those sales originating outside Illinois, nor does UDITPA. The taxpayer included the amounts in the denominator of the sales factor but did not include them in the numerator in the computation of its Illinois Income Tax liability.

[14]*GTE Automatic Electric, Incorporated* v. *Robert H. Alphin* 369 NE 2d 841 (1977) Illinois S. Ct.
[15]*Kennecott Copper Corporation* v. *State Tax Commission of Utah* 493 P.2d 632 (1972) Utah S. Ct.

The MTC and 11 states filed an amicus curiae brief maintaining that the sales in question should be included in the Illinois numerator through an interpretation of the Illinois statute. Failure to include the sales in the numerator would allow the taxpayer to enjoy a tax loophole, contrary to legislative intent. Alternatively, it was suggested that the sales be excluded from both numerator and denominator.

The court rejected the MTC suggestions and recognized a legislative intent that the business income of a multistate corporation be apportioned in such a manner that 100 percent of its income, no more or no less, would be taxable. It then invoked the Illinois equivalent of Rule 18 of UDITPA and held that the sales be included in the Illinois numerator.

However, the loophole remains to be closed in UDITPA and other state statutes. Failure to provide for this type of shipment could subject the taxpayer to multiple taxation, since each state in which it files an income tax return could claim that the sales in question belong in the numerator of the sales factor.

In *Kennecott,* the taxpayer filed returns for the years 1967 and 1968 that reflected the following apportionment factors:

	1967	1968
Property	0.4246	0.3565
Payroll	0.4288	0.3336
Sales	0.00831	0.00568

The Utah Tax Commission was of the opinion that the returns did not fairly reflect the extent of Kennecott's business activity in Utah and made a redetermination of the sales factor under Rule 18. The Tax Commission deviated from the destination rule of UDITPA and used as a numerator the "net income from the property" (for purposes of calculating depletion allowable for Federal income taxation), less depletion.

In a strong dissenting opinion this was noted:

> In the instant action the Tax Commission, in defiance of express legislative policy and in disregard of the balancing purpose of the sales factor in a production jurisdiction, in effect apportioned the sales of Utah Cooper division to this state.

It was forcibly voiced that the relief provisions of Rule 18 should be given a narrow construction.

> . . . If a choice of methods is permitted, different administrators in different states inevitably will choose different methods. As a result, even if all the states imposing taxes on or measured by income should adopt the Uniform Act, the chaotic condition heretofore existing would continue to exist.

Also, reference was made to Professor Pierce's statement that if UDITPA were adopted in every state having a tax measured by income, 100 percent of such income, no more and no less, would be taxed. It was observed by the dissenting justice that this statement would not be true if Rule 18 were widely applied by the taxing states. Therefore, it was the intent that the formula be altered only in unusual cases.

COMPLIANCE PROBLEMS

Determination of Total Taxable Income for a Member of an Affiliated Group Filing a Consolidated Federal Income Tax Return

As discussed earlier, a common starting point for the computation of state income tax liability for a corporation is Federal Taxable income. From here, the various modifications to fulfill state requirements are made. The end result is income subject to state income taxation. If the entire activity of the taxpayer corporation is within one state, the state income tax is computed on this base. If the activities of the taxpayer corporation are partly within and partly without the taxing state, apportionment of the business income portion of the base is required. The most common method of apportionment is the three-factor base previously outlined. The percentage derived is applied to the business income portion of the base to arrive at the portion of income subject to state tax. Nonbusiness income is allocated to a specific state.

Where a corporation files a separate Federal income tax return, there is little problem in determining total taxable income. Where a corporation is a member of a group of corporations filing a consolidated Federal income tax return, the total taxable income is not as easily determined. To perceive this problem, an understanding of a consolidated Federal income tax return is useful. An outline of the computation of consolidated Federal taxable income follows. This outline is not intended to be all-inclusive but is presented to give an understanding of the mechanics of arriving at Consolidated Federal Taxable Income.

Step I—Computation of Separate Taxable Income (Reg. Sec. 1.1502–12)

Compute the Federal taxable income of each member as if a separate Federal income tax return were being filed.

ELIMINATE TO REMOVE FROM SEPARATE RETURNS (REG. SEC. 1.1502–12)

1 Intercompany dividends (Reg. Sec. 1.1502–14(a)).
2 Disallowed built-in deductions (Reg. Sec. 1.1502–15).
3 Excess mine exploration expenditures (Reg. Sec. 1.1502–16).

ELIMINATE SEPARATE RETURN CALCULATIONS IN ORDER TO RESTATE LATER ON A CONSOLIDATED BASIS (REG. SEC. 1.1502–12)

1 Net operating loss deductions (Reg. Sec. 1.1502–12(h)).
2 Capital gains and losses (Reg. Sec. 1.1502–12(j)).
3 Section 1231 gains and losses (Reg. Sec. 1.1502–12(k)).
4 Charitable contributions deductions (Reg. Sec. 1.1502–12(1)).
5 Section 922 deductions (Western Hemisphere trade corporations. (Reg. Sec. 1.1502–12(m)).
6 Dividends received deductions (Reg. Sec. 1.1502–12(n)).
7 Dividends paid deductions (Reg. Sec. 1.1502–12(n)).
8 Casualty and theft gains and/or losses.

ADJUST PRIMARILY TO REMOVE INTERCOMPANY GAINS AND LOSSES (REG. SEC. 1.1502–13)

1 Deferred intercompany gains and losses (Reg. Sec. 1.1502–13).
2 Intercompany profits in inventory (Reg. Secs. 1.1502–13 and 1.1502–18).
3 Nondividend distributions on intercompany-held stocks, bonds, notes, and other obligations and related gains and losses on disposal (Reg. Sec. 1.1502–14).
4 Excess losses of affiliates (on disposition of the stock of a subsidiary) (Reg. Sec. 1.1502–19).

The result of Step I is a computation that results in the separate taxable income of a member of a group of corporations filing a consolidated Federal income tax return, as required by Reg. Sec. 1.1502–12.

Step II—Computation of Consolidated Taxable Income (Reg. Sec. 1.1502–11)

Combine the separate taxable incomes computed in Step I.

ADJUST THE COMBINED TAXABLE INCOMES TO A CONSOLIDATED BASIS (REG. SEC. 1.1502–11)

1 Consolidated net operating loss deduction (Reg. Sec. 1.1502–21).
2 Consolidated charitable contributions deduction and limitation (Reg. Sec. 1.1502–24).
3 Consolidated Section 922, Western Hemisphere Trade Corporation deduction (Reg. Sec. 1.1502–25).
4 Consolidated dividends received deduction (Reg. Sec. 1.1502–26).
5 Consolidated dividends paid deduction (Reg. Sec. 1.1502–27).

6 Consolidated casualty and theft net loss.
7 Consolidated Section 1231 net loss (may include net gain from casualties and theft) (Reg. Sec. 1.1502–23).

ADD TO RESTATE ON A CONSOLIDATED BASIS (REG. SEC. 1.1502–11)

1 Consolidated net capital gain (Reg. Sec. 1.1502–22).
2 The consolidated net capital loss and limitations on carry-overs and carrybacks.

The result of Step II is a computation that results in consolidated Federal taxable income pursuant to Reg. Sec. 1.1502–11.

From the foregoing outline, it can be seen that Form 1120 is not necessary for each member of the group. Only one return is filed, and that is on a consolidated basis. The only requirement is a computation of separate taxable income for each company as shown in Step I of the outline.

Defining Federal Taxable Income

Many of the states have provisions to require the member of a consolidated Federal Income Tax Return to compute its Federal taxable income on a separate return basis. For example, the Illinois Income Tax Act makes the following provision[16]:

> . . . the taxable income properly reportable for Federal income tax purposes shall mean: Consolidated Corporations. In the case of a corporation which is a member of an affiliated group of corporations filing a consolidated income tax return for the taxable year for federal income tax purposes, taxable income is determined as if such corporation had filed a separate return for Federal income tax purposes for the taxable year and each preceding taxable year for which it was a member of an affiliated group.

Although seemingly a practical approach, it causes some difficulty at times for such a taxpayer. If a separate return were being filed by a member, then such a taxpayer might be planning Federal tax consequences on a different basis than it would as a member of a consolidated group. Consider the following examples:

1 The consolidated group might elect to claim foreign income taxes as a credit against U.S. tax liability, whereas the members might elect to claim these taxes as deductions.
2 The consolidated group might want to maximize deductions such as depreciation and research and experimental costs, whereas the member

---

[16]Illinois Income Tax Act, Chapter 120, Article 2, Section 203.

might want to minimize in order to utilize separate basis net operating loss carry-overs.

3 Transactions that become deferred intercompany transactions on a consolidated return, and thus not currently taxable, may be unattractive on a separate return basis. An illustration is this: Company A has land with a basis of $10 M, fair market value $85 M that Comapny B would like to purchase. If the sale is made and a consolidated Federal return is filed, the $75 M gain is deferred for Federal income tax purposes. If the sale were made and A filed a separate return, the gain would be taxable.

If Federal taxable income is defined on an "as if" basis, then consideration should at least be given to the following items for special handling.

Dividends Traditionally, dividend income has been considered non-business income. Accordingly, taxpayers allocated this income to the commercial domicile. The taxability then depended on the income tax law of the state where the company had its commercial domicile.

However, Multistate Tax Compact members take a dim view of dividends being treated as nonbusiness income. In those states, dividends would be considered business income. As such they are apportioned to the various taxing states and become subject to state tax to the extent so apportioned.

Dividend income is one type of income that is subject to state tax even though it may be deductible for Federal income tax purposes. For Federal income tax purposes, assuming separate returns are being filed, a 100 percent dividend received deduction for domestic intercompany dividends is available, and an 85 percent deduction is available for other domestic dividends. For state tax purposes, most states do not recognize either of these deductions; that is, the tax base is line 28 of the Federal income tax return. For those that recognize a deduction, the 100 percent deduction for intercompany dividends should be recognized even where the taxpayer is included in a consolidated Federal return. If a consolidated return is being filed, these dividends will be eliminated (see preceding outline). If a consolidated return is not filed, a 100 percent dividend received deduction could be elected.[17] This election can be made even if a consolidated return is filed.[18] Therefore, if dividend received deductions are allowed by a state, they should be allowed at 100 percent with respect to intercompany distributions. A taxpayer could assure this treatment by making the election under Section 243, IRC.

[17]IRC Section 243.
[18]Revenue Ruling 73–484 CB 1973–2 78.

Deferred Intercompany Gains and Losses

The Federal consolidated return regulations allow the deferral of gain or loss on specified deferred intercompany transactions. Restoration of such gain or loss is required when some subsequent event occurs. Events triggering restoration of deferred gain or loss include such events as the subsequent sale of the property by the buying member outside the affiliated group or subsequent deductions by the buying member, for example, depreciation in the case of depreciable property.

The timing of the taxability of gain or loss on deferred intercompany transactions should be the same for state tax purposes as it is for Federal purposes. Thus deferred gain on a sale by one member to another would not become part of taxable income for state purposes until restored to income for Federal income tax purposes.

In the preceding examples (item 3), Company A sold land with a basis of $10 M and fair market value of $85 M to Company B, both being members of an affiliated group filing a consolidated Federal income tax return. In the year of sale, Company A would otherwise have a $75 M gain for state tax purposes and no gain for Federal income tax purposes. Likewise, if Company B sold the land to a party that is not a member of the affiliated group in a subsequent year, Company B would have no gain for state tax purposes, but this event would trigger a gain of $75 M for Federal income tax purposes. It would seem that the year of taxability should be the same. However, with the common definition among the states, the taxability for state purposes will be different from the Federal.

Charitable Contributions   The limitation on charitable contributions is based on consolidated Federal taxable income. In some cases, the total consolidated deduction may be limited. Arguably, only the portion utilized in the consolidated return should be reflected as a deduction for state purposes. However, since it is usually not possible to relate an excess consolidated deduction to a specific member company, the practical solution is to deduct the amount that would be allowed on a separate return basis. Any carry-over would be reflected on a separate return basis even though it may have previously been utilized in full or in part in the consolidated return. As an illustration, assume a member company has a charitable contribution of X dollars in a year in which its contribution is above the allowable deduction on a separate return basis. None of this would be utilized by such member in the loss year for state purposes but would carryforward to subsequent years for state purposes. For Federal tax purposes, X dollars may have been utilized in the consolidated return.

Notification to the States of Changes in Federal Taxable Income

The degree to which the states reference their income taxes to Federal taxable income is very extensive. This direct tie-in to Federal taxable income has the advantage of establishing a firm starting point for the computation of state tax. It has an additional advantage in that the states, insofar as large corporate returns are concerned, may largely rely on the Internal Revenue Service (IRS) to perform most of the audit function with respect to taxable income. Thus a state does not need to greatly concern itself with the determination of taxable income from the books and records. Without the need to examine the state starting point, before adjustments, state audits can be limited to factors that only apply to state taxation, such as modifications to Federal taxable income, apportionment factors, distinctions between business and nonbusiness classifications, and other specific state tax issues.

The reliance on the IRS to determine a starting point for state income taxes would not be complete without some provision to adjust state taxable income for any change to Federal taxable income initiated by the taxpayer or required by the IRS. This gap is filled by the requirement of all the states: that some form of notification to the state be made within a specified time after a certain event. Exhibit 2.2 provides a general guide to these notification requirements among the various states.

Exhibit 2.2   Requirements for Notification to States of Changes in Federal Taxable Income

Category I after Final Determination (Due)	Category II after Change or Notice of Change (Due)	Category III Other (Due)	
Arizona (90 days)	Alaska (30 days)	Alabama	(on request)
California (90 days)	Arkansas (30 days)	Indiana	(on request)
Colorado (30 days)	Connecticut (90 days)	Kentucky	(30 days after knowledge of examination)
Delaware (90 days)	Washington, D.C. (30 days)	South Carolina	(30 days after start of examination
Florida (60 days)	Hawaii (90 days)	Tennessee	(required by regulation to be reported on return)
Georgia (180 days)	Illinois (20 days)	Iowa	(if amended Federal return filed, amended state return required)
Idaho (immediately)	Kansas (90 days)		
Louisiana (60 days)	Michigan (120 days)		
Maine (90 days)	Minnesota (90 days)		
Maryland (90 days)	Nebraska (90 days)		
Massachusetts (3 months)	New Mexico (30 days)		
Mississippi (30 days)	North Carolina (2 years)		
Missouri (90 days)	Oklahoma (1 year)		
Montana (90 days)	Pennsylvania (30 days)		
New Hampshire (due date of next return)	Vermont (30 days)		
New Jersey (90 days)			
New York (90 days)			
North Dakota (90 days)			
Ohio (120 days)			
Oregon (90 days)			
Rhode Island (60 days)			
Utah (90 days)			
Virginia (90 days)			
West Virginia (90 days)			
Wisconsin (90 days)			

Source: All States Tax Guide Prentice-Hall, Englewood Cliffs, N.J., 1977, paragraph 232.

Example of Notification by Company F for the Year 1975

1   Company F filed its Federal income tax return on June 15, 1976.
    Company F filed its various state income tax returns in accordance with
    state requirements about what constitutes Federal taxable income.
2   On September 15, 1976, the IRS commenced an audit of the 1975
    return.
3   The results of the audit revealed several issues that increased Federal
    taxable income. Regarding some of these issues, Form 870–C—
    "Waiver of Restrictions on Assessment and Collection of Deficiency in
    Tax and Acceptance of Overassessment"—was executed. The execu-
    tion of this form resulted in additional Federal income tax, being
    assessed and paid. The form was executed April 1, 1977. A Revenue
    Agents Report (RAR), dated May 15, 1977, was forwarded to Company
    F.
4   Regarding the contested issues, Company F chose to file a petition in
    U.S. Tax Court. These issues were reflected in the RAR, and Company
    F chose not to pay the tax on these issues pending the outcome of its
    litigation.

Company F would comply with those states in Category III of Exhibit 2.2
in accordance with the special requirements of those states. For example,
Kentucky and South Carolina would have been notified within 30 days
after September 15, 1976, which was the date the IRS examination began.

Regarding Category II of Exhibit 2.2 since a Notice of Change in
Federal taxable income has been received in the form of a RAR, Company
F would be compelled to notify the applicable states. Illinois, for example,
specifically states that the execution of Form 870 is an act that constitutes
an alteration in income required to be reported (Illinois Regulation Section
903–1(a)(3)). The specified time period for Illinois would date from April 1,
1977, the date Form 870 was executed.

Many of the states listed in Category I of Exhibit 2.1 require notification
only when a final determination of Federal income tax liability has occurred. A final determination for Company F will not occur until the litigation on the unagreed issues is completed and all time periods for appeal
have expired for both parties. Therefore, notification to these states would
not be required until the litigation had ended.

As a practical matter though, a final determination on the agreed issues
has occurred with the signing of Form 870, since Company F is certain
about these issues. It may desire to notify those states where applicable to
minimize interest on the deficiencies. If interest is not material to the
decision, it may choose to wait until litigation is settled before notification.

The methods of notification take different forms. Most commonly, a
statement itemizing the changes, prepared from the RAR, or a copy of the
RAR itself is forwarded to the state. This information will then be used to

recompute the tax liability, and an assessment, plus interest, will be issued by the state. Increasingly, an amended return or the equivalent computation is required. This latter method places the burden on the taxpayer to (1) give notification of change, (2) compute the additional tax, plus interest, and (3) remit the amount due, all in a single communication.

Adjustments to Taxable Income as a Result of the Renegotiation Act of 1951*

Under the Renegotiation Act of 1951 as amended, certain governmental deparments or agencies are authorized and directed to require contractors to renegotiate the contract price with respect to designated contracts and subcontracts. Excess profits associated with the contracts are required to be repaid to the government.

The determination of excess profits associated with governmental contracts is made by the Renegotiation Board, which was created as the enforcing body of the Act. The Renegotiation Board administers the Act and conducts audits of contracts and subcontractors subject to the Act to determine the amount, if any, of the excess profits.

The IRS has no authority to function in the determination or collection of excess profits. This is a function of the Renegotiation Board. The District Director, IRS, however, on the request of the parties to the renegotiation, will advise them of the manner in which the renegotiation affects the Federal income tax for the year in which there is a determination of excess profits by the Renegotiation Board. For illustration, assume that Builder Corporation performed contracts with the U.S. government during 1972 that fell within the jurisdiction of the Renegotiation Act of 1951. Assume further that the Renegotiation Board found in its examination of the profits earned on those contracts that profits were excessive and that the parties agree that the excess profit is $1 million.

The effect of this assessment is a reduction of the 1972 Federal taxable income of Builder of $1 million. Since taxable income has been reduced, it follows that the Federal income tax liability should be reduced accordingly. This reduction is provided for in Section 1481 of the Internal Revenue Code of 1954. Administratively, to determine the Federal income tax offset, Builder and the Board would request the District Director of the IRS to advise them of the amount by which 1972 Federal income tax liability would be reduced by the excess profit determination. The Renegotiation Board would reduce the assessment by the amount of tax reduction. Builder would then receive and pay a net amount to the U.S. govern-

---

*Note: The Renegotiation Board has been terminated. After a final two-hour debate on April 2, 1979, the U.S. Senate decided against appropriating more funds for the Board, and this agency's activities abruptly ceased. Efforts are underway to have the Board's function reinstated in a different form.

ment.[19] Assuming a 48 percent tax rate, the net amount would be as follows:

Excess profits	$1,000,000
Mitigation of tax effect pursuant to Section 1481 IRC	480,000
Amount payable to government	$ 520,000

In cases of renegotiation agreements for a year for which an income tax return has not yet been filed and for which income tax has not been paid, the procedure would be different from the foregoing. In such a case, the Federal income tax return would be filed reflecting the lower income and tax paid accordingly.[20]

The significance of the Renegotiation procedure is that an assessment of excess profits triggers the possibility of refund of state income taxes. Since Federal taxable income is reduced, the starting point for state taxes has also been reduced. Consider the following illustration:

Total taxable income for State A as reflected on the return filed for 1975	$180,000
Apportionment to State A (10%)	18,000
Excess profits of $30,000 are determined; thus total taxable income becomes	150,000
Apportionment to State A (10%)	15,000
Change in State A taxable income	3,000
Refund due based on a 6% state tax rate	$ 180

Partnerships

None of the states having an income tax imposes its tax directly on the partnership. Rather the individual partners are taxed to the extent of their partnership profit interests or taxable distributions from the partnership.

For state purposes, the income of a partnership may be taxed on the "entity theory." The term "entity" is here used to indicate that although the organization itself is not directly taxed, the division of the income for state tax purposes is done at the partnership level by application of the state allocation and apportionment rules. To illustrate how this would be applied, assume that Baron Corporation is a partner with two other parties in Partnership A doing part of its business in Illinois. Partnership A will prepare Form 1065, the Partnership Return, which is an information return.

[19]For additional discussion, see Revenue Ruling 71–415, 1971–2 CB 322 and Revenue Ruling 74–259, 1974–1 CB 250.
[20]See Revenue Ruling 74–259, 1974–1 CB 250.

Exhibit 2.3   Determination of Partnership Taxes

Method 1

Partnership A's total income: $70,000

Apportionable income distribution:

Illinois	25% × $64,000 =	$16,000
Indiana	10% × $64,000 =	6,400
Iowa	15% × $64,000 =	9,600
Missouri	50% × $64,000 =	32,000
		$64,000

Allocable income distribution:

Iowa	1,000
Illinois	5,000
	$6,000

Baron's partnership interest: 50%
Income allocable to Illinois by Baron Corporation:

50% ×	16,000 =	8,000
50% ×	5,000 =	2,500
		10,500

Method 2

Partnership A	Payroll	Sales	Property
	800,000	25,000,000	15,000,000
Interest in Partnership A	50%	50%	50%
Baron's portion of apportionment factors	400,000	12,500,000	7,500,000

For Federal income tax purposes. this return provides information to the partners necessary to the preparation of their respective Federal income tax returns. Thus Baron would report the applicable share of income and deductions on its corporate return, Form 1120.

Partnership A will also prepare Illinois Form IL–1065, the Partnership Return of Income. (Form IL–1065 must be used in Illinois if any of the partners are nonresidents. In Illinois the term "nonresident" includes all corporations.)

Partnership A will determine its Illinois taxable income as if it were a taxable entity. Baron, a nonresident partner, will then report its share on the corporate return. Partnership A will determine the allocable or nonbusiness income for Illinois based on the rules of that state. Next, the apportionable or business income attributable to Illinois will be determined based on the three-factor formula, using only the factors of the partnership. Baron's share of allocable income and apportionable income is reflected on its Illinois corporate income tax return as allocable income and is thus fully taxable.

In summary, the partnership determines its Illinois allocable and apportionable income as if it were a separate entity, and each corporate partner reports its share of both as income allocable to Illinois. (See Exhibit 2.3.)

Care should be taken to assure that partnership income is not taxed twice. Partnership income will already be reflected in the corporation's Federal income tax return that is used as the starting point for state income tax returns. This amount should be removed prior to allocation and apportionment of the corporate income. Partnership income will then be brought in as allocable income as previously stated. The tax forms provide for this adjustment.

An approach that views the partnership under the "aggregate theory" is also used. This method assumes that the partners all have an undivided interest in the activity of the partnership. The mechanics of applying the allocation and apportionment rules under this method for Baron with respect to the previously mentioned Partnership A would be as follows:

1 Determine the undivided interest in the sales, property, and payroll of the partnership. Usually, this would be on the basis of the partners' profit interest.
2 Determine the state breakdown of each of the apportionment factors of the partnership.
3 Combine the apportionment data, in state and everywhere, as determined in step 2 with the corporate apportionment data of Baron.

Since Federal taxable income already reflects the distributive share of gain or loss, no adjustment is required before application of the allocation and apportionment procedure of Baron as was necessary under the entity concept. The aggregate approach is more commonly used where the partnership is determined to be "unitary" to the operations of the corporate partner. (See Exhibit 2.3.)

The apportionment values from Partnership A are combined with the apportionment values of Baron. For example, the $400,000 payroll amount would be combined with the total payroll of Baron to form the denominator of that factor for Baron. Likewise, the Illinois portion of the $400,000 would be combined with Baron's Illinois payroll to form the numerator of the payroll factor.

Net Operating Losses (NOLs)

Section 172, IRC, allows corporate taxpayers a carryback and carryforward of net operating losses (NOLs). The sequence is a carryback to the third year previous to the year in which the loss was incurred then to the second and first. Thereafter, the loss is carried forward for five years. For net operating losses incurred after December 31, 1975, the carryover period is seven years instead of five.

A special election is available with respect to NOLs incurred after December 31, 1975. This election allows a taxpayer to forego the carryback provisions. Such an election, once made for any taxable year, is irrevocable for that taxable year. For Federal income tax purposes, a taxpayer may find this election useful if there were tax credits utilized in preceding years that would expire unused as a result of the NOL carryback, or the taxes saved as a result of the carryback would be less than obtained by a carry-over. This could result from differences in tax rates or alternative computations.

The extent to which the states allow corporate taxpayers a carryover of NOLs is quite varied.[21] A few specifically allow no adjustments to other years or have no provision for NOL deductions. Some follow the Federal provisions, and it is presumed that these states would recognize the Federal election to forego the carryback. The rest of the states have provisions for NOLs with varied restrictions. For example, the time periods are different, or the NOL may be limited to a new industry as in the case of South Carolina. (See S. B. 449 for the recent amendment regarding NOLs.)

When confronted with a NOL for Federal income tax purposes, it is, of course, important to recognize and apply the NOL provisions of the states. If a carryback is involved, it will be necessary to file a claim for refund with the states involved in the manner prescribed by that state. Filing such a claim will ordinarily result in the proper refund, except that, in some instances, an audit by the state may result in an order for the taxing jurisdiction to verify the amount. Needless to say, timely filing of the claim should be closely observed.

There is some inconsistency with respect to how the NOLs are calculated by the states. For example, assume the following data for Pollox Company, which is subject to the income tax of State M. Further assume that State M has a three-year carryback.

	1976	1975	1974	1973
Federal taxable income modified for State M	(3,000)	10,000	8,000	11,000
Apportionment % of Pollox to State M	43%	20%	16%	18%

---

[21]See *All States Tax Guide*, Prentice-Hall, paragraph 228–E.

Method 1

The NOL is carried back in its entirety to 1973, similar to the Federal income tax procedure. State tax is computed on the net for 1973 after application of the NOL carryback.[22]

Income	11,000
1976 NOL carryback	(3,000)
Revised apportionable income	8,000
Revised M taxable income @ 18%	1,440

Method 2

The state portion of the NOL for 1976 is first determined and then carried back to 1973.[23]

State M NOL for 1976	
3000 × 43%	(1,290)
State M Taxable Income for	
1973 before NOL 11,000 × 18%	1,980
Revised State M taxable income	590

In this example, the income taxable by State M as revised by application of the NOL carryback is different under the two methods:

Method 1	1,440
Method 2	590

This difference is due to the fluctuation of the apportionment percentage. Of the two methods, Method 2 would appear to be the most equitable, since it properly matches the loss incurred within State M with income earned in that state.

A noteworthy situation arises where a company included in a consolidated federal income tax return has a NOL but where the consolidated return has taxable income. As mentioned earlier, most states permit or require such a member to file state returns based on what Federal taxable income would have been had the member company filed a separate return for the current year and all previous years. Thus a member of an affiliated group having a NOL would, under this concept, be entitled to state

---

[22]See Section 39–22–504 Colorado Income Tax Act.
An NOL deduction shall be allowed in the same manner that it is allowed under the IRC, except as is otherwise provided in this section. The amount of the NOL that may be carried forward and carried back for Colorado income tax purposes shall be that portion of the Federal NOL allocated to Colorado under this article in the taxable year that the NOL is sustained.
[23]See 1978 General Instruction for Form M–4, Minnesota Corporation Income Tax Return Line 17, which allows the apportionment ratio of the loss year, or the apportionment ratio of the year to which the loss is carried, whichever is smaller.

carrybacks and carryforwards the same as any other corporate taxpayer. This puts the member of an affiliated group on a par with taxpayers filing separate federal income tax returns. In either case, the NOL is applied against Federal taxable income. For the member of an affiliated group, the NOL is applied in the current year through the mechanism of the consolidated Federal income tax return. In the case of a taxpayer filing separately, the NOL is applied by way of the NOL provisions of Section 172, IRC. It follows that such NOLs should likewise be applied in both instances for state tax purposes. However, since the mechanism of the consolidated return is not available for state tax purposes, the carryback and carryforward rules produce the equitable result.

Pollution Control Facilities

Section 169, IRC permits taxpayers to elect a five-year amortization of qualified costs of air and water pollution control facilities. The purpose of this IRC section is to provide tax relief to taxpayers that were required to make substantial investments in facilities necessary to meet Federal clean air and clean water standards. A penalty was imposed on those that made the election with respect to property which would have qualified for investment credit. The election to take amortization under Section 169 precluded a taxpayer from claiming investment credit. The investment credit penalty was modified by the Tax Reform Act of 1976 to require that only 50 percent of the property be excluded from the investment credit base. Finally, full investment credit was allowed under the Revenue Act of 1978, except where the facilities are financed by tax exempt Industrial Development Bonds.

Many taxpayers have determined that the election under Section 169 is undesirable for one or more of the following reasons:

1 Loss of investment credit.
2 Requirements for state and Federal certifications to take advantage of the election.
3 Five-year amortization not a substantial incentive over accelerated depreciation, SYD, or 200 percent DB, for assets with relatively short lives.
4 The amortization under Section 169 generates a tax preference item entering into the computation of the minimum tax under Section 56, IRC.

Thus, overall, many taxpayers found the intended incentive of Section 169 to be a financial penalty and declined to make the election, except for Section 1245 property having a relatively long depreciable life, say, more than 15 years, and with respect to depreciable real property that has a long depreciable life.

If a state permits amortization in accordance with Section 169, IRC, the deductions reflected in Federal taxable income automatically flow into the state return. However, if a particular state does not permit Section 169 amortization, and such a deduction is reflected for Federal tax purposes, an adjustment will be necessary. The adjustment for that state tax will be to remove the amortization from total taxable income and substitute a deduction, that is, depreciation permitted by the state. Such an adjustment would be necessary so long as the asset is being depreciated for state purposes.

If Section 169 amortization is not being taken for Federal purposes but is desired for state purposes, a similar adjustment is required. In this case, the Federal depreciation deduction is removed from total taxable income, and the state amortization deduction is taken for state purposes. This adjustment is necessary for as long as the asset is being depreciated for Federal income tax purposes. Consider this example of an asset costing $550 having a 10-year life being amortized under Section 169 for Federal tax purposes, but State E allows depreciation only (SYD):

Year	Federal Amortization Taken	Depreciation Allowed by State E	State Adjustment
1	110	100	−10
2	110	90	−20
3	110	80	−30
4	110	70	−40
5	110	60	−50
6		50	50
7		40	40
8		30	30
9		20	20
10		10	10
	550	550	0

Deductions for Federal Income Tax

Only a few states allow a deduction for Federal income taxes. In general, the deduction is accomplished by treating the amount as an addition to those deductions shown on the Federal income tax returns. The amount deductible is, in some instances, on a cash basis, even though the taxpayer may be on an accrual method of accounting. A taxpayer filing a Federal income tax return on a calendar year basis will have the Federal tax applicable to a given year reflected on Line 31, Form 1120, U.S. Corporation Income Tax Return. This amount will be the total tax paid with respect to the income for the year. Since the tax shown thereon relates to the taxable income, the tax reflected on Line 31 will ordinarily be the deduction. The deduction against state taxable income is determined by application of the apportionment percentage used to determine state taxable income.

The Federal income tax deduction for a member of an affiliated group filing a consolidated Federal income tax return was the controversy in an Alabama case involving Western Grain Company[24] (Western).

Western filed its Alabama income tax return, taking a deduction for Federal income tax based on the amount shown on its books as accrued Federal income tax. It joined with the parent company and other affiliated subsidiaries in filing a consolidated Federal income tax return. The amount it paid to the parent was the amount accrued on its books that was the tax calculated as if the corporation had filed a separate Federal return. While a separate return was not prepared, a statement of taxable income showing Federal tax thereon was prepared and forwarded to the parent. In this instance, the affiiliated group had a consolidated loss, and no federal income tax was actually paid. However, by agreement with the parent Western paid to the parent the sum it had calculated on the statement submitted.

The Alabama Department of Revenue denied the deduction, saying, in effect, that Western neither paid nor accrued any Federal income tax because of its joining on the consolidated return. The Alabama Court of Civil Appeals upheld the disallowance, and the taxpayer's appeals to the Alabama Supreme Court and the U.S. Supreme Court were denied.

Precedent for the decision in Western had been established in the *Standard Oil Company (California)* case.[25] The factual situation in this case was much the same as in Western. The subsidiary (Kyso) was a member of an affiliated group filing a consolidated return. It did not prepare a separate return but filed an accounting statement with the parent showing how much it would have had to pay to the IRS if it had filed directly. The *Kyso* situation was different from *Western* in that the consolidated group incurred a liability. Kyso, although not allowed to deduct the separate tax, was allowed a deduction but only to the extent of a percentage of the actual cash paid to the IRS by the parent. Further, the amount paid to the IRS could not be considered the amount before investment credit. The taxpayer had contended that the Federal tax paid should be viewed as the amount prior to credits on the theory that the "credit" was part of the payment.

The *Kyso* and *Western* decisions hinged on the interpretation of the phrase "Federal income taxes paid or accrued" as contained in the Alabama regulations. The court sustained the Department of Revenue's

[24]*State of Alabama* v. *Western Grain Company* 318 So. 2d 719 (Appeal dismissed U.S. Supreme Court).
[25]*Standard Oil Company* v. *State* (1975) 313 So. 2d 526 cert. denied. Alabama S. Ct. 313 So. 2d 540.

interpretation that "paid" or "accrued" meant the amount paid from the parent to the IRS. Thus the filing of an accounting statement with the parent, followed by payment of tax to the parent, would not meet the test. The court was also influenced by the state's consistent policy of refusing to allow any corporation or any person to take a deduction for Federal income tax in an amount in excess of the amount actually paid to the IRS. The amount to be deducted was the amount shown to be due by the final Federal income tax return filed with the U.S. government.

Kyso had relied, in part, on the *Cities Service* decision of the Kansas courts.[26] This was a case involving similar facts and the same legal issue in which the Kansas Supreme Court held that the subsidiary corporation actually incurred and paid Federal income tax when it filed a statement with the parent and then discharged its tax liability by payment to the parent rather than the IRS. However, the state of Alabama cited *Trunkline Gas Company*[27] in which the Louisiana court reached the result as the Alabama court did in *Standard Oil*.

Consider this example in which companies A, B, C, and D are members of an affiliated group, all owned 100 percent by Parent M. Company A files a tax return with State K that permits a deduction for Federal income tax. The income and separate return tax are shown here:

	Taxable Income	Separate Return Tax
Parent M	10,000	5,000
Company A	100,000	50,000
Company B	50,000	25,000
Company C	(25,000)	0
Company D	(85,000)	0
Consolidated	50,000	25,000

1 Company A files a return with State K, and the affiliated group does not file a consolidated return. Company A's deduction would be the amount reflected on the return, $50,000.

2 Company A files a return with State K, and the affiliated group files a consolidated return, and Company A pays its separate return liability to the parent.

(a) If the interpretation by the state for allowance of the deduction follows the Kansas decision, Company A would be allowed a deduction of $50,000, just as if it had filed a separate return and paid the amount to the U.S. government.

---

[26]*Cities Service Gas Company* v. *McDonald* 466 P. 2d 277.
[27]*Trunkline Gas Company* v. *Collection of Revenue* 182 So. 2d 674.

(b) If the interpretation by the state for allowance of the deduction follows the Alabama and Louisiana decisions, Company A would be allowed only a portion of the consolidated tax of $25,000, typically, in proportion to other profit companies.

Profit Companies	Amount
Company M	10,000
Company A	100,000
Company B	50,000
Total profit companies	160,000

Company A profit $\dfrac{100,000}{160,000} \times 25,000 = \$15,635$
Total profit companies

The Missouri Supreme Court more recently held in the *Armco* case[28] that under the Missouri statute as it existed at the time (1969) that the Western approach was applicable. (In 1973, the Missouri code was revised to allow a deduction on a separate return basis.)

---

[28]*Armco Steel Corporation* v. *State Tax Commissioner* 580 S.W. 2d 242.

CHAPTER THREE

Combined Reports

BACKGROUND

Problems in the Taxation of a Business with Activities within and without a State

Corporations conducting a trade or business for profit will be subject to an income tax at both the Federal and state levels. Compliance at the Federal level necessitates the adoption of a common set of tax regulations. Compliance at the state level differs in that it requires an understanding and application of numerous state tax regulations. When a corporation has operations within only one state, a more simplistic approach to this subject can be taken. All revenue and expense producing activities are performed within specific geographic boundaries, assuring that a state can tax no more than 100 percent of corporate net income. Furthermore, there is no other state having the jurisdiction to tax this same income. Therefore, there are no Federal constitutional problems involving interstate tax burdens simply because all the business activities are intrastate.

If a business does have operations in more than one state, it will be subject to taxation within several jurisdictions and must comply with each state's tax. These are the corporations referred to as having activities partly within and partly without a taxing state. Uniformity is harder to achieve in these cases because each state will have its own unique method for determining the corporation's taxable income. The income subject to taxation is based on each state's interpretation of the amount of business activity transacted within its boundaries in relation to the total activities of the corporation. The corporations operating in these states may not view the nature and frequency of their activities in the same manner. There is a fine line between a reasonable basis for a tax and a basis that could eventually become a burden to interstate commerce. Each state wants to assess a reasonable tax liability as compensation for the legal and economic protection provided to all business. Each corporation wants to legally minimize its state tax burden through effective tax planning. Many important issues have arisen because of this basic conflict of interests. To present an unbiased discussion of these issues, the situation is analyzed from both viewpoints.

As Viewed by the States

As previously stated, each state wants to receive compensation for the privileges and benefits granted to the corporations conducting business within its borders. This compensation is a very important revenue source that directly affects state budgeting. When a corporation pays what a state believes is less than its fair share of tax, the state revenue department might consider alternative taxing procedures to amend this situation. The larger the tax a corporation must absorb in its operating costs, the more inclined it will be to practice tax planning. At this point, it is crucial to realize that although tax evasion is illegal tax avoidance is an accepted planning tool. As long as there is no fraudulent denial of a tax, any legal means may be used to minimize the tax burden. There have been two commonly used techniques for minimizing the burden of state taxation.

INCOME SHIFTING UNDER SEPARATE ACCOUNTING

The first technique involves a shifting of income between operating states. Income is reported to the state with the lower tax rate or to the state that does not have a tax based on or measured by income. This can be easily accomplished by those corporations with manufacturing and selling divisions located in different states. When the manufacturing operations are in the state with the higher tax rate, the taxable income reportable to that state can be decreased by charging the selling division with the total costs of production, or with reasonable, but often subjective, transfer prices. If the total costs of manufacturing are equal to the charge to the selling division, no income will be attributable to the state of manufacturing, and, accordingly, no taxes will be paid. If the total costs of manufacturing are offset by a nominal transfer price, there will be a loss or relatively little taxable income. This transaction between the two divisions will be journalized as a charge to the selling division from the manufacturing division. The manufacturing division's books of account will then reflect the taxable income as computed for state taxation purposes. The selling division's books of account will also reflect the charge for the manufactured goods.

The corporation could try to justify charging a selling division with the total cost of manufacturing by stating that a manufacturing division cannot earn revenue and that only a selling division can recognize and then realize revenue after a sale has been made. The corporation could also justify the transfer price between its two divisions by claiming and illustrating it to be representative of a fair market value. This may be difficult to disprove because of the subjective nature of many market prices and the inability to put a price tag on certain products. Consider this example in which B&T, Incorporated, manufactures electronic games that are sold throughout the country. All production occurs in State X, and all sales are made from State Y. Both states impose income taxes based solely on intrastate activities. Tax rates of 8 percent and 4 percent are imposed by states X and Y, respectively. Illustrated next are Exhibits 3.1, a Cost of Goods Manufactured Statement, and 3.2, an Income Statement; both statements are used in determining and computing the state income tax liabilities.

Computation of State Taxes—Separate Accounting by Divisions

	Manufacturing Division State X		Selling Division State Y
Net sales or gross receipts		$150,000	$500,000
Less expenses		150,000	375,000
Income subject to state taxes		0	$125,000
State adjustments		0	15,000
State taxable income		0	$110,000
Taxes due	(8%)	0	(4%) 4,400

As illustrated in the example, the manufacturing division in State X charges the selling division in State Y with the total costs of manufacturing or

Exhibit 3.1 B&T, Incorporated, Statement of Cost of Goods Manufactured for the Year Ended December 31, 1979

Materials		
Beginning inventory, December 31, 1978		$ 15,000
Net purchases		85,000
Total inventory and purchases		$100,000
Ending inventory, December 31, 1979		10,000
Cost of materials used		$ 90,000
Direct labor		50,000
Manufacturing overhead		
Indirect labor	$10,000	
Heat, light, and power	2,000	
Machinery repairs	4,000	
Depreciation	8,000	
Insurance	1,000	
Property taxes	2,000	
Small tools	3,000	
Miscellaneous expenses	2,000	
Total overhead		$ 32,000
Total costs of manufacturing		172,000
Add beginning goods in process, December 31, 1978		25,000
Total		$197,000
Deduct ending goods in process, December 31, 1979		47,000
Cost of goods manufactured		$150,000

Exhibit 3.2 B&T, Incorporated, Income Statement of Selling Division for the Year Ended December 31, 1979

Gross sales			$525,000
Sales returns and allowances			25,000
Net sales			$500,000
Cost of goods sold			
Beginning finished goods			
inventory, December 31, 1978	$ 30,000		
Cost of goods manufactured			
(Exhibit 3.1)	150,000		
Total merchandise available			
for sale	$180,000		
Ending finished goods			
inventory, December 31, 1979	20,000		$160,000
Gross profit on sales			$340,000
Operating expenses			
Selling expenses			
Salaries	$ 25,000		
Advertising	15,000		
Depreciation on delivery			
equipment	5,000	$45,000	
General and administrative			
expense			
Officers and office salaries	$ 50,000		
Insurance	3,000		
Taxes	5,000		
Depreciation of office furniture	5,000		
Miscellaneous	10,000	73,000	118,000
Net operating income			$222,000
Other revenue and expense items			
Dividend income	$ 5,000		
Interest income	4,000	$ 9,000	
Interest expense		11,000	2,000
Net income before taxes			$220,000
Income taxes			95,000
Net income			$125,000

$150,000. No income is attributed to operations in State X; therefore, all income taxes are paid to State Y. If a $160,000 transfer price were charged to the selling division representing the costs of manufacturing, plus a $10,000 fixed charge, total income taxes would increase $400, with $800 payable to State X ($160,000 − 150,000) × 0.08 and $4,000 payable to State Y ($500,000 − 385,000 − 15,000) × 0.04.

This type of tax avoidance is possible when a state's tax is based only on the business activity transacted in that state. The underlying assumption is that each division functions as a separate and independent operation. If both state taxes were to be based on the apportioned earnings from the entire corporate operations, regardless of the transfer prices used, neither division would be able to avoid these taxes. This explains why many states insist on income apportionment from every corporation instead of a so-called "separate accounting" system as just illustrated.

INCOME SHIFTING UNDER FORMULARY APPORTIONMENT

Even when a state tax is based on the apportioned income of a corporation, there is another mechanism that can be used to minimize taxes. A corporation can modify its structure and create a new subsidiary corporation by incorporating a division of the original parent corporation. The new corporation can be domiciled where the old division was domiciled. If feasible, the operations could even be moved to a state with lower tax rates or one that does not presently have a tax based on or measured by income.

Let us consider once again the corporation with a manufacturing and selling division in different states. If this corporation were to create a new subsidiary corporation in lieu of its selling division, the corporation's sales of manufactured goods produced by the manufacturing division would now be transacted with the new subsidiary corporation instead of with the selling division. The sale price can be fixed at the exact cost of manufacturing each period or for the cost of manufacturing, plus a fixed percentage. This will eliminate taxable income for the original manufacturing corporation or fix the taxable income at a certain level.

It is probably evident at this point that the same underlying tax planning concept has been used in both situations discussed, whether there is a "shifting of income" under separate accounting or a "shifting of income" under income apportionment. These two planning techniques cannot be used interchangeably, although the end result in both cases is a minimization or elimination of taxes paid by a manufacturing division or corporation. In the example, the taxing states based their income taxes only on the activities performed within their borders. No relationship to other divisions or corporations is considered, so the use of transfer pricing between divisions was the only action that was necessary to decrease the tax liability. When the state taxes are based on activities of each separate corporation, regardless of whether all the activity occur within a state's borders, a new type of tax plan is needed. In these cases, the creation of a subsidiary corporation will aid in decreasing the state tax burden. The type of tax used by the states will control the tax planning techniques used by any corporation.

From the viewpoint of taxing states, the accepted usage of these tax planning tools by so many corporations has provoked them into searching for taxing methods that would close such loopholes. The use of income shifting under separate accounting and the use of shifting under formulary income apportionment through the modification of corporate structures are two examples of loopholes claimed to have been used by taxpayers.

As Viewed by the Interstate Corporation

Every corporation with interstate operations is entitled to a nondiscriminatory tax system that extends to all the states in which it has contact. These interstate businesses require protection so that they will not have to bear the burden of paying taxes on more than 100 percent of their income. However, local corporations should not be penalized at the expense of these interstate companies. It is necessary that both local and interstate businesses absorb the tax burden of a state in an equitable manner. This will help to insure that an interstate business does not have a competitive advantage over a local business simply because its operations extend beyond a state's borders.[1]

Practically, this type of tax system in which no more than 100 percent of a corporation's income can be taxed may not be feasible within the limits of the current tax system. There are differences in the nature of the state taxing systems, in addition to the differences in the nature of the state taxes, their coverage, and the tax rates.

ANALYSIS OF APPORTIONMENT FACTORS

Although the tax planning used by a corporation will reduce the burden of interstate taxation, many corporations still view some state taxes as restrictive and biased. Primarily, this accusation is directly against the states that base their taxes on the apportioned earnings of a corporation. Basically, it is argued that the apportionment formulas are the causes of the bias against foreign corporations, because they tend to favor resident businesses.[2] We can see how this occurs through a discussion of the three-factor formula and its inherent weaknesses.

Property

First, consider the property factor. The items most commonly included in this factor are inventories, supplies, property, plant, equipment, and rented property expense times eight. It is possible for slight variations in the factor to occur, depending on the corporation and the state involved. Each property item included in the formula is an asset owned or rented by a corporation that offers potential benefits for increasing revenue or can be sold or exchanged for other assets. A factory and the land on which it is built are both needed for the factory to manufacture products for a profit. Similarly, inventory is needed to earn a profit from sales transacted in the regular course of business. The assets not included in the property factor,

---

[1]Jerome R. Hellerstein, "An Academician's View of State Taxation of Interstate Commerce," 16 *Tax Law Review* 2 (January 1961), pp. 162–163.
[2]Floyd E. Britton, "Taxation without Representation Modernized," 38 *Taxes* 8 (August, 1960), p. 631. Subsections 1, 2, and 3 are based on Britton's thesis presented in this article.

as defined by most states, include the intangible assets of a corporation. These intangibles are also working assets of the corporation as are the properties and inventories. Each contributes to the potential earnings of the corporation and, perhaps, should also be included in the property factor. Excluding the intangibles from the factor provides a tax advantage for the resident corporations. The reason for this is that most intangibles are located in the state of domicile or where the main headquarters are located, which would place these assets in the numerator of the factor for the resident taxpayers. This would increase the apportionable income of the corporation and, accordingly, the tax burden.[3] It is easy to understand why a foreign corporation would feel that it is unjustly overtaxed to compensate for this undertaxation of the domestic corporations.

Sales

The sales or gross receipts factor is also subject to some controversy. The factor is usually determined by the ratio of destination sales in the taxing state in relation to the total sales for a company. When a nonresident business transacts a sale in one state to be delivered to the taxing state, this sale will be includable in the numerator of the sales factor because the destination of the product is the taxing state. When a resident business transacts a sale in the taxing state to be shipped to a neighboring state, the sale will be excluded from the numerator of the factor because the destination of the product is to a different state. In effect, the sales ratio becomes a measure of the proportion of the shipment into a state in relation to total shipments by the company. This causes a larger tax for nonresident businesses because "except for the direction of the purchaser to ship the goods into the taxing state, there would be no tax in the state of destination on the nonresident seller measured by the sale. The tax in practical effect is on account of and proportionate to shipment into the state. It is a direct deterrent to the search for, and acceptance of, orders requiring shipment interstate."[4]

A DIFFERENT VIEWPOINT

Professor Jerome Hellerstein disagrees with this position taken by Floyd Britton against the apportionment factors being used by the states. To begin with, Professor Hellerstein does not accept the underlying principle inherent in Britton's thesis that out-of-state businesses are being penalized or that they should be substantially relieved of the danger of the corporation's being taxed unfairly. Furthermore, he does not believe that states

---

[3]Britton, "Taxation without Representation Modernized." p.632.
[4]Britton, "Taxation without Representation Modernized," pp. 633–634.

have the tendency to rig their apportionment factors for the purposes of attacking or penalizing these out-of-state businesses.[5]

Concentrating just on the sales factor, Professor Hellerstein, first, disagrees with any commerce clause objection to the destination test, based on previous Supreme Court decisions.[6]

Federal and state courts have upheld a state's power to tax income derived solely from interstate selling within a state, particularly when the corporation is engaged in substantial income-producing activities through its selling efforts within that state. Therefore, Professor Hellerstein concludes that ". . . it is too late in our constitutional development to contend that the commerce clause presents any barrier to a state to apportionment of receipts derived from sales solicitation and shipment of goods into the state."[7]

Second, any economic argument stating that selling produces no wealth and should not be taxed through the destination rule is also dismissed by Professor Hellerstein. The reason being simply that factors relevant in an economic model for determining what creates wealth are not relevant to the factors which determine a company's income productivity that will be subject to state income taxes.[8]

Third, from a practical viewpoint, Professor Hellerstein believes the destination test to have some merit, particularly when considered as part of a multifactor formula. He observes: "The states in which manufacturing and warehousing take place, the states in which executive, accounting, and administrative personnel carry on their functions, obtain a heavy weighting in most multi-factor apportionment formulas, and therefore there is apportioned to such states a substantial part of existing tax measures. If the market state is to share to any significant extent in the tax revenues, the sales factor and the destination test afford a workable means to achieve that result. Moreover, that test sets up a standard not easily avoided under a properly drafted formula, a fact of no little significance in this area."[9]

Finally, it should be noted that both Britton and Professor Hellerstein are in agreement that when any out-of-state business regularly sends

---

[5]Hellerstein, "An Academician's View of State Taxation of Interstate Commerce," pp. 171–172.
[6]See the *Northwestern States Portland Cement* and *Stockham Valves* cases and the *West Publishing* case cited and examined in Chapter 1.
[7]Hellerstein, "An Academician's View of State Taxation of Interstate Commerce," p. 174.
[8]Hellerstein, "An Academician's View of State Taxation of Interstate Commerce." Professor Hellerstein has diverted his comments toward those who also share Britton's view. See Harris, "Interstate Apportionment of Business Income," 49 *American Economic Revue* 399 (1959); Harris, "Economic Aspects of Interstate Apportionment of Business Income," 37 *Taxes* 327 (1950); Paul Studenski and Gerald Glasser, "New Threat in State Business Taxation," 36 *Harvard Business Review* 77 (1958).
[9]Hellerstein, "An Academician's View of State Taxation of Interstate Commerce," p. 175.

salesmen into a state there is no due process objection to the taxation of this business or the implementation of the destination test for the sales factor.[10]

A CASE IN POINT — MOORMAN MANUFACTURING COMPANY V. G. D. BAIR 57 L. ED. 2D 197

The previous discussion has concentrated on the use of the sales factor as part of a multifactor formula. However, there is a recent Supreme Court case dealing with the issue of the constitutionality of apportionment by the single sales factor. The holding by the court in the case of *Moorman Manufacturing Company*[11] was that the use of a single sales factor for the apportionment of income by the state of Iowa was constitutionally sound.

Moorman Manufacturing was an Illinois corporation engaged in the manufacture and sale of animal feeds. The corporation's manufacturing activities occurred in Illinois, but some of its sales were made to Iowa residents. In addition, the company had over 500 salesmen located in Iowa, and it owned six warehouses in the state. Iowa imposed an income tax on all foreign and domestic corporations doing business within the state. For those corporations conducting their operations in several states, the tax was imposed on the portion of income "reasonably attributable" to business activities in Iowa. This amount was computed by use of an apportionment method that apportioned income using a one-factor sales formula equal to gross sales made within Iowa over the total gross sales transacted everywhere.

According to the Iowa Code, Section 422.33(i)(B), any taxpayer could file a statement with the Director of Revenue suggesting an alternative method of taxation if it believed that the one-factor sales formula created an unjust burden. Since the one-factor sales formula gives only an approximation of the income earned or attributable to operations in Iowa, it is possible that the formula could attribute more than a reasonable amount of income to the state. If the taxpayer can provide sufficient evidence to persuade the Director of Revenue that the one-factor sales formula incorrectly calculates income deemed to be earned in Iowa, taxable income may be recalculated. What is presumably necessary is the clear evidence as demonstrated by Hans Rees' Sons, Incorporated, in its Supreme Court case against the state of North Carolina (283 U.S. 123) (1931). Income attributed to the state through formulary apportionment was demonstrated by Hans Rees' Sons to be unreasonable when compared to income actually earned in the state. The courts found that no such convincing evidence was

---

[10]Once again, see the *Northwestern States Portland Cement* and *Stockham Valves* cases in Chapter 1. Where a company regularly solicits sales into a state, ships goods within the states borders to receive payments from residents of the state, and can utilize the local courts to enforce payments, the states have an adequate basis for taxing this company on its income from sources within the state.

[11]*Moorman Manufacturing Company* v. *G. D. Bair*, 57 L. Ed. 2d 197 (1978).

presented by Moorman in its proceedings and that the taxpayer therefore failed in its attempt to overcome the single-factor method of apportionment.[12]

Payroll

Finally, payroll the one factor that does seem to account for all business conducted within each state. This is due to the fact that all payments made to officers, supervisors, or employees in each state must be included in the numerator of that factor. Although this ratio is considered an appropriate measure of payroll activities, the balancing effect of the payroll factor is cut by one-third when payroll is averaged with the property and sales factors. To illustrate, apportionment data are provided next in Exhibit 3.3 for the

Exhibit 3.3 Apportionment Data for the Taxing State of Zeta

Corporation	Alpha	Beta
a. Property—exclusive of intangibles		
Location in Zeta	$ 90,000	$ 10,000
Total everywhere	$ 100,000	$ 100,000
% ratio	90%	10%
b. Intangible Property		
Zeta	$ 50,000	$
Everywhere	$ 50,000	$ 50,000
% ratio	100%	0%
c. Total Property—(including intangibles)		
Zeta	$ 140,000	$ 10,000
Everywhere	$ 150,000	$ 150,000
% ratio	93%	6.7%
d. Payroll		
Zeta	$ 45,000	$ 5,000
Everywhere	$ 50,000	$ 50,000
% ratio	90%	10%
e. Sales		
Destination—Zeta	$ 5,000,000	$ 500,000
Everywhere sales	$10,000,000	$10,000,000
% ratio	50%	5%
f. Sales		
Transacted and shipped to Zeta	$ 5,500,000	$ 50,000
Everywhere sales	$10,000,000	$10,000,000
% ratio	55%	0.5%

[12]For a discussion of Justice Powell's and Justice Blackman's dissenting views, see J. Nelson Young, "The Single Factor Sales Formula and the Moorman Manufacturing Company Decision—A Backward Step in the Apportionment of Income of Interstate Business," 56 *Taxes* 11 (November 1978) p. 659.

Exhibit 3.4 Apportionment factors for the Alpha and Beta Corporations

Apportionment %	Alpha	Beta
1 UDITPA		
$\dfrac{a + d + e}{3}$	$\dfrac{0.9 + 0.9 + 0.5}{3}$	$\dfrac{0.1 + 0.1 + 0.05}{3}$
	$= 76.7\%$	$= 8.3\%$
2 Possible alternative		
$\dfrac{c + d + f}{3}$	$\dfrac{0.93 + 0.9 + 0.55}{3}$	$\dfrac{0.067 + 0.1 + 0.005}{3}$
	$= 79.3\%$	$= 5.7\%$

Exhibit 3.5

	Alpha	Beta
Taxable Income	$1,000,000	$1,000,000
Apportioned to Zeta using formula 1 from Exhibit 3.4	767,000	83,000
Tax @ 1%	$ 7,670	$ 830
Apportioned to Zeta using formula 2	793,000	570,000
Tax @ 1%	$ 7,930	$ 570

Alpha and Beta corporations. The Alpha Corporation is incorporated and domiciled in the taxing state of Zeta, but the Beta Corporation only has one branch office in Zeta. Two different apportionment factors are computed for each company, as illustrated in Exhibit 3.4, one using a regular three-factor formula, the other applying the concepts discussed in this section. Note how the taxable income and tax attributable to Alpha increases when intangible property is included in the property factor and when the sales factor is based only on sales transacted and shipped within a state. (See Exhibit 3.5.) Conversely, notice how the taxable income of the foreign corporation, Beta, decreases as these same adjustments are made to its property factor.

Conflicts in the Methods for Computing the Tax for a Business with Operations within and without a State

The problems concerning the taxation of interstate commerce has introduced the reader to some basic struggles existing between corporations and state taxing agencies. All the topics mentioned earlier in this chapter have

dealt with corporate income that is either apportioned or separately allocated to these taxing states. These two accounting methods seldom, if ever,
give the same results when applied to the same set of accounting data. The
ever-present conflict between the use of separate accounting and formulary
apportionment has opened the door for the introduction of the combined-
return concept. However, before any discussion of combined reports is
presented, a better understanding of separate accounting and formulary
apportionment is required.

Separate Accounting

The separate accounting method treats business activity within a state just
as the name implies; it is considered separate, distinct, and unconnected
with the business activity outside the state. This method is only applicable
when each function performed by the business in a state is conducted and
can be accounted for apart from those activities outside a state. Suppose,
for example, a corporation has two divisions, each operating in a different
state. Each division carries out its duties independently, using different
organizational policies to guide its corporate planning. If both states
required or permitted separate accounting, both the gross receipts and
operating expenses for each branch would be determined without regard to
the receipts and expenses received or incurred outside the state. It is
possible that the corporation may also incur general overhead expenses
attributable to both divisions. These costs should be allocated to each
division on an equitable basis.

   Computing taxable income using the separate accounting basis will not
always be appropriate or practical, particularly for those corporations with
complex organizational structures. The increasing number of highly diversified companies located in several states would most likely fall into this
category. Such corporations are often marked by common management
and financial control throughout the states of operation. Under these
circumstances, an accounting for each branch or division operating in a
state as if it were an independent entity could provide erroneous results.
Even if a business does not have a highly complex organizational structure,
the same standards for applying an accounting method will hold true.
Operational independence for any corporate subsidiary or branch conducting business in a separate state cannot be assumed to exist merely because
these subsidiaries or branches are located within different geographic
boundaries.

   Another reason why separate accounting may not be practical is because of the extensive recordkeeping required to maintain separate accounts. It is usually a very costly and time-consuming process for a
corporation to separately accumulate all the necessary accounting data for
each state of operation or to maintain a record of all transactions on a
state-by-state basis.

Finally, separate accounting requires the determination of a reasonable sale price for goods bought and sold from commonly owned or controlled corporations. An unrealistic price can inflate or deflate the purchasing company's cost of goods sold, thereby decreasing or increasing its taxable income. the same time, this sales price can inflate or deflate the selling company's revenue, thereby increasing or decreasing its taxable income. Problems are often encountered in computing these fair sales prices because of the difficulty in obtaining the necessary objective, verifiable data.[13]

One way a comparable price can be derived is by evaluating the market conditions to determine what the produce would sell for in an arm's-length transaction. The trouble with this seemingly easy approach is that comparable conditions for specific product quality and quantity and credit and shipping terms are difficult to find, even when corporations are within the same basic industry group.

The second approach involves the construction of an imputed price requiring the addition of a reasonable profit to the cost of goods manufactured or sold.[14] The actual cost of a product, whether manufactured or purchased, does provide an objective starting point, but the varying methods for determining a reasonable profit to be added to these costs will make these values less than perfect. It is a difficult task to calculate these profits, because profit margins can vary according to the product, product line, the company, and even the geographic location of the company. Furthermore, sufficient data for comparative purposes for products unique to a certain company may be nonexistent. Hopefully, the many educated guesses that must be made would provide a relatively undistorted profit figure.

These methods for constructing reasonable sales prices or an arm's-length price for goods are essentially the same methods as those prescribed by the IRS for administering Section 482 for the sale of goods between members of a controlled group.[15] These are the "comparable uncontrolled price method," "resale price method," and the "cost plus method" in the Income Tax Regulations under Section 482.[16]

An important distinction should be made between the use of the Section 482 techniques for Federal purposes and its applicability with separate

[13]Jerome Hellerstein, "The Unitary Business Principle and Multicorporate Enterprises: An Examination of the Major Controversies," 17 Tax Executive Institute 4 (July 1975) p. 316.
[14]Hellerstein, "The Unitary Business Principle and Multicorporate Enterprises: An Examination of the Major Controversies," p. 317.
[15]Section 482, Allocation Of Income and Deductions Among Taxpayers, reads as follows: "In any case of two or more organizations, trades, or businesses (whether or not incorporated, whether or not organized in the United States, and whether or not affiliated) owned or controlled directly or indirectly by the same interests, the Secretary may distribute, apportion, or allocate gross income, deduction, credits, or allowances between or among such organizations, trades, or businesses, if he determines that such distribution, apportionment, or allocation is necessary in order to prevent evasion of taxes or clearly to reflect the income of any of such organizations, trades, or businesses."
[16]Income Tax Regulation Section 1.482–2(e).

accounting for purposes of state taxation. The purpose of Section 482 is to prevent tax avoidance from occurring where members of a controlled group are concerned. All the income from the members of the group will ordinarily be subject to the Federal tax. The manner in which the income is divided among the corporate group members may not materially alter the total tax liability, except perhaps if there are questions concerning surtax exemptions or loss carry-overs.[17] However, for purposes of state taxation, the use of these Section 482 adjustments will directly affect the amount of income subject to tax in any given state. For example, assume a corporation with several subsidiaries is operating in several states. If separate accounting techniques are used, each state taxing authority may attempt to make these Section 482–type adjustments. This increases the possibility of there being a tax on more than 100 percent of the corporate income. Furthermore, there is also the possibility of some administrative difficulties in accumulating sufficient data to make the adjustments. It may be possible that the required information is only available from a subsidiary corporation over which a state taxing authority has no jurisdiction.[18]

Although these problems associated with the use of separate accounting do present some obstacles that must be overcome, separate accounting cannot be totally discouraged. There are many companies whose operations can be more accurately measured when separate accounting is used.

Many corporations, particularly those in natural resource industries, prefer the use of separate accounting.[19] In fact, some states not only permit but also prefer the use of separate accounting.

Formulary Apportionment

The formulary method for determining taxable income treats all business activity within a state as being an essential and integral part of the business activity outside the state. The total operations of a business are considered as one economic unit rather than as separate divisions in various states. The formulary approach to interstate taxation can be compared to a jigsaw puzzle, with each piece being necessary for completing an entire picture. Similarly, each division of a company, regardless of the company's location, is considered a necessary part in viewing the total picture of a corporation's operations.

The use of formulary apportionment developed from the necessity of the state to find a way to fairly measure the portion of a multistate corporation's activity taking place within that state's boundaries.[20] It has

---

[17]George Rudolph, "State Taxation of Interstate Business: The Unitary Business Concept and Affiliated Corporate Groups," 25 *Tax Law Review* 2 (January 1970), p. 207.

[18]Rudolph, "State Taxation of Interstate Business."

[19]The *Superior Oil* case is an example of an exception to this statement. The case is discussed subsequently.

[20]Jerome R. Hellerstein, "Recent Developments in State Tax Apportionment and the Circumscription of Unitary Business," 21 *National Tax Journal* (1968), p. 487.

generally been held to satisfy both the Due Process Clause prohibition against a state's taxation of corporate income generated outside a state's borders and the Commerce Clause prohibition against a state's taxation of activities that would create an undue burden on interstate commerce.[21] Also, the use of formulary apportionment can simplify the recordkeeping requirements of a company, thus having some practical benefits as well. A company using formulary apportionment may not have the need to keep a complete set of books and records in each state where it has operations.

The starting point for apportioning taxable earnings attributable to the activities in each state of operation is the total earnings of the corporation. Each state may use a different apportionment formula, provided the factors in the formula can reasonably identify the activities within the state. The most common formula is the three-factor Massachusetts formula. The use of the three-factor formula is required for apportioning business income under UDITPA to encourage uniformity in apportionment procedures.[22]

Separate Accounting v. Formulary Apportionment

The best way to illustrate the differences between separate accounting and formulary apportionment is through an example. Exhibits 3.6 and 3.7 illustrates data the Gamma Corporation uses for computing its taxable income attributable to operations in State Z.

Notice that $2224 is taxable in State Z using separate accounting before any allocation of deductions is made from the main office. If these deductions were not made, a $111 tax liability would result ($2224 × 5%).

A situation existing under the foregoing circumstances would explain why a corporate taxpayer would prefer to compute taxable income by separate accounting. It would also explain why many states prefer formulary apportionment when it can produce a larger tax revenue. Although the issues of proper taxation of interstate commerce are of extreme importance to all parties involved, the issues of tax dollars paid and tax dollars received are also in the foreground of this controversy.

There is, however, one point to which both the proponents of separate accounting and formulary apportionment will agree. Each state is only entitled to tax the income of a corporation derived from business done

[21]Hellerstein, "Recent Development in State Tax Apportionment and the Circumscription of Unitary Business."

[22]Prior to the Adoption of UDITPA the National Tax Association sought to obtain uniform state apportionment policies for several decades. The Association has therefore been primarily responsible for the widespread use of the Massachusetts three-factor formula. For a historic perspective, see Proceedings of National Tax Association 190, 195 (1939), "Second Preliminary Report of the Committee on Tax Status and Allocation" in Proceedings of National Tax Association 349 (1950), "Interim Report of Committee on Interstate Allocation of Business Income" in Proceeding of National Tax Association 349 (1950). "Interim Report of Committee on Interstate Allocation of Business Income" in Proceedings of National Tax Association 372 (1958).

Form **1120**

Department of the Treasury
Internal Revenue Service

U.S. Corporation Income Tax Return

For calendar year 1979 or other taxable year beginning _____ , 1979, ending _____ , 19 ___

1979

Check if a—		
A Consolidated return ☐	**Use IRS label.**	Name **Gamma Corporation**
B Personal Holding Co. ☐	**Other-wise please print or type.**	Number and street **1122 East Pontiac**
C Business Code No. (See Page 8 of instructions)		City or town, State, and ZIP code **Chicago, Illinois 60600**

D Employer identification number (see instruction W) **36-1440513**

E Date incorporated **January 1, 1952**

F Enter total assets (see instruction X) $ _____

Gross Income

1 (a) Gross receipts or sales $ .... (b) Less returns and allowances $ .... Balance ▶	1(c)	5,700,045
2 **Less:** Cost of goods sold (Schedule A) and/or operations (attach schedule)	2	4,865,757
3 Gross profit	3	834,288
4 Dividends (Schedule C)	4	2,250
5 Interest on obligations of the United States and U.S. instrumentalities	5	--
6 Other interest	6	39,655
7 Gross rents	7	66,180
8 Gross royalties	8	
9 (a) Capital gain net income (attach separate Schedule D)	9(a)	2,787
(b) Net gain or (loss) from Form 4797, line 11, Part II (attach Form 4797)	9(b)	2,198
10 Other income (see instructions—attach schedule)	10	49,815
11 TOTAL income—Add lines 3 through 10	11	997,173

Deductions

12 Compensation of officers (Schedule E)	12	1,259
13 (a) Salaries and wages .... 13(b) Less WIN and jobs credit(s) .... Balance ▶	13(c)	--
14 Repairs (see instructions)	14	72,157
15 Bad debts (Schedule F if reserve method is used)	15	29,013
16 Rents	16	58,530
17 Taxes	17	164,064
18 Interest	18	17,019
19 Contributions (**not over 5% of line 30 adjusted per instructions—attach schedule**)	19	294
20 Amortization (attach schedule)	20	443
21 Depreciation from Form 4562 (attach Form 4562) ...., less depreciation claimed in Schedule A and elsewhere on return ...., Balance ▶	21	90,096
22 Depletion	22	--
23 Advertising	23	14,316
24 Pension, profit-sharing, etc. plans (see instructions) (enter number of plans ▶ ....)	24	46,507
25 Employee benefit programs (see instructions)	25	13,624
26 Other deductions (attach schedule)	26	419,221
27 TOTAL deductions—Add lines 12 through 26	27	926,543
28 Taxable income before net operating loss deduction and special deductions (subtract line 27 from line 11)	28	70,630
29 **Less:** (a) Net operating loss deduction (see instructions—attach schedule) 29(a)		
(b) Special deductions (Schedule I) 29(b)	29	2,249
30 Taxable income (subtract line 29 from line 28)	30	68,381

Tax

31 TOTAL TAX (Schedule J)	31	
32 Credits: (a) Overpayment from 1978 allowed as a credit		
(b) 1979 estimated tax payments		
(c) Less refund of 1979 estimated tax applied for on Form 4466 (...............)		
(d) Tax deposited: Form 7004 .... Form 7005 (attach) .... Total ▶		
(e) Credit from regulated investment companies (attach Form 2439)		
(f) Federal tax on special fuels and oils (attach Form 4136 or 4136–T)	32	
33 TAX DUE (subtract line 32 from line 31). See instruction G for depositary method of payment .	33	
(Check ▶ ☐ if Form 2220 is attached. See page 3 of instructions.) ▶ $		
34 OVERPAYMENT (subtract line 31 from line 32)	34	
35 Enter amount of line 34 you want: Credited to 1980 estimated tax ▶ .... Refunded ▶	35	

Please Sign Here

Under penalties of perjury, I declare that I have examined this return, including accompanying schedules and statements, and to the best of my knowledge and belief, it is true, correct, and complete. Declaration of preparer (other than taxpayer) is based on all information of which preparer has any knowledge.

Signature of officer	Date	▶ Title

Paid Preparer's Information	Preparer's signature and date ▶		Check if self-employed ▶ ☐	Preparer's social security no.
	Firm's name (or yours, if self-employed) and address ▶		E.I. No. ▶
			ZIP code ▶

Exhibit 3.6 Corporate tax return.

Exhibit 3.7

(a) Apportionment Data

	Operations in State Z	Total Company	Ratio—State Z Total Company
Property	125,189	1,181,255	0.105980
Payroll	73,125	292,500	0.250000
Sales and other	750,000	5,700,044	0.131578
Total ratios			0.487558
Average ratios			0.162519

(b) State Z: Income and Expense Separately Accounted for

Sales	$750,000
Cost of goods sold	(695,725)
Gross profit	54,275
Other income	25,675
Total income	79,950
Salaries	73,125
Depreciation	2,975
Other deductions	1,626
Total deductions	77,726
Taxable income	$ 2,224

(c) Expenses of Gamma Allocated to Operations in State Z

Advertising	$3,579
Other services from main offices	3,407
	$6,986

(d) Taxable Income of Gamma—1979 1120 Tax Return

Note: The total sales used in the apportionment data in Section a ties in to Line 1 of the 1120 of the Gamma Corporation. The total payroll in the apportionment data does not tie in to the 1120, because this cost is buried in several items, such as the cost of goods sold.

(e) Computations of Tax

	Separate Company	Formulary Apportionment
Total taxable income	$79,950	$997,173
less direct expenses	77,726	926,543
Income before special deductions	2,224	70,630
Special deductions or allocated deductions	6,986	2,249
Income or loss subject to tax	($4,762)	$ 68,381
Apportionment % applied to taxable earning	—	0.162519
Taxable income in State Z	0	11,113
Tax @ 5%	0	$ 556

within that state. When separate accounting is used, it must clearly be the most accurate and appropriate method for measuring the activity within a state. When formulary apportionment is used, the formula must be reasonable in order to reach only the profits earned within a state. When a conflict between these methods arises, the issues center primarily on the constitutional question, "Have the Due Process and Commerce clauses been violated?"

Many of these disputes between the taxpayers and the states have gone to court. In most instances, the courts have accepted and approved the state's formulary apportionment methods because the taxpayers have been unable to show that the formula used produced an unreasonable result. Furthermore, these apportionment formulas are seldom found to be unconstitutional. Although there have been numerous U.S. and State Supreme Court cases that set precedents in the taxation of businesses with operations in more than one state, discussion is limited now to two of the more important U.S. Supreme Court cases which focus on the dispute between separate accounting and income apportionment.

UNDERWOOD TYPEWRITER COMPANY V. CHAMBERLAIN 254 U.S. 113 (1920)

The *Underwood Typewriter Company* v. *Chamberlain* case was one of the earliest U.S. Supreme Court cases to deal with the separate accounting and income apportionment controversy. (See Chapter 2 for a review of more details of this case.)

When the Underwood Company filed its 1916 tax return in Connecticut, it reported a net profit of $42,942.18 as being attributable to the activities within the state and a net profit of $1,293,643.95 as being attributable to all its activities. Underwood relied on its separate accounting data for determining the $42,942.18 Connecticut profit. The company's manufacturing activities in Connecticut were considered separate from the selling activities outside the state.

The Connecticut Tax Commissioner recomputed Underwood's tax using an apportionment percentage that acknowledged the relationship between the operations in Connecticut and the operations occurring in all other states. This relationship was evident from a review of Underwood's business cycle that consisted of a series of transactions beginning in Connecticut with the manufacture of the products and ending in other states with the sale of these same products. The application of an apportionment percentage consisting of the fair cash value of real and tangible personal property in Connecticut in relation to the value of this property located in all states was deemed to be a satisfactory means of reaching only the profits earned within Connecticut as contrasted with what the Commissioner believed to be an impossible task when using separate accounting. Underwood did not attempt to disprove that the 47 percent of its total earnings apportioned to Connecticut was unreasonable or arbitrary; consequently, the U.S. Supreme Court observed that the amount actually earned in the state could have been even larger. The U.S. Supreme Court upheld the state's formulary apportionment procedures.

BASS, RATCLIFF, AND GRETTON, LIMITED V. STATE TAX COMMISSION 266 U.S. 271 (1924)

Bass, Ratcliff, and Gretton, Limited v. *State Tax Commission* is another U.S. Supreme Court case that upheld a state's use of formulary apportionment over separate accounting. The emphasis on profits accruing through a series of transactions is once again an important factor as it was in the *Underwood Typewriter Company* v. *Chamberlain* case.

Bass, Ratcliff, and Gretton was a British corporation that brewed Bass' ale in England and then distributed this ale internationally. Two branch offices were located in the United States—in New York and Chicago—for U.S. distribution of the ale. The company had relied on its separate accounting data for determining and reporting taxable earnings attributable to these branch offices. The lack of any earnings reportable to the New York office triggered this case in a conflict over the best means of calculating the company's New York Franchise Tax Liability.

The New York Franchise Tax was imposed on foreign corporations operating in New York for the privilege of transacting business in the state. The tax was measured by the previous year's income that was then apportioned to the state. The apportionment factor was a one-factor ratio to be computed on the basis of real and tangible personal property, bills, and accounts receivable resulting from the manufacture and sale of merchandise and services performed and the shares of stock owned in other corporations not exceeding the percent of the real and tangible property located in New York, over the total of these assets wherever located.

This formula was not used by Bass, Ratcliff, and Gretton when computing its franchise tax for the year beginning on November 1, 1918. No taxable earnings were attributed to the New York and Chicago offices or even reported as earned in the United States on the Federal tax return that was filed. There was, however, a $2,185,600.00 net income computed for this same year from the operations of the entire business. This amount was shown on the Federal return as a result of a provision stating that when a corporation is organized under the laws of another country it is required to state its entire net income.

Using the information that Bass, Ratcliff, and Gretton's total income from operations was $2,185,600.00, the New York Tax Commission recomputed the company's tax liability by apportioning $27,537.68 of this income to New York. The apportionment formula for the company consisted of $44,117.00 of property in New York to the $3,501,483.00 located everywhere. A 3 percent tax rate was applied to the $27,537.68 figure which resulted in a $286.14 tax assessment that was paid under protest.

The company argued that New York was taxing the property and business income out of its jurisdiction, thereby violating the Due Process clause of the Fourteenth Amendment and the Commerce Clause of the Constitution. The Commission, however, felt that these earnings were, in fact, attributable to the business conducted in New York.

The Commission had looked beyond the local and Federal net income computed on a separate accounting basis to the combined earnings that had accrued because of the foreign and U.S. operations. They believed that this method attributed to the state its just proportion of net profits earned by the business as a whole. Total profits were considered to be earned throughout a series of transactions, not only at the time of a sale. The first step in this earning cycle began in England with the manufacturing of ale, and the last step ended with the sale of the ale in England, New York, and Chicago. The *Underwood Typewriter* case was cited by the Court as an example as it stated that "the legislature in attempting to put upon this business its fair share of the burden of taxation was faced with the impossibility of allocating specifically the profits earned by the processes conducted within its borders. It, therefore, adopted a method of apportionment which, for all that appears in this record, reached, and was meant to reach, only the profits earned within the State." The Court went on to state that Bass, Ratcliff, and Gretton conducted a unitary business and that to get a true picture of the activities within New York all the foreign and domestic activities must also be considered. The state may look to all the property of a company when it "can be seen in some plain and fairly intelligible way that it adds to the value of the (property) and the rights exercised in the State."

The final decision by the Court to approve the income apportionment is important for two reasons. First, the concept of conducting a business within and without a state had included foreign activities as well as the domestic activities as part of the operations outside a state. Second, this decision helped to pave the pathway for combining earnings for a business operating as one economic unit or having unitary characteristics.

ORIGINS AND DEVELOPMENT OF COMBINED REPORTING

Creation of the Combined Return to Promote Uniformity

The *Underwood Typewriter* and *Bass, Ratcliff, and Gretton* cases were instrumental in illustrating the merits of income apportionment in determining the income attributable to corporate activities within a state. The use of income apportionment represented a reasonable and viable alternative to a system of state taxation that was formerly dominated by the use of separate accounting. Gradually, many more states began to tax single corporations on their apportioned earnings.

The concept of apportionment for a single corporation has been expanded by the state of California to include a group of corporations, or a parent corporation and its subsidiaries, for determining the income base subject to apportionment. This was the introduction of the combined report concept. Income was to be determined from economic units, whether the unit was composed of one corporation, one corporation with six branches, or one corporation with six subsidiaries. Separate entities, as defined for legal and technical purposes, were to be ignored. The purpose of the combined report was to look beyond these imposed limitations to create more uniformity and equity in state taxation. Regardless of the numerous reasons for operating a business with 1, 3, 30, or even 300 separate corporations, for purposes of state taxation, the combined report computes taxable income in all these instances as if only one corporation were being taxed. The key factor in applying the combined return concept is to restrict the combination to those companies carrying on a unitary business. These are the only companies that can justly be treated as a single economic unit.[23] A combination that includes a nonunitary business would provide erroneous tax results. The establishment of a working definition for a unitary business is documented after a review of the important features and mechanics of a combined return.

Features of the Combined Return

The combined return for state purposes should not be confused with a consolidated return under Federal income tax concepts. The basic difference between these returns is that on a consolidated return separate entities are disregarded; the parent and its subsidiary companies are taxed as one unit. On a combined return, each company is taxed but only on its own income that is apportioned to a state from earnings reflecting the operations of the entire business. Although both of these returns do require the combination of income and then the elimination of intercompany transactions, the similarities end there. For purposes of the combined return, intercompany items such as dividends, are eliminated to the extent that they are paid from unitary income subject to apportionment. Intercompany eliminations for dividends in a consolidated return covers all dividends between corporations in the consolidated group. Furthermore, a combined return requires an ownership of more than 50 percent before a combination can take place, whereas a consolidated return requires at least an 80 percent ownership. Also, when filing a combined report, the affiliated corporations must report income determined on the basis of the same accounting period. For example, if all the unitary corporations on a

---

[23]From the speech by Frank M. Keesling presented at the June 25, 1974, Annual Meeting of the Multistate Tax Commission, "The Combined Report and Uniformity in Allocation Practices," reproduced in the Seventh Annual Report, Multistate Tax Commission, June 30, 1974, p. 33.

combined return have a December 31 year-end and one corporation has a March 31 income year, the latter must assign $\frac{9}{12}$ of its unitary income of one year and $\frac{3}{12}$ of its unitary income from its preceding fiscal year to the total unitary income reportable on the return. When a parent-subsidiary relationship exists, income from a subsidiary is usually determined on the basis of the parent's taxable year. Finally, the acknowledgment of a minority interest is visible on a consolidated return, but for a combined return, minority interests are not even recognized. This means that the tax attributed to a corporation on a combined return would be the same, regardless of whether there is a 51 percent, 75 percent, or 100 percent ownership. Exhibit 3.8 highlights the characteristics of combined and consolidated returns.

When the combined report was introduced in California, there was no California law that specifically authorized its usage. The combined report was created by the commissioners as a means of determining income attributable to the source within California. In subsequent years, it was upheld by the California Supreme Court as a reasonable method of apportionment. There are still no particular provisions existing in any state's law insisting on the usage of a combined report, although several states have upheld this return as a reasonable and fair method for apportioning income.

Mechanics of the Combined Return

The starting point for filing a combined return is the determination of the combined income from a unitary group. There has been some debate about whether income from companies incorporated outside the United States

Exhibit 3.8

	Combined Return	Consolidated Return
Intercompany eliminations	To the extent that they are paid from unitary income subject to apportionment	All dividend income
Companies included in return	Unitary companies with more than 50% ownership	Those owned 80% or more
Accounting period	Income year to coincide with the corporation expected to have the largest amount of unitary income on a recurring basis	Income year to coincide with parent corporation
Minority interest	Not considered in computing tax	Visible on consolidated returns

should also be included in this combined unitary income. According to the creators of the combined return, all income from a unitary business is to be included on the return, regardless of whether the unitary company is incorporated in the United States or in a foreign country. In practice, however, some combined returns include only those companies incorporated in the United States. Once the combined income for any unitary group is determined, all intercompany eliminations from unitary income must be made to arrive at the unitary income subject to apportionment.

ADDITIONAL CONSIDERATIONS—FOREIGN SOURCE INCOME

California's practice of including foreign and nonforeign unitary income in the combined return can create some additional complexities. Most states have taxable income based on Federal taxable income, plus or minus various adjustments. This aids both the taxpayer and the state tax administrator, since they can rely on the Federal audit procedures for determining changes in many state tax liabilities. Most states, in fact, require notification from a corporation if there is any change in Federal taxable income as a result of a Federal tax audit.[24] (See Chapter 2.) By including foreign source income with other unitary income, more data must be accumulated by the taxpayer, thereby making tax compliance more costly and time consuming. As the following example illustrates, (after the discussion of the treatment of dividends), all intercompany transactions of the unitary group for Kapco Industries must be eliminated.

This means all transactions between U.S. affiliated corporations as well as its foreign incorporated affiliates must be considered before combined unitary income subject to apportionment can be properly computed. The proper computation of the apportionment factors of property, payroll, and sales also requires additional data and records to be maintained to include the amounts from any foreign unitary business. Furthermore, the ability to audit and verify the foreign source data presents some additional obstacles for the state auditor. It has also been suggested that including foreign source income in the unitary computations makes it necessary for the taxpayer to compute a hypothetical Federal net income for each foreign corporation.[25]

TREATMENT OF DIVIDENDS

The treatment of dividends on a combined return creates some problems in the application of the unitary concept. First, there is the question of how to handle the elimination of dividends from related companies. At the Federal

---

[24]Peter Miller, "State Income Taxation of Multiple Corporations and Multiple Businesses," 49 *Taxes*, 2 (February 1971), p. 106.
[25]Miller, "State Income Taxation of Multiple Corporations and Multiple Businesses," p. 113. Also see IRC Reg. Section 1.964–1, illustrating the conversion of net profit according to the books of a controlled foreign corporation into earnings and profits for Federal income tax purposes.

level, the problems of intercorporate dividends have been resolved by allowing the corporation receiving dividends a deduction of 85 percent of dividends received from other domestic corporations.[26]

Furthermore, dividends received from a member of an affiliated group are 100 percent deductible. These Federal provisions can carry over to the states, for example, by having their statutes refer to taxable income as defined by Section 63 of the IRC. For purposes of a consolidated return for Federal purposes, all intercompany dividends are eliminated in the process of determining consolidated income.[27]

For a combined return, it would seem reasonable on first considerations to follow Federal consolidated guidelines and to eliminate all intercompany dividends. However, since the combined return only combines income of unitary businesses, dividends are eliminated only to the extent that they are paid from unitary income.[28]

Previously, in California, a dividend paid by a subsidiary to its parent would be specifically allocated to California, providing the payee's commercial domicile was in California. This was true even if the operations of the parent and subsidiary were considered unitary and reported on a combined return.[29] Since this procedure obviously promoted double taxation, California amended its statute to provide for the elimination of intercompany dividends to the extent that the dividends are paid from unitary business income.[30]

Second, there is also a problem in terms of promoting uniformity in the treatment of dividends and avoiding multiple taxation. Historically, dividend income received by a corporation would be allocated to and taxed in the state of commercial domicile. This would preclude double or multiple taxation from occurring. More recently, however, states have begun to treat dividends received by nondomiciliary corporations as business income subject to apportionment. The basis of this type of taxation may stem from the adoption of UDITPA by various states. Under UDITPA, dividend income is to be allocated to the state of commercial domicile only if such dividends constitute nonbusiness income. All other dividend income would be subject to formulary apportionment, since it would fall under the definition of business income.[31] As discussed in Chapter 2, the definitions

---

[26]IRC, Section 243.

[27]IRC, Reg. 1.1502–14.

[28]See Exhibit 3.8, highlighting the distinctions between a combined and a consolidated return.

[29]Warren Keesling, "The Unitary Concept in the Allocation of Income," 12 *Hastings Law Journal* 42 (1960), p. 60; and Rudolph, "State Taxation of Interstate Business: The Unitary Business Concept and Affiliated Corporate Groups," p. 200.

[30]California Revenue and Tax Code, Article 1, Section 25 106.

[31]Business income in UDITPA is defined in Section 1(a) as "income arising from transactions and activity in the regular course of the taxpayer's trade or business and includes income from tangible and intangible property if the acquisition, management, and disposition of the property constitute integral parts of the taxpayer's regular trade or business operations."

of business versus nonbusiness income are subject to controversy in their interpretations. Thus nonuniform interpretations are possible under the provisions that were designed to promote uniformity.

There are also the practical problems between taxpayers and state tax administrators.[32]

This example is presented for purposes of illustrating the potential problems in administering the UDITPA provisions. In studying the example assume the following facts:

1 State X does not exempt dividend income from taxation.
2 Corporation 1 is domiciled in State X.
3 Corporation 2 is domiciled in State Z but has operations in State X.

In the process of analyzing and interpreting their corporate operations, particularly in State X, Corporation 1 could seek to apportion its dividend income as business income to another state with a lower tax rate. Corporation 2, on the other hand, could seek to allocate its dividend income to its state of domicile (Z) on the basis that it is nonbusiness income and should be allocated to this state rather than apportioned to the nondomiciliary State X. Obviously, this type of situation promotes varied interpretations between taxpayers seeking to decrease their tax liabilities and tax administrators seeking to increase the tax dollars. Both parties are working within the same system that is designed to promote uniformity, although the system's applicability may promote nonuniformity.

One possibility for promoting more uniformity in the treatment of dividends would be to adjust the definition of business income in UDITPA. For example, business income could be defined to include only those dividends received on stocks that a corporation dealing in securities is holding for investment purposes. This would permit dividends received from subsidiaries to be classified as nonbusiness income. These dividends would then be allocated to the corporation's state of domicile.[33]

Whereas there are strong arguments for treating dividends as allocable nonbusiness income and for treating them as apportionable business income, any realistic solution to this problem cannot overlook the following facts:[34]

1 Dividend income from affiliated corporations is declared on earnings that have been subjected to foreign, Federal, or state taxation.

---

[32]S. C. Nemeth, Jr., and H. O. Agee, Jr., "State Taxation of Multistate Business: Resolution or Stalemate?," 48 *Taxes* 237 (April 1970), p. 246.
[33]Miller, "State Income Taxation of Multiple Corporations and Multiple Businesses," p. 113.
[34]Agee, Nemeth, "State Taxation of Multistate Business: Resolution or Stalemate?" p. 247.

2 The concept of specifically allocating dividend income to the corporation's state of domicile has a long history under state income taxation.

3 Because the taxation of nondomiciliary corporation dividend income is a relatively recent concept, Federal legislation denying state power to tax these dividends should not materially affect state revenues.

(For a comprehensive example, see Appendix B.)

Kapco Industries, Incorporated, is one of the largest manufacturers and distributors of industrial chemical products. It is incorporated and headquartered in Illinois and operates throughout the midwestern states. Kapco is the parent company for eight subsidiary companies, all owned 100 percent, three of which are qualified to do business in California. There are also two foreign-incorporated affiliated companies that manufacture and distribute products in Europe. Kapco and all its U.S. subsidiaries file a consolidated Federal income tax return and all other necessary returns required for reporting income of foreign affiliates.

The operations of Kapco and its affiliated companies are to be considered unitary for the purpose of this example.

The earning data and intercompany eliminations for determining combined income subject to apportionment in California are shown in Exhibit 3.9.

Exhibit 3.9   Determination of Combined Income

Income or Expense	Kapco	U.S. Affiliates	Foreign Incorporated Affiliates	Total before Eliminations	Less Intercompany Eliminations	Total
Sales and Operating revenue	38,550	26,725	10,500	75,775	3,075	72,700
Other income	250	175	35	460	35	425
Total revenue	38,800	26,900	10,535	76,235	3,110	73,125
Operating expenses	9,650	4,675	3,905	18,230	55	18,175
Administrative expenses	850	150	350	1,350	—	1,350
Taxes	1,050	975	2,750	4,775	—	4,775
Miscellaneous expenses	2,000	860	1,010	3,870	15	3,855
Net income	25,250	20,240	2,520	48,010	3,040	44,970[a]

[a]Combined unitary income subject to apportionment.

After unitary income is calculated, it is apportioned to the taxing state subject to various state adjustments and then taxed at the appropriate tax rate. Exhibits 3.10 through 3.14 are miniaturized worksheets used for preparing the three-factor Massachusetts formula. The data are for the three subsidiaries of Kapco Industries subject to the California franchise tax.

Exhibit 3.10 Worksheet for Determining the Property Factor

Property within California	Subsidiary 1	Subsidiary 2	Subsidiary 3	Total
Beginning of Year				
Land	20,000	750	17,980	38,730
Inventory (net of intercompany profits)	163,750	1,500	155,250	320,500
Equipment	350,000	10,000	1,875,320	2,235,320
Total beginning of year	533,750	12,250	2,048,550	2,594,550
End of Year				
Land	22,000	1,750	17,980	41,730
Inventory	174,860	1,950	220,150	396,960
Equipment	350,000	15,500	1,540,321	1,905,821
Total end of year	546,860	19,200	1,778,451	2,344,511
Total beginning and end of year	1,080,610	31,450	3,827,001	4,939,061
Average value of property in California	540,305	15,725	1,913,501	2,469,531
Rent expense for year × 8	8,000	26,000	14,800	48,800
Total property in state	548,305	41,725	1,928,301	2,518,331
Average value of property from all locations — "everywhere" value				$67,954,766
Ratio of California property to all property	0.008069	0.000614	0.028376	0.037059

Exhibit 3.11 Worksheet for Determining the Payroll Factor

	Subsidiary 1	Subsidiary 2	Subsidiary 3	Total
California payroll	100,000	500,000	350,000	950,000
Total payroll paid by Kapco and all its affiliates at all locations	10,000,000	10,000,000	10,000,000	10,000,000
Ratio of California payroll to all payroll	0.01	0.05	0.035	0.095

Exhibit 3.12 Worksheet for Determining the Sales Factor

	Subsidiary 1	Subsidiary 2	Subsidiary 3	Total
California sales	5,555,250	2,105,750	6,345,200	14,006,200
Less intercompany sales	550,000	750,250	3,200,000	4,500,250
California sales to trade	5,005,250	1,355,500	3,145,200	9,505,950
Total sales by Kapco and its affiliates' net of intercompany transactions				152,684,097
Ratio of California sales to total sales	0.032782	0.008878	0.020599	0.062259

Exhibit 3.13 Worksheet Summarizing Factor Information

	Subsidiary 1	Subsidiary 2	Subsidiary 3	Total
Property	0.008069	0.000614	0.028376	0.037059
Payroll	0.01	0.05	0.035	0.095
Sales	0.032782	0.008878	0.020599	0.062259
Total	0.050851	0.059492	0.083975	0.194318
Average % (÷ 3)	0.016950	0.019831	0.027992	0.064793

Exhibit 3.14 Computation of Tax

Combined Income Subject to Apportionment $44,970,000 (from Exhibit 3.9)	Subsidiary 1	Subsidiary 2	Subsidiary 3	Total
Apportionment %	0.016950	0.019831	0.027992	0.064773
Combined income apportioned to California	762,242	891,800	1,258,800	2,912,842
Allocable (nonbusiness) income	1,500	4,500	10,000	16,000
California taxable income	763,742	896,300	1,268,800	2,928,842
Tax @ 9%	$ 68,737	$ 80,667	$ 114,192	$ 263,596

After the apportionment factor is determined the final worksheet can be prepared. This will show the application of the factor to the combined unitary income. A tax is computed representing both the total tax liability due to the state and the tax attributable to each subsidiary's operations within the state.

Determination of Unitary Business

The controversy over the use of separate accounting and income apportionment discussed earlier has been important for two reasons. First, by displaying the merits and difficulties of both methods, combined reporting can be accepted as an understandable extension of income apportionment. Second, the justification for the use of apportionment has introduced the important term "unitary business." Numerous court cases have reinforced the position that when a corporation is engaged in a unitary business, with operations encompassing several states, formulary apportionment is an acceptable means for determining state taxable income. One of the first times the term was actually used to describe the nature of a business was in *Bass, Ratcliff, and Gretton.* No definition or qualification of this term was made at that time, since Bass, Ratcliff, and Gretton agreed with the courts that its business was "unitary" in nature. Two important California cases which have created judicial guidelines that serve as standards for evaluating the unitary nature of a business are reviewed after the background of the term is considered.

The unitary business concept is based on the real property law known as the "unit rule."[35] This unit rule was first applied in the taxation of railroads, express companies, and other transportation companies.[36]

In the early 1890s, the Supreme Court used a rail mileage formula to apportion the capital stock of a company.[37] To fairly assess the value of a railroad in a state, the in-state rail mileage is considered as a part of the total rail mileage in all states. Each mile of rail by itself was considered valueless, unless it was part of a system or network of railroads. Other common carriers were also being treated as part of a single economic unit. In each of these instances, an apportionment formula was used to properly attribute a segment of the taxable property to the state. For example, if a railroad had 500,000 miles of rail with 20,000 miles in a particular state, then 4 percent of the total system would be taxable property in that state.

If this track mileage method of apportionment resulted in a ratio that greatly exceeded the ratio of car mileage actually traveled by the rolling stock of a tank car line in the state, the tax levied using this system would be considered unconstitutional.[38] This is because the use of the rail apportionment factor resulted in the taxation of out-of-state activities.

The physical connection of assets found in railroads and carriers was not necessarily required for the unit rule to be applied. The concept has

---

[35]The unit rule was approved by the U.S. Supreme Court in the *Union Pacific Railway Company* v. *Cheyenne* case 113 U.S. 516 (1884).
[36]Wilbur LaVelle, "What Constitutes a Unitary Business," *Southern California Tax Institute* Mathew Bender, New York, 1973, p. 241.
[37]*Pullman's Palace Car Company* v. *Pennsylvania* 141 U.S. 18 (1891).
[38]*Union Tank Line Company* v. *Wright* 249 U.S. 275 (1919).

gradually expanded to include companies where the connection between the states of operations was composed only of common management ties.[39]

By 1920, however, the nature of the cases brought to the Supreme Court had changed, since there were many more manufacturing and mercantile businesses. Whereas the application of the unit rule theory in these cases, which lead to the unitary business theory, did not change, the judicial atmosphere did. For nearly four decades, virtually no taxpayer could convince the Court that the apportionment percentage used by a state was unconstitutional.[40]

What is essential in all these cases based on a unity in a business is the need for some link between in-state and out-of-state activities. The use of formulary apportionment takes into account the entire range of activities of a multistate company and is constitutionally permissible only where a unitary business exists. According to Rudolph, "A unitary business may apparently be defined either as an interstate business, which is so integrated as to make separate accounting for the in-state business impossible, or as an interstate business in which the in-state activities contribute to the out-of-state activities, and the out-of-state activities contribute to the in-state business."[41]

Butler Brothers v. McColgan 315 U.S. 501 (1942)—Three Unities Test

The *Butler Brothers* case was the first Supreme Court case that provided a working definition of a unitary business. It also ranks as one of the leading cases on the use of formulary apportionment (the other two cases are *Underwood Typewriter* v. *Chamberlain* and *Bass, Ratcliff, and Gretton* v. *State Tax Commission*) and helped to initiate the combined reporting concept in California.

The pertinent facts of the case are as follows: Butler Brothers was a distributor of wholesale dry goods and other merchandise that was purchased from manufacturers and sold only to retailers. It operated seven stores, or houses, located in seven different states. Each house operated independently from the other houses by maintaining its own books of account, separate stocks of inventory, and separate handling of sales and credit arrangements. Accordingly, sales and expenses were directly attributed to the house that made the sale or incurred the expense. There were also some general expenses that were allocated to each house because these expenses were incurred for the benefit of all the houses. Included in this category were costs of operating a central buying division, central advertising fees, executive salaries, and miscellaneous overhead items.

---

[39]*Adams Express Company* v. *Ohio State Auditor* 166 U.S. 185 (1897).

[40]Hellerstein, "Recent Developments in State Tax Apportionment and the Circumscription of Unitary Business," p. 489.

[41]Rudolph, "State Taxation of Interstate Business: The Unitary Business Concept and Affiliated Corporate Groups" p. 184.

Butler Brothers filed a tax return in California for the taxable year 1936 by accounting for activity at its San Francisco house on a separate accounting basis. Sales revenue consisted of sales originating from the San Francisco office, and deductions from revenue consisted of both the direct expenses of the house and an allocated share of the common expenses. A loss of $82,851.00 was reported. The Franchise Tax Commissioner reviewed the operations of Butler Brothers making an additional $3,798.43 assessment after considering the following additional circumstances.

The central buying division of Butler Brothers was able to purchase inventory in large enough quantities to receive a purchase saving not realizable by each house in purchasing its own inventory. The reason the goods could be purchased in such large amounts was because of the company's ability to sell these very items, thus creating a tie between the purchasing and selling activities of all Butler Brothers' houses. The interdependency of these activities confirmed the Commissioner's belief that a single unitary business was being conducted. Furthermore, the maintenance of central advertising, accounting, and management divisions enabled Butler Brothers to spread these costs over more units. This would enable the company to take advantage of advertising opportunities not affordable to a single house and accounting and management services of a quality and cost also not as affordable to a single house. Based on this evidence, the Commissioner concluded that Butler Brothers was conducting a unitary business illustrated by the existence of three unities:

1　A unity of ownership—all divisions or distributing houses were owned 100 percent.
2　A unit of operation—evidenced by the central purchasing, advertising, accounting, and management division.
3　A unit of use—evidenced by the central executive force and general system of operation.

To fairly assess a tax on Butler Brothers' operations in California, the Commissioner combined the income from the entire operation and then apportioned an amount to California. The three-factor Massachusetts formula was used. The total earnings realized from the operations of all the houses were $1,149,677.00, of which 8.1372 percent was apportioned to California. The basis for these calculations was Section 10 of the Bank and Corporate Franchise Tax Act (General Laws, Act 8488, Vol. 2, p. 3851, Stats. 1929, pp. 19, 24, amended by Stat. 1931, p. 2226, Stat. 1935, p. 965) providing in part:

> . . . if the entire business of such bank or corporation is not done within this State, the tax shall be according to or measured by that portion thereof which is derived from business done within this State. The portion of net income derived from business done within this State shall be determined by an allocation upon the basis of sales, purchases, expenses of manufacturer,

payroll, value and situs of tangible property, or by reference to these or other factors, or by such other method of allocation as is fairly calculated to assign to the State the portion of net income reasonably attributable to the business done within this State and to avoid subjecting the taxpayer to double taxation.

The Commissioner, therefore, felt justified in assessing Butler Brothers' California operations by apportioning its total earnings.

The main conflict between Butler Brothers and the Commissioner centered on the question, could the tax commission insist on the use of formulary apportionment according to this franchise act? Butler Brothers argued that it was entitled to use separate accounting for determining the income to California and that the use of formulary apportionment was unlawful because it resulted in extraterritorial taxation. Insufficient evidence was offered to support this position in the opinion of the courts. In the courts' view, each factor of the apportionment formula used would have had to have been shown to be inappropriate or the cause of a severe and unfair tax burden. This was not done by Butler Brothers in its protest against the tax commission. Conversely, the Commissioner argued that the unit rule of assessment was appropriate for taxing this unitary business because the activities within the state were not truly separate and distinct from business without the state. The courts upheld the Commissioner's assessment by recognizing that where a unitary business exists the apportionment of income with a reasonable formula can be properly sustained.

It is evident that the same basic concepts of the *Underwood Typewriter* and *Bass, Ratcliff, Gretton* cases also reappeared in this case. There were a series of transactions occurring for each of these corporations that contributed to the earning of profits. For the Underwood Typewriter and Bass, Ratcliff, and Gretton corporations, there was a cycle, starting with the manufacture of the product and ending with its sale. In *Butler Brothers,* this cycle began with the purchase of the product and ended with the sale of the product. The *Butler Brothers* case, however, was the first to provide a working definition of a unitary business with the three unities test. This definition enabled the combined report concept to be expanded beyond a combination of a corporation and its divisions to also include several corporations and their subsidiaries, as illustrated in the discussion of another important case.

*Edison California Stores, Incorporated v. McColgan 183 P. 2d 16
(1947)—Contribution or Dependency Test*

The *Edison California Stores* case is the second important California case cited for providing a working definition of a unitary business. This case also reaffirmed the stand taken in the *Butler Brothers* case: that apportioning the income of a unitary business operating in several states to California by using a reasonable formula will not result in the taxation of extraterritorial values. The unitary business concept was also expanded in this case to include a group of commonly owned corporations as well as the previously employed group of commonly owned divisions of a single corporation.

Edison California Stores, Incorporated, was a Delaware corporation and was the parent of 15 subsidiaries located in 15 different states. The stock of the parent and subsidiary corporations was completely owned by members of the Edison family who were also the officers and directors of these corporations. The parent corporation purchased ladies' shoes, accessories, handbags, hosiery, and costume jewelry for retail distribution by itself and all the subsidiaries. The amount of merchandise shipped to each subsidiary store was statistically determined from the daily reports sent in by all store managers. A specified percentage charge for this service was then added on to the cost of the merchandise to each store. There were also a central management division, central purchasing department, central distributing department, central store operations department, and central advertising department and various other central administrative departments.

In reporting taxable income to the state of California in 1937 and 1938, the California corporation computed its income on a separate accounting basis. Although the Edison California company sold merchandise exclusively in the state of California, its business activities were not separate from the business conducted outside California. Realizing this fact, the Commissioner recomputed Edison's income on a combined return basis for the two years in question. This was done to insure a fair apportionment of taxable income to the state of California. Once again, the three-factor formula, based on property, payroll, and sales, was used. An additional assessment of $5,161.09 and $6,313.35, plus interest, was made for the first and second years, respectively. The tax commission believed the combined return was justified because of the unitary nature of Edison Stores. The three unities test from the *Butler Brothers* case was determined to be applicable. There was a unity of ownership; each subsidiary was completely owned by the parent company that, in turn, was owned by the Edison family. A unity of operations also existed as evidenced by central departmental control over corporate policies. Finally, there was a unity of use in the centralized executive force and general system of operation. The new unitary test introduced with this case concerns a "contribution" or "dependency" test or a "unity of use and management." The California courts stated:

> If the operation of the portion of the business done within the state is dependent upon or contributes to the operation of the business without the sate, the operations are unitary. . . .

Edison Stores failed to disprove the fairness of the combined return computed for the two years in question. Any taxpayer that attacks this formula has the burden of showing it resulted in extraterritorial taxation. The only evidence provided by the Edison California Stores was a demonstration that its separate accounting books were also accurate and reasonable. This type of evidence does not discredit a formula for income apportionment for state taxation.

Similarities in the Butler Brothers and Edison Stores Cases

Both of these important cases have provided a statutory basis for the use of combined reports. They are often cited in essays concerning the taxation of a unitary business and have demonstrated that specific state legislation is not needed for a state to apply combined reports. In the *Butler Brothers* case, the U.S. Supreme Court approved the application of the unitary concept to a group of commonly owned divisions. Originally, the unitary concept only dealt with single corporations, such as Butler Brothers, that were engaged in a business being operated in several states. Several years later, the California Supreme Court approved the same concept with respect to a group of commonly owned corporations in the *Edison California Stores* case. The unitary concept had been expanded to apply to all economic units rather than just single corporations. The taxable economic unit in the *Edison Stores* case consisted of a group of 15 subsidiary corporations and a parent corporation.

The primary emphasis in each of these cases was determining a reasonable method for clearly reflecting income attributable to the business activities within California. Butler Brothers and the Edison California Stores accounted for all their activities on a separate accounting basis. The California Tax Commissioner recomputed these amounts using a combined report. Separate accounting information was not disregarded in either case as being incorrect; rather combined reporting was demonstrated to more accurately reflect California taxable income. Furthermore, no specific evidence was provided in either case to sufficiently disprove the results of apportionment on a combined return.

Combined reporting was deemed to be the appropriate means for computing taxable income because both corporations were conducting a unitary business. Butler Brothers and the Edison Stores each had a "unity of ownership." Although Butler Brothers had a branch office operating in California and Edison Stores had a subsidiary operating in California, both the branch office and subsidiary corporation were totally owned by a corporation incorporated and operated outside California. There was also a "unity of operation" for both corporations, evidenced by central service activities located outside California. The head office of Butler Brothers and the parent corporation of Edison California Store interacted with California operations, providing such services as accounting, advertising, and centralized purchasing. The centralized purchasing was influential in determining the cost of goods sold in California. The cost of the goods sold by Butler Brothers was affected by the purchase discounts received by the head office that could purchase in large quantities. The cost of the inventory sold by the Edison California Stores was affected by the percentage charge added to the original cost paid by the parent corporation. Finally, there was also a "unity of use," illustrated through the employment of a centralized executive force and in the general system of operations.

Recent Trends and Developments in Combined Reporting

Although the *Butler Brothers* and *Edison Stores* cases have provided judicial guidelines for determining a unitary business, it is still possible to fall into the trap of labeling every large corporation a "unitary business." For example, the existence of the corporation having a common management group working for some of its divisions or subsidiaries does not necessarily indicate the existence of a unitary business. Similarly, a group of corporations bearing the same trade name could also mislead one into believing that a unitary business must exist. The situation for each corporation must be considered and evaluated before any assumptions about a unitary business are dictated to be fact. This requires the examination of a diverse array of indicators for each corporate organization. Exhibit 3.15 is an example of the types of questions a state would ask for determining whether a unitary business existed.

A New Consideration

This type of questionnaire can be informative and can be a useful tool for determining whether a unitary business exists. Several other unitary tests have also been suggested, including the operational interdependency test.[42] For this test, a business would be considered part of a unitary group if the basic corporate operations are interdependent on functions of other controlled companies in the same group. (A controlled company is one in which the parent company owns more than 50 percent of the corporate voting stock.) Any other relationship between affiliated companies—such as common legal counsel, advertising, and accounting services—would not be considered, even though they do affect the profitability of a company. Operational interdependency would be the extent of intercompany purchases and sales, an amount easily quantifiable. The establishment of a percentage of purchases and sales between affiliates would be the only requirement for this test. For example, if more than 20 percent of a corporations sales are to an affiliated corporation, the two corporations would be engaged in a unitary business. Although many other aspects of a companies operations are overlooked, this test is intended to "narrow the scope of a unitary business."

Superior Oil Company v. Franchise Tax Board 60 Cal. 2d 406
(1963)—Expansion of the Unitary Concept

In the past two decades, there has been an expansion of the scope of the unitary approach. Whereas the earlier court cases have concentrated on an

Exhibit 3.15   Indicators of a Unitary Business—Unitary Checklist

Management

1   Business operated in divisions?
Separate corporate entities?

   (a)   Why operated this way?

   (b)   Why was affiliate acquired or created?

2   Overall policies formulated and decisions made in what areas?

   (a)   Were specific goals sought?

   (b)   General in nature?

3   Was it involved in product development? Operations development? Marketing? Search for new businesses?

4   Any fiscal controls?

   (a)   What type?

   (b)   Budgetary controls?

   (c)   Reports?

5   Meetings with managers and other personnel of affiliates?

   (a)   Frequency?

   (b)   Purpose?

6   Approval of promotions, salary increases, bonuses, and so on, of affiliates?

7   Selection of board of directors and officers of affiliates?

8   Extent of supervision of

   (a)   Home office personnel?

   (b)   Affiliates' management personnel?

Financing

1   Sources for parent and affiliates?

2   Better rates by volume borrowing?

3   Direction and negotiation of financing for affiliate?

4   Participation in financing for affiliate by furnishing advice, guarantee, and the like?

5   Intercompany loans?

6   Who makes borrowing decisions?

Reports to Parent

1   Types of reports or accounting?

2   Purpose of such reports or accounting?

3   Frequency?

4   Originator and recipient of reports?

5   If no reports or accounting, how does parent keep itself apprised of affiliates' operations?

Exhibit 3.15 continued

6 Visits to parent's offices or vice versa? By whom? Frequency? Purpose for such visits?

Intercompany Sales

1 What percentage of affiliates' sales were sales of parent's products? What was the dollar volume?

2 What percentage of affiliates' sales were sales to parent? Dollar volume?

3 Likewise, what percentage of parent's sales were sales of affiliates' products, and what percentage of its sales were to its affiliates? Dollar volumes?

4 Types of products or services sold by parent and affiliate?

5 Were products purchased by parent from affiliate used by parent or sold to others and vice versa?

6 Were similar products purchased from competitors? If so, why such purchases?

Central Service by Parent

1 Maintenance of corporate records and minutes?

2 Uniform accounting procedures and central recruitment and training of accounting personnel?

3 Assistance in budget preparation and central review by parent?

4 Central review of all audits (internal and independent), tax returns, and so on?

5 Central electronic data processing?

6 Credit investigations?

7 Credit cards, car rental, and so on?

Personnel

1 Centralized or by each corporation, division, and the like?

2 Intercompany exchange of employees? If so, what classification of employees?

3 Intercompany training services?
   (a) Who attends classes?
   (b) Type of training?
   (c) Mandatory
   (d) Promotional purposes?

4 Common benefits?
   (a) Each type of benefit or plan?
       (1) Health, life, insurance?
       (2) Pension plans?
       (3) Vacations?
       (4) Stock purchase plan?
       (5) Employee loans?
   (b) What employees covered?
   (c) Managed by whom?

Exhibit 3.15 continued

Common Facilities

1 Administrative offices, sales office, manufacturing plants, storage warehouses, transportation?

2 Reason for common use?

3 Intercompany exchanges, leases or sales of equipment, property, and so on.

4 Common lease service?

Advertising

1 To public and to customers?

2 Direction, assistance, or advice from parent to affiliate?

3 Intercompany exchange of ad information?

4 Cooperative ads?

5 Same ad agency?

Technical and Research

1 Common design, patent, trade name, and patterns?

2 Common planning and engineering data?

3 Intercompany exchange of information?

4 Sharing of research expense and/or facilities?

Insurance

1 Types—property, payroll, and the like?

2 Administered and purchased by whom for parent and affiliate?

3 Common agency or insurer?

4 Common policy for parent and affiliate?

Manuals

1 Type—sales, accounting, management, and so on?

2 Prepared by whom?

Common Purchasing/Leasing

1 What? Labels, containers, raw materials, and the like?

2 Master purchase agreement?

3 Centralized purchasing?

4 Benefit by use of same service?

5 Common import brokers?

Common Selling Effort and/or Facilities

1 Same salesmen, brokers, and so on?

Exhibit 3.15 continued

---

2 Servicing of same customers?

3 Joint marketing efforts or agreements?

4 Cooperative marketing?

Other Centralized Services

1 Common legal service—house counsel and outside counsel?

2 Common accounting, tax, and audit services?

3 With respect to outside legal, accounting, tax, and auditing services
   - **(a)** Who contracted for the services?
     - (1) Tax problems?
     - (2) Local operating problems?
     - (3) Independent accountants?
   - **(b)** Who paid for them?
     - (1) Tax problems?
     - (2) Local operating problems?
     - (3) Independent accountants?
   - **(c)** How were charges prorated between parent and affiliates?
     - (1) Tax problems?
     - (2) Local operating problems?
     - (3) Independent accountants?

4 Central administrative services?
   - **(a)** How were affiliates charged for such services?
   - **(b)** What did the services consist of?

Conclusion

With respect to these other factors, the final question is what benefit was there to the corporate group as a result of these factors:

1 Lower cost?

2 Efficiency?

3 Increased sales?

---

interstate flow of goods between affiliates, the new court cases have proved the unitary concept to be dynamic. This interstate flow of goods is no longer considered an essential factor for the establishment of a unitary business, as illustrated in the *Superior Oil* case.

The Superior Oil Company was a California corporation. The company's principal place of business was in Los Angeles. The company

---

[42]Hellerstein, "The Unitary Business Principle and Multicorporate Enterprises: An Examination of the Major Controversies," p. 322.

produced and sold petroleum and petroleum products in California and various other states and foreign countries. Most of the raw petroleum was sold at the well site, with only a minor portion of the production processed or refined. There was also a realty subdivision located in California that contributed to the California income with its sales of capital assets and dividends on stock investments. The real estate activities strictly in California were accounted for on a separate accounting basis as were the other intrastate activities. Income from all the petroleum operations were computed on a combined return basis. The California Franchise Tax Commission, however, insisted that separate accounting procedures would be more appropriate because Superior Oil was not an integrated oil company. (The company did not refine and process a substantial portion of its production.) It should be noted that the tax resulting from the use of separate accounting was approximately $381,000.00 higher than the tax computed on apportioned income on a combined return.

The following was cited by Superior Oil as conclusive evidence of the unitary nature of its operations to support the use of a combined return:

1   The business activities transacted inside California were not separate or distinct from those conducted outside California. There were a central executive office, functions for central accounting and purchasing services, and personnel transfers among the states of operations.
2   The three unity elements existed for the Superior Oil Company. There was a unity of ownership, as well as a unity in the operations for executive, financial, and various other activities of the company. Finally, there was a unity of use in the general operations.
3   The operations in California were dependent on the operations outside the state for financial and legal services, technical services, and materials and equipment. Funds were borrowed on assets located outside California to finance projects in California. There was also a transfer of funds from outside California to finance projects in California. Fiscal control was exercised by the Texas office, and legal counseling was received from attorneys in Texas and Washington. Texas laboratories and offices supply geophysical technical information and services and land lease controls. The Texas office also controlled and supplied the tubular materials needed. Skilled personnel were transferred to California to perform any necessary services. Also, technical information was supplied daily to the California offices for decision-making purposes.
4   California's operations also contributed to the operations outside the state. To aid in Superior Oil's petroleum production, there was a coordination of exploration activities, well production, and land acquisition in California. Economic contributions were made in terms of accounting, the filing of tax returns, manufacturing, selling, and purchasing in California. Finally, overall business strategies and adminstrative controls were coordinated in California.

After an evaluation of this evidence, the California Court of Appeals ruled in favor of the taxpayer. Superior Oil had shown its unitary nature according to the guidelines from the *Butler Brothers* and *Edison Stores* cases. The sale of oil in interstate commerce was not required for proving a unitary operation.

Another Nonuniform Interpretation—Kennecott Cooper Corporation v. State Tax Commission 493 P.2d 632 (1972)

The existence of a unitary business will not always signal the use of a combined report. A state that has adopted UDITPA for the apportionment of unitary business income can still choose to apply the act in a nonuniform manner. The concept of using combined reporting to promote uniformity would thus be overlooked. This is illustrated in the *Kennecott Cooper* case in the state of Utah.

The Kennecott Corporation exemplified a unitary business according to the standard illustrated in the previous cases discussed. It had worldwide operations engaged in the mining, recovering, refining, and fabricating of metals. Mining properties were located in New Mexico, Arizona, and Nevada, as well as in Utah. There were also numerous sales outlets in other states and countries. Financial and management control of all Kennecott's subsidiaries was based at the New York City headquarters.

For the 1967 and 1968 taxable years, franchise tax returns were filed in the state of Utah using a combined return. The state of Utah had adopted UDITPA and regulations for the apportionment of combined earnings from a unitary business. Considering all the previous landmark decisions in this area, it would seem appropriate for the Kennecott Corporation to file in this manner. The Utah Tax Commission questioned the validity of these returns and redetermined Kennecott's tax liability using a method that altered the sales factor.

The original franchise returns filed were calculated in the manner prescribed in UDITPA; the three-factor formula of property, payroll, and sales, was applied to apportionable income. The sales factor would include all sales in Utah if the tangible personal property were delivered to a purchaser in Utah. Any other terms of the sale were not considered. The Utah Tax Commission believed the sales factors on Kennecott's combined return distorted the true picture of the company's activities in the state. A comparison was made between Kennecott's gross receipts in Utah as computed for determining the depletion allowance and the sales figure as computed for determining the three-factor apportionment percentage. For the 1967 taxable year, gross income for depletion purposes was $155,960,165.49 higher than the sales attributable to Utah. Despite this rather large discrepancy, an explanation can be given. The gross receipts' figure included sales delivered to purchasers both within and without the state of Utah. According to the Utah regulations, the sales computed as part of the three-factor formula should not have included sales to pur-chasers outside Utah. The gross income computed for the determination of a depletion allowance was also much larger than the net income shown on the franchise returns.

Problems Identifying a Unitary Business

There has been a substantial amount of controversy concerning the meth-ods for determining a unitary business and the implementation of a com-bined return. However, once it is conceded that the use of apportionment for a unitary business applies to both a multistate corporation with several subsidiaries or branches and a multistructured corporation,[43] the focus can be directed to the practical considerations of applying the unitary concept. Once again, there has been much controversy concerning the administra-tion of the unitary apportionment concept. More specifically, the majority of the criticism has been directed against the unitary doctrine as developed by the California taxing authorities,[44] since they are considered the pioneers in this area.[45]

LACK OF A WORKING OBJECTIVE DEFINITION

The California tests for determining a unitary business as examined in the *Butler Brothers* and *Edison California Stores* cases create unitary bound-aries so large that it seems as if every corporation with interstate activities and operations in California would appear to be a unitary corporation.[46] Furthermore, after reading the checklist for the indicators of a unitary business (see Exhibit 3.15), the subjectiveness involved in classifying a company as unitary becomes even more apparent.

Frank M. Keesling and John S. Warren, two of the most knowledgeable authorities on the unitary concept, have also addressed the difficulties involved in providing an objective definition of a unitary business, as illustrated by their following examples.

---

[43]For a multistate corporation, "This unitary concept [the operational interdependence test] has the same theoretical justification that applies to the taxation of a corporation with unitary divisions . . . " For additional information, see Industry Statement, "Hearings on State Taxation of Interstate Commerce," Mondale Subcommittee of Senate Finance Committee, p. 260, 282 (93rd Congress, First Session, September 18, 1973), presented on behalf of the Committee on State Taxation of the Council of State Chambers of Commerce, the National Association of Manufacturers, and other organizations.

[44]Hellerstein, "The Unitary Business Principle and Multicorporate Enterprises: An Examina-tion of the Major Controversies," p. 318.

[45]For the history of the unitary concept considered along with its current applications, see Frank Keesling, "A Current Look at the Combined Report and Uniformity in Allocation Practices," 42 *Journal of Taxation* 106 (1975).

[46]Hellerstein, "The Unitary Business Principle and Multicorporate Enterprises: An Examina-tion of the Major Controversies," p. 318.

Is the growing of oranges a different kind of business than the growing of grapefruit, or are they one business inasmuch as both oranges and grapefruits are citrus fruits? Is a company which manufactures insecticides in California, fertilizer in West Virginia, and chemicals for use in textile manufacturing in Georgia engaged in three separate businesses, or is it engaged in the single business of manufacturing chemicals? Again, is a company which operates oil wells in California and mines in a number of other states engaged in two different businesses or in the single business of extracting mineral substances from the earth?[47]

Kessling and Warren suggest that the solution is to determine whether the activities within a taxing state are economically interdependent on those outside that state. If the in-state activities are economically interdependent on the outside of one and if the latter contribute materially to the earning of profits in-state, then the business should be considered to be unitary.[48] However, the use of this test—which relies on these three unities: (1) unit of ownership, (2) unity of operation, and (3) unity of use—and the contribution or dependency test could place all large corporations with operations in California in the unitary category. This means that if a company with activities outside a state provides substantial services or substantial capital to a subsidiary operating within another state the corporation would be classified as unitary. Furthermore, this unitary concept appears to be equivalent to a combination for apportionment purposes based simply on common ownership.[49] This interpretation has actually been approved and used in several courts, because "under the recent California and Utah cases, centralized management, without more, may be sufficient to support a finding a unitary business. Under such a test practically every interstate corporation would appear to be unitary. But the question is ultimately a Federal one, and this goes considerably beyond the holdings in any of the Supreme Court cases."[50]

PRACTICAL PROBLEMS AS ILLUSTRATED BY COURT CASES

The practical problems of determining whether a corporation is unitary have also been illustrated by the conflicting decisions in the *Superior Oil* case[51] and the *Skelly Oil* case.[52] The *Superior Oil* case decided by the California Supreme Court was discussed earlier. As previously stated, the court concluded that Superior's operations outside California were an

---

[47]Frank M. Keesling and John S. Warren, "California's Uniform Division of Income for Tax Purposes Act," 15 *UCLA Law Review* 156 (1967) and 655 (1968).
[48]Miller, "State Income Taxation of Multiple Corporations and Multiple Businesses," p. 106.
[49]Miller, "State Income Taxation of Multiple Corporations and Multiple Businesses," p. 107.
[50]Rudolph, "State Taxation of Interstate Business: The Unitary Business Concept and Affiliated Corporate Groups," p. 192.
[51]See p. 94 for a complete discussion of this case.
[52]*Skelly Oil Company* v. *Commissioner of Taxation* 131 N.W. 2d 632 (1964).

integral part of its operations within California and that therefore unitary treatment was appropriate. This allowed Superior Oil to utilize losses sustained from operations in Arkansas and Louisiana by offsetting the company with income from California sources.

At least one authority in the field believes the findings in the *Superior Oil* case to be incorrect.[53] Hellerstein questions whether Superior's activity should have been considered unitary merely because its in-state and out-of-state production operations benefited from common nonoperating activities such as fiscal control, technical, and laboratory assistance and information, legal counseling, and the transfer of employees from other branches. Hellerstein's conclusion is based on the fact that all Superior's oil was sold in crude form at the wellhead and that no sales were made to customers in one state from oil produced in another state.[54] Hellerstein, therefore, concludes that the "crucial factor that underlines the rationale for reaching out to take into account activities in other states, the segregation of the profits from producing and from selling, is missing."[55]

In the *Skelly Oil* case, the Supreme Court of Minnesota held that Skelly's activities within Minnesota were separate and distinct from its activities outside the state. Accordingly, the company's operations were deemed to be nonunitary. The only activity of Skelly Oil in Minnesota was the marketing of refined products. This activity was deemed to be separate and distinct from the company's refining and production activities. The Commissioner argued that part of Skelly's production income should be included in the total income to be apportioned, since a percentage of Skelly's production went to its own refineries. The Commissioner held that Skelly's business was integrated and accordingly believed that part of the out-of-state operations should be taken into account in arriving at the company's Minnesota taxable income. The court, however, concluded that the production activities of Skelly constituted an entirely separate business. Professor Hellerstein once again disagrees with this conclusion. He concludes that Skelly's activities in Minnesota should have been found to be part of a unitary business on the basis that Skelly Oil made oil sales to customers in Minnesota from oil that it had produced within other states.[56]

It is evident that although the factual distinctions of each case are not to be ignored, the possibility for varied interpretations of the unitary concept does exist.

---

[53]Hellerstein, "The Unitary Business Principle and Multicorporate Enterprises: An Examination of the Major Controversies," p. 323.
[54]Hellerstein, "Recent Development in State Tax Apportionment and the Circumscription of Unitary Business," p. 497–503.
[55]Hellerstein, " The Unitary Business Principle and Multicorporate Enterprises: An Examination of the Major Controversies," p. 323.
[56]Hellerstein, "The Unitary Business Principle and Multicorporate Enterprise: An Examination of the Major Controversies."

PROBLEMS IN ALTERNATIVES—ANOTHER POSSIBILITY STILL LEAVES
UNANSWERED QUESTIONS

The possibility for an alternative unitary test based on operational interdependency was mentioned earlier. The key factor needed to classify a
business as unitary under this system is the interdependence of operating
functions—such as the production of goods in one state that are sold from
a location in another state. Under this method, nonoperating functions such
as common management, legal, or marketing departments would not be
sufficient to characterize a business as unitary. However, even if this
"operational interdependency" test is accepted as a means for determining
a unitary business, it has been noted that there would still be some
unresolved questions in evaluating how and if operating functions should
be grouped into a series of separate businesses rather than a single
business.[57] Miller poses this question: "For example, a manufacturer of air
conditioning equipment may produce single-room window units, larger
units to cool one-family homes, and still larger units to cool entire high-rise
apartment houses. Should the classification of these activities into one,
two, or three businesses depend on whether or not the several products
(i) are manufactured at one rather than at separate factories, (ii) utilize
similar or dissimilar productive processes and components, (iii) are sold
under a single brand name or several names, or (iv) are marketed through
one or several channels of distribution?"[58] This type of situation along with
many other questions which may arise, would require a certain amount of
judgment in evaluating the significance of certain facts. This would once
again provide for the possibility of varied interpretations.

CONCLUSION

Miller identifies these problems: "One of the major problems in the 'unitary' business approach is the almost impossible task of establishing understandable and uniform tests or criteria for determining the basis requiring or
permitting the filing on other than a single corporate basis. A review of
only a few of the numerous cases involved in the 'unitary' business concept
clearly evidences the difficulties inherent in the subjective tests presently
utilized. Further, the preoccupation of some state income tax administrators with the unitary business theory has undoubtedly caused them to
venture far beyond the scope of the original income shifting problems
which gave rise to the theory. The point may have already been reached
where affiliated corporations meeting the subjective tests are forced to file
combined or consolidated returns even though in some instances the
complicance and audit costs may well exceed the additional tax liabilities
generated."[59]

[57]Miller, "State Income Taxation of Multiple Corporations and Multiple Businesses," p. 108.
[58]Miller, "State Income Taxation of Multiple Corporations and Multiple Businesses." p. 108.
[59]Nemeth and Agee, "State Taxation of Multistate Business: Resolution or Stalemate?," p.
247–248.

Because of this absence of a completely objective criteria, a state taxing authority could attempt to invoke the unitary treatment using a California-type combined return whenever he finds that a combined return results in higher tax dollars payable to the state. On the other hand, a corporation could also claim its operations were unitary in the states where a combined return would aid in reducing the company's tax liability. Furthermore, the extensive knowledge that taxpayers have concerning their corporate operations gives them an advantage over state taxing authorities in determining which combinations of activities will produce the smallest tax liability in each taxing jurisdiction.

Both the taxpayer and tax administrator must accept the fact that the application of the combined report and unitary concepts involves the exercise of a high degree of judgment on the part of both. This is particularly true since the financial and nonfinancial data for each corporation are so different, and this opens the door for variations in applying the unitary concept.

Finally, it must be remembered that combined reporting originated with simple structured companies, that is, *Butler Brothers* and *Edison Stores*. These companies had a single line of business, and application of a combined report was easily applied to such operations and was supportable through the precedents set by earlier cases, that is, *Underwood* and *Bass Ratcliff* that were also companies with a single line of business. However, attempts to apply the principles to the large ultracomplex operations of the present-day multistate and often times multinational corporations could very well be a case of principle misapplied, combined theory run rampant.

CHAPTER FOUR

The Multistate Compact

CREATION OF THE MULTISTATE TAX COMPACT

Reasons for the Creation of the Compact

In the last two and one-half decades, there has been a noticeable increase in the number of problems focused on the taxation of interstate commerce. Business and state taxing agencies were becoming involved in a tug of war over the income taxes levied on corporate activities within a state. This situation had prompted extensive studies to be conducted by both Federal and state officials, as well as by business and tax administrators.

As the American economy flourished, interstate merchants and manufacturers became prominent in economic systems. There was an increase in large complex businesses because of natural growth and the growing number of mergers. Many of these larger corporations eventually found it necessary to become qualified to do business in the majority of states where their products were sold, thereby becoming taxpayers in those states. There was also an increase in corporations that maintained offices in relatively few states but that continued to take advantage of the markets of other states. These companies managed to avoid being subjected to the corporate income or franchise taxes of these latter states. For many years, the states fought to subject these smaller out-of-state companies to a share of the tax burden. Local businesses in these states complained that their operations were at an unfair advantage, since out-of-state companies did not bear any of the state tax burden.[1]

One reason this situation existed was because until 1959, a corporation could assume that a state would not tax its interstate commerce if it did no intrastate business with that state. Since the concepts of "business location" and "doing business" within a state were somewhat ambiguous, each state could almost set its own criteria. Gradually, more and more states were taxing a larger proportion of the corporate activities within their borders. The states believed that these businesses were obligated to pay their fair share of the tax burden. Many businesses became discontented at

---

[1]Jerome R. Hellerstein, "Allocation and Nexus in State Taxation of Interstate Businesses," 20 *Tax Law Review* 2 (January 1965), p. 259.

the idea that so many states could tax their activities, no matter how minimal, and feared that more than 100 percent of their income could and would be subject to taxation.

In 1959, the U.S. Supreme Court determined what constituted sufficient activity within a state to subject a business to taxation. The *Northwestern States Portland Cement Company* and *Stockham Valves and Fittings, Incorporated* decisions (see Chapter 1) maintained that a business with a sales office used for solicitation purposes in a state represented a sufficient amount of activity for a business to be liable for that state's taxes, even though the business was otherwise exclusively engaged in interstate commerce. The business community was greatly disturbed by these Court decisions. Corporate taxpayers faced with the prospect of larger tax liabilities felt that these state taxes would absorb an exorbitant percentage of their profits. They were also apprehensive of being faced with greater time-consuming compliance responsibilities because of the necessity to report their activities to more states.

These two landmark cases stressed the need for an increase in uniformity in state taxation. Definite tax guidelines stating the obligations of in-state as well as multistate businesses were needed to provide an equitable tax system that could discourage multiple taxation. These guidelines would be the starting point for providing systematic control over a diversified taxation system. Both the Federal and state governments have attempted to provide such guidelines.

Federal Attempts to Provide Uniformity

The first efforts by the Federal government to resolve the problems of state taxation of interstate commerce were in 1959, shortly after the controversial *Northwestern* and *Stockham* cases. Within weeks of the Supreme Court decisions handed down in these cases, the Senate Select Committee on Small Business held a series of public hearings.[2] Meanwhile, the House Judiciary Committee and Senate Finance Committee considered various bills that could provide temporary relief for interstate companies obliged to pay numerous state taxes. The result was the introduction of P.L. 86-272. (A reproduction of P.L. 86-272 is in Chapter 1.) P.L. 86-272 provides a minimum standard for the taxation of multistate businesses when the tax is based on or measured by income. The law applies only to the income tax and does not afford protection to any corporation incorporated under the laws of the taxing state. The law was designed to prevent a state from levying an income tax on a corporation engaged in interstate commerce when its only business activity within that state consists of the solicitation of orders for the sale of tangible personal property. These orders must be sent outside the state for approval or rejection and must be filled by

[2]"Hearings on State Taxation on Interstate Commerce before the Senate Select Committee on Small Business," 86th Congress, 1st Session (1959).

shipment or delivery from any point outside the state. Each of these factors must be present for the corporation to be exempt from taxation under this law.

Example

The H-K Corporation is a Delaware corporation qualified to do business in Illinois, Indiana, and Iowa. It is engaged in the manufacture and distribution of farm machinery. The machinery is produced in Illinois, where the company's main offices are located. Sales offices are also maintained in Indiana and Iowa. The only activity in Delaware is the solicitation of orders made by a representative of the corporation. P.L. 86-272 will not prevent Delaware from assessing an income tax on the H-K Corporation, because the law does not provide any minimum taxation standards for corporations acting within the state of incorporation.

Example

Widget, Incorporated, sells hardware to various distributors on the West Coast. A representative of Widget, Incorporated, solicits orders in Colorado that are sent to the central offices in Texas for approval. Once an order is approved, the hardware is shipped to the customers from a small warehouse in Colorado. P.L. 86-272 would not prevent Colorado from imposing an income tax, because an inventory of goods is maintained in the state. This is clearly beyond the business activity permitted in the law.

The acceptance of P.L. 86-272 appeared to be the solution to the "nexus" problem, even though the law never explicitly defines "solicitation of an order." The law, however, was an attempt to appease the business community by providing the quota for the minimum standards for income taxes, but there was still uncertainty relative to the collection of sales and use taxes.[3] In 1961, Congress passed an amendment to P.L. 86-272 that authorized Congress to make an examination of all pertinent matters regarding the state taxation of interstate commerce and to issue a report with proposals to the Congress.[4]

The main objectives of this study were as follows:

1   Develop statistical and factual data concerning the activities of interstate companies.

2   Determine the ability of these companies to comply with the numerous state tax laws.

---

[3]S. C. Nemeth, Jr., and H. O. Agee, Jr., "State Taxation of Multistate Business: Resolution or Stalement?," 48 *Taxes*, 4 (April 1970), p. 239.

[4]For further information see the following: "Hearings before Select Committee on Small Business of United States Senate," 86th Congress, 1st Session (1959); State Taxation of Interstate Commerce, Senate Report No. 453, 86th Congress, 1st Session (1959); and State Taxation of Income Derived from Interstate Commerce, Senate Report No. 658, 86th Congress, 1st Session (1959).

3 Determine the actual costs of compliance.

4 Consider new proposals and evaluate their effects.

The four and one-half year study was conducted by the Special Subcommittee on State Taxation of Interstate Commerce headed by Congressman Edwin Willis of Louisiana.

During the study, the subcommittee received information from both businessmen and tax officials. The public was also kept informed by members of the subcommittee through various speeches, meetings, and articles. The results of the study and the recommendations that were published in four volumes led to the proposed legislation commonly known as the "Willis Bills."

The first two volumes of the study were published in June 1964 and dealt with the general findings of the study and net income taxes. Volume three was published in June 1965 and dealt with sales and use taxes, gross receipts taxes, and capital stock taxes. Volume four was published in September 1965 and contained the legislative recommendations.[5]

SPECIAL CONGRESSIONAL STUDY

Before a review of bills introduced in Congress as a result of this study, the initial Report or volumes 1 and 2 issued by the Subcommittee should be considered. The Report substantiated the fact that there is a need for uniformity in the taxation of income for state tax purposes. This viewpoint has been accepted by both businessmen and tax administrators. Yet for numerous reasons that include conflicting economic interests among the states the Report states that voluntary adoption of any type of uniform system by the states would be a slow process, if not an impossible one.[6]

To begin with, the Report deals primarily with the taxation of income from manufacturing and mercantile companies. The need for uniformity in these cases exists, because according to the Report, there are diversities in the income tax bases used by the states and in the methods of dividing this income among the states.

The Report recommends that a substantially uniform net income tax base be established. Variations would be permitted however, but only for important local policy differences. The result of such an income tax base would be simplified reporting procedures, a reduction in compliance costs, and a simplification in the administration of these taxes.[7] The Report has acknowledged that there is already substantial conformity here with the states because of the adoption of the Federal tax base for many items.[8] The

---

[5]"Report on State Taxation of Interstate Commerce," House Report 1480, 88th Congress, 2nd Session, Vols. 1 and 2 (1964); House Report 565, 89th Congress, 1st Session (1965); House Report 952, 89th Congress, 1st Session (1965).

[6]House Report 1480, p. 355.

[7]House Report 1480, pp. 588–590.

[8]House Report 1480, p. 279.

Report also examines the diversities in the methods used by the states in the division of income, which consists of the use of the following:

1   Specific allocation.
2   Separate accounting.
3   Formulary apportionment.
4   Varying jurisdictional and nexus requirements.[9]

The implementation of all these methods has resulted in the overtaxation of some companies and the undertaxation of others.[10] Although the use of these methods could have created excessive compliance costs for the multistate company, the Report has shown the opposite to be true, stating: "What has happened is that the complexity of the multistate tax system, instead of producing large amounts of compliance cost, has resulted in noncompliance and in the inequities which come with a tax system in which formal requirements have been abandoned."[11]

What the Report eventually gives support to is the use of a congressionally prescribed apportionment formula based on the two factors of property and payroll. The suggested elimination of the receipts factor, and more particularly the destination test for sales, is based on the fact that the apportionment of sales receipts is by far the most difficult and troublesome factor to deal with.[12] This is because a multistate company must keep sufficient records for all its sales to show the place of origin, destination, acceptance of the order, and the sales office location involved. This places two requirements on the company involved: the need to have a sufficient bookkeeping system and the need to have knowledge concerning the varying state laws and rules.[13] If, in fact, the use of a two-factor formula is accepted, multistate manufacturing and mercantile companies that maintain no inventories in a state but exploit that state's markets might be able to avoid an income tax in that state. Exactly what effect this would have on the revenue of the states was also examined in the Report.

Based on its study of manufacturing and mercantile companies, the Report concludes that there will be very little revenue difference to the states if the receipts factor were eliminated from the three-factor formula or if the origin or destination test for receipts were used under this three-factor formula.[14] Therefore, since heavy compliance problems can be eliminated without any significant revenue effects, the implementation of the two factors of property and payroll is suggested for consideration. The

---

[9]House Report 1480, pp. 157–249.
[10]House Report 1480, p. 249.
[11]House Report 1480, p. 384.
[12]House Report 1480, p. 247.
[13]House Report 1480, pp. 319–327.
[14]House Report 1480, pp. 560–563.

Report does acknowledge, however, that although the revenues involved may not be significant the heavy manufacturing states would gain some additional revenues from an origin test of sales or from a two-factor formula and that the less industrial states would lose some revenues by eliminating the destination test or the sales factor itself.

The conclusion that there will be a minimal revenue effect should be questioned. The percentage of the revenue losses in the Report is misleading, since it deals with the percentage of a state's total tax revenue and not the percentage of the lost corporate income tax revenue. As noted in the Report, the choice of a formula could have substantial revenue effects on a company if viewed in terms of taxable income gained or lost from the manufacturing and mercantile operations.[15] Furthermore, to judge the revenue impacts by the effects on total collections results in distortive figures.

If the study used total revenue because it was concerned with a state's ability to meet all its obligations, perhaps an even broader standard could have been used. The effect of the apportionment factor change could have been viewed in terms of a state's total revenues that include such items as Federal grants and aid. Using such a larger base would make it even easier to conclude that any change in the factors would have no significant revenue effects.[16]

Whereas many other questions can be proposed concerning the statistical methods, estimates, and assumptions made in the Report, the Report does represent the efforts of numerous competent individuals who have studied the historical and economic data available. The Report is essentially the first extensive attempt by the Federal government to study the problems of uniformity in state taxation. It has also lead to the numerous proposed tax bills in this area that are highlighted next.

HOUSE REPORT 11798

"The first bill, House Report 11798 was introduced in Congress in October, 1965.[17] It provided recommendations for determining which corporation should be subject to state taxation, the method of taxation, and the means of administering these taxes. Jurisdiction was to be granted for the imposition of state taxes based on or measured by income if a corporation had a business location within that state. A business location was deemed to exist if real property were owned or leased or one or more employees were

[15]House Report 1480, p. 539.

[16]Hellerstein, "Allocation and Nexus in State Taxation of Interstate Businesses," pp. 269–270.

[17]House Report 11798, 89th Congress, 2nd Session (1966). Also see Taxation of Business with Multistate Operations House Report 11798, comments of Honorable Fred L. Cox, Director, Interstate Affairs, Georgia Department of Revenue, before the House of Representatives, Committee of the Judiciary, Special Subcommittee on State Taxation of Interstate Commerce, Washington, D.C., Thursday, March 10, 1966.

located within the state. The taxable base was to consist of the taxable income as previously determined for federal taxation purposes. Each state could make its own unique adjustments to this base. A two-factor apportionment formula consisting of a property and payroll factor was to be applied to the adjusted Federal tax base. Finally, the aforementioned taxing procedures were to be administered by the U.S. Treasury Department, which would also have the responsibility for handling the state tax forms, coordinating regulations, and arbitrating any tax disputes.

Various hearings were held so that other government officials and business and community leaders could voice their reactions to the proposed legislation.[18] Perhaps the most controversial item of this proposed legislation was the use of a two-factor apportionment formula. Most states preferred the three-factor property, payroll, and sales formula they were presently using. Demanding all states to enforce this two-factor formula would ignore accounting theories that consider manufacturing, distributing, and selling all important variables and prerequisites to the earning of a profit. Also, the use of a two-factor formula in all the states could tend to be discriminatory. Those states with businesses requiring heavy outlays of capital investments that are also labor intense industries would be in an enviable situation. The tax revenues of these states would tend to be larger than those for a state with businesses predominately oriented toward marketing and sales promotion or with relatively minor manufacturing operations. An overview of the revenue receivable by all states from this two-factor formula would vary not only on a state-by-state basis but also by segments of the country as well. Eastern states predominantly known for their manufacturing industries would most likely show the largest revenue intake from the income taxes.

Another questionable aspect of House Report 11798 was the choice for the taxable income base. Using the Federal taxable income as the starting point for computing the state tax liability does provide uniformity; however, this process ignores all other unitary income earned but not computed under the IRC. Chapter 3 examined the existence of foreign source unitary income often included on combined returns. Although the activities producing the foreign income may be instrumental to the entire business unit in the United States, the foreign operations would be totally ignored and not taxed with other segments of the business. Whereas many still believe that foreign earnings should never be taxable by a state, the proponents of combined reporting would insist that all income from any unitary operation, regardless of its source, be included for taxation by a state enforcing the combined reporting concept.

Finally, the choice of who shall be the administrator of the state taxes on interstate commerce provides another debatable topic. Allowing the

---

[18]"Hearings before the Special Subcommittee on State Taxation of Interstate Commerce of the House Committee on the Judiciary," 89th Congress, 2nd Session, Series 14 (1966).

U.S. Treasury Department full administrative control would shift important functions away from state officials who are more knowledgeable of the peculiarities of their state. Using the Treasury Department as a final arbitrator or policymaker would probably be a more acceptable and viable alternative.

HOUSE REPORT 16491 AND HOUSE REPORT 2158

Although House Report 11798 was not passed in Congress, a new bill, House Report 16491, was introduced in 1966 to supercede House Report 11798. Since the 89th Congress adjourned shortly after the bill was introduced, the House did not have sufficient time to consider its adoption. However, the bill was reintroduced in the 90th Congress the following year as House Report 2158.[19] House Report 2158 varied from the original bill, House Report 11798, in several aspects. There was a change in the standards for determining when a corporation was considered to be doing business in a state, a change in the apportionment methods allowable, and in the method of administering the taxes. The bill specifically made provisions for the adoption of P.L. 86-272 for all taxpayers.

The definition of "doing business" in a state was expanded by House Report 2158 to include those corporations maintaining a regular stock of inventory in a state. Also, employees were not considered to be located in a state if their only activities were the solicitation of orders to be accepted out of state and shipped from out of state. The strongly debated two-factor apportionment formula originating from House Report 11798 was not made mandatory; instead, an option was granted permitting either a two- or three-factor apportionment formula. Finally, the provisions for the Federal administration of these state taxes were eliminated. It should be noted that this bill was not all-encompassing and did exclude many companies from its legislative purview. The excluded companies included transportation, insurance, utility, and investment companies and banks and any corporation with a net income over one million dollars.

This bill, passed by the House of Representatives in May 1968 after several months of hearing, did not reach the Senate in sufficient time for an analysis of the bill's proposed remedies. The 90th Congress adjourned before consideration was given to House Report 2158.

HOUSE REPORT 7906

In 1969, a new bill, House Report 7906, was introduced in the 91st Congress by Representative Peter Rodino in lieu of House Report 2158.[20] The bill's content was identical to House Report 2158, with the exception of one section on double taxation of personal incomes that was deleted. House Report 7906 is divided into five topical categories directed toward

---

[19]House Report 2158, 90th Congress, 1st Session (1967).
[20]House Report 7906, 91st Congress, 1st Session (1969).

eliminating the burdensome areas of interstate commerce but still allowing states to maintain or possibly increase their revenue intake. Procedural uniformity was stressed and hopefully achievable through compliance with the standards of House Report 7906.

The first section of House Report 7906 concerned a state's jurisdiction to levy a tax, whether a tax on gross receipts and capital stock or a sales and use tax. Once again, the basic theory of maintaining a business location within a state was defined to encompass those owning or leasing real property in the state, cases where one or more employees were located in the state, or instances when a stock of tangible property to be sold in the regular course of business was maintained in the state.

The second section of the bill introduced an optional two-factor property and payroll factor to function as a guide limiting the maximum amount of income or capital that a state could tax. Each state would be able to apportion income or capital by various formulas or, perhaps, by actually using the two-factor formula for apportionment. For determining the maximum amount taxable, the two-factor formula would be applied against the taxable base before state adjustments were made. The denominator for the factor would be limited to domestic values only for setting the maximum percentage within the reach of a state's jurisdiction. Otherwise, factors located outside the United States may be used. This bill contained no provision for a definition of an income tax base to be subject to apportionment. In addition, although a business is protected from being taxed beyond a certain limit, there was no mechanism in the bill for providing uniformity for the apportionment of income or capital between states.

The last three segments of the bill were devoted to a discussion of sales and use taxes, an evaluation of state progress, and the necessary definitions and miscellaneous provisions. Also, if substantial progress were not made within four years after enactment of the bill, action would be taken to solve any problem areas and perhaps introduce some new measures.[21]

HOUSE REPORT 669—PROPOSED LEGISLATION, A DECADE LATER

One of the more recent bills introduced in the House of Representatives is House Report 669.[22] This bill was proposed by Representative Peter Rodino in January 1977 and has provisions for jurisdictional standards, taxation based on income or capital, sales and use taxes, evaluation of state progress, taxation of individuals, and definitions and miscellaneous provisions. For all practical purposes, this bill is a reinstatement of House Report 7906, introduced in 1969. The taxable income apportioned to a state according to House Report 669 is limited once again by an optional two-factor formula of property and payroll. For purposes of determining

---

[21]"Interstate Taxation Bill Goes to House Floor," 47 *Taxes* 7, (July 1969), pp. 406–407.
[22]House Report 669, 95th Congress, 1st Session, (1977).

the property factor, the denominator shall include the corporation's property located in all states and shall exclude any property located in a state in which the corporation has no business location. If either the property or payroll factor has a denominator of zero, then the other factor will be used for apportioning income to the state. When the denominators of both the property and payroll factors are zero, the apportionment percentage will be 100 percent in the state where the corporation maintains its business location. This proposal, as well as the many others introduced since the mid-1960s, has provided a viable alternative for determining when a state has jurisdiction to tax and how the state may determine the tax. Although none of these bills has ever been passed, it is evident that the subject of interstate taxation is still a pressing issue for the Federal government. (See Exhibit 4.1.)

Action by the States to Provide Uniformity

The states have also been actively pursuing a means for regulating taxation of interstate commerce. They have not taken a back seat to the Federal government on this issue and have arrived at a different alternative through

Exhibit 4.1 Summary of Proposed Legislation in the 1960s

Proposed Legislation	Requirements of "Doing Business" in a State	Apportionment Method	Administrators of the Tax
(1965) House Report 11798	1. Own or lease real property 2. One or more employees	2-factor formula— property and payroll	U.S. Treasury Department
(1966) House Report 16491 and (1967) House Report 2158	1. Own or lease real property 2. Employees with activities beyond solicitation 3. Maintenance of a regular stock of inventory	Optional 2- or 3-factor formula	State departments of revenue
(1969) House Report 7906	Same as above	2-factor formula to function as a guide to set the maximum tax limit	Same as above

their own observations, investigations, and evaluations. There were three forces influencing the states to take some action:

First, the major impetus of the states to create some feasible plans and control over the taxation of interstate commerce stemmed from the threats of the pending Federal legislation in the 1960s. The states believed that Federal intervention would violate their rights under the Tenth Amendment which reserves power for the states that is not specifically delegated to the Federal government. There was also a fear that Federal legislation would fall under the influence and control of lobbyists from large corporations desiring preferential tax status.

Second, the states were responding to the taxpayers who had numerous occasions to voice their views during the congressional examinations of the Willis and Rodino bills. Many industry leaders openly supported the proposed Federal legislation believing compliance with past and present tax laws to be the cause of multiple taxation. Finally, there was a strong desire by the states to regulate this area on their own, since some of the difficulties of interstate taxation were generated by state activities. Also, it is only natural for each state revenue department to want to remain the ruler of its own geographic domain.[23]

In January 1966, the states had a special meeting of the National Association of Tax Administrators. Representatives from the National Association of Attorneys General, the National Legislation Council, and various state officials and tax administrators met to discuss the business and tax climate at the time and to combine their resources. The concept of a Multistate Tax Compact was first introduced at this meeting, and a draft of the compact was written during that year for presentation in January 1967. (Presently, 19 states are members of the interstate compact.[24])

Analysis of the Multistate Tax Compact

The Multistate Tax Compact is an interstate compact created to promote equity and uniformity in state taxation and to facilitate the compliance and administration of the state tax regulations. The four purposes of the compact are as follows:

1 To facilitate proper determination of state and local tax liability of multistate taxpayers, including the equitable apportionment of tax bases and the settlement of apportionment disputes.

---

[23]Carlyle O. Livingston and Michael I. Hepler, "The Multistate Business Taxation Jungle: Will Congress Take Remedial Action?," *Tax Adviser* (July 1974).
[24]The 19 member states as of January 1, 1980 are Alaska, Arkansas, California, Colorado, Hawaii, Idaho, Kansas, Michigan, Missouri, Montana, Nebraska, Nevada, New Mexico, North Dakota, Oregon, South Dakota, Texas, Utah, and Washington.

2 To promote uniformity or compatibility in significant components of tax systems.

3 To facilitate taxpayer convenience and compliance in the filing of tax returns and in other phases of tax administration.

4 To avoid duplicative taxation.[25]

The compact was not designed to conflict with any state or Federal regulations. It was also not designed to impose or promote any additional taxes on a business not previously existing. The Multistate Compact is reproduced in Appendix C.

Multistate Tax Commission

The Multistate Tax Commission is the vehicle used to coordinate and administer the proper controls over the Multistate Tax Compact. The Commission was created by all the states that have adopted the Compact as part of their state laws.[26] The members of the Commission consist of one tax administrator from each state that has adopted the Compact. These members meet on a regular basis, and seven of them also serve on the Executive Committee that conducts the daily activities of the Compact from their Colorado headquarters.

The members of the Commission do not have equal voting powers for making policy decisions. Membership voting power is according to the member state's population. A state with 15 million residents will have three times the voting power of a state with five million residents.[27]

There are also others who can also participate in the activities of the Commission. These are the representatives from states that have not enacted the Compact into law but have either made an effective adoption of the Compact, dependent on a subsequent condition, or have merely applied for an associate membership. The Commission has made this provision for associate member states for two reasons. First, it allows all states to learn about the Commission by attending the various meetings. For those representatives who want to learn more about the Compact, this provides a perfect opportunity for an update and expansion of their information through active participation. Second, the Commission can receive greater feedback concerning its activities by seeking the active participation from

---

[25]Multistate Tax Compact, Article I, *Purposes,* (See Appendix C.)

[26]Multistate Tax Compact Article VI, the Commission. (See Appendix C.)

[27]The original voting procedures in the Compact's bylaws provided an equal value for every Commission member's vote. However, in 1974, the state of California conditionally adopted the Compact to be effective on January 1, 1976, if the bylaws were changed to require voting based on the member state's populations. Subsequently, this amendment was made. All proposals may now be passed if approved by the member states with a majority of the total population of all member states.

associate members. Hopefully, this will encourage the associate members to adopt the Compact and become a full member.

The Commission acts on behalf of each of the states enforcing the rules, regulations, and the agreements between the member states. Uniformity is actively pursued by stressing the cooperation between these member states. One example of this state cooperation is the existence of the joint auditing services that are explained in the following section. Some of the other important powers of the Commission granted in Article VI, Section 3 of the Compact are that it can do the following: "a) Study state and local tax systems and particular types of state and local taxes, b) Develop and recommend proposals for an increase in uniformity or compatibility of state and local tax laws with a view toward encouraging the simplification and improvement of state and local tax law and administration, c) Compile and publish information as in its judgment would assist the party states in implementation of the compact and taxpayers in complying with state and local tax laws, d) Do all things necessary and incidental to the administration of its functions pursuant to this compact."

Although the Multistate Tax Commission cannot legally enforce the regulations of the Compact, each member state is able to make such enforcement, since the Compact is a part of each state's law. This does not, however, make the Commission incapable of promoting uniform practices in administering each of its member states' taxes.

It is the policy of the Commission to recommend the use of formularly apportionment. The apportionment would be applied to all corporate business income in states that tax corporations directly on their income or have taxes measured by the income. This income apportionment is not limited to only certain types of income. Rental income, interest income, royalty income, and gross proceeds from the sale of business assets would all be apportioned to the states, depending on the classification of business or nonbusiness income. This deviates from the widely used concept of allocating certain types of income to the corporation's state of commercial domicile. The total apportionment concept for determining the source of a taxpayer's income has become a controversial topic for the Multistate Tax Commission, particularly over the treatment of dividend income. Many believe dividend income should be completely immune from taxation because the income from which dividends are paid has already been taxed. Other alternatives would be to allocate all dividend income to the state of commercial domicile or to apportion all dividends, whether from investments, controlled domestic subsidiaries, or foreign-related corporations.

Another policy endorsed by the Commission is the use of the unitary business concept for businesses affected by UDITPA. Adopted by the National Conference of Commissioners on Uniform State Laws in 1957, UDITPA does not refer to the application of combined reporting for unitary operations. This concept developed from the Commission's interpretations of UDITPA as reflected in the MTC's own proposed regulations for the apportionment and allocation of income. There are no citations in the Commission's regulations requiring a mandatory application of combined reporting. Instead, the usage of combined reporting is implied from these regulations and backed by the courts in their support of this California concept.[28] In those instances where a state's law is contradictory with any of the policies used by the Commission, it is suggested that the state make an effort to amend its laws to be in agreement with the Commission's policies.

Joint Audit Committee

The Joint Audit Committee is the Multistate Tax Commission's answer to the problem of corporate taxpayer compliance with the various state tax regulations.[29] The Committee consists of a group of auditors representing the member states of the Compact. It will audit a corporation at the request of the member states with taxing authority over the corporation. The purpose of the Committee is to audit the records of a large corporation for several states at one time, encouraging a more efficient system for both the taxpayer and the taxing states. The work of the Committee is particularly beneficial for those states lacking the expertise for conducting such an audit.[30]

One or two auditors are able to audit a large corporation as representatives for 2 or 3 or, say, 13 states at one time. The corporation only has to supply its financial books and records at one time instead of at 13 separate audit engagements. The corporations most likely to be audited by the Joint Audit Committee are the ones that are the largest revenue producers for the state. A small error in the calculations for such a corporation may mean thousands of dollars in additional state tax revenue. These large corporations with operations within Compact member states represent the major opposition to the joint audit programs.

The audit is conducted in a manner similar to that of a single state testing and verifying the revenue and expenses of a corporation. Since the Commission usually audits a corporation using the combined theory for reporting, the types of information collected and analyzed will tend to be illustrative of the facets needed to conclude a business is unitary in nature. The tests for a unitary business, discussed in Chapter 3, will be the tools to decipher which corporations are affiliated in their operations. These are the three unities test and the dependency or contribution test. The data

[28]*Butler Brothers* v. *McColgan* 17 Cal 2d; 315 U.S. 501 (1941).
Edison California Stores v. *McColgan* 30 Cal 2d 472; 183 P.2d 16 (1947).
[29]Multistate Tax Compact Article VIII, Interstate Audits. (See Appendix C)
[30]See the Speech by Frederick P. Cappetta, Audit Coordinator of the Multistate Tax Commission (1974), "The Joint Audit Program of the Multistate Tax Commission," presented at the 33rd Annual Institute on Federal Taxation of the New York University School of Continuing Education, November 11, 1974.

collected will not only be numerical in nature but also informative of the details of the incorporation, merging, control, and operation of the business.

The data and other information the auditors request the taxpayers to have available usually consist of the following:

1 The corporation's Federal tax return, Form 1120, and the supporting schedules.
2 Federal revenue agent reports.
3 Federal Form 940.
4 Quarterly employment records and reports for each state.
5 Annual reports and any other supplementary information.
6 Information provided to stockholders.
7 Documentation supporting information disclosed in state tax returns.
8 Schedules of property, payroll, and receipts for the preparation of an apportionment formula.
9 Identification of all consolidated corporations if a Federal consolidated return is filed (80 percent ownership).
10 Identification of affiliated corporations where more than 50 percent common ownership is involved.
11 Any other pertinent information that will help to evaluate the nature of the corporation being audited.

Numerical data used in the audit must provide sufficient competent, evidential matter. This entails verification of items composing total taxable income of a corporation in arriving at income to be apportioned to a state. The income apportioned to a state can only be as accurate and reliable as the apportionment factors. This necessitates the auditing of the components that constitute the property, payroll, and sales factors for both the numerator and denominator of the apportionment formula.

The payroll factor is usually the easiest to audit because it involves an examination of only the Federal 940 and 941 forms and the quarterly state unemployment compensation forms. Form 940 is used to prove the accuracy of the denominator or "everywhere" value of the factor. The quarterly unemployment compensation forms are used to verify the numerator of the factor showing the payroll data on a state-by-state basis. Auditing the property factor will be a more time-consuming task, since each type of property owned or rented must be attributed to its proper situs in a state. The total property figure can usually be documented using the balance sheet included in the Federal tax return. The sales factor is verified by a tie-in of the net sales attributed to each state, to the total net sales figure on Line 1 of the Federal tax return. When a state breakdown of other receipts is available, this information will also be included in the sales factor. If there is an error in the corporation records, the correction is treated in terms of its effects on the taxable income reportable to each member state participating in the audit.

After the Multistate Tax Commission's auditor has recomputed the new taxable income attributable to the member state, work papers are completed showing the amount due a state or the refund to be received from a state. These work papers are to be approved by the state; that is, a given state evaluates the accuracy and consistency of the audit information with respect to its law.

Once state approval is received, the taxpayer has the right to evaluate the assessment or refund computation and make an appeal to the state concerning any disputable items. This procedure is also followed for joint audits on sales and use taxes.

Agreement between Member States

The audit program provides many benefits for the member states and demonstrates the practicability of joint audits conducted by one organization, the Multistate Tax Commission. The strength of the Commission and all its programs is dependent on the bonds between the member states. To insure proper communications and open channels for activities, an agreement on the exchange of information between states is necessary. Such an agreement is provided for in the Compact.

This agreement is to be signed by a state official from each of the member states of the Compact and is not to be considered a means for revoking or superseding any other agreements of a similar nature. Each member state that signs this agreement must inform the other states of the statutory provisions concerning the use of confidential information and of any penalties for the misuse of this information. Any information received in accordance with the terms of this agreement is only to be used to aid the state in its tax administration. State officials have the option of refusing to disclose any information that is in the process of being litigated. This right can be exercised anytime it is considered in the best interest of the state to wait until a final determination is made on the litigation.

All these rules are applicable to the information obtained by a state in the process of verifying or recomputing the income tax of a taxpayer. This means that the actual return of the taxpayer can be inspected by another state or that one specific questionable item on the return may be furnished for a review. There is no specific time limit on this agreement. The only limitation placed on the states concerns the sharing of information. The restriction is placed on information dealing with agreements between any of the states and the IRS. Also, any information received on account of this agreement may not be shared with anyone who is not authorized in the member states' agreement.

The following represents the Agreement on Exchange of Information among the member states of the Compact.[31]

Agreement on Exchange of Information

In the interest of furthering the mutual interests of the undersigned states represented by the undersigned officials through benefits which can be derived from the exchange of information among said states, each of said officials does hereby enter into the following Agreement for the exchange of information with every other undersigned official.

The undersigned hereby mutually agree to exchange information, to the full extent permitted by their respective laws, in accordance with the terms and limitations below:

1. For purposes of this Agreement, income tax means a tax imposed on or measured by net income, including any tax imposed on or measured by an amount arrived at by deducting expenses from gross income, one or more forms of which expenses are not specifically and directly related to particular transaction.

2. This Agreement shall be applicable with respect to:
   a. The inspection of income tax returns of any taxpayer; and
   b. The furnishing of an abstract of the return of income of any taxpayer; and
   c. The furnishing of any information concerning any items contained in any return of income of any taxpayer; and
   d. The furnishing of any information disclosed by the report of any investigation of the income or return of income of any taxpayer, exclusive of any information obtained through an agreement between any of the undersigned states and the Internal Revenue Service.

3. For purposes of this Agreement, taxpayer includes any individual, corporation, partnership or fiduciary subject to an income tax or required to file an income tax return.

4. This Agreement is not limited to a specific period of time or to returns, documents or information relating to any specific years or periods; and it will be considered to be in effect until revoked.

5. Additions and changes, including definitions, in the provisions of this Agreement, may be made by mutual consent of the proper officials of the undersigned states, and shall become an attachment to this Agreement.

6. No information obtained pursuant to this Agreement shall be disclosed to any person not authorized by the laws of the undersigned states.

7. The information obtained pursuant to this Agreement shall be used only for the purpose of administration of the income tax laws of the undersigned states.

[31]This agreement was shown in the Seventh Annual Report of the Multistate Tax Commission, Appendix F.

8. This written Agreement shall not become effective between any two states until the authorized officials for both such states have signed it in the space provided below.

9. This written Agreement is not intended to revoke or supersede any other similar agreement that may have been previously entered into between any two or more of the states represented below.

10. The undersigned agree to inform each other of the current statutory provisions of their respective states concerning the confidentiality of the material exchanged and the penalties for unlawful disclosure thereof.

11. Any of the undersigned state officials may, at their discretion, refuse to furnish information disclosed in the report of any investigation while such investigation is still in progress or during such time as litigation is contemplated or in process, if the official of the state making the investigation deems it in the best interests of his state for such information to be withheld pending determination of litigation.

12. Each of the undersigned state officials hereby affirms that he is the proper official charged with the administration of the income tax laws of his state.

Rules and Regulations

There is another facet of the Compact to be considered, aside from the various committees and agreements. This consists of the rules and regulations adopted by the Multistate Tax Commission for use in state taxation of interstate commerce. These rules and regulations are important for two reasons. First, they must be realistic and generally accepted by the business community, since the Compact initially represented ammunition against the proposed Federal legislation in this area. The overall effectiveness of the Compact, the Commission, and the multistate auditors inevitably rest on the foundation set by these rules and regulations. Second, in providing an alternative to the states for regulating and administrating state taxes, these rules must be logical and practical. If there is no consistency or fairness in the method of taxation, there will be no support from the group that this Compact was designed for, namely, all the taxing states.

The regulations adopted by the Multistate Tax Commission with respect to income taxes are the Uniform Allocation and Apportionment Regulations.[32] These regulations are interpretations of UDITPA. The Multistate Tax Commission cannot demand that the states accept these regulations, because presently it does not have the power to do so. The adoption of the regulations by the Commission is only a recommendation that each state which is a party to the Compact endorse and adopt them as well. Some of the more important and commonly used aspects of the regulations are explained next. These regulations are reproduced in full in Appendix A.

---

[32]The Multistate Tax Commission has adopted the allocation and apportionment regulations under Article IV of the Multistate Compact. The regulations are reproduced in Appendix A.

DETERMINING A TAXPAYER'S TRADE OR BUSINESS

A phrase frequently used in the discussion of taxable entities is "a taxpayer's trade or business." Although many ambiguous definitions can be applied, a more direct and sophisticated approach was explained in the regulations of the Compact.[33] The regulations list three factors to serve as a guide in determining whether the activities of a taxpayer constitute a single trade or business. Since a taxpayer may have more than one trade or business, it is important to know where one business ends and another begins. It is usually presumed that a single business exists if any one of the following factors is applicable.

The first indication of a single business occurs when the activities of the business are in the same general line of work.[34] The regulations give an example of a taxpayer that operates a chain of retail grocery stores. The grocery stores are all the same type of business, just as the operations of several McDonald restaurants would be considered the "same type of business." The second indicator of a single business is one having steps that are a part of a vertical process.[35] Each step may or may not be totally independent from the other steps completed by separate departments, divisions, or segments in a business. There is usually some general supervision over all the departments from an executive office. The example used to illustrate this type of business concerned a company that explored and mined for copper ores. Several different steps were completed independently, starting from the concentrating, smelting, and refining of the ores to the fabrication of the refined copper. The taxpayer's executive offices provided the supervisory controls necessary over each of the segments. The third indication of a single business is the existence of a strong central management,[36] coupled with centralized departments for such functions as financing and purchasing. The numerous conglomerates so prevalent today would fall into this category. Central executive officers would be involved in the operation of each division, and centralized offices would perform such work as the accounting, purchasing, and financing for each division.

WHAT IS BUSINESS AND NONBUSINESS INCOME?

The ever-present controversy over determining whether income should be classified as business or nonbusiness income has often been settled in a manner that classifies the income according to its label. For example, rent income and interest income would be considered income because these terms have been so often associated with nonbusiness income in the past. This basis for determining business income is not used in the regulations, because a label for the income, whether rent, interest, or dividend, cannot

---

[33]Multistate Tax Commission, Regulation IV.I (b) under Article IV of the Compact.
[34]Multistate Tax Commission, Regulation IV.1(b)(1).
[35]Multistate Tax Commission, Regulation IV.1(b)(2).
[36]Multistate Tax Commission, Regulation IV.1(b)(3).

serve as a dependable index for classification purposes. The regulations adopted by the Commission define business income to encompass all income arising from transactions that occur in the regular course of a taxpayer's business.[37] The taxpayer's business must be investigated in evaluating whether a transaction producing income is a necessary and integral part of the business. The general rule is that whenever an activity is dependent on or contributes to the operations of the entire business, the activity will be considered a transaction in the regular course of a trade or business. Nonbusiness income is defined in the negative sense; that is, all income that is not business income is nonbusiness income.[38]

Rental Income from Real and Tangible Personal Property   In determining how to classify the rent income from real and tangible personal property, the use of the property must be considered.[39] The same kind of property held by two different corporations may produce nonbusiness rent income for one company and business income for the other. Property is usually acquired for its potential income-producing or cost-reducing effects. When the property is acquired to be used in the regular course of the taxpayer's business, the rent income is to be considered business income. The effect this will have on the taxpayer's state income tax return is as follows: the property is included in the "property factor" in calculating the apportionment factor, and the rent income is included with all other business income that will be apportioned to the state. When the property is not used in the regular course of the taxpayer's business, the rent income flowing from this property is to be considered nonbusiness income. The effect this will have on the taxpayer's state income tax will be the reverse of the situation previously stated. Property used in the production of nonbusiness income is excluded from the "property factor," and rent income is handled as all other nonbusiness income would be, that is, allocated to the states. Two examples from the regulations that illustrate the distinction of rental income as business versus nonbusiness income are these: (1) The taxpayer operates a multistate chain of men's clothing stores. The taxpayer purchases a five-story office building for use in connection with its trade or business. It uses the street floor as one of its retail stores and the second and third floors for its general corporate headquarters. The remaining two floors are leased to others. The rental of the two floors is incidental to the operation of the taxpayer's trade or business. The rental income is business income.[40] (2) The taxpayer operates a multistate chain of grocery stores. It purchases as an investment an office building in another state with surplus funds and leases the entire building to others. The net rental income is not

---

[37]Multistate Tax Commission, Regulation IV.1(a)(1).
[38]Multistate Tax Commission, Regulation IV.1(a)(1).
[39]Multistate Tax Commission, Regulation IV.1(c)(1).
[40]Multistate Tax Commission, Regulation IV.1(c)(1) (Example iii).

business income of the grocery store trade or business. Therefore, the net rental income is nonbusiness income.[41]

Gain or Loss from the Sale of Assets   A similar procedure is applied for determining whether a gain or loss from the sale of an asset should be considered as business or nonbusiness income. Although the facts and circumstances of each company will be unique, the criterion to be used will be the same. The actual determination rests on the nature and use of the asset in the taxpayer's business. If the asset were used in the business while it was owned, its sale will result in an increase in taxable business income. If the asset were used in the production of nonbusiness income, its sale will result in an increase in taxable nonbusiness income.[42]

Interest, Dividends, Patents, and Copyright Royalties   The same type of analysis used in the previous sections is applicable for all other types of income as well, including interest, dividends, patent, and royalty income. The evaluation rests on three factors: an asset appearing on the corporate balance sheet, the use of this asset in the business, and the revenue item appearing on the corporate income statement. Whenever the asset is used in the business for the production of business income, the revenue shown on the income statement is considered business income.

Interest income can be classified as business or nonbusiness, depending on the nature of the intangible asset that produces the income.[43] If the asset were created, acquired, or held for purposes related to or incidental to the operation of the business, the income arising from these assets will be business income. The following two examples are based on examples in the regulations. The first example concerns a taxpayer in a multistate manufacturing and selling business. This taxpayer usually has excess funds of $200,000 that it regularly invests in short-term, interest-bearing securities. Since the interest is received from activities related to maintaining the operations of the business, the interest income is business income.[44] The second example concerns a different taxpayer also receiving interest income. However, in this case, the taxpayer received $20,000,000 from the sale of the stock of a subsidiary. The funds were placed in an interest-bearing account until management could determine the best means for utilizing this amount. The interest income received from the account is considered nonbusiness income. The interest received resulted from a possible one-time occurrence that was not incidental to the operations of the business.[45]

Similar examples are given to illustrate when dividend, patent, and

[41]Multistate Tax Commission, Regulation IV.1(c)(1) (Example iv).
[42]Multistate Tax Commission, Regulation IV.1(c)(2).
[43]Multistate Tax Commission, Regulation IV.1(c)(3).
[44]Multistate Tax Commission, Regulation IV.1(c)(3) (Example v).
[45]Multistate Tax Commission, Regulation IV.1(c)(3) (Example vi).

royalty income should be classified as business income.[46] When stock, patents, or copyrights are acquired or held for purposes related to or incidental to the business, business income results. Taxpayers receiving dividends from the stock of their subsidiaries that act as the marketing agents for the products sold by the taxpayers will be getting business income. If, however, a taxpayer engaged in the manufacture of radios holds a stock portfolio, dividend income received from this portfolio will be nonbusiness income. The holding of the portfolio is unrelated to the business of manufacturing radios. If this same corporation also held a patent for a special chemical machine, the royalties received on the patent would also be nonbusiness income.

Allocation of Nonbusiness Income under UDITPA   Exhibit 4.2 describes the means for allocating nonbusiness income to a state.[47]

Exhibit 4.2

Income Source	Allocation
Capital gains and losses from the sale of real property	To the state where the real property is located
Capital gains and losses from the sale of tangible personal property	To the state of the property's situs at the time of the sale or to the state of the company's commercial domicile if it is not subject to tax in the state of the property's situs
Capital gains and losses from the sale of intangible personal property	To the state of the company's commercial domicile
Dividend income	To the state of the company's commercial domicile
Interest income	To the state of the company's commercial domicile
Net rents and royalties from real property	To the state where the real property is located
Net rents and royalties from tangible property	To the state where the property is used
Patent and copyright royalties	To the state where the patent or copyright is used or to the state of commercial domicile if not subject to tax in the state where they are used

[46]Multistate Tax Commission, Regulation IV.1(c)(4), IV.1(c)(5).
[47]Sections 5–8 of UDITPA.

The Multistate Tax Commission's Interpretation of Business Income versus Nonbusiness Income under UDITPA   As discussed in the previous sections, there are specific provisions in UDITPA dealing with nonbusiness income of a corporation. However, the Multistate Tax Commission contends that all income of a large multinational corporation should be classified as business income. This position was recently stated by William D. Dexter, General Counsel for the Commission.

> . . . any large segments of the resources of large multinational corporations are devoted to produce what is characterized under Section 1(a) of UDITPA as nonbusiness income is difficult to conceive. . . . business corporations engage in business transactions for the purpose of producing income. All of the income should qualify as apportionable income, and the states should act to bring this about as quickly as possible.[48]

If all income is to be considered as business income, Section 4 of UDITPA (that defines nonbusiness income) and Sections 5 through 8 of UDITPA (that describe the allocation of nonbusiness income) would be totally ignored.

(a)   Administrative Interpretations

To understand the basis of the Multistate Tax Commission's administrative interpretations of Section 1(a) of UDITPA, we must first look to the requirements of this section. Two basic conditions must be satisfied for income to be defined as business income:

1. The income must arise from transactions and activities in the regular course of the taxpayer's trade or business.
2. Business income includes income arising from the acquisition, management, and disposition of tangible and intangible property if these assets constitute an integral part of the taxpayer's trade or business operations.

The first requirement concentrates on a taxpayer's trade or business. The primary considerations are how a taxpayer's trade or business is to be defined and the relationship between this trade or business and the income it generates. More specifically, is there a unitary connection between the business activities and the income from, or investment in, the business property.[49]

---

[48]William D. Dexter, "The Business v. Nonbusiness Distinction under UDITPA," 10 *Urban Lawyer* 2 (Spring 1978).

[49]Gary J. Hansen, "Business v. Nonbusiness Income of Large Multinational Corporations under UDITPA," 57 *Taxes* 6 (June 1979), p. 366.

The Commission has basically relied on two cases[50] for determining whether income does, in fact, arise in the regular course of a taxpayer's business.

Although the definition of a taxpayer's trade or business is not contained in UDITPA, the regulations of the Multistate Tax Compact make these provisions:

> The determination of whether the activities of the taxpayer constituted a single trade or business or more than one trade or business will turn on the facts in each case. In general, the activities of the taxpayer will be considered a single business if there is evidence to indicate that the segments under consideration are integrated with, dependent upon or contribute to each other and the operations of the taxpayer as a whole.[51]

While this regulation recognizes that a taxpayer may have more than one trade or business, generally a taxpayer is considered to have only one business when all its activities are subject to a strong centralized management or its activities depend on or contribute to the economic enterprise as a whole.[52] This broad interpretation covers almost any income-producing activity, since any such activity can be considered as contributing to the taxpayer's operations. This is considered to be a reasonable administrative interpretation of Section 1(a) of UDITPA, even though on its face it appears that there can never be nonbusiness income, since all income will be business income contributing to the taxpayer's trade.[53]

The second requirement of Section 1(a) of UDITPA concerns whether or not income is derived from any property that is acquired, managed, and disposed of as an integral part of taxpayer's business. Once again, this aspect will not hinder the Commission from classifying all income as business income. Specifically, the requirement that the property be managed as an integral part of the taxpayer's business poses no additional administrative problems for the Commission. This is because the Commission considers investment portfolios and other property owned by large multinational corporations to be clearly managed in the regular business operations of any company.[54]

---

[50]The two Minnesota cases are *Flint* v. *Stone Tracy Company* 220 U.S. 107 (1911) and *Montgomery Ward and Company* v. *Commissioner of Taxation* 151 N.W. 2d 294 (1967). See Hansen, "Business v. Nonbusiness Income of Large Multinational Corporations under UDITPA." Hansen believes that the Commission's reliance on these cases should be questioned. The *Flint* case was decided in 1911 and could not have taken the complex UDITPA requirements into account. The *Montgomery Ward* case was based on Minnesota's interpretation of business income according to its own law, since it has not adopted UDITPA and is not a member of the Multistate Tax Compact.

[51]Multistate Tax Commission, Regulation V.1(b).

[52]Multistate Tax Commission, Regulation IV.1(a).

[53]See Dexter, "The Business v. Nonbusiness Distinction under UDITPA."

[54]See Dexter, "The Business v. Nonbusiness Distinction under UDITPA."

(b)   Evaluation of the Multistate Tax Commission's Position

Under the unitary theory of operations, the Multistate Tax Commission has sought to subject all the income of a corporation to taxation in the taxing state. It has interpreted the provisions of UDITPA in such a way that any multistate or multinational corporation would be considered to have only business income. From the viewpoint of these corporations being taxed, the decision not to acknowledge the existence of nonbusiness income appears to be discriminatory and arbitrary.[55]

These corporations could be subject to large taxable income in each taxing jurisdiction. For many years prior to the creation of the Multistate Tax Compact, items such as interest and dividend income from out-of-state subsidiaries would normally have been viewed as nonbusiness income and assigned to the corporation's state of domicile for taxation. This procedure would follow the Due Process requirements of having a definite link or connection between the state and the corporation, property, or transaction the state is seeking to tax.[56] The commercial domicile is considered to be sufficient nexus. However, since the Multistate Tax Commission has interpreted the business versus nonbusiness income issue in a different manner, a corporation that considers its tax liabilities unfair might want to consider the alternatives it has available.

First, a corporation could accept the Multistate Tax Commission's position. In many states it may not be a prime issue if the tax dollars involved are minimal.

Second, a corporation which totally rejects the interpretation that all income is business income could file its state tax returns under the assumption that it does, in fact, have nonbusiness income if it is prepared to litigate the issue. It may also be possible for a corporation to arrive at a compromise position with the state authorities involved.

Third, a corporation may rely on the provisions of Section 18 of UDITPA and the Multistate Tax Compact's special regulations that provide alternative methods for a taxpayer if the allocation and apportionment provisions required do not fairly represent the extent of the taxpayer's business activity within a state.[57]

A corporation seeking to adjust its apportionment factors under this section might want to consider a change that reflects the consideration of intangible properties or the income from these properties. For example,

---

[55]Hansen, "Business v. Nonbusiness Income of Large Multinational Corporations under UDITPA," p. 368.

[56]*Miller Bros. Co.* v. *Maryland* 347 U.S. 340 (1954).

[57]Multistate Tax Commission, Regulation IV.18(a) allows the taxpayer to petition for, or the tax administrator to require, if reasonable, the following: (1) separation accounting, (2) the exclusion of any one or more of the factors, (3) the inclusion of one or more additional factors which will fairly represent the taxpayer's business activity in this state, or (4) the employment of any other method to effectuate an equitable allocation and apportionment of the taxpayer's income.

since dividend and interest income are being considered as apportionable business income, such could also be considered for inclusion in the denominator of the sales factor.[58]

Or a corporation might attempt to include the intangible property in the property factor. However, because the Commission holds the position that even though income from intangibles is considered as business income and because the UDITPA property factor only considers tangible property, such views do not in themselves prove the UDITPA formula to be arbitrary or unreasonable.[59]

Finally, the Commission's position concerning the adjustment of apportionment factors may present some additional obstacles for the corporation involved. The Multistate Tax Commission has followed the position from various case law, where the courts have essentially stated that even though intangible income is being taxed the Commission had no authority to consider intangible property in the apportionment formula, since such an adjustment is not provided for in the statutes.[60]

Litigation—Mobil Oil Corporation v. Commissioner of Taxes of Vermont 394A.2d 1147 (1978) Mobil Oil filed its Vermont income tax return for the years 1970 through 1972 by treating its investment income, that is, dividends from foreign subsidiaries, dividends from nonsubsidiary versus corporations, and interest, as nonbusiness income. After deducting nonbusiness income from total income, the remainder, business income, was apportioned to Vermont on the basis of the three-factor formula used by that state.

The state of commercial domicile of Mobil Oil was New York. Mobil maintained that New York had the power to treat the investment income as nonbusiness income allocable to New York for purposes of a New York tax based on income. If New York could tax 100 percent of such income and Vermont (or any other state) were permitted to tax some apportioned

---

[58]See Hansen, "Business v. Nonbusiness Income of Large Multinational Corporations under UDITPA," pp. 371 and 372, where he points out that this may also not be the optimal solution. For example, he says: "Take, for instance, a dividend paid by an affiliated corporation to a parent. The MTC contends the dividend received by the parent corporation is business income and apportionable. Adjusting the denominator of the sales factor by the dividend income alone does not appear to resolve the problem since consideration needs to be given to the total sales by the parent corporation made to earn its other business income, as well as to the payroll and property of the parent. It appears to make more sense to include all sales of an affiliated corporation that were utilized in earning the dividend income classified as business income by the MTC to the parent corporation in the denominator of the parent corporation's sales factor. If a more equitable result was desired, sales, property, and payroll of an affiliated corporation paying the dividend should be used in adjusting the apportionment formula since they were utilized in the actual earning of that income."

[59]See Dexter, "The Business v. Nonbusiness Distinction under UDITPA."

[60]See *Gulf Oil Corp. v. Morrison* 120 Vt. 324, 141 A. 2d 671 (1958); *F. W. Woolworth Co. v. Commissioner of Taxes* 133 Vt. 93, 328 A. 2d 671 (1958); and In re Goodyear Tire and Rubber Co., Corporate Income Tax 1966, 1967, 1968, 133 Vt. 132, 135 A. 2d 310 (1975).

amount of the same income, the investment income would be taxed at more
than 100 percent. Thus the issue came down to whether Vermont's tax on
an apportioned amount of the investment income would constitute multiple
taxation prohibited by the Commerce Clause.

Treating investment income as allocable to New York for Vermont
income tax purposes produced unusual results. For the year 1971, after
subtracting investment income, only 8 percent of Federal taxable income
remained as business income to be apportioned to Vermont. For the year
1972, investment income exceeded Federal taxable income so that no
business income remained to be apportioned to Vermont. This end result
was a practical consideration that the Vermont Supreme Court viewed as
reinforcing its conclusion that the Commerce Clause was not violated.

In fact, New York did not treat the investment income as allocable
income for purposes of its tax based on income. Mobil's argument was that
New York had the constitutional power to treat the income in such a
manner and that this was sufficient to raise the multiple tax risk. The
Vermont Supreme Court held that Mobil had failed to establish this latter
point and thus no multiple taxation was shown. In any event, even if New
York had taxed the income at 100 percent, it would not, in the court's
opinion, prevent Vermont from taxing some apportioned amount. It was
ventured that in such a conflict New York might very well have to yield.
The *Johns Manville Products Corporation* v. *Commissioner of Revenue
Administration* decision 115 N.H. 428, 430–31; 343A.2d 221, 223 (1975)
(appeal dismissed for want of a substantial federal question, 423 U.S. 1069,
96S. Ct. 851, 47L.Ed.2d 79 (1976)) was cited in support.

This opinion, after holding that Mobil had failed to meet the burden of
demonstrating a risk of multiple taxation, concluded with the following:

> The Court has said repeatedly that where a state tax is fairly apportioned, not
> discriminatory, related to state services provided, and where the entity taxed
> has a substantial nexus to the taxing state, the Court will not void the tax on
> Commerce Clause grounds on an argument that is an abstraction or is based
> on mere speculation. That is, where the tax is of a type that is not inherently
> burdensome, the Court is requiring proof in the record of multiple taxation
> and not merely the argument that such a tax could hypothetically occur.
> (Citing *Moorman* 437 U.S. 267, *Complete Auto Transits* 430 U.S. 274,
> *General Motors Corporation* 377 U.S. 436, *Northwestern States* 358 U.S.
> 450).

The U.S. Supreme Court affirmed the decision of the Vermont Supreme
Court (*Mobil Oil Corporation* v. *Commissioner of Taxes of Vermont*,
Docket No. 78-1201, March 19, 1980).

In Summary:

> Appellant is a corporation organized under the laws of New York, where it
> has its principal place of business and its "commercial domicile." It does
> business in many States, including Vermont, where it engages in the wholesale

and retail marketing of petroleum products. Vermont imposed a corporate income tax, calculated by means of an apportionment formula, upon "foreign source" dividend income received by appellant from its subsidiaries and affiliates doing business abroad. Appellant challenged the tax on the grounds, inter alia, that it violated the Due Process Clause of the Fourteenth Amendment and the Commerce Clause, but the tax ultimately was upheld by the Vermont Supreme Court.

Held:

1. The tax does not violate the Due Process Clause. There is a sufficient "nexus" between Vermont and appellant to justify the tax, and neither the "foreign source" of the income in question nor the fact that it was received in the form of dividends from subsidiaries and affiliates precludes its taxability. Appellant failed to establish that its subsidiaries and affiliates engage in business activities unrelated to its sale of petroleum products in Vermont, and accordingly it has failed to sustain its burden of proving that its "foreign source" dividends are exempt, as a matter of due process, from fairly apportioned income taxation by Vermont. Pp. 10–16.

2. Nor does the tax violate the Commerce Clause. Pp. 16–22.

   (a) The tax does not impose a burden on interstate commerce by virtue of its effect relative to appellant's income tax liability in other States. Assuming that New York, the State of "commercial domicile," has the authority to impose some tax on appellant's dividend income, there is no reason why that power should be exclusive when the dividends reflect income from a unitary business, part of which is conducted in other States. The income bears relation to benefits and privileges conferred by several States, and in these circumstances apportionment, rather than allocation, is ordinarily the accepted method of taxation. Vermont's interest in taxing a proportionate share of appellant's dividend income thus is not overridden by any interest of the State of "commercial domicile." Pp. 16–19.

   (b) Nor does the tax impose a burden on foreign commerce. Appellant's argument that the risk of multiple taxation abroad requires allocation of "foreign source" income to a single situs at home, is without merit in the present context. That argument attempts to focus attention on the effect of foreign taxation when the effect of domestic taxation is the only real issue; its logic is not limited to dividend income but would apply to any income arguably earned from foreign commerce, so that acceptance of the argument would make it difficult for state taxing authorities to determine whether income does or does not have a foreign source; the argument underestimates this Court's power to correct discriminatory taxation of foreign commerce that results from multiple state taxation; and its acceptance would not guarantee a lesser domestic tax burden on dividend income from foreign sources. *Japan Line, Ltd. v. County of Los Angeles,* 441 U.S. 434, which concerned property taxation of instrumentalities of foreign commerce, does not provide an analogy for this case. Pp. 19–22.

136 Vt. 545, 394 A, 2d 1147, affirmed.

Mobil had offered three principal arguments for the exclusion of dividends from apportionment. First, there was no "nexus" between Vermont and either its management of investments or the business activities of the payor corporations. Second, taxation of the dividends in Vermont would create an unconstitutional burden of multiple taxation because the dividends could be taxable in full in New York, the state of commercial domicile. Third, Mobil argued that the "foreign source" of the dividends precluded state income taxation, at least in states other than the commercial domicile, because of the risk of multiple taxation at the international level.

The court examined the first argument from two potential factors: (1) the foreign source aspect and (2) the "form" of the income, that is, dividends. The former was seen as having no basis, since Mobil was viewed as a unitary business and it was not shown that foreign activities were distinct in any business or economic sense from those in Vermont. Neither was the Supreme Court impressed with the latter factor, stating that "so long as dividends from subsidiaries and affiliates reflect profits derived from a functionally integrated enterprise, those dividends are income to the parent earned in a unitary business. One must look principally at the underlying activity, not at the form of investment, to determine the propriety of apportionability."

The door was not completely closed to allocation of dividends, but the burden is on the taxpayer to demonstrate that the dividends are separate and distinct in the case of a unitary operation:

> We do not mean to suggest that all dividend income received by corporations operating in interstate commerce is necessarily taxable in each State where that corporation does business. Where the business activities of the dividend payor have nothing to do with the activities of the recipient in the taxing State, due process considerations might well preclude apportionability, because there would be no underlying unitary business. We need not decide, however, whether Vermont's tax statute would reach extraterritorial values in an instance of that kind. Cf. *Underwood Typewriter Co. v. Chamberlain,* 254 U.S., at 121. Mobil has failed to sustain its burden of proving any unrelated business activity on the part of its subsidiaries and affiliates that would raise the question of nonapportionability. See *Norton Co. v. Department of Revenue,* 340 U.S. 534, 537 (1951); *Butler Bros. v. McColgan,* 315 U.S., at 507. We therefore hold that its foreign source dividends have not been shown to be exempt, as a matter of due process, from apportionment for state income taxation by the State of Vermont.

On the matter of multiple taxation Mobil had maintained that the Commerce Clause required allocation of dividend income to a single situs. This was unacceptable to the Court:

Taxation by apportionment and taxation by allocation to a single situs are theoretically incommensurate, and if the latter method is constitutionally preferred, a tax based on the former cannot be sustained. See *Standard Oil Co. v. Peck,* 342 U.S. 382, 384 (1952). We find no adequate justification, however, for such a preference. Although a fictionalized situs for intangible property sometimes has been invoked to avoid multiple taxation of ownership, there is nothing talismanic about the concepts of "business situs" or "commercial domicile" that automatically renders those concepts applicable when taxation of income from intangibles is at issue. The Court has observed that the maxim mobilia sequunter personam, upon which these fictions of situs are based, "states a rule without disclosing the reasons for it." *First Bank Stock Corp. v. Minnesota,* 301 U.S., at 241 (1937). The Court also has recognized that "the reason for a single place of taxation no longer obtains" when the taxpayer's activities with respect to the intangible property involve relations with more than one jurisdiction. *Curry v. McCanless,* 307 U.S. 357, 367 (1939). Even for property or franchise taxes, apportionment of intangible values is not unknown. See *Ford Motor Co. v. Beauchamp,* 308 U.S., at 335–336; *Adams Express Co. v. Ohio,* 166 U.S. 185, 222 (1897). Moreover, cases upholding allocation to a single situs for property tax purposes have distinguished income tax situations where the apportionment principle prevails. See *Wheeling Steel Corp. v. Fox,* 298 U.S., at 212.

Mobil also relied on *Japan Line, Ltd. v. County of Los Angeles,* 441 U.S. 434 (1979) to argue that at least dividends from foreign incorporated subsidiaries should be allocated to situs. The Court held that reliance on this case was weak:

Appellant's attempted analogy between this case and Japan Line strikes us as forced. That case involved ad valorem property taxes assessed directly upon instrumentalities of foreign commerce. As has been noted, the factors favoring use of the allocation method in property taxation have no immediate applicability to an income tax. Japan Line, moreover, focused on problems of duplicative taxation at the international level, while appellant here has confined its argument to the wholly different sphere of multiple taxation among our States. Finally, in Japan Line the Court was confronted with actual multiple taxation that could be remedied only by adoption of an allocation approach. As has already been explained, in the present case we are not similarly impelled.

EVALUATION OF THE COMPACT AND CURRENT LITIGATION

Current Review

When the idea of a Multistate Tax Compact was first introduced, there was some doubt in the business community concerning the Compact's potential effectiveness. Many believed the Compact was created solely as a diversionary tactic to pull attention away from proposed Federal legislation and possibly prevent any further congressional attempts to legislate this area. It cannot be denied that the states do have the common goal of avoiding Federal legislation; however, the willingness of the states to direct themselves toward solving interstate taxation problems has been demonstrated to also be a priority of the Compact.

The Compact, like any other writing subject to changing economic pressure over the passage of time, has undergone several changes. It was not until 1973 that the Commission approved the revised Uniform Allocation and Apportionment Regulations interpreting UDITPA for tax administration purposes. The voting procedures of the Commission, mentioned earlier in this chapter, were also changed with the admission of California as a member state. Another section of the Compact that had to be changed before California would become a member was the enforcement of a new agreement not to use the arbitration clause. This has been a controversial area because the arbitration clause could have provided a mechanism for helping to eliminate the occurrence of multiple taxation. Since California's membership will be automatically revoked if either the original voting or arbitration clauses are reinstated, many fear the Commission will or has already become a puppet to the state of California.

There are also several other controversial issues facing the Commission that must be resolved. The most pressing of these is the implementation of combined reporting with respect to foreign earnings. The unitary concept dictates that earnings of an economic unit be taxed as a single entity regardless of whether there are operations located in foreign territories. States trying to stimulate foreign investment and trade within their borders are particularly wary of this combined reporting approach. As an alternative, combined reports with only domestic operations are used. Although both methods have their merits, it would be advantageous for the Commission to administer uniform reporting practices in all member states. Two other frequently debated subjects are the allocation and apportionment practices followed by the Commission and the methods for handling dividend income. The allocation and apportionment controversy is directed toward a total apportionment concept for all income. This practice is welcomed in those states with little industry or income allocated within their borders. The states with heavy capital investments and numerous corporations within their borders prefer an allocation of nonbusiness income, placing this revenue source only within their own grasp. Corporation opinion fluctuates, depending on the potential changes in a corporation's tax burden. Finally, a consistent and uniformly accepted procedure for taxing dividends must be decided on. The possible alternatives to be considered have already been discussed in this chapter.

The past Chairmen of the Commission have made glowing comments concerning the Compact—such as "The Multistate Tax Compact offers the most exciting promise for progress in the field of taxation. Its possibilities for good are unlimited. It is not a new mechanism for dominating the states, but rather an association to stimulate action, state-by-state, by providing the necessary information which is not now available regarding many important problems; and by providing a vehicle for cooperative state action,"[61] and the Compact is "the most significant effort that the states have made in the last 50 years to improve state taxation of interstate business. . . . The Multistate Tax Compact deserves Congressional blessing."[62]

There have been many other worthy comments praising the Compact, but there have also been many critical comments concerning the Compact's past and present problems. Since all the considerations are needed for making any type of evaluation, it would be appropriate at this point to consider the advantages as well as the disadvantages the Compact has already provided in all the member states and the business community.

Advantages of the Multistate Tax Compact

One of the important advantages of the Multistate Tax Compact is that it was created and is maintained by the states to solve their similar tax problems. It is only reasonable for a state to take an active role in molding its tax structure, since a state's budget is directly affected by the tax structure. The increase or decrease in revenues resulting from changes in tax regulations determines the amounts expendable for various state and municipal projects, such as increased educational benefits and more efficient health care facilities. There is also an important noneconomic factor behind a state's desire to resolve any respective tax problems. This is the attainment of a business community with an atmosphere conducive and stimulating to trade. Corporations will be more inclined to remain in a state, and other corporations will be encouraged to set up residences in a state where numerous benefits are provided. The state and its residents can, in turn, receive benefits from these businesses. Since the states are in a position where they can receive continual feedback from the businesses, the states are able to periodically evaluate their tax structures. This introduces another advantage of the Multistate Tax Compact. The Multistate Tax Commission is available to respond to the needs of each state and provide possible solutions as the circumstances dictate. By having many states partake in the Commission's activities, each state can benefit individually through the mutual efforts of all states working jointly. The Commission makes continual studies of various tax areas, so theoretically there will not be too great a time lag between the onset of a tax problem and its possible resolution.

Another advantage of the Multistate Tax Compact is that it has the potential for eventually providing a source to turn to for guidance and to look to for setting precedents in the field of interstate commerce. As various problems arise, whether they be centered on jurisdictional rights of

---

[61]George Kinnear, Chairman, June 1967—January 1970, from the Seventh Annual Report of the Multistate Tax Commission.
[62]Byron L. Dorgan, Chairman, July 1972—June 1974, from the Seventh Annual Report of the Multistate Tax Commission.

a state or proper methods of apportionment and allocation, the standards set by the Multistate Tax Commission may be used as an indicator of the proper action to be taken.

Disadvantages of the Multistate Tax Compact

A frequently noted disadvantage of the Multistate Tax Compact is its inability to legally enforce its own rules. The Multistate Tax Commission has no jurisdictional power to insure that its goal can be achieved. Although each member state of the Commission can enforce the Compact if it so chooses, these states can also choose not to follow the Compact when the results prove to be disadvantageous. This can cripple the Multistate Tax Compact's image in the business community and at the same time prove its ineffectiveness when a state chooses to ignore the generally accepted interpretations of the Compact. The best example of this was cited by Frank Keesling in his speech at the 1974 Annual Meeting of the Multistate Tax Commission.[63] Keesling noted that the state of Utah had adopted the Compact and the Uniform provisions for the apportionment of unitary income. However, the Utah Tax Commission and the Utah Supreme Court disregarded the uniform provisions use when separate accounting procedures brought about a higher taxable income.

The example of the Utah Supreme Court voting separate accounting procedures superior to combined reporting points to yet another problem of the Compact: a lack of uniform interpretations and administration practices. Unless all the member states agree on the proper interpretation of the Compact, each state will interpret the Compact in a manner most beneficial to that state. The administration functions also need more coordination, particularly when considering the audit program. Definite rules are needed and should be followed in all states instead of implementing audit strategy on a state-to-state or company-by-company basis. For example, the methods of handling business and nonbusiness income are often inconsistent, as are some determinations of the accounts to be used in the factors composing a company's apportionment formula.

Other disadvantages that can be cited about the Compact are that it will have difficulty achieving uniformity in state taxation because it promotes nonuniformity in its application of the allocation and apportionment of income (this issue was discussed earlier),[64] and because not all states have adopted the Compact. Most of the members of the Compact are western or midwestern states that are primarily agricultural states. The capital invest-

---

[63]"The Combined Report and Uniformity in Allocation Practices," presented on June 25, 1974, by Frank M. Keesling at the Annual Meeting of the Multistate Tax Commission.

[64]Also, see the September 20, 1971, notification from the Committee on State Taxation, Council of State Chambers of Commerce, entitled "Multistate Tax Commission Adds to the Interstate Tax Confusion."

ments and manufacturing activities of these states are relatively minor when compared to the eastern industrial nonmember states. One explanation for this is that the use of the Commission's total income apportionment concept is advantageous to the western states because more taxable income will be apportioned to these states. Previously, income that was allocable only to the corporation's state of domicile could not have been taxable in a western state, since the corporation was not domiciled there. Conversely, an eastern state would prefer to have certain types of income still allocated to the state of domicile, so the tax would only be paid to that state. By not joining the Compact, this income can still be taxed only within its borders.[65]

The Compact could possibly be more effective in facilitating the determination of tax liabilities and preventing duplicative taxes if the eastern states would also join. However, this criticism may not be as valid as the others, because any organization uniting those with common interests or problems does not always include all the parties eligible to participate. The lack of participation by these parties does not make these organizations any less effective.

Litigation—U.S. Steel Corporation v. Multistate Tax Commission 54 L Ed 2d 682 (1978)

Although the Multistate Tax Compact was designed to promote uniformity in the state taxing system, it has received only nominal support from the business sector. One of the biggest complaints has been about the activities of the Joint Audit Committee because of its policy of combined reporting and the fact that a state is not bound by the audit results if it finds they are unfavorable.[66] This resistance has been strong enough to promote a suit against the Multistate Tax Commission. The case involved the United States Steel Corporation and 15 other companies in a suit seeking to declare the Multistate Tax Compact invalid under the U.S. Constitution. The case was heard in the U.S. District Court for the Southern District of New York, with the judgment resulting in favor of the Multistate Tax Commission. The U.S. Steel Corporation appealed this decision to the U.S. Supreme Court. The Supreme Court confirmed the district court's decision. The highlights of this important case are examined next.

The first contention by the U.S. Steel Corporation was that the entire Compact was invalid, because it had not been approved by the Congress as required by Article I, Section 10, Clause 3 of the Constitution.

---

[65]See the Statement in Support of the Withdrawal of the State of Indiana from Membership in the Multistate Tax Compact, March 1977.
[66]Richard Krol, "Taxpayers Balking at Submitting to Audits of Multistate Tax Commission," 50 *Journal of Taxation* 5 (December 1975).

This section states:

> No State shall, without the Consent of the Congress . . . enter into any
> Agreement or Compact with another State, or with a Foreign Power. . . .

This clause was not interpreted by the courts as requiring congressional
approval for all interstate agreements. The courts applied the rules used in
two other Supreme Court cases dealing with interstate agreements which
state that congressional approval was not necessary for agreements or
compacts if the political power in the states were not increased to encroach
on the supremacy of the United States.[67] The Compact does not permit
member states to exercise powers they could not formerly exercise without
the Compact. Furthermore, each state is able to adopt or reject the rules of
the Commission and is free to withdraw at any time from the Compact.
Therefore, the courts concluded that the Multistate Tax Compact does not
increase the political power of the states, because the Commission has no
legislative or taxing authority. The Commission does have the power to
conduct audits, but this is only when an audit is first requested by a
member state. It is interesting to note that shortly after the formation of the
Compact in 1967 the Commission formed a special committee for considering whether congressional consent was needed for the Compact. Many
state officials were obviously concerned, since their state funds would be
affected. The committee appointed to make this study also relied on the
court cases cited by the Federal courts and arrived at the same conclusions. Congressional consent was not considered necessary, because several other interstate agreements had been made and put into operation
without receiving congressional consent.

The second argument by the U.S. Steel Corporation was that the
Multistate Tax Compact imposed an undue and unreasonable burden on
interstate commerce. Although the compact does promote ideology for
allocation and apportionment rules among the states, this in itself does not
create an undue burden on interstate commerce.

Each state already had the rights to enforce similar tax legislation and
has done so through the enactment of UDITPA. Also, any agreements by
the states to enforce the same principles would only promote uniformity, as
encouraged by the Multistate Tax Compact.

The third argument was directed to the compact's invalidity under the
Commerce, Equal Protection, and Due Process clauses. The three discriminatory areas cited in this issue were, first, that the Multistate Tax
Commission auditors are not subject to the civil service requirements of the
member states; second, that the auditors were not subject to state criminal

---

[67]*Virginia* v. *Tennessee* 148 U.S. 503 (1893).
New Hampshire v. *Maine* 426 U.S. 363 (1976).

penalties for disclosure of confidential audit information; and, third, the subpoena powers of the Commission exceed those of the individual states.

The fact that an auditor from the Multistate Tax Commission does not have a civil service status does not make him or her any less competent as an auditor. Every auditor is required to apply the same laws of the state, and the auditor's work can always be questioned and reviewed through the same tax appeal procedures. The Multistate auditor is also subject to the same penalties as a state auditor for disclosure of confidential audit information. Finally, the subpoena powers of the Commission are no greater than those of each member state. The process of auditing a corporation's accounting data does necessitate the use of subpoena powers to obtain the corporation's books and records supporting this data. However, the Commission does not have a power separate and distinct from the powers of the states for which it is performing the audit, even though a single state cannot use its powers in the same manner as the Commission.

The last contention by the U.S. Steel Corporation was that the portion of the Compact that relates to the producing of records for a joint audit violates the Fourth Amendment by requiring a corporation to disclose data to an unlawful body. The courts held the Multistate Tax Compact and the Commission to be lawfully created and, therefore, also found no merit in the issue of the Fourth Amendment being violated.

CHAPTER FIVE

Taxes Based on Capital

GENERAL DESCRIPTION

Taxes based on capital are commonly referred to as "franchise taxes." In its everyday meaning, the tax is on the right to be and to exercise the powers of a corporation. The state having granted the corporate charter or certificate to do business imposes these taxes against the value of the company. The term does not always have reference to a tax measured by capital. Franchise taxes are frequently measured by the income of the company rather than its capital. To further confuse the terminology, all taxes measured by capital are not called franchise taxes. These taxes may be levied under various other names such as "Corporation License Tax" or "Corporation Business Tax." For simplicity, the term "taxes based on capital" is used and is always in reference to a tax on the privilege to exercise a corporate charter or certificate to do business.

Taxes based on capital are old in the states as compared to income or sales and use taxes.[1] Such taxes first appeared when corporations were few in number. As early as 1805, Georgia imposed a tax on the capital stock of banks. This and other early taxes were regarded somewhat as a logical extension of the property tax. By 1900, the corporation was the dominant form of business in manufacturing and was increasingly more important with respect to interstate business activity. By 1929, nearly all the present-day taxes on capital had been established.

Initially, the tax was imposed on domestic corporations. Typically, the taxing state would then extend the levy to foreign corporations qualified to do business in the state.

The significance of taxes based on capital is minor when compared with other forms of taxation such as sales and use or income taxes. Capital stock tax as a percentage of total tax revenue in 1963 nowhere exceeded 15 percent and in only one state was it more than 8 percent. As pointed out by the Willis Committee,[2] this was not always the case in much earlier years, when the percentage ranged as high as 43 percent. The statistics may be

---

[1]See the Report of the Special Subcommittee on State Taxation of Interstate Commerce, June 30, 1965, Vol. 3, p. 909.
[2]Report of the Special Subcommittee on State Taxation of Interstate Commerce, p. 931.

misleading, however, when examined from the viewpoint of the interstate corporation. The foregoing statistics reveal the significance to the state of such revenue in terms of total revenue. Total revenue, in turn, includes all state taxes, such as individual income and sales and use tax revenue. The better comparison if statistics were readily available would be to compare total taxes based on capital to total corporate taxes.

In any event, the individual interstate corporate taxpayer will often find taxes based on capital very significant. First, the nature of the tax is such that it continues as a fixed charge rather than fluctuating with income. Second, for any particular state, it can be a substantial levy in itself, growing in proportion to the increased value of the firm.

NEXUS

General Jurisdictional Standards

The protection given to interstate taxpayers by the provisions of P.L. 86-272 does not extend to taxes measured by capital. The principles in P.L. 86-272 cannot be relied on by taxpayers to determine whether they are or are not subject to tax.

A domestic corporation, and a foreign corporation that has been issued a certificate of authority (qualified to do business) will both virtually always be subject to this type of tax. However, in some states, even if the corporation does possess a certificate of authority, its taxability will depend on whether it is actually doing business in the state.[3] The problem of jurisdiction arises, therefore, only in the case of a foreign corporation that is not qualified in the taxing state but has some degree of intrastate activity. The real question this foreign corporation must ask itself is whether its activities in the state are such that they require the corporation to qualify to do business there. The answer lies in the corporation licensing law of the particular state.

In general then the degree of intrastate activity will determine whether the corporation will be required to obtain a certificate of authority. Usually, the statutes and cases provide no clear-cut answer to the question of when it would be compelled to qualify, and there are no regulations to provide guidance. Also, the Willis Committee brought out the following[4]:

> . . . even if the corporation determines that it is legally immune from qualification requirements, it must weigh the practical consequences. By remaining unqualified, it may run the risk of having to litigate the issue of its immunity when it asserts its right to enforce a contract. At the same time, if it

[3]Report of the Special Subcommittee on State Taxation of Interstate Commerce, p. 931.
[4]Report of the Special Subcommittee on State Taxation of Interstate Commerce, p. 931.

qualifies without being legally required to, it will be forced to pay a capital stock tax, a burden for which it otherwise would not be liable. Furthermore, in many states foreign corporations are barred from bidding on state contracts unless they are qualified to do business in the state. Again, the relationship between qualification to do business and the applicability of the capital stock tax results in a company, in effect, being forced to volunteer to contribute a capital stock tax in the absence of any independent basis for liability.

Perhaps the most comprehensive attempt to determine the nexus standards applicable to taxes based on capital used by the states was the study conducted by the Willis Committee.[5] Portions of the published findings applicable to nexus are reproduced in Appendix D. The *Nexus Questionnaire* that was used to produce Appendix E is also shown as Appendix F.

Colonial Pipeline Company v. Traigle 421 U.S. 100 (1975)

In *Colonial Pipeline* v. *Traigle* the question of jurisdiction is closely examined. Colonial owned and operated a major pipeline moving petroleum products from Texas to destinations as far north as New York City, with deliveries to 14 states and the District of Columbia. Some 258 miles of this pipeline, of a total mileage of 3400 miles, were within the state of Louisiana. Colonial's in-state property at the time the controversy arose consisted of the 258 miles of pipeline and other necessary property such as pumping stations and tank storage facilities. To operate the facilities in Louisiana, the company needed 25 to 30 employees. All the business done in Louisiana was considered interstate, that is, bringing products into Louisiana or moving them out of state through the pipeline.

Based on these circumstances, the controversy arose about whether Colonial was subject to Louisiana's tax based on capital. The tax in question was imposed by Section 47:601 La. Rev. Stat. that contained the following pertinent provisions:

1 A tax is imposed based on the amount of capital stock, surplus, undivided profits, and borrowed capital employed in the state.
2 The tax is imposed on every domestic corporation and every foreign corporation qualified to do business, or actually doing business in the state.
3 The tax is levied on the qualification to carry on or do business in the state in corporate form.
4 The stated purpose of the levy is for the right granted to exist as a corporation and for the enjoyment under the laws of Louisiana of the

[5]Report of the Special Subcommittee on State Taxation of Interstate Commerce, Part IV, Chapter 30.

powers, rights, privileges, and immunities derived by reason of the corporate form of existence and operation.

Colonial had previously run afoul of the Louisiana franchise tax. In an earlier case, the Louisiana Supreme Court refused to review the lower court decisions which had found that Section 47:601 as it was then written violated the Commerce Clause of the U.S. Constitution. At the time of the earlier litigation, Section 47:601 was imposed on "the privilege of carrying on or doing business. . . ." The language here was fatal as far as the Louisiana courts were concerned because this imposed a tax squarely on the privilege of doing interstate business. Following this decision, Louisiana changed Section 47:601 as outlined in the foregoing.

The facts and circumstances with respect to Colonial's operations in Louisiana were no different in the first case as opposed to the second. The only element that was different was the change in the wording of Section 47:601. However, this mere change in wording was sufficient to correct the flaw, with the result being that Colonial now found itself subject to the tax. This wording change caused Mr. Justice Blackmun to comment in his concurring opinion that the distinctions have little substantive difference and it results in taxation by semantics.

This case illustrates the fact that a state can so word its statute so as to impose a tax on the privilege or right to do business in the corporate form and not violate the Commerce Clause. The first *Colonial* decision followed the rule of law from *Spector Motor*[6] which stated that a tax imposed on the "privilege" of doing interstate business was unconstitutional, being in violation of the Commerce Clause. *Spector,* as far as this rule of law is concerned, was overruled in *Complete Auto Transits.*[7] Thus changing the Louisiana statute would not now be necessary.

The similarity between the present case and that of Memphis Gas Company[8] was appropriately commented on in the opinion. In this decision, Memphis Gas Company was found to be doing business in the state of Mississippi:

Memphis Natural Gas Company, a Delaware corporation, owned and operated a natural gas pipeline extending from Louisiana, through Arkansas and Mississippi, to Memphis and other parts of Tennessee. Approximately 135 miles of the pipeline were located in Mississippi and two of the corporation's compressing stations were located in that state. The corporation engaged in no intrastate commerce in Mississippi, and had only one customer there. It had not qualified under the corporation laws of Mississippi. It had neither an

---

[6]*Spector Motor Service* v. *O'Connor* 340 U.S. 602 (1951).
[7]*Complete Auto Transits, Incorporated* v. *Brady, Chairman, Mississippi State Tax Commission* 51 2d 236 (1977).
[8]*Memphis Gas Company* v. *Stone* 335 U.S. 80 (1948).

agent for the service of process nor an office in that state, and its only employees there were those necessary for the maintenance of the pipeline.

The corporation paid all ad valorem taxes assessed against its property in Mississippi. In addition to these taxes, however, Mississippi imposed a "franchise or excise tax" upon all corporations "doing business" within the state. . . . The Supreme Court of Mississippi held . . . that the tax was "an exaction . . . as a recompense for . . . protection of . . . the local activities in maintaining, keeping in repair, and otherwise manning the facilities of the system throughout the 135 miles of its line in this state."

The U.S. Supreme Court opinion upholding the Mississippi court said:[9]

We think that the state is within its constitutional rights in exacting compensation under this statute for the protection it affords the activities within its borders. Of course, the interstate commerce could not be conducted without these local activities. But that fact is not conclusive. These are events apart from the flow of commerce. This is a tax on activities for which the state, not the United States, gives protection and the state is entitled to compensation when its tax cannot be said to be an unreasonable burden or a toll on the interstate business.

It was further noted that Colonial had voluntarily qualified under Louisiana law and therefore enjoyed the same rights and privileges as a domestic corporation; that is, Colonial had the legal status to sue and be sued in Louisiana courts and benefited from continuity of business, advantages of the corporate form of doing business, and general absence of individual liability. It was concluded that these privileges obviously enhanced the value of Colonial's activities within Louisiana.

COMPUTATIONAL DECISIONS

Ford Motor Company v. Beauchamp 308 U.S. 331 (1939)

Ford Motor Company was qualified to do business in Texas, and there was no question about the company being subject to the Texas franchise tax. The company had substantial activity in-state, principally the ownership and operation of assembly plants. None of the parts for the automobiles was manufactured in Texas, but after assembly, the autos were sold intrastate. Other autos and parts were shipped to Texas from out of state and there sold intrastate.

The tax base for the Texas franchise tax was capital stock, surplus, undivided profits, and long-term debt. The apportionment of the tax base consisted of a single factor of Texas business as a proportion of total

---

[9]*Memphis Gas Company* v. *Stone*, p. 84.

business. Application of the apportionment formula to the taxpayer resulted in approximately $23 million taxable by Texas. The value of all assets located in Texas was somewhat over $3 million as calculated by the taxpayer. The taxpayer claimed that (1) the tax was being applied to out-of-state values used in interstate commerce and thus was in violation of the Commerce Clause and (2) tax was being assessed on property and activity beyond the borders of Texas in violation of the Due Process Clause. The reasonableness of the apportionment formula was not contested.

The decision in this case was that the tax as applied by Texas was not unconstitutional. Citing *Bass, Ratcliff*[10] (see Chapter 3) the court reasoned that Ford Motor Company, being a unitary business, was not being taxed unfairly. The tax base as computed by the Texas formula was not an unreasonable result (see *Underwood Typewriter*[11] Chapter 3).

International Harvester Company v. Evatt 329 U.S. 416 (1946)

This is also a case where there was no question about nexus. International Harvester Company (IHC) had factories, branch-selling establishments, warehouses, and retail stores within the taxing state of Ohio. The tax base was the value of capital stock. The apportionment of the tax base was determined as follows:

One-half the tax base was multiplied by the ratio of Ohio property to total property.

One-half the tax base was multiplied by the Ohio business done to total business done.

The tax rate was then applied to the values so determined to arrive at the tax due.

The issue was whether sales proceeds of goods manufactured in Ohio plants and shipped to customers outside Ohio should be included in apportionment computations. IHC contended that the state had taxed sales made outside Ohio in violation of the Due Process Clause. The company also argued that the inclusion of these sales was an undue burden on interstate commerce:

Held:

(a) The fact that the state chose to measure the tax on the business of manufacturing done in the state by the value of the products (including

---

[10]*Bass Ratcliff and Gretton, Limited* v. *State Tax Commission* 266 U.S. 271 (1924).
[11]*Underwood Typewriter Company* v. *Chamberlain* 254 U.S. 113 (1920).

those sold out of the state) does not transform the tax on that business to a tax on sales out of the state.

(b) Treatment of sales within Ohio of products manufactured elsewhere as "business done" in Ohio did not result in violation of the Due Process Clause, since the business of Ohio customers were intrastate activities.

1. This does not constitute a tax on sales made outside Ohio in violation of the Due Process Clause of the Fourteenth Amendment, since it is a franchise tax for the privilege of doing business in the state.

2. The tax does not violate the Commerce Clause, since the purpose of the formula was to arrive at a fair conclusion as to what was the value of the intrastate business and it has not been demonstrated that it achieves an unfair result.

a. A state's tax law is not to be nullified merely because the result is achieved through a formula which includes consideration of interstate and out-of-state transactions in their relation to the intrastate privilege.

b. No multiplication of this tax through its imposition by other states is involved, since the tax is levied only against the privilege of doing local business of manufacturing and selling in Ohio and no other state can tax that privilege.

TAX BASE AND APPORTIONMENT METHODS

The cases dealing with taxes based on capital demonstrate that a tax for the privilege of doing business will be upheld without regard to the measure of the tax. That is, the state will be entitled to impose such a tax, and the method devised to compute the amount will not generally run afoul of the Commerce and Due Process clauses. Thus a state enjoys considerable freedom in its selection of the tax base and the apportionment of that tax base to determine the taxable amount. This freedom is best illustrated by an examination of the variety that exists in the different statutes. A review of the taxes based on capital of the states of Illinois, Texas, Ohio, Pennsylvania, and Alabama demonstrates this. (See Exhibits 5.1 and 5.2.)

Illinois Franchise Tax

The Illinois franchise tax is a tax on the privilege to do business in the state for a fiscal period ending June 30. The tax rate is 0.001 of taxable value with a maximum tax of $1 million.

The taxable base is comprised of two elements: stated capital (capital stock) and paid-in capital as shown on the balance sheet of the company at year-end. A taxpayer may elect to have its franchise tax computed on the entire stated and paid-in capital, or it may elect to be taxed on an apportioned amount.

If the apportionment method is elected, the taxable portion is determined by multiplying total stated capital and paid-in capital by a single fraction, the numerator of which is the total of Illinois business done, plus Illinois property, and the denominator of which is total business everywhere, plus total property everywhere.

The term "business" is poorly defined and could mean sales, services, commissions, dividends, and so on. The term Illinois business is even more vague. In the case of sales of tangible property it could mean Illinois sales on a destination, origin, or negotiated basis. The "property" term is clearly defined as being virtually all property tangible and intangible, as shown on the financial balance sheet. Notes and accounts receivable would thus be included, but a few specific items such as goodwill and deferred changes are not included. Illinois property is comprised of those tangible and intangible assets located in Illinois at December 31 (for a calendar year taxpayer).

Interim filings and proportionate additional payments are required for any additions to either elements of the tax base during the privilege year. The tax is administered by the Office of the Secretary of State rather than the Illinois Department of Revenue.

Texas Franchise Tax

The Texas franchise tax is levied on the privilege of doing business in Texas, the privilege year being the calendar year. The tax base is expanded over that of Illinois to include retained earnings; in other words, the tax base is comprised of total net worth.

The apportionment of the tax base is by means of a single receipts factor. *Receipts* are defined to include sale of tangible property, services, rentals, royalties, other business receipts, and a share of net earnings of partnerships operating in Texas. The determination of the Texas portion of receipts is also clearly defined. In the case of sales of tangible property, the Texas portion is determined on a destination basis.

The tax rate is 0.00425 and is applied to the apportioned net worth. However, there is an alternative computation to be made before the final franchise tax is determined. The alternative computation requies that a Texas tax base be derived by summing the county assessed value of all real and tangible personal property in Texas. Such amounts are reflected on the various county ad valorem tax bills of the previous year. If the alternative tax base is higher than the apportioned tax base, the tax rate is applied to the higher value.

Ohio Franchise Tax

The Ohio tax is a privilege tax for doing business for the calendar year. As in the case of Texas, the tax is the higher of two computations. One is a computation based on income of the previous year, apportioned on the basis of the three-factor formula. The other is a tax based on capital apportioned on the basis of a two-factor formula. Only the latter computation is described here, since the income tax computation would be as described in Chapter 2.

The base for the tax based on capital includes capital stock, retained earnings, paid-in capital, and reserves (except valuation reserves against specific assets). A typical reserve to be included would be a timing difference such as deferred Federal income tax.

The total of the foregoing may be reduced by goodwill and air and water pollution control facilities to the extent these are reflected on the financial balance sheet.

The total tax base so computed is apportioned to Ohio by means of the two factors of property and business. The business factor is similar to the UDITPA requirement. The property factor is similar to that of Illinois. Year-end values are used rather than average, and all property—tangible and intangible—is included. Property and business and the Ohio portion of each are clearly defined, including the refinement to cite investments in subsidiaries as Ohio property. The Ohio portion of investments in subsidiaries is determined by multiplying the balance sheet investment by the ratio of the subsidiaries' Ohio tangible property to the toal tangible property as shown on the Ohio franchise tax reports of the subsidiaries.

The tax rate to determine the capital based portion of the franchise tax is 0.005.

Pennsylvania Franchise

The Pennsylvania franchise tax is for a privilege year covering the calendar year. The franchise tax is in addition to the income tax.

The total tax base is the value of the capital stock as appraised by the officers of the company. Considerations to arrive at the value include the average selling price of stock, average book earnings, and average dividends paid. In practice, the value of capital stock for franchise tax purposes is the value as appraised by the Pennsylvania Department of Revenue.

Apportionment of the total tax base is by means of a three-factor UDITPA-type formula. A very important manufacturing exemption is provided, however, in that salaries and wages, property, sales attributable to manufacturing, processing, and research and development within Pennsylvania are excluded from the numerator of the appropriate factor. For example, the salaries and wages and property connected with a Pennsylvania research facility would not be included in the numerators of those factors but would be included in the denominators. Similarly, a manufacturing or processing facility would have an exclusion for Pennsylvania sales, payroll, and property. The sales factor has a peculiar rule known as the "throw-out" rule. This rule deals with sales originating in Pennsylvania and shipped to a state where the seller would not be subject to tax by that state. (See the "throw-back" rule under UDITPA, Chapter 2). Such sales are removed from the denominator of the sales factor.

The tax rate applied to the apportioned value is 0.01.

Alabama Franchise Tax

The Alabama franchise tax is for the privilege of engaging in business for the calendar year.

The total tax base is very broad. It includes capital stock, retained earnings, paid-in surplus, accelerated depreciation or amortization, indebtedness maturing in more than one year, and indebtedness no matter when maturing to certain related parties.

Exclusions from the total capital base are allowed for investments in domestic corporations and investments in capital of foreign corporations subject to Alabama franchise tax.

Apportionment of the total tax base depends on the type of activity in which the taxpayer is engaged. The factors to be considered as shown on the return are these:

1 Sales by place of manufacture.
2 Destination sales.
3 Gross revenue by source.
4 Dollar volume of contracting work.
5 Transportation mileage.
6 Salaries and wages and/or commissions.
7 Tangible property (original cost).
8 Tangible property (book value).
9 Inventories.
10 Cost of manufacturing.

The apportionment formula for an interstate manufacturing and selling company would be as follows:

Three factors are involved. The first is to develop the ratios of each of the factors 1 and 2 and average the two.

The second is factor 6.

The third is to develop the ratios of each of the factors 7 and 9 and average the two.

The final apportionment ratio is the sum of these three factors divided by three.

Alabama allows important deductions to be applied to the apportioned tax base. Included is a deduction for the book value of Alabama air and water pollution control devices.

The tax rate is 0.003.

It is obvious from these comparisons that substantial variations of the tax base and the apportionment of that tax base exist among the states. Since a tax based on capital is a privilege-type levy, there is no need for uniformity inasmuch as it amounts to strictly a state matter. Unlike taxes based on income, which often run afoul of U.S. Constitutional constraints, privilege taxes relate only to state jurisdiction. The states are free to devise their own computational methods so long as these methods are applied uniformly to all taxpayers.

In some states, the franchise tax is a major revenue-producing levy, for example, the Pennsylvania franchise. In those states economic constraints are present; that is, the tax cannot be so high that it influences the decision of the interstate taxpayers to do business there or to select some other state in which to locate business facilities. When this happens, offsetting incentives are offered, such as the manufacturing exemption of Pennsylvania.

In other states, for example, Illinois, the franchise tax does not appear to be designed as a revenue source. The income generated is more related to offsetting the cost of administering the corporate regulatory law than meeting fiscal budgetary needs. These states have designed their tax on capital accordingly.

COMBINED REPORTING FOR TAXES BASED ON CAPITAL

Thus far, the principles of combined reporting that have been applied with respect to taxes based on income have not been applied to taxes based on capital. However, certain similarities exist that would appear in theory, to make such an application possible.

Exhibit 5.1 Comparison of Total Tax Base — Five Taxes Based on Capital

Balance Sheet Categories	Illinois	Texas	Ohio	Pennsylvania	Alabama
Capital stock	X	X	X		X
Paid-in capital	X	X	X		X
Retained earnings		X	X		X
Long-term debt					X
Indebtedness to related parties					X
Reserves (other than valuation)			X		X
Facts and circumstances				X	
Exemptions on deductions,					
manufacturing, or processing				X	
Research and development				X	
Pollution control		X			X
Goodwill		X			

Exhibit 5.2 Comparison of Apportionment Data and Tax Rates—Five Taxes Based on Capital

Categories	Illinois	Texas	Ohio	Pennsylvania	Alabama
Sales					
Destination		X	X	X	
Origin					
Other or undefined	X				X
Property					
Similar to UDITPA				X	
Year-end values					
Tangibles	X		X		
Intangibles	X		X		
Average values					X
Tangibles					X
Salaries and wages				X	X
Tax rates	0.001	0.00425	0.005	0.01	0.003

Combined reporting originated with the unitary concept, as illustrated in various court decisions.[12] If a taxpayer is found to be part of a unitary business operation, then a state's attempt to apply the combined report procedures to the unitary income has been upheld. This is applicable whether the unitary business is conducted in a single corporate organization or in the form of a number of corporations.[13] When combined reporting is applied to a unitary business, the in-state apportionment data of the taxpayer are used as the numerators of the apportionment factors and the everywhere data of the apportionment factors will include that of the taxpayer and all other parties to the unitary business. The factors so determined are then applied to the entire income of the unitary business. (See the Comprehensive Example, Appendix B Chapter 3.) In the decisions on unitary operations, the courts refused to attempt to overturn formula apportionment, reasoning that an exact determination of in-state income could not be accomplished so that any formula that produced a "reasonable" result was upheld.

In most instances a unitary business was seen to be a series of transactions beginning with the manufacture of a product in one state and its ultimate sale elsewhere. This type of enterprise exemplified the concept that intrastate income could best be measured by formula.

The unitary concept has been expanded now to apply to the multinational corporation, and the unitary business can be on a worldwide scale.

[12]*Underwood Typewriter Company* v. *Chamberlain* 254 U.S. 113 (1920).

Bass Ratcliff and Gretton, Limited v. *State Tax Commission* 266 U.S. 271 (1924).

Norfolk and Western Railway Company v. *North Carolina* 297 U.S. 682 (1936).

Butler Brothers v. *McColgan* 315 U.S. 501 (1942).

[13]See *Edison California Stores, Incorporated* v. *McColgan* 183 P.2d 16 (1947).

The criteria specified in *Butler Brothers*[14] and *Edison California Stores, Incorporated,*[15] that is, unity of ownership, operation, and use, make it extremely difficult for a group of corporations to avoid classification as a unitary business.

With combined reporting firmly entrenched in state income taxation, what is to prevent the same application to taxes based on capital? It would appear that there is ample basis for such an extension.

Initially, taxes based on capital were not considered a radical departure from the then-prevailing method of state taxation: the property tax. These taxes existed within the framework of the property tax and were regarded as a natural extension of property taxation. It later came to be recognized that the tax on tangible property was failing to reach the real economic value of a corporation, that is, the intangible portion of its value. This began the trend of the states to turn to various forms of tax imposed on capital stock or "capital." These taxes can be thought of as intangible property taxes.

In the *Ford*[16] decision the taxpayers contended that the in-state value of its assets in Texas was approximately $3 million, whereas the value allocated to Texas by that state's statutory formula was over $23 million. The U.S. Supreme Court viewed this case very much like *Bass Ratcliff:*[17]

> It is much like that upheld in *Bass Ratcliff and Gretton v. Tax Commission.* In that case a tax was laid for the privilege of doing business in New York determined, for corporations which did not transact all their business within that state, by a percentage of that part of the net income which is calculated by the proportion which the aggregate of specified classes of property within the state bears to all the property of the corporation.[18]

The similarities between *Ford* and *Bass* are as follows:

1   Both involved a tax on the privilege of doing intrastate business.
2   Both taxpayers were found to be engaged in a unitary business.
3   Both claimed separate accounting as a better measure of the tax base.
4   Formula apportionment by the state was not overcome by showing of separate accounting.

The dissimilarities are as follows:

1   Tax base   Ford: Capital
                          Bass: Previous year's income

---

[14]*Butler Brothers* v. *McColgan.*
[15]*Edison California Stores, Incorporated* v. *McColgan.*
[16]*Ford Motor Company* v. *Beauchamp* 308 U.S. 331 (1939).
[17]*Bass Ratcliff and Gretton, Limited* v. *State Tax Commission.*
[18]*Ford Motor Company* v. *Beauchamp* p. 335.

2 Apportionment   Ford: Single sales factor
                                 Bass: Single property factor

The similarities between the two cases are apparent, and the dissimilarity comes down to a single element—only the tax base is different. This would not seem to bar the extension of combined reporting to this type of tax.

Assume that combined reporting could be applied to a tax based on capital. As illustrated in Exhibit 5.3 the results can fluctuate, depending on the circumstances.

In this example, Company S is subject to a franchise tax measured by an apportioned amount of its capital stock and earned surplus. The taxing state uses the single factor of sales for apportionment purposes. In-state sales are derived on a destination basis.

Company P is not qualified to do business in the taxing state. The total sales of Company P for the year amount to $3,000,000.

Company S is subject to the Franchise tax. Company S's shipments to customers in the taxing state amount to $1,000,000, and its sales everywhere amount to $2,000,000.

The tax base on a nonunitary basis for Company S would be as shown here:

$$\frac{1,000,000}{2,000,000} \times \$231,000 = \$115,500$$

The tax base on a unitary basis for Company S would be the following:

$$\frac{1,000,000}{5,000,000} \times \$410,000 = \$82,000$$

Under this set of circumstances, Company S would have a smaller tax base on a unitary basis than on a separate company basis. However, assume

Exhibit 5.3

	Parent P	Subsidiary S	Eliminations	Consolidated
Investment in subsidiary	1,000		1,000	
Other assets	190,000	300,000		490,000
Total assets	191,000	300,000	1,000	490,000
Liabilities	11,000	69,000		80,000
Capital stock	50,000	1,000	1,000	50,000
Earned surplus	130,000	230,000		360,000
Total liabilities and capital	191,000	300,000	1,000	490,000

that Company S had paid a $200,000 dividend to Company P during the year. Company S's earned surplus would then have been $30,000, and Company P's earned surplus would have been $330,000.

The tax base on a nonunitary basis for Company S would be this:

$$\frac{1,000,000}{2,000,000} \times \$31,000 \ = \$15,500$$

The tax base on a unitary basis for Company S would be the following:

$$\frac{1,000,000}{5,000,000} \times \$410,000 = \$82,000$$

In the foregoing example, it is apparent that Company S can minimize its tax by paying dividends to the parent, thereby reducing the taxable base. Whether Company S would do so to avoid the impact of the tax would depend on several considerations—for instance, taxability of the dividend income to the parent or increase in taxes based on capital for the parent.

CHAPTER SIX

Michigan Single Business Tax (Value Added)

A NEW APPROACH TO STATE TAXATION

The first five chapters of this text have introduced the various theories and methods used by those states levying an income tax on intrastate and interstate commerce. The three basic techniques previously discussed are separate accounting, combined reporting, and consolidated reporting. Other states not levying a tax based on or measured by income usually use a tax based on a corporation's capital. These taxes were discussed in Chapter 5. Finally, there is another approach to state taxation presently used only by Michigan. It is called the Michigan Single Business Tax and is regarded as a value added tax (VAT) on business activity within that state.

Background

The value added tax was developed after World War II as a means of taxing business without interfering in internal business decisions. It is based on various economic criteria and designed for modern industrial markets. Although this type of tax had not been used in the United States,[1] the European Common Market countries adopted a VAT tax in the 1960s as did several other countries. The growth of the VAT in Europe is attributable to its adoption by the Council of the European Economic Community as an acceptable method of indirect taxation that would not distort trade within the common market. The VAT would hopefully equalize the position of integrated and nonintegrated companies, thereby avoiding conditions that could distort competition. The tax's use would

---

[1] The possibility of introducing a value added tax in the United States had been discussed in the early 1970s. See Dan Smith, "When-If-We Have the VAT," *Volume 51 Harvard Business Reveiw* Number 1 (January–February 1973); Kenneth Sanden, "VAT: What, How, Where," *Tax Advisor* (March 1973); "Value Added Tax, A Business View," Association of New York, Incorporated, Commerce and Industry, New York, 1970. Currently, a VAT bill is before the House Ways and Means Committee, H.B. 5665, having been introduced by Chairman Ullman on October 22, 1979.

also permit tax collections to be made at each stage of production, and this would reduce the possibilities of tax evasion. The VAT would be simple and neutral in its applicability. Part of the preamble of the First Directive of the Council of the European Economic Community, dated April 11, 1967, states:

> . . . that a system of tax on value added will achieve the highest degree of simplicity and neutrality when the tax is levied in as general a manner as possible and when its scope of application includes all stages of production and distribution as well as the realm of the rendition of services; and that it is, accordingly, in the interest of the Common Market and of the Member States to adopt a common system the scope of which also extends to retail trade.

Michigan's first attempt at a VAT was in 1972. A constitutional amendment was proposed that included provisions for this tax, but the proposal was defeated. Prior to this time, from 1953 to 1967, Michigan had in effect a business activities tax that was similar to a gross receipts tax, but was administered as an income tax.

In 1968 the business activities tax was repealed and a corporate income tax was introduced, but this type of tax structure was not compatible with the state's revenue needs. It was finally decided in 1975 that a new tax system was needed which could stabilize tax revenues and, at the same time, promote economic growth. A bill was drafted by the House of Representatives after numerous meetings with business and governmental leaders and finally enacted into law. The Single Business Tax (SBT) became effective in Michigan on January 1, 1976.

To fully appreciate the effects and implications of the Michigan Single Business Tax, a basic understanding of the VAT is necessary.

What is the VAT?

The VAT is a tax imposed on the value added to a product by the producer or vendor. When there is no tangible product involved, the tax is on the value of services that have been rendered. The result of this system is a tax that is paid on wages, interest, rent, profits, and any other cost of production not previously subjected to the tax. Using a more simplistic economic system, this would be equivalent to taxing the value added to a commodity by determining the profits accrued by a company and the payments a company makes to those who are not VAT taxpayers, usually the company's employees. In effect, it is the end product or service that is to be taxed, not the operations of the entire business, as with an income tax. The transfer of a product or performance of a service is material to income tax assessment only to the extent that it affects the net profits of a company.

A comparison of an income tax and a VAT imposed on a manufacturing concern can best illustrate the impact of the VAT.

Exhibit 6.1   MGW Corporation, Income Statements

	Year 1	Year 2
Sales	$10,000	$25,000
Cost of goods manufactured	15,000	20,000
Net loss	$(5,000)	$ 5,000

Exhibit 6.2   MGW Corporation, Statements of Manufacturing Costs

	Year 1	Year 2
Cost of raw material supplies	$ 8,000	$12,000
Costs incurred by MGW Corporation	7,000	8,000
Total manufacturing costs	$15,000	$20,000

The data of exhibits 6.1 and 6.2 represent a condensed income statement and statement of manufacturing costs for the MGW Corporation for the first two years of its operations.

An income tax and a VAT imposed at a 10 percent rate would yield the following results:

	Year 1	Year 2
Income tax	$ 0	$ 500
VAT	$700	$1,300

An income tax would only be incurred in year 2 where the MGW Corporation has a net income of $5000 subject to tax. A liability for a VAT, however, would be incurred in both years, since the corporation has added to the value of the manufactured goods that it sells. This value added represents a tax on the wages and profits and any other cost of manufacturing that was not passed on to the MGW Corporation from another corporation subject to the VAT. In this example, the corporation supplying the raw materials would have been subject to the VAT.

In year 1, the value added for the MGW Corporation consisted of the $7000 of additional manufacturing costs. In year 2, the value added consists of the $8000 of additional manufacturing costs, plus the $5000 of profits.

Variations of the VAT

The previous example computed the VAT by adding both the value added to the manufacturing costs by the MGW Corporation and the company's profits. This example ignored the possibility of additional transactions—such as the purchase of manufacturing equipment—that may or may not influence the amount of the VAT to be paid, depending on the method of computing the tax.

Actually, three types of VATs can be used:

1 Consumption type VAT.
2 Income type VAT.
3 Gross product type VAT.

Although the general concept of taxing the "value added" remains the same in each of the three methods, the primary difference is based on the treatment of capital expenditures.

Consumption Type VAT

The consumption type of value added tax is essentially the method used in computing the Michigan SBT. It is also the method used in Europe. The tax on value added is basically determined by taxing a company's sales, less its purchases from other businesses so that the ultimate burden of the tax would be on the final consumer.

There are three basic approaches to the consumption type tax. The first is the credit method that imposes a tax on the sale of goods and services and allows a credit for all purchases whether they are purchases of raw materials or capital assets.[2]

Company and transaction	VAT
Company A — Sells Product X to Company B for $5,000 = (sales × rate) − (purchases × rate)	Tax paid = $5,000 × 10% = $ 500
Company B — resells Product X purchased from Company A to Company C for $8,500 = (sales × rate) − (purchases × rate)	Tax paid = 8,500 × 10% = $ 850 − 5,000 × 10% = 500 $ 350
Company C — sells Product X to customer for $10,000 + (sales × rate) − (purchases × rate)	Tax paid = 10,000 × 10% = $1,000 − 8,500 × 10% = 850 $ 150

[2]Samuel J. McKim, III, "Michigan Single Business Tax Seen as a VAT," *Tax Executive* 29 (October 1976).

The total tax paid on the sale of Product X is $1000 or 10 percent of the $10,000 sales price.

This credit method or invoice method is the approach to the VAT used in Europe. Each taxpayer multiplies the total sales prices on all products by the appropriate tax rate. A credit is then applied against this tax that is equivalent to the amount of tax paid by a company to its suppliers. The amount of credit is readily ascertainable on all the invoices received by each company purchasing from another VAT taxpayer. This system provides a certain degree of self-policing, since each purchaser benefits by insuring that all VATs paid are shown on the invoices.[3]

The second method for computing the consumption type tax is the subtraction method. Under this method, a business subtracts the amount paid to other VAT taxpayers for its goods and services from its sales and applies the appropriate tax rate to this tax base.

The third method is the addition method that consists of adding together all the components of the value added base, which would be wages, rents, interest, profits, and other payments made to non-VAT taxpayers. The Michigan SBT uses the addition method.

Regardless of which of the three methods is used to compute the consumption type tax, in each case there is no VAT paid on the purchase of capital assets. A credit on the purchase of capital assets would be given, or the purchase of the asset would be deducted from a company's sales, or in the addition method, the cost of such an asset would not be added to the VAT base.

Income and Gross Product Types of VATs

These two methods of computing VATs differ from the consumption method in their treatment of capital expenditures. Under the income method, a purchase price of a capital asset would be ratably amortized over the economic life of the asset as an offset to the company's sales. This treatment is similar to the depreciation deducted from sales in computing a tax base for net income tax purposes.

The gross product VAT differs from the consumption and income methods in that the acquisition of capital goods is totally included in the tax base. It allows no deductions for the cost of capital expenditures and no amortization of the asset. The gross product type of VAT obviously penalizes capital intense industries and therefore has not received much attention except from a theoretical standpoint. If every business firm were to be subject to such a VAT, the tax would be on the gross national product.[4]

Exhibit 6.3 is a summary of the consumption, income, and gross product VAT bases.

[3]McKim, "Michigan Single Business Tax Seen as a VAT," p. 153.
[4]Smith, "When-If-We Have the VAT."

Exhibit 6.3   Three Different VAT Bases

Consumption	Sales, less purchases from taxpayers subject to the VAT
Income	Sales, less purchases from taxpayers subject to the VAT, plus capital expenditures, less amortization of capital items
Gross product	Sales, less purchases from taxpayers subject to the VAT, plus capital expenditures

Neutrality of a VAT

Aside from the simplistic concept embodied in a VAT system, the VAT is also appealing because of its inherent neutrality. In evaluating the neutrality of the VAT, or any other tax, it is important not to view the tax in comparison with any tax system already being imposed. To do so would place the tax system in use as the standard for an economy, with any deviations from it being considered as good or bad. The neutrality of a tax can be objectively reviewed and will not be distorted if one assumes an economy with no taxes being imposed as the focal point. In this context, the VAT is neutral because of the following[5]:

1 It does not discriminate between capital-intensive and labor-intensive industries, because the tax is based on the selling price of the product and looks only to the value added to the product.
2 An efficient company will not be penalized and have to carry the burden for an inefficient company. An income tax would require only the profitable and efficient company to pay a tax, whereas a VAT would require all companies to pay the tax regardless of their efficiency.
3 The use of equity or debt financing would not distort the amount of tax paid. An income tax discriminates against equity financing by allowing interest expenses to be deducted from income before computing a tax. The VAT does not favor one form of financing over the other.
4 The size or form of business organization does not affect the amount of taxes to be paid. A large conglomerate, a small corporation, a partnership, and a proprietorship must all bear the same tax burden. The imposition of a VAT is not an influencing factor in determining business decisions or in deciding on a business form.

The neutrality results from the VAT because it is the end product and service that is taxed and not the business itself. The profitability, capitalization, and form of the business are not influencing factors in reducing the

[5]Smith, "When-If-We Have the VAT", p.131.

tax to be paid. The reduction of the total costs of the business as reflected in the selling price would be the way to reduce the VAT paid.[6]

The Michigan SBT can be understood more easily if these basic VAT concepts are kept in mind.

The Michigan SBT—Federal and Constitutional Limitations

The SBT is levied on the privilege of doing business within the state and not on net income. Federal limitations preventing any state from levying income taxes on foreign businesses whose only in-state activity is the solicitation of orders for approval outside the state will not apply to the SBT.

More specifically, the state of Michigan is not bound by the Federal limitations of P.L. 86-272 and is able to set its own limitations. The nexus standards that will be enforced by the Michigan Treasury Department in the taxation of foreign business activity are those set by the U.S. Supreme Court in the *Northwestern* case (see Chapter 1) before the enactment of P.L. 86-272. Any person using the Michigan market for a business activity that includes the sale of property, rental of property, or performance of a service will be responsible for paying a tax in Michigan if the activity can be fairly apportioned to the state.[7]

Two other landmark cases, *National Bellas-Hess* and *Scripto,* will also provide taxation guidelines (see Chapter 7). Accordingly, any interstate corporation that solicits orders in-state through independent salesmen or by means of its own employees will be considered to be doing business within the state and will be subject to tax, and any out-of-state mail order activities will not be subject to the tax.

A company using the Michigan market would be required to apportion its business activity to Michigan if it is represented in Michigan by an employee, broker, or independent salesman who exclusively represents that company. Solicitation or the mere presence in Michigan will be considered sufficient nexus to subject the activity to be fairly apportioned to the state.[8]

The Michigan Court of Appeals has upheld the constitutionality of the SBT in the case of *Stockler* v. *State of Michigan* 255 N.W. 2d 718 (1977), since the tax is levied on the privilege of doing business and not on net income. The tax was not considered a violation of the Federal Constitution's interstate Commerce Clause, and there was no proof that it caused an undue burden on interstate commerce. The court indicated that ''al-

---

[6]Kenneth Sanden, ''VAT: What, How, Where,'' *Tax Advisor* (March 1973).

[7]See Commerce Clearing House Publications, Michigan Single Business Tax Division Releases, Single Business Tax Bulletin 1978-3, *Jurisdictional Standard* (March 24, 1978).

[8]Commerce Clearing House Publications, Michigan Single Business Tax Division Releases, Single Business Tax Bulletin 1978-3, ¶ 19-503, Jurisdictional Standard (March 24, 1978).

though federal taxable income is used as the starting point in computing the tax base, it is possible that a taxpayer may have no income and still be subject to the payment of the SBT. Other components of the tax base, e.g., wages, include expenses incurred, a theory not synonomous with income taxes.''

The absence of a specific reference to this tax in Michigan's state constitution also does not invalidate it. The enumeration of possible taxes in the state's constitution is not intended to be an exclusive listing of permissible taxes. Furthermore, the tax does not violate the state constitution's prohibition against graduated income taxes, because the SBT is not an income tax and it is not a graduated tax.[9]

Purpose of the SBT

The SBT was created to provide an economy in Michigan that would be conducive to industrial growth. It is designed to promote rather than discourage economic expansion within the state and, at the same time, stabilize the state's tax revenues.

The important feature of the tax is that all businesses will be paying a tax proportional to the economic size of their businesses. Furthermore, the amount of the tax payable will not be dependent on the legal form chosen. The SBT is applicable to corporations, partnerships, sole proprietorships, financial institutions, and estates and trusts. All the business activity will be apportioned or allocated to Michigan according to provisions similar to those of UDITPA.[10] This discussion is primarily limited to the corporate implications of the tax.

When the SBT was enacted, eight taxes previously being levied were repealed. These taxes were the corporate income tax, corporate franchise tax, the business portion of the intangibles tax, the financial institutions tax, the personal property tax on inventory, the savings and loan association privilege tax, the domestic insurance carrier privilege tax, and the business portion of the individual income tax. The SBT was designed to take the place of all these taxes. The revenue provided by these taxes was approximately $800 million, and the estimated revenue to be provided by the SBT was approximately the same.[11]

Effect on Michigan Economy

A comparison of the old system of taxation with the new SBT helps to reveal the reasons behind the adoption of this unique tax. The corporate

[9]See Commerce Clearing House Publications, Michigan Tax Reports, No. 240 (June 27, 1977).
[10]Sydney D. Goodman, ''Michigan's Single Business Tax,'' *Tax Executive Institute,* Volume XXVIII (April 1976) 3, p. 214.
[11]Goodman, ''Michigan's Single Business Tax,'' ·p. 214.

income tax, adopted in 1968, was affected by the fluctuating tax base of corporate net income. If the general business climate presented favorable economic opportunities, corporate profits would increase, creating a larger taxable base in Michigan. This would also provide a large revenue supply to the state. If there were a recessional period, corporate taxable incomes would tend to decrease as would the potential revenue for the state. The SBT, however, would stabilize Michigan's tax receipts, thereby decreasing the possibility of any more tax increases similar to what had occurred under the Income Tax Act of 1968. The possibility of the Michigan Treasury department having periods of budget deficits followed by budget surpluses should be dimished with the prolonged use of the SBT.

More Equity in the Tax System

It was also believed that the old system of taxation permitted tax inequities to flourish in Michigan. Successful companies with large profits had an increasing corporate income tax burden to deal with and would, therefore, be penalized, whereas unprofitable companies would escape the income tax. Under the SBT, most companies would be paying a tax regardless of whether they are operating at a profit or loss. Profit companies would not have to subsidize unprofitable business ventures. It should be noted that although an unprofitable corporation could previously escape the income tax, it would still be subject to the franchise, property, and intangibles taxes.

Another change introduced with the SBT is the similar tax treatment designed for both labor-intense and capital-intense companies. In actuality, the tax may be slightly unfavorable for labor-intense industries, which is not surprising, since the capital-intense industries are the core of the Michigan economy. The tax incentive for capital-intense operations are provided through an immediate recovery of capital expenditures. By attempting to encourage and develop an even stronger manufacturing base in Michigan, this will, hopefully, provide for a stronger market for service-oriented industries as well.

The results should be of an operating nature. As the heavy burden on capital is removed, more capital investments can occur that can promote more job opportunities in the state, thereby increasing productivity and the potential for more capital investments.

Finally, the SBT should discourage businesses from making any unsound economic decisions in an effort to reduce tax liabilities. Under the previous system of taxation, action taken by a business to minimize one of Michigan's taxes could tend to be contrary to any actions that could economically benefit the community. For example, the corporate franchise tax would represent a greater burden for large manufacturing industries, with the tax liability being influenced by the accounting practices used by the company. The property tax on inventory would be more restrictive for retail and wholesale concerns. By the very nature of both of these taxes, any management decision to reduce these tax liabilities would also have an impact on various internal business policies. In contrast, the SBT is designed so that it will not be a major consideration in any "uneconomic decisions" to reduce tax liabilities. The tax base is the amount of income paid by a company to its owners (profits, interest, and depreciation) and to its employees (wages and fringe benefits) to make its product or to provide a service.[12] The tax base will be representative of the economic size of each business.

Who Is Subject to the Michigan SBT?

The Michigan SBT is imposed on the adjusted tax base of every person that has business activity within Michigan which is allocated or apportioned to the state.[13] Two requirements must be met before a SBT return is required to be filed. First, a potential taxpayer must fall within the definition of a "person"; second, this taxpayer must have business activity within Michigan.

A "person" is defined in Section 6(1)[14] as including the following:

1   Individual.
2   Firm.
3   Bank.
4   Financial institution.
5   Limited partnership.
6   Copartnership.
7   Partnership.
8   Joint venture.
9   Association.
10   Corporation.
11   Receiver.
12   Estate.
13   Trust.
14   Or any other group or combination acting as a unit.

Since a corporation is clearly a "person," it will be subject to the SBT if it can meet the business activity test.

Section 3(2)[15] provides a very broad definition for business activity that includes the following:

---

[12]Goodman, "Michigan's Single Business Tax", p. 215.
[13]Michigan Single Business Tax Act Section 208.31.
[14]Michigan Single Business Tax Act Section 208.6.
[15]Michigan Single Business Tax Act Section 208.3

. . . a transfer of legal or equitable title to or rental of property, whether real, personal, or mixed, tangible or intangible, or the performance of services, or any combination thereof, made or engaged in, or caused to be made or engaged in, within this state, whether in intrastate, interstate, or foreign commerce, with the object of gain, benefit, or advantage, whether direct or indirect, to the taxpayer or to others, but shall not include the services rendered by an employee to his employer or a casual transaction. Although an activity of a taxpayer may be incidental to another or other of his business activities, each activity shall be considered to be business engaged in within the meaning of this act.

The two types of activities clearly not covered by this definition are the services rendered by an employee to his employer or any casual transaction engaged in other than in the ordinary course of business. If the casual transaction is incidental to that person's regular business activity, it will fall within the limits of the business activity definition.[16] All other transactions engaged in or "caused to be made or engaged in" Michigan in intrastate, interstate, or foreign commerce will also fall within the limits of this definition. The ability of Michigan to tax any transaction falling into this category will depend on its constitutional rights.[17]

Once it is determined that a corporation's activities can constitutionally be subject to the Michigan SBT, data can be accumulated for the tax base and the necessary tax computations can be made.

MECHANICS OF THE SBT

The first step in computing the SBT is the determination of the tax base. The *tax base* is defined as meaning business income, even if it is zero or a negative amount.[18] *Business income* is then defined for a corporation as meaning Federal taxable income,[19] as it is defined in Section 63 of the IRC.[20] This means that for a corporation the distinction between business and nonbusiness income, which has been a very important issue in state taxes, is no longer used. All corporate income is deemed to be business income. For persons other than a corporation, business income is defined to mean that part of Federal taxable income derived from business activity.

Since the SBT is essentially a consumption type VAT, the tax base consists of economic profits and the cost of goods and services purchased from those who are not SBT taxpayers.

[16]Michigan Single Business Tax Act, Section 208.4.
[17]See the section in this chapter concerning the Federal and constitutional limitations of the Michigan SBT.
[18]Michigan Single Business Tax Act Section 208.9
[19]Michigan Single Business Tax Act Section 208.3(3).
[20]Michigan Single Business Tax Act Section 208.5(3).

Economic Profits as a Part of the Michigan Tax Base

The corporation's Federal taxable income (Line 30, Form 1120, or Line 28, Form 1120S) is the starting point in the conversion of taxable income into economic profit. Exhibit 6.4 represents a list and explanation of the adjustments[21] necessary to convert Federal taxable income into an economic profit.

All these 12 adjustments are a necessary step in changing Federal taxable income into the Michigan SBT base. However, as previously stated, this listing represents only one component of the tax base. The amount paid for goods and services to non-SBT taxpayers, namely, compensation paid to employees, must now be added to the economic profit. This is the second step in arriving at the SBT base.

Compensation as a Part of the Michigan Tax Base

Compensation deals with amounts paid to employees and former employees, since all other persons engaged in business activities would be SBT taxpayers themselves.

Compensation is defined[22] as follows:

> . . . all wages, salaries, fees, bonuses, commissions, or other payments made in the taxable year on behalf of or for the benefit of employees, officers, or directors of the taxpayers and subject to or specifically exempt from withholding under section 3401 of the internal revenue code. Compensation includes, on a cash or accrual basis consistent with the taxpayer's method of accounting for federal income tax purposes, payments to state and federal unemployment compensation funds, payments under the federal insurance contribution act, and similar social insurance contribution act, and similar social insurance programs, payments, including self-insurance, for workmen's compensation insurance, payments to individuals not currently working, payments to dependents and heirs of individuals because of current or former labor services rendered by those individuals, payments to a pension, retirement, or profit sharing plan, and payment for insurance for which employees are the beneficiaries. Compensation does not include discounts on the price of the taxpayer's merchandise or services sold to the taxpayer's employees, officers, or directors which are not available to other customers or payments to an independent contractor.

Compensation is perhaps one of the most unusual items to compute, since the definition of compensation for the SBT is unlike the definition of compensation for income tax purposes. However, the Michigan Department of Treasury has indicated the accounting methods to be used in adding compensation to the tax base for the SBT.

---

[21]Michigan Single Business Tax Act Section 208.9.
[22]Michigan Single Business Tax Act Section 208.4(3).

Exhibit 6.4

Adjustment	Explanation

Additions to Federal Taxable Income

1 Depreciation and other write-offs of tangible assets

This includes all depreciation, amortization, or immediate or accelerated write-off of tangible assets that have been deducted on the Federal return. Prior to 1977, 100 percent of the depreciation was added back for only those assets for which a capital acquisition deduction was claimed under Section 23 of the SBT Act and 72 percent for other depreciation, amortization, or immediate or accelerated write-offs related to the cost of other tangible assets.[a]

The 100 percent add-back is consistent with a consumption type value added tax where the entire cost of acquiring a capital asset is deducted in the year it is paid for or accrued. If this add-back were not made, a double deduction would result. The 72 percent add-back in use only during 1976 was inconsistent with the consumption type VAT, since no capital acquisition deduction was permitted for this group of assets, and it therefore placed a tax on depreciation.

2 Taxes imposed on or measured by income from city, state, or foreign sources

This addition is designed to eliminate an artificial deduction that was allowed in computing Federal taxable income. The add-back of these taxes, along with the others in this list, allows the Federal taxable income to become more in line with the concept of computing economic profits. Note that the taxes based on capital, sales taxes, or intangible taxes are not included in this list, since they are not taxes based on or measured by income.

3 SBT

The SBT deducted on the Federal tax return must be added back to arrive at economic profits on which the current SBT will be based.

4 Dividends, interest, royalties

Dividends are added back to Federal taxable income, since the deduction permitted for Federal purposes once again is arbitrary in terms of the economic profit concept. The add-back simply allows a reduction in taxable income subject to a net income tax, and

Exhibit 6.4 *(continued)*

Adjustment	Explanation

the SBT is concerned with a value added concept. Dividends that represent reductions of premiums to policy holders of insurance companies are excluded[b] from this add-back, since they cannot be considered in the same category as those other "arbitrary" dividend deductions.

Most interest and all royalties are added back, since they are nonproductive expenses, and therefore, this add-back is consistent with the theory behind the VAT. Interest paid, credited, or reserved by insurance companies as amounts necessary to fulfill the policy and other contract liability requirements of sections 805 and 809 of the IRC are not added back.[c] Also, interest payments made by a financial organization would not be added back, since these would be productive expenses.

There is an inconsistency with the VAT concept here, in that rent expenses are not included in this category of add-backs.

5 Capital loss carryover or carryback

Any carryback or carryforward of a capital loss incurred after January 1, 1976 (the date the SBT became effective) is added back so that there will be complete inclusion of capital income in the SBT base.[d] (Individuals only would also add back any capital gains related to business activities that were excluded under Section 1202 of the IRC. This add-back would hopefully eliminate another deduction allowed by the IRC that is not pertinent to the SBT computation.)

6 NOL, carryover or carryback

Once again, the adding back of the NOL can be considered a step in eliminating artificial adjustments or deductions acceptable in computing Federal income taxes.[e] To not add back an NOL incurred by a company would be straying from the purpose of these adjustments: to compute economic profits of the company.

Since the SBT became effective on January 1, 1976, any unused Michigan Corporate Income Tax NOL as of December 31, 1975,

Exhibit 6.4 *(continued)*

Adjustment	Explanation

could only be carried forward five years or through December 31, 1980.[f]

7 Gross interest and dividend income from bonds and similar obligations derived from states other than Michigan and political subdivisions thereof

Interest income and dividends derived from obligations or securities of states other than Michigan not previously included in Federal taxable income, less related expenses not deducted in computing Federal taxable income because of Section 265 of the IRC, must be added back to Federal taxable income.[g] This provision is inconsistent with the theory of a VAT and seems to be politically motivated by favoring and encouraging the sale of Michigan municipals and other obligations to the SBT taxpayer.

Except for financial organizations, interest income that has been included in computing Federal taxable income must be excluded in computing the SBT base.[h] This provision is the only exception to this rule.

8 Disc, Western Hemisphere Trade Corporation, China Trade Act Corporation

The add-back of these special exclusions or deductions is done because they were specifically designed to reduce or postpone the Federal income tax liability. The add-back will eliminate these artificial deductions. This section does not apply to the special provisions of Sections 805, 815(C)(2)(A), 809, 823(C), and 824(A) of the IRC.[i]

9 Losses from partnerships

For all partners that are corporations, the pro rata share of partnership losses deducted in arriving at business income must be added back to Federal taxable income.

The Michigan Department of Treasury has administratively decided to permit a corporate partner to deduct its pro rata share of partnership income and add back its pro rata share of partnership losses.[j]

Subtractions from Federal Taxable Income

10 Dividends, interest, and royalty income

All royalty, interest, and dividends received or deemed received, including all foreign dividend gross up provided for in the IRC, are deducted to the extent included in Federal taxable income.[k]

Exhibit 6.4 *(continued)*

Adjustment	Explanation
	This does not include interest income received by a financial organization or dividends allowed as a dividend received deduction on the Federal return.
	The purpose of these deductions is to eliminate passive income. These items should not be considered in determining the value added by the taxpayer simply because they
11 Capital losses not deducted computing Federal taxable income	This provision allows for the deduction of capital losses not deducted in computing Federal taxable income in the year the loss occurred.[l] Theoretically, all capital gains should be included in the tax base, and all capital losses should be deducted, since Section 208.9(4)(b) of the Michigan law requires the add-back of capital losses deducted in computing Federal taxable income.
	The tax base is still going to include the capital losses deducted in computing Federal taxable income as opposed to capital losses not so deducted which discriminate in favor of taxpayers that had no capital gains against which to offset capital losses.[m]
12 Income from partnerships	The Michigan Department of Treasury has administratively elected to permit a corporation's pro rata share of income to be excluded from the SBT base. See item 9.

[a]Michigan Single Business Tax Act Section 208.9(4).
[b]Michigan Single Business Tax Act Section 208.9(4)(d).
[c]Michigan Single Business Tax Act Section 208.9(4)(f).
[d]Michigan Single Business Tax Act Section 208.9(4)(b).
[e]Michigan Single Business Tax Act Section 208.9(4)(a).
[f]Commerce Clearing House Publications, *Michigan State Tax Reporter*, Michigan Single Business Tax Division Releases, Single Business Tax Questions and Answers Volume II, 19-002, Question 12: (October 20, 1975).
[g]Michigan Single Business Tax Act Section 208.9(2).
[h]Michigan Single Business Tax Act Section 208.21.
[i]Michigan Single Business Tax Act Section 208.9(4)(e).
[j]Michigan Department of Treasury SBT Returns and Instructions.
[k]Michigan Single Business Tax Act Section 208.9(7)(a)(b)(c).
[l]Michigan Single Business Tax Act Section 208.9(8).
[m]McKim ''Michigan Single Business Tax Seen as a Vat,'' p. 34.

Wages, salaries, fees, bonuses, commissions, or any other payments made on behalf of or for the benefit of employees, officers, or directors and subject to or specifically exempt from Federal income tax withholding must be reported on a cash basis. The amount subject to withholding can be obtained from U.S. tax Form 941. Payroll taxes and all other fringe benefits are reported on either a cash or accrual basis, whichever is consistent with a taxpayer's method of accounting for Federal income tax purposes.[23]

The following are some of the items included in the definition of compensation.[24]

1   Payroll taxes.

2   Employee insurance plans.

3   Salaries, wages.

4   Gifts to employees.

5   Reimbursement of employee's expense.

6   Payroll paid from a Federal grant.

7   Tips reported to the employee and considered in determining the employee's compensation under the minimum wage law.

8   Automatic service charges when paid to the employee.

9   Directors' fees.

10   Fringe benefits included in an inventory of work in progress, whether on a cash or accrual basis.

11   Capitalized labor costs.

12   Labor included in inventory and work in process.

13   Employers' cost of training programs determined to be compensation for the purpose of Federal income tax withholding.

From the total of all payments made on behalf of or for the benefit of employees or officers, a special exemption was given that expired December 31, 1979. This was a 50 percent exemption for the compensation directly related to the completion of construction contracts for the planning, designing, construction, alteration, repair, or improvement of real property. A bid must have been submitted or a contract signed before September 1, 1975, for this exemption to have applied.[25]

---

[23]Commerce Clearing House Publications *Michigan State Tax Reporter,* Michigan Single Business Tax Division Releases, Single Business Tax Questions and Answers Volume III, 19-003, Question 7.

[24]Michigan Single Business Tax Act Section 208.4(3), Single Business Tax Questions and Answers, Vol. I (September 15, 1975), Volume 4 (April 21, 1976), Vol. 5 (June 15, 1976), Vol. 6, (August 23, 1976), Vol. 7 (October 22, 1976), Vol. 11 (March 24, 1978), Commerce Clearing House, *Michigan State Tax Reporters.* Michigan Single Business Tax Division Release.

[25]Michigan Single Business Tax Act Section 208.35(f).

Tax Base for Financial Organizations

Once the necessary computations have been made, as illustrated in Exhibit 6.5, the tax base will be defined for the SBT. However, for financial organizations, there will be a special base that does not exclude interest income and does not require interest expenses to be added back.[26] If this special adjustment were not made, many financial institutions could possibly have escaped being subject to the SBT.

Exhibit 6.5 Computation of a Michigan Tax Base

The following data are for the Western Corporation for the taxable year ended December 31, 1979:

Federal taxable income	$150,000
Depreciation	20,000
Depreciation computed using the Asset Depreciation Range (ADR)	50,000
Taxes based on income and SBT	40,000
Capital loss not deducted in computing Federal taxable income	60,000
Interest income	85,000
Dividend income (net of dividends received deduction)	25,000
Interest expense	15,000
Royalties paid	5,000
Wages and salaries	50,000
Director fees	15,000
Payroll taxes	15,000
Employee insurance plans	10,000

The Michigan tax base would be computed as follows:

Federal taxable income and compensation		$150,000
Wages and salaries	$50,000	
Director fees	15,000	
Payroll taxes	15,000	
Employee insurance plans	10,000	90,000
+ Additions: Depreciation	$20,000	
Depreciation using ADR	50,000	
Taxes based on income and SBT	40,000	
Interest expense	15,000	
Royalties paid	5,000	130,000
− Subtractions: Capital loss	$60,000	
Interest income	85,000	
Dividend income (net)	25,000	(170,000)
Michigan tax base		$200,000

---

[26]Michigan Single Business Tax Act Section 208.21.

A financial organization is defined to include the following[27]:

> . . . a bank, industrial bank, trust company, building, and loan or savings and loan association, bank holding company as defined in 12 U.S.C. 1841, credit union, safety and collateral deposit company, regulated investment company as defined in the internal revenue code, and any other association, joint stock company, or corporation at least 90% of whose assets consist of intangible personal property and at least 90% of whose gross receipts income consists of dividends or interest or other charges resulting from the use of money or credit.

Therefore, for any financial organization falling within this definition, the gross receipts would include all interest and dividend income. This means the gross interest income derived from obligations of states and their political subdivisions, including Michigan, that was excluded from Federal taxable income would be included in the gross receipts.[28]

Allocation and Apportionment of the Tax Base

Once the tax base is computed, the entire amount can be allocated or apportioned to Michigan. If a corporation has all its business activities solely within Michigan, the entire tax base will be allocated to the state tax.[29] If a corporation has taxable activities both in Michigan and another state the entire tax base will be subject to apportionment.[30] A corporation is taxable in another state if it is subject to a business privilege tax, a net income tax, a franchise tax measured by net income, a franchise tax for the privilege of doing business, a corporate stock tax, or a tax similar to the SBT or if a state simply has the jurisdiction to subject the corporation to one or more of these taxes.[31] Note the similarity between this provision and that provided for in UDITPA's Section 3, The SBT provisions also follow substantially the UDITPA apportionment formula or the three-factor Massachusetts formula or property, payroll, and sales, with some important variations that are noted in Exhibit 6.6.

Based on the data of Exhibit 6.7, the schedule for the Michigan SBT apportionment formula, Form C-8000H, can be completed as shown in Exhibit 6.8.

---

[27]Michigan Single Business Tax Act Section 208.10(4).
[28]Commerce Clearing House Publications *Michigan State Tax Reporter,* Michigan Single Business Tax Division Releases, Single Business Tax Questions and Answers Volume XII (August 10, 1978).
[29]Michigan Single Business Tax Act Section 208.40.
[30]Michigan Single Business Tax Act Section 208.41.
[31]Michigan Single Business Tax Act Section 208.42.

Exhibit 6.6

Factor	Comments
Property[a] Average value real and tangible personal property owned or rented in Michigan <hr> Average value of all real and tangible personal property owned or rented everywhere	This property factor is almost the same as the UDITPA formula, except that the UDITPA provisions refer to property that not only is owned or rented but also is used by the taxpayer in the regular course of trade or business.[b] The reason for this distinction is related to the tax base being apportioned. UDITPA deals with the apportionment of business income, whereas the SBT deals with the apportionment of an entire tax base. Since the SBT base does not distinguish between business and non-business income for the corporation, the requirement that property be used in the business is not necessary.
Payroll[c] Wages paid in state by taxpayer <hr> Wages paid everywhere	This factor is the same as the UDITPA provision. However, the concept for determining this payroll factor is completely different from the concept for determining "compensation" that is required to be added to business income in computing the apportionable tax base. The wages used in the payroll factor deal only with wages as they are defined in Section 3401 of the IRC. For example, an item such as fringe benefits would be included in the definition of compensation but would be excluded from the payroll apportionment formula.[d] Furthermore, the wages are to be included in the factor on a cash or accrual basis consistent with the taxpayer's method of accounting.[e] Compensation included in the tax base must be on a cash basis.
Sales[f] Total sales within Michigan <hr> Total sales everywhere	The sales factor varies the most from the UDITPA factor. First, sales are defined differently in each case. UDITPA defines *sales* to mean all gross receipts derived by the taxpayer from transactions occurring in the regular course of business that are not allocated.[g] The SBT defines *sales* as meaning gross receipts arising from a transaction in which gross receipts constitute consideration: "...a) for the transfer of title to, or possession of, property that is stock in trade

Exhibit 6.6 *(continued)*

Factor	Comments
	or other property of a kind which would properly be included in the inventory of the taxpayer if on hand at the close of the tax period or property held by the taxpayer primarily for sale to customers in the ordinary course of its trade or business, or b) for the performance of services, which constitute business activities other than those included in (a), or from any combination of (a) or (b)."[h]
	The SBT then goes on to define gross receipts as follows:
	"The sum of sales, as defined in subsection (1) and rental or lease receipts..."[i]
	This means that the sales factor for the SBT will not include passive income such as rent, interest, or dividend income. Capital gain proceeds will also not be included.
	In addition to this distinction between the much narrower SBT sales factor and the all-encompassing UDITPA sales or gross receipts factor, there is a distinction in the SBT law itself. In Section 208.3(2) of the SBT Act, *business activity* is defined to mean a transfer of legal or equitable title to or rental of property. In Section 208.7(1), *sales* is defined to mean gross receipts from the transfer of title to or possession of property that is stock in trade or inventory. The transfer of title is more narrow in the definition of the sales factor. However, the Section 208.7(1) definition of gross receipts received as consideration for the performance of services would cover all services that involved a business activity as defined in Section 208.3(2).[j]
	Second, the throw-back provision of the sales factor specifically defines the term "state."[k] This means that property shipped from a location in Michigan and not taxable in the state of the purchaser would be considered a sale in Michigan only if the other "state" were a state in the United States, the District of Columbia, the commonwealth of Puerto Rico, or any territory or possession

Exhibit 6.6 *(continued)*

Factor	Comments
	of the United States. Accordingly, a sale to a foreign country would not be included in the sales factor numerator but would be included in the denominator.[l]
	Finally, careful attention should be given to the section which deals with sales other than tangible personal property.[m] The sales are deemed to be in Michigan if the business activity is performed in the state, and a cost of performance is used to evaluate whether a greater proportion of the business activity is performed inside or outside Michigan. Furthermore, there is a specific provision that receipts derived from services performed for planning, design, or construction activities within the state will be deemed to be Michigan receipts.

[a]Michigan Single Business Tax Act Section 208.46.

[b]UDITPA—Paragraphs 10, 11, 12.

[c]Michigan Single Business Tax Act. Section 208.49.

[d]Commerce Clearing House Publications, *Michigan State Tax Reporter,* Michigan Single Business Tax Division Releases, Single Business Tax Questions and Answers Volume I (September 15, 1975).

[e]Commerce Clearing House Publications, *Michigan State Tax Reporter,* Michigan Single Business Tax Division Releases, Single Business Tax Questions and Answers Volume XII (March 24, 1978).

[f]Michigan Single Business Tax Act. Section 208.51.

[g]UDITPA—Section 1(g).

[h]Michigan Single Business Tax Act Section 208.7(1).

[i]Michigan Single Business Tax Act Section 208.7(3).

[j]McKim "Michigan Single Business Tax Seen as a Vat."

[k]Michigan Single Business Tax Act Section 208.52(b).

[l]Commerce Clearing House Publications, *Michigan State Tax Reporter,* Michigan Single Business Tax Division Releases, Single Business Tax Questions and Answers Volume I, No. 15 (September 15, 1975) and Volume III, No. 9.

[m]Michigan Single Business Tax Act Section 208.53.

Special Apportionment Procedures

In addition to the apportionment formula previously reviewed, there are several special apportionment formulas that will be used in the appropriate circumstances. For transportation companies, the ratio used is dependent

Exhibit 6.7

Apportionment Data			

Property *Michigan*	Beginning of the Year Values	End of Year	Average
Owned and not in use	$ 50,000	$ 50,000	$ 50,000
Owned and used	$135,000	$225,000	$ 180,000
			$ 230,000
Michigan Rentals		$ 3,000 × 8 =	24,000
			$ 254,000
Everywhere			
Owned and not in use	$300,000	$400,000	$ 350,000
Owned and used	$750,000	$850,000	$ 800,000
			$1,150,000
Total rentals		$ 15,000 × 8 =	120,000
			$1,270,000
Payroll		*Sales*	
Michigan	$125,000	Michigan: Sales of	
Everywhere	$650,000	Tangible	
		Property	$ 75,000
		+ Throw-back sales	2,000
			$ 77,000
		Everywhere:	$ 950,000

on the product being transported.[32] Domestic insurers will also have a variation in the formula,[33] as will financial organizations,[34] and some companies with sales not exceeding $100,000.[35]

Finally, there is an alternative method that can be used if the apportionment provisions of the SBT Act do not fairly represent the extent of a taxpayer's business in the state. A taxpayer can petition for, or the Commissioner could require, if reasonable, separate accounting, the exclusion of one or more factors, the inclusion of one or more additional factors that will fairly represent the taxpayer's business activity in Michigan, or the use of any other method to effectuate an equitable allocation and apportionment of the tax base.[36] This provision is almost the same as the

[32]Michigan Single Business Tax Act Sections 208.56, 208.57, 208.58.
[32]Michigan Single Business Tax Act Section 208.62.
[34]Michigan Single Business Tax Act Section 208.65.
[35]Michigan Single Business Tax Act Section 208.68.
[36]Michigan Single Business Tax Act Section 208.69.

MICHIGAN SINGLE BUSINESS TAX
APPORTIONMENT FORMULA

1979 ■

1. Name:	2. Account Number:
Example	XXXXX

To be used only by those taxpayers doing business in Michigan and one or more other states or foreign countries and who are taxable both within and without this state **(see instructions on reverse side)**

PART I Computation of apportionment percentage:

PROPERTY FACTOR*
3. Average Michigan property	**3.**	230,000 00	
4. Michigan rentals x 8	**4.**	24,000 00	
5. Total Michigan property (ADD lines 3 and 4)	5.	254,000 00	
6. Average total property	**6.**	1,150,000 00	
7. Total rentals x 8	**7.**	120,000 00	
8. Total property (ADD lines 6 and 7)	8.	1,270,000 00	
9. Percentage (DIVIDE line 5 by line 8)	9.		20 %

PAYROLL FACTOR
10. Michigan payroll	**10.**	125,000 00	
11. Total payroll	**11.**	650,000 00	
12. Percentage (DIVIDE line 10 by line 11)	12.		19.23076 %

SALES FACTOR
13. Michigan sales	**13.**	77,000 00	
14. Total sales	**14.**	950,000 00	
15. Percentage (DIVIDE line 13 by line 14)	15.		8.10526 %

16. Total percentage (ADD lines 9, 12 and 15)	16.		47.33602 %
17. Apportionment percentage (DIVIDE line 16 by 3, if less than 3 factors, divide by number of factor(s)**)	**17.**		15.778673 %

*The commissioner may require the periodic averaging of values during the tax year, if reasonably required to reflect properly the average value of the taxpayer's property.

**Number of factors are those factors (property, payroll, or sales) which have denominators (lines 8, 11 or 14, respectively) greater than zero.

PART II

TRANSPORTATION SERVICES, DOMESTIC INSURERS, FINANCIAL ORGANIZATIONS, OR
IF TAXPAYER IS AUTHORIZED TO USE A SPECIAL FORMULA, USE THE LINES PROVIDED BELOW
(Attach Explanation)

18. Michigan	**18.**	00	
19. Total	**19.**	00	
20. Apportionment percentage (DIVIDE line 18 by line 19)	**20.**		%

PART III

CAPITAL ACQUISITION APPORTIONMENT
(Apportionment Percentage For Capital Acquisition)

21. Property factor (from line 9)	21.	%	
22. Payroll factor (from line 12)	22.	%	
23. Total (ADD lines 21 and 22)	23.		%
24. Average percentage (DIVIDE line 23 by 2, if only 1 factor enter line 23)	**24.**		%

Exhibit 6.8 Michigan single business tax apportionment formula.

Section 18 provision of UDIPTA, allowing for possible alternative methods of allocation and apportionment.

Adjustments to the Apportioned Tax Base

After the taxpayer's tax base has been apportioned to Michigan, the appropriate adjustments can be made to arrive at the adjusted tax base. There are three basic types of adjustments. The first is related to a taxpayer's cost of depreciable or amortizable personal property and real property. The second concerns any business loss incurred by the taxpayer, and the third deals with an NOL.

Capital Asset Acquisition and Disposition

The capital acquisition adjustment allows the taxpayer to exclude the entire amount paid or accrued for capital assets from the apportioned tax base. This provides a cash flow advantage, since it allows the entire deduction in the year that the capital expenditure was incurred rather than depreciating the asset over its economic life. This concept follows the principles of a consumption type VAT that provides for the complete deduction on capital expenditures in the year incurred, thereby providing an advantage for a capital-oriented business. In this case, it is the taxpayers with capital in Michigan that receive the benefit. However, since the entire cost of the asset is excluded initially, the entire gross proceeds from the eventual sale of these assets will be added back when received or accrued.

DEPRECIABLE PERSONAL PROPERTY

The first deduction from the tax base is for the cost of depreciable or amortizable tangible personal property. The deduction is for the cost of tangible assets, including the cost of fabrication and installation, that are eligible for depreciation or amortization for Federal income tax purposes. Note than any capitalized fabrication and installation charges that were previously added back in computing the tax base as compensation are now being deducted from the apportioned tax base. Also, the cost of assets defined in Section 1250 of the IRC are excluded from this category of depreciable personal property.

Once the total amount of depreciable personal property is determined, it is multiplied by the following fraction:

$$\frac{\text{Payroll factor } + \text{ property factor[37]}}{2}$$

This formula is applied to the cost of these assets in an effort to establish situs. Since it is possible to shift the situs of assets every year, the use of

[37]Michigan Single Business Tax Act Section 208.23(a).

the formula allows a reasonable method for apportionment by the taxpayer. The use of this two-factor formula instead of the three-factor formula used in apportioning the SBT tax base provides a larger capital acquisition exclusion for those taxpayers with more property and payroll rather than sales activity in the state.

Since a deduction is provided for the acquisition of these assets, a recapture of the capital acquisition deduction must be made. This is accomplished by adding to the tax base the gross proceeds or benefit derived, minus the gain or plus the loss reflected in Federal taxable income, from the sale or other disposition of these tangible assets. Once the total amount subject to recapture is determined, it is multiplied by the following fraction:

$$\frac{\text{Payroll factor } + \text{ property factor}^{38}}{2}$$

The use of this two-factor formula for capital asset acquisition and disposition promotes several inconsistencies in the SBT computations.

As required in computing the tax base,[39] depreciation, amortization, or any other immediate or accelerated write-offs are added back to the base, and capital gains on the disposition of these same assets remain in the base, whereas capital losses not deducted in computing Federal taxable income are deducted. These adjustments are all made prior to apportionment using the three-factor formula.

The requirements of this section[40] have the gross proceeds from the sale of depreciable personal property adjusted by deducting any gain and adding any loss from the sale. It is illogical that this adjustment is to be apportioned by a two-factor formula before being added back to the tax base. Furthermore, if an alternative method to the three-factor formula for computing the apportioned tax base is used because of the nature of the company,[41] or by the provisions of Section 208.69 that allows alternative methods, an even greater inconsistency between the tax base and the adjustments to the tax bases will exist.

Finally, the property factor used considers both real and personal property owned or rented, which is substantially different from the amount being apportioned—only depreciable personal property.

DEPRECIABLE REAL PROPERTY

The second provision for the capital adjustment requires the taxpayer to do the following:

---

[38]Michigan Single Business Tax Act Section 208.23(b).
[39]Michigan Single Business Tax Act Section 208.9.
[40]Michigan Single Business Tax Act Section 208.23(b).
[41]Michigan Single Business Tax Act Sections 208.56, 208.57, 208.58, 208.62, 208.65.

Deduct the cost, including fabrication and installation, excluding the cost deducted under subdivision (a) paid or accrued in the taxable year of tangible assets of a type, which are, or under the internal revenue code will become eligible for depreciation or amortization for federal income tax purposes, provided that the assets are physically located in Michigan.[42]

This provision intends to allow the deduction for the entire cost, including fabrication and installation, of any Section 1250 property (referred to as depreciable real property), located in Michigan. Although the law does not specifically refer to Section 1250 property, the Michigan Department of Treasury has looked to the legislative intent of the law and even refers to Section 1250-type property on the tax Form C-8000D, SBT Capital Acquisition Adjustment.

There is no need to use a two-factor apportionment formula on the total depreciable real property located in Michigan, since there is no situs problem to contend with.

When the real property for which a capital acquisition exclusion deduction was claimed is finally sold, the gross proceeds or benefit derived from the sale are to be added to the tax base. Any gain will be deducted, and any loss will be added to the base after being multiplied by the three-factor apportionment formula. A capital gain that was included in computing Federal taxable income and in computing the tax base is subtracted here to prevent a double inclusion. Consider these two examples: (1) the construction of a building located in Michigan began July 1, 1977, and was completed June 30, 1978. A total cost of $100,000 was paid or accrued in 1977 and $200,000 was paid or accrued in 1978. The cost of $200,000 qualifies for the capital acquisition deduction for the taxable year 1978.[43] (2) During 1978, the XYZ Corporation made the following acquisitions:

Real property	$125,000
Machinery	$ 50,000
Office furniture	$ 15,000

Using this information, Form C-8000D would be completed as illustrated in Exhibit 6.9.

Business Loss

After a taxpayer has made the capital acquisition adjustment to the apportioned tax base, it may be possible for a taxpayer to arrive at a negative adjusted tax base. If a substantial amount of capital acquisition expenditures are made during the year, this would account for a significant deduction from the apportioned tax base, resulting in a loss figure. This

[42]Michigan Single Business Tax Act Section 208.23(c).
[43]Michigan Department of Treasury Single Business Tax Returns and Instructions, 1978, Instructions for C-8000D: Capital Acquisition Adjustment.

SINGLE BUSINESS TAX
CAPITAL ACQUISITION ADJUSTMENT

(see instructions, page 9)

1979 ■

1 Name	2 Account Number
XYZ Corporation	12345

CAPITAL ACQUISITION DEDUCTION

PART I Acquisition of depreciable real property located in Michigan and acquired during taxable year (section 1250 IRC type property).

a Description	b Location	c Date Acquired	d Cost Paid or Accrued During Taxable Year
3 3-5 Acres of Farm Land	125 West Northside Rd.	5-15-79	125,000

4 TOTAL depreciable real property located in Michigan	4	125,000	00

PART II Acquisition of depreciable personal property acquired during taxable year (other than section 1250 IRC type property).

a Description	b Location	c Date Acquired	d Cost Paid or Accrued During Taxable Year
5 Manufacturing Machinery	1074 East Pontiac	3-10-79	50,000
Office Furniture	1074 East Pontiac	11-24-79	15,000

6 TOTAL depreciable personal property	6	65,000	00
If taxable in another state complete line 7.			
7 Apportioned depreciable personal property—Multiply line 6 by % from C-8000H, line 24	7	6,825	00

PART III Total Deduction

8 TOTAL CAPITAL ACQUISITION DEDUCTION (Add lines 4 and 6 or 7, whichever is applicable, enter here and on C-8000, page 1, line 13a)	8	131,825	00

Note: If more space is needed, submit a separate schedule and enter totals on lines 4 and 6.

Exhibit 6.9 Form C-8000D: Michigan capital acquisition adjustment.

negative amount is defined as a "business loss."[44] This business loss can be carried forward as a deduction for the next 10 years.

Net Operating Loss (NOL)

While the Michigan income tax was in effect prior to the enactment of the SBT, a taxpayer could have incurred a substantial NOL. The SBT allows these losses to be carried forward as a deduction from the tax base but only through the year ended December 31, 1980.[45]

Exemptions

Standard Exemption

After the adjusted tax base has been computed, it can be adjusted even further with certain exemptions provided in the law. There is an annual exemption of $40,000 for every person in 1977 and the following years.[46] This exemption is then increased $12,000 for each partner of a partnership or shareholder of a Subchapter S corporation or professional corporation in excess of one providing that these conditions are met:

1 The partners or shareholders are full-time employees.
2 Business income from the business is at least $12,000.
3 The taxpayer owns at least 10 percent of the business.

The total increased exemption cannot exceed $48,000. Also, the exemption is reduced $2 for each $1 that business income exceeds the amount of the exemption.

The business income is computed as follows:

Business income for a corporation = Federal taxable income

    + compensation and director's fees of shareholders of a corporation

    + Any carryback or carryforward of an NOL or capital loss to the extent deducted in arriving at Federal taxable income

For those taxpayers whose business activity is for a fractional part of the year, the exemption must be prorated for the period of the taxpayers business activity.

---

[44]Michigan Single Business Tax Act Section 208.23(e).
[45]Michigan Single Business Tax Act Section 208.23(f).
[46]Michigan Single Business Tax Act Section 208.35(1). This exemption was $34,000 in 1976 and $36,000 for 1977 before Act 273, Laws 1977.

Exempt Organizations, Payroll, and Compensation Exemptions

The SBT also exempts the United States, a state, an agency and political subdivisions or enterprises of each;[47] certain persons not required to pay Federal income tax,[48] and foreign insurance companies whose tax base is derived from the business activities of insurance carrier services.[49] An organization exempt under the IRC would still be subject to the SBT, based on its activities that create any unrelated taxable business income.

The SBT also exempts a portion of the payroll of domestic insurers or of some marketing corporations primarily concerned with the adjustment of claims.[50] Also, 50 percent of the compensation related to the completion of construction contracts for the planning, design, construction, alteration, repair, or improvement of real property is exempted, if a bid had been submitted on a contract signed on or before September 1, 1975.[51]

Special Adjustments

There are two basic benefits from the original SBT that act as "circuit breakers" to limit the size of the adjusted tax base. These were designed to alleviate any harsh treatment the SBT presented for certain groups. There are also special adjustments available that are of interest on a more limited basis. Although a corporation may be eligible for more than one special adjustment, only one may be used in any given tax year.

Gross Receipts Limitation

The first special adjustment is a gross receipts limitation. The gross receipts limitation provides that if the adjusted tax base of a taxpayer exceeds 50 percent of the gross receipts of the taxpayer that have been apportioned to Michigan, plus the adjustments for the recapture of the capital acquisition deduction, the taxpayer may reduce the adjusted tax base by such excess.[52] Once again, gross receipts would include only the sum of sales, as defined in Section 208.7(1), and rental or lease receipts.[53]

Gross receipts limitation = adjusted tax base − (50% of gross receipts + adjustments)

Labor-Intensity Adjustment

The second adjustment is particularly beneficial for those taxpayers with an intense labor involvement within Michigan. The labor-intensity deduction

[47]Michigan Single Business Tax Act, Section 208.35(b).
[48]Michigan Single Business Tax Act, Section 208.35(c).
[49]Michigan Single Business Tax Act Section 208.35(d).
[50]Michigan Single Business Tax Act Section 208.35(e).
[51]Michigan Single Business Tax Act Section 208.35(f). This subsection expired December 31, 1979.
[52]Michigan Single Business Tax Act Sections 208.23(b) and (d).
[53]Michigan Single Business Tax Act Section 208.7(3).

allows the taxpayer to reduce the adjusted tax base by the percentage that the compensation divided by the tax base exceeds 63 percent. However, this deduction cannot exceed 37 percent of the adjusted tax base.[54]

Labor-intensity deduction = labor-intensity deduction factor − 63 percent × Michigan adjusted tax base

Labor-intensity deduction factor = total compensation added

$$\frac{\text{to Federal taxable income}}{\text{Michigan tax base}}$$

Note that when the total tax base is being considered for the labor-intensity factor just illustrated, any depreciation, amortization, or immediate or accelerated write-off related to tangible assets which was not previously added to Federal taxable income in computing the tax base must be added back.[55] Furthermore, when the term "tax base" is used, it shall not include the effect of the capital acquisition deduction, business loss carry-over, or NOL carry-over.[56] This is true not only for the labor-intensity deduction but also for the special interest deductions explained in the next section. Since these three Section 23 adjustments (capital acquisition, business loss, NOL) are made to the tax base rather than the adjusted tax base the reference to them in this section is superfluous. As explained earlier, these three adjustments are not made until after the tax base has been computed.

As an example of the foregoing discussion, consider the following data for the Crane Corporation for its taxable year ended December 31, 1978. With the information provided one can compute both the gross receipts and labor-intensity reductions on Form C-8000S (Exhibit 6.10). The reduction that is more beneficial will be the one used.

Tax base	$300,000
Adjusted tax base	195,000
Compensation	100,000
Gross receipts	100,000
Recapture of capital acquisition deduction	5,000
Three-factor apportionment percentage	18.75%

The gross receipts limitation will be applicable in this example, since the adjusted tax base greatly exceeds 50 percent of the apportioned gross receipts added to the capital acquisition recapture. The labor-intensity reduction is not even applicable.

Other Special Interest Adjustments

There are also other adjustments to the adjusted tax base available to special interest groups. For example, there is an adjustment for a person

[54]Michigan Single Business Tax Act Section 208.31(5).
[55]Michigan Single Business Tax Act Section 208.31(8).
[56]Michigan Single Business Tax Act Section 208.31(8).

C-8000S

SINGLE BUSINESS TAX
REDUCTIONS TO ADJUSTED TAX BASE

See instructions on reverse side

1979

1 Name:	2 Account Number:

PART I COMPENSATION REDUCTION

PERCENT OF TAX BASE

3	Compensation (from C-8000, page 1, line 8)...	3	100,000 | 00
4	Tax base (from C-8000, page 1, line 12a)...	4	300,000 | 00
5	Percentage—Divide line 3 by line 4	5	33.3333 %

COMPUTATION OF REDUCTION

6	Adjusted tax base (from C-8000, page 1, line 20)..	6	195,000 | 00
7	Percentage on line 5 that exceeds 63% (not to exceed 37%)	7	0 %
8	Reduction to adjusted tax base—Multiply line 6 by line 7, enter here and on C-8000, page 1, line 21....	8	None | 00

PART II RETAIL FOOD STORE   If 75% or more of gross receipts is retail sales of food exempt from sales tax. (Complete lines 3-5 of Part I)

9	Adjusted tax base (from C-8000, page 1, line 20)..	9	| 00
10	Percentage on line 5 that exceeds 40% (45% for 1980) but not to exceed 60% (55% for 1980)	10	%
11	Reduction to adjusted tax base—Multiply line 9 by line 10, enter here and on C-8000, page 1, line 21....	11	| 00

PART III SPECIAL REDUCTIONS   Granted in Sec. 31(7) (See instruction on reverse side) (Complete lines 3-5 of Part I)

12	Adjusted tax base (from C-8000, page 1, line 20)..	12	| 00
13	Percentage on line 5 that exceeds 45% (50% for 1980) but not to exceed 55% (50% for 1980)..	13	%
14	Reduction to adjusted tax base—Multiply line 12 by line 13, enter here and on C-8000, page 1, line 21....	14	| 00

PART IV GROSS RECEIPTS REDUCTION

ADJUSTED GROSS RECEIPTS

15	Gross receipts (from C-8000, page 1, line 6) (If taxable in another state, complete line 16).............	15	100,000 | 00
16	Apportioned gross receipts—Multiply line 15 by % from C-8000H, line 17 or line 20, whichever is applicable	16	18,750 | 00
17	Recapture of capital acquisition deduction (from C-8000, page 1, line 13b).............................	17	5,000 | 00
18	Adjusted gross receipts—Add lines 15 or 16, whichever is applicable, and line 17—..................	18	23,750 | 00
	If short method elected, enter 50% of line 18 on C-8000, page 1, line 22		

COMPUTATION OF REDUCTION

19	Adjusted tax base (from C-8000, page 1, line 20)	19	195,000 | 00
20	Gross receipts limitation—Multiply line 18 by 50%	20	11,875 | 00
21	Reduction to adjusted tax base		
	(Subtract line 20 from line 19, enter here and on C-8000, page 1, line 21—**cannot be less than zero**)..... 21		183,125 | 00

PART V RENTAL INVESTMENTS (Complete lines 15-18 of Part IV)

22	Adjusted tax base (from C-8000, page 1, line 20)..	22	| 00
23	Gross receipts limitation—Multiply line 18 by 41% (44% for 1980)...............................	23	| 00
24	Reduction to adjusted tax base		
	(Subtract line 23 from line 22, enter here and on C-8000, page 1, line 21—**cannot be less than zero**)..... 24		| 00

NOTE: PLEASE IDENTIFY REDUCTION METHOD BY CHECKING APPROPRIATE BOX ON C-8000, PAGE 1, LINE 21.

Exhibit 6.10   Single business tax reductions to adjusted tax base.

whose interest paid and depreciation on assets acquired before January 1, 1976, comprise 70 percent of more of the adjusted tax base derived from rental investments. The taxpayer would be entitled to a "rental investment reduction" that is limited to the amount in excess of the following amounts that have been apportioned to Michigan[57]:

> 38% of gross receipts in 1978.
>
> 41% of gross receipts in 1979.
>
> 44% of gross receipts in 1980.
>
> 47% of gross receipts in 1981.
>
> 50% of gross receipts in 1982.

For those taxpayers whose business includes the retail sale of food for human consumption, there is a different adjustment, provided the gross receipts from these taxpayers' equal 75 percent or more of total gross receipts. The reduction to the adjusted tax base is the percentage that compensation divided by the total tax base exceeds the following:

> 35% in 1978 but does not exceed 65%.
>
> 40% in 1979 but does not exceed 60%.
>
> 45% in 1980 but does not exceed 55%.
>
> 50% in 1981 but does not exceed 50%.
>
> 55% in 1982 but does not exceed 45%.
>
> 60% in 1983 but does not exceed 40%.[58]

Finally, certain lifeguard services are also permitted to reduce their adjusted tax base by the percentage by which compensation divided by the total tax base exceeds the following:

> 40% in 1978 but does not exceed 60%.
>
> 45% in 1979 but does not exceed 55%.
>
> 50% in 1980 but does not exceed 50%.
>
> 55% in 1981 but does not exceed 45%.
>
> 60% in 1982 but does not exceed 40%.[59]

A Practical Approach to the SBT

Now that the theory and law of the SBT has been reviewed, a practical approach to the SBT will be easier to follow. The sample problem in Exhibit 6.11 illustrates a basic worksheet approach to computing the SBT. Exhibit 6.12 is a worksheet showing the computations of the Michigan

[57]Michigan Single Business Tax Act Section 208.31(3).
[58]Michigan Single Business Tax Act Section 208.31(6).
[59]Michigan Single Business Tax Act Section 208.31(7).

Exhibit 6.11   Basic Worksheet to Compute the SBT

Federal taxable income		$ 943,200
Add		
Compensation		
Wags	$15,210,300	
Payroll taxes	550,600	
Workmen's compensation	100,000	
Contributions to savings plan	150,000	16,010,900
Depreciation		450,600
Interest expense		35,000
State and local income taxes		90,000
Subtract		
Dividend received		(78,000)
Interest income		(120,000)
Michigan tax base		17,331,700
Capital acquisition deduction		(1,321,400)
Add		
Gross proceeds of property sold less gain		16,250
Michigan adjusted tax base		16,026,550
Less		
Labor-intensity deduction		
Compensation		
16,010,900		
(a) Michigan tax base = 92.38%		
17,331,700		
(b) 92.38% − 63% × 16,026,550 =		
Michigan adjusted tax base		(4,708,600)
Michigan adjusted tax base		$11,317,950
Tax at 2.35%		$ 265,972

Single Business Tax for the Wells Corporation, a labor-intensive company operating exclusively in Michigan.

Illustrative Example

Exhibit 6.12 represents a single business tax return filed by a corporation for the taxable year ended December 31, 1979.

C-8000	**SINGLE BUSINESS TAX ANNUAL RETURN**	**1979**

IDENTIFICATION 1 Taxable year beginning _____ 1979, ending _____ 19___

2 Check organization:	**PLEASE TYPE OR PRINT**	Account Number
		XXXX
Individual a ☐	Name XY Corporation	**5b** If no account number, enter Social Security number
Fiduciary b ☐		
Professional Corp. c ☐	d/b/a	
Sub S Corp. d ☐	**(PLACE LABEL HERE)**	
Other Corp. e ☐	Number/Street 1234 S. Third	**5c** Business Start Date
Partnership f ☐		
3 Check if consolidated ☐	City or town, state and ZIP code Westville, Illinois	1-1-78
4 **Is your organization a member of a controlled group?** .... Yes ☐ No☒ (Controlled group is defined on page 5)		**5d** Principal business activity Sales

TAX BASE

6	Gross Receipts (50% Method—see instructions, page 5)	3,675,150	00	
7	Business income (see instructions, page 5)		75,425	00
8	Compensation (from page 2, line 46)		394,071	00
9	Additions (from page 2, line 57)		190,618	00
10	Subtotal—Add lines 7, 8, and 9	10	660,114	00
11	Subtractions (from page 2, line 61)		4,811	00
12a	TAX BASE—Subtract line 11 from line 10		655,303	00
	(If taxable in another state, see instructions for C-8000H and complete line 12b)			
12b	APPORTIONED TAX BASE—Multiply line 12a by % from C-8000H, line 17 or line 20 31.71646%	12b	207,839	00

ADJUSTMENTS

13a	Capital acquisition deduction (from C-8000D, line 8)	13a	17,651	00
13b	Recapture of capital acquisition deduction (from C-8000D, line 24)		–	00
14	Net capital acquisition deduction—Subtract line 13b from line 13a		17,651	00
15	ADJUSTED TAX BASE BEFORE loss deductions and statutory exemption Subtract (if negative add) line 14 from line 12a or 12b whichever is applicable		190,188	00
16	Business loss carry forward from single business tax	–	00	
17	Net operating loss carry forward from Mich. Corp. Income Tax	–	00	
18	Statutory exemption (from page 2, line 71)	–	00	
19	Total—Add lines 16, 17, and 18	19	–	00
20	ADJUSTED TAX BASE—Subtract line 19 from line 15. If line 19 is greater than line 15, enter NONE	20	190,188	00

REDUCTIONS, CREDITS, TAX

21	Reduction to adjusted tax base, if applicable (see instructions on C-8000S) Check if from C-8000S a. ☐ Part I, b. ☐ Part II, c. ☐ Part III, d. ☐ Part IV, or e. ☐ Part V	21	–	00
22	Subtotal—Subtract line 21 from line 20	22	190,188	00
23	TAX BEFORE credits—Multiply line 22 by 2.35% (.0235)		4,469	00
24	Small business credit (from C-8000I, line 25; C-8000P, line 22; or C-8000C, line 19)		–	00
25	Other credits for corporations (from C-8000C, line 26)		–	00
26	Subtotal—Subtract lines 24 and 25 from line 23	26	4,469	00
27	Unincorporated/Subchapter S Corp. tax credit—Multiply line 26 by % from table, page 8	27	4,469	00
28	TAX—Subtract line 27 from line 26			00

PAYMENTS

29	Overpayment credited from 1978	–	00	
30	Estimated tax payments	4,500	00	
31	Tax paid with request for extension	–	00	
32	Total—Add lines 29, 30 and 31	32	4,500	00
33	TAX DUE—Subtract line 32 from line 28			00
34	Penalty ___% ☐ 00 plus interest ___% ☐	00		
35	Add lines 33 and 34—**PAY THIS AMOUNT**		31	00
36	OVERPAYMENT—Subtract line 28 from line 32	00		
37	Amount of overpayment to be refunded	00		
38	Amount of overpayment to be credited to 1980 estimated tax	31	00	

Exhibit 6.12 Single business tax data.

COMPENSATION List all payments made on behalf of or for the benefit of employees or officers. (see instructions, pages 5 & 6)

39	Salaries, wages, and other payments to employees	39	200,575 | 00
40	Payroll taxes—FICA, state and federal unemployment payments	40	85,400 | 00
41	Employee insurance plans—workmen's compensation, health, life	41	60,450 | 00
42	Pension, retirement, profit sharing plans	42	35,350 | 00
43	Other payments—supplemental unemployment benefit trust, etc.	43	12,296 | 00
44	Subtotal—Add lines 39 through 43	44	394,071 | 00
45	Special exemptions (see instructions—contractor's exemption expires 12-31-79)	45	– | 00
46	Compensation (Subtract line 45 from line 44, enter here and on page 1, line 8)	46	394,071 | 00

ADDITIONS (see instructions, page 6) To the extent deducted in arriving at federal taxable income

47	Depreciation, and other write-off of tangible assets	47	105,768 | 00
48	Taxes imposed on or measured by income (city, state and foreign)	48	4,400 | 00
49	Single business tax	49	| 00
50	Dividends, interest and royalties	50	73,700 | 00
51	Capital loss carryover or carryback	51	250 | 00
52	Net operating loss carryover or carryback	52	– | 00
53	Excluded capital gains (Individuals only)	53	– | 00
54	Gross interest and dividend income from bonds and similar obligations issued by states other than Michigan and political subdivisions thereof	54	6,500 | 00
55	Any deduction or exclusion due to classification as DISC, Western Hemisphere trade corporation, China trade act corporation, and similar classifications	55	– | 00
56	Losses from partnerships—Account No.	56	– | 00
57	Total Additions (Add lines 47 through 56, enter here and on page 1, line 9)	57	190,618 | 00

SUBTRACTIONS (see instructions, page 7)

58	Dividends, interest and royalty income included in business income, page 1, line 7	58	4,811 | 00
59	Capital losses not deducted in arriving at business income, page 1, line 7	59	– | 00
60	Income from partnerships included in business income—Account No.	60	– | 00
61	Total Subtractions (Add lines 58 through 60, enter here and on page 1, line 11)	61	4,811 | 00

STATUTORY EXEMPTION Business income averaging available to noncorporate taxpayers in 1980 (see instructions, page 7)

62	Statutory exemption—Enter $40,000 or the amount allocated from C-8009, line 6	62	| 00
	Partners or Shareholders (Sub S or Professional Corp.) Exemption		
63	Number qualified (from C-8000KP, line 5 or C-8000KC, line 4) **63a**_____ LESS 1 ☐		
64	Multiply line 63b by $12,000 (maximum $48,000)	64	| 00
65	Total Statutory Exemption—Add lines 62 and 64	65	| 00
	Short-period/Part-year Exemption		
66	Number of months covered by this return **66a**_____ ÷ 12 = **66b**_____ %		
67	Multiply line 65 by percentage on line 66b	67	| 00
68a	Business income (from page 1, line 7—1980, see instructions) **68a**_____ | 00		
68b	Loss carryover or carryback (from lines 51 and 52) **68b**_____ | 00		
68c	Compensation and Director fees of **ALL** shareholders (from C-8000KC, Line 5) ☐_____ | 00		
69	Total—Add lines 68a, 68b, and 68c	69	00
70a	Excess business income—Subtract line 65 or 67 from line 69 (**cannot be less than zero**)	70a	| 00
70b	Reduction factor—Multiply line 70a by 2	70b	00
71	Allowable Exemption (Subtract line 70b from line 65 or line 67, enter here and on page 1, line 18)	71	– | 00

RETURN DUE On or before the last day of the 4th month after close of your tax year. Make remittance payable to STATE OF MICHIGAN (Please write account number on remittance.) Mail to Michigan Department of Treasury, P.O. Box 30059, Lansing, MI 48909.

PREPARER'S AND TAXPAYER'S DECLARATION:

Under penalties of perjury, I declare that I have examined this return, including accompanying schedules and statements, and to the best of my knowledge and belief it is true, correct and complete. If prepared by a person other than the taxpayer, declaration is based on any known information.

Signature of Taxpayer	Date	Signature of Preparer other than Taxpayer	Date
Title		Business Address	

Exhibit 6.12 *(continued)*

SINGLE BUSINESS TAX
CAPITAL ACQUISITION ADJUSTMENT
(see instructions, page 9)

1979 ■

1 Name	2 Account Number
XY Corporation	XXXX

CAPITAL ACQUISITION DEDUCTION

PART I Acquisition of depreciable real property located in Michigan and acquired during taxable year (section 1250 IRC type property).

a Description	**b** Location	**c** Date Acquired	**d** Cost Paid or Accrued During Taxable Year
3			

4 TOTAL depreciable real property located in Michigan	**4**		00

PART II Acquisition of depreciable personal property acquired during taxable year (other than section 1250 IRC type property).

a Description	**b** Location	**c** Date Acquired	**d** Cost Paid or Accrued During Taxable Year
5			
Executive Desks	Anywhere USA	3-05-79	2,750
Calculators	Anywhere USA	4-06-79	1,050
Machinery	Anywhere USA	7-04-79	12,000
Office Furniture	Anywhere USA	8-16-79	40,000

6 TOTAL depreciable personal property	**6**	55,800	00
If taxable in another state complete line 7.			
7 Apportioned depreciable personal property—Multiply line 6 by % from C-8000H, line 24	7	17,651	00

PART III Total Deduction

8 TOTAL CAPITAL ACQUISITION DEDUCTION (Add lines 4 and 6 or 7, whichever is applicable, enter here and on C-8000, page 1, line 13a)	8	17,651	00

Note: If more space is needed, submit a separate schedule and enter totals on lines 4 and 6.

Exhibit 6.12 *(continued)*

RECAPTURE OF CAPITAL ACQUISITION DEDUCTION

PART IV Sales and other dispositions of depreciable real property acquired on or after 1/1/76 (section 1250 IRC type property located in Michigan).

a Description	b Location	c Date Acquired	d Date Sold	e Gross Sales Price	f Gain or (loss)
9					
10 Totals..10				None	

11 Adjusted proceeds—Line 10, column (e) LESS gain, or PLUS loss on line 10, column (f)......... 11 _____ | 00
   If taxable in another state, complete lines 12-19
12 Gross proceeds (from line 10, column (e)).. 12 _____ | 00
13 Total gains or (losses) (from line 10, column (f))........... 13 _____ | 00
14 Excluded gains attributable to line 13 and entered on
   C-8000, page 2, line 53............................... 14 _____ | 00
15 Reported gains or (losses)—Subtract line 14 from 13........ 15 _____ | 00
16 Apportioned gains or (losses)—Multiply line 15 by % from C-8000H, line 17 or line 20,
   whichever is applicable................................. 16 _____ | 00
17 Subtotal—line 12 LESS gain, or PLUS a loss on line 16.............. 17 _____ | 00
18 Excluded gains (from line 14)................................. 18 _____ | 00
19 Adjusted proceeds—Subtract line 18 from line 17................ 19 None | 00

PART V Sales and other dispositions of depreciable personal property acquired on or after 1/1/76 (other than section 1250 type property).

a Description	b Location	c Date Acquired	d Date Sold	e Gross Sales Price	f Gain or (loss)
20					
21 Totals.................................. 21					

22 Adjusted proceeds—line 21, column (e) LESS gain, or PLUS loss on line 21, column (f)..... 22 _____ | 00
   If taxable in another state, complete line 23
23 Apportioned adjusted proceeds. Multiply line 22 by % from C-8000H, line 24............. 23 None | 00

PART VI Total Recapture

24 TOTAL RECAPTURE OF CAPITAL ACQUISITION DEDUCTION (Add lines 11 and 22 **or**
   lines 19 and 23, whichever are applicable, enter here and C-8000, page 1, line 13b)................24 – | 00

Exhibit 6.12 *(continued)*

MICHIGAN SINGLE BUSINESS TAX
APPORTIONMENT FORMULA

1979 ■

1. Name:	2. Account Number:
XY Corporation	XXXX

To be used only by those taxpayers doing business in Michigan and one or more other states or foreign countries and who are taxable both within and without this state (**see instructions on reverse side**)

PART I Computation of apportionment percentage:

PROPERTY FACTOR*

3. Average Michigan property **3.**	125,600 00			
4. Michigan rentals x 8 **4.**	35,000 00			
5. Total Michigan property (ADD lines 3 and 4)	5.	160,600 00		
6. Average total property **6.**	800,350 00			
7. Total rentals x 8 **7.**	40,000 00			
8. Total property (ADD lines 6 and 7)	8.	840,350 00		
9. Percentage (DIVIDE line 5 by line 8)			9.	19.11108 %

PAYROLL FACTOR

10. Michigan payroll **10.**	135,000 00			
11. Total payroll **11.**	305,750 00			
12. Percentage (DIVIDE line 10 by line 11)			12	44.15372 %

SALES FACTOR

13. Michigan sales **13.**	805,325 00			
14. Total sales **14.**	2,525,750 00			
15. Percentage (DIVIDE line 13 by line 14)			15	31.88458 %

16. Total percentage (ADD lines 9, 12 and 15)		16.	95.14938 %
17. Apportionment percentage (DIVIDE line 16 by 3, if less than 3 factors, divide by number of factor(s)**) **17.**			31.71646 %

*The commissioner may require the periodic averaging of values during the tax year, if reasonably required to reflect properly the average value of the taxpayer's property.

**Number of factors are those factors (property, payroll, or sales) which have denominators (lines 8, 11 or 14, respectively) greater than zero.

PART II

**TRANSPORTATION SERVICES, DOMESTIC INSURERS, FINANCIAL ORGANIZATIONS, OR
IF TAXPAYER IS AUTHORIZED TO USE A SPECIAL FORMULA, USE THE LINES PROVIDED BELOW**
(Attach Explanation)

18. Michigan **18.**	00		
19. Total **19.**	00		
20. Apportionment percentage (DIVIDE line 18 by line 19) **20.**			%

PART III

CAPITAL ACQUISITION APPORTIONMENT
(Apportionment Percentage For Capital Acquisition)

21. Property factor (from line 9)	21.	19.11108 %		
22. Payroll factor (from line 12)	22.	44.15372 %		
23. Total (ADD lines 21 and 22)			23.	63.2648 %
24. Average percentage (DIVIDE line 23 by 2, if only 1 factor enter line 23) **24.**				31.6324 %

Exhibit 6.12 *(continued)*

Consolidated Returns

The SBT will permit or the Commissioner may require the filing of a consolidated or combined return by an affiliated group of corporations. However, the following three conditions must first be met:

1 All members of the affiliated group are Michigan taxpayers.
2 Each member of the affiliated group maintains a relationship with one or more members of the group that includes intercorporate transactions of a substantial nature other than control, ownership, or financing arrangements or any combination thereof.
3 The business activities of each member of the affiliated group are subject to apportionment by a specific apportionment formula contained in this act. This specific formula also is applicable to all other members of the affiliated group. The formula would be applicable to each member even if it were not part of the affiliated group.[60]

An *affiliated group* is defined to mean:

. . . Two or more corporations, one of which owns or controls, directly or indirectly, 80 per cent of more of the capital stock with voting rights of the other corporation or corporations.[61]

There is no longer any optional use of a consolidated return, and a noncorporate taxpayer will not be able to combine or consolidate its income with any other taxpayer. A taxpayer can file only one SBT return, even if it engages in 15 different businesses.[62] Every time a taxpayer combines with another to engage in a business activity, a new entity comes into being and a separate return is required.

Conclusion

The SBT has entirely replaced the old system of taxation of business activity within Michigan, with the exception of some minor taxes. Although the SBT has incorporated all types of taxes into one tax, an SBT return does not supply the state with all the necessary business information. Therefore, annual reports and reports on personal property must still be filed with the state, even though the franchise tax and personal property tax on inventory have been repealed.

[60]Michigan Single Business Tax Act Section 208.77.
[61]Michigan Single Business Tax Act Section 208.3(1).
[62]Commerce Clearing House Publications, *Michigan State Tax Reporter,* Michigan Single Business Tax Division Releases, Single Business Tax Questions and Answers Volume I (September 15, 1975).

The SBT is a tax on the privilege of doing business and is not an income or gross receipts tax. The SBT will be administered like an income tax in that information on the Federal income tax returns will be used, and IRS definitions and dates will be enforced. It was designed to affect all businesses in the same manner, regardless of size, form, or nature of the business. Basically, it is a tax on profits, payroll, interest expenses, and depreciation, less any expenditures for capital investments. It was initiated to encourage job development in Michigan by providing tax benefits to industries capable of making job-creating investments.

CHAPTER SEVEN

Sales and Use Taxes

BACKGROUND

Overview

Sales and use taxes as they are known today were introduced in the 1930s amid a climate of scarce resources and capital. It was the financial difficulties of the depression that motivated the states to consider these taxes as a revenue source. Mississippi was the first state to take action in the early 1930s by eliminating a substantial portion of its multiple state tax levied on production and distribution. At the same time, Mississippi's tax rate on retail sales was raised from less than 1 percent to 2 percent, eventually making this tax that state's major source of revenue.[1] It did not take long for the other states to realize the revenue advantages of a higher tax on retail sales. Large amounts of revenue could be realized based on tax rates that were low enough so as not to antagonize the taxpayers. A state could now maintain or even increase its spending as these taxes created a steady or an increased flow of revenue dollars.

During the 1930s, the retail sales taxes were basically taxes on the sale of tangible personal property.[2] The burden of the tax was placed on the purchaser of the property. As the country's economic outlook improved, the number of taxable transactions increased. By 1960, 34 states were imposing a sales tax, and consumer services were also being included within the boundaries of taxable transactions. At the end of that decade, 45 states were levying a sales tax.[3]

There are several reasons for the widespread use and popularity of these taxes. First, it was not feasible for the states to rely too heavily on income taxes, since this was and still is an area dominated by the Federal government. Second, consumption taxes (sales taxes) presented new opportunities for the states to take complete advantage of, considering that the Federal government had no tax of this nature. This was a chance to tap a previously untouched revenue source. It is interesting to note that

---

[1]State and Local Sales Tax, Tax Foundation, Incorporated, New York, p. 8.
[2]State and Local Sales Tax, p. 8.
[3]State and Local Sales Tax, p. 10.

consumption taxes have also played an important role for local governments that have used these revenues to supplement their property tax revenues, which have traditionally been their primary source of tax revenue. Finally, part of the appeal of a consumption tax was that it was possible for the states to administer these taxes and to keep them within their control.[4]

Sales and Use Taxes Defined

The *sales tax* is a tax on the transfer, sale, or exchange of property and is imposed only on intrastate sales. A *use tax* is a tax imposed on property that is stored or consumed in a state and has not previously been subject to a sales tax.[5] Although these taxes are usually referred to in conjunction with one another, they are taxes on different types of transactions. Whereas a sales tax is a tax on the purchase of property, a use tax is a complementary tax on the enjoyment of the property. Each tax must be constitutionally sound in its own right.[6] However, because the provisions for both of these taxes are so similar, they are often confused with one another. Although it cannot be denied that these taxes are interrelated, caution must be exercised, because it is possible for a transaction to be subject to a sales tax and not subject to a use tax. To avoid any problems, references to sales taxes throughout this chapter do not imply sales and use taxes jointly. Furthermore, when only a use tax is being discussed, such is explicitly stated.

For classification purposes, there are five basic categories of sales taxes.[7] These are retail sales taxes, general sales taxes that are not restricted only to retail sales, gross proceeds taxes that are based on sales and services, gross receipts taxes that are discussed in Chapter 8, and various selective sales taxes on items such as alcohol, tobacco, and gasoline. This chapter is devoted to the more common retail and general sales taxes.

The Need for Both Sales and Use Taxes

Before any discussion covering the jurisdictional guidelines for sales and use taxes, it is worthwhile to first consider why each state that levies a sales tax also has a complementary use tax. The necessity for levying both of these taxes stems from a basic constitutional objective discussed in connection with taxes based on or measured by income. Essentially, it is

---

[4]State and Local Sales Tax, p. 12.
[5]Richard Krol, "Minimizing the Corporate Interstate Tax Burden," American Institute of Certified Public Accountants Continuing Education Program.
[6]*McLeod v. J. E. Dilworth* 322 U.S. 327 (1944).
[7]Thomas J. Barrett, "Multistate Sales & Use Taxation," *Journal of Taxation,* Vol. 3, No. 1 (Spring 1976) p. 9.

the philosophy that a balance should exist between the taxes levied on companies with only intrastate operations and those with interstate activities as well. In other words, a sales tax, like an income tax, should not be discriminatory by enabling an interstate or intrastate business to profit at the expense of the other. If a state only levied a sales tax, intrastate business could be at a disadvantage. This example illustrates this point: The Zeus Company is a retail operation that sells foreign handicrafts imported from all over the world. It is incorporated, domiciled, and has operations only with State X. The Poseidon Company is another retail concern also engaged in the business of importing and selling foreign handicrafts and is located in State Y. The Poseidon Company is not domiciled and it does not have sufficient nexus within State X to require it to collect a sales tax. State X imposes a sales tax but not a use tax. When a buyer decides to make a purchase, he could either make the purchase from the Zeus Company, subject to sales tax, or he could order the same item from the Poseidon Company without the burden of a sales tax. Needless to say, the customer will be inclined to make the purchase from the Poseidon Company.

Although the example is rather simplistic, it illustrates the inequity that could be created by a sales tax levied in a state without a use tax. Such a tax would be disadvantageous to businesses in the state because of sales lost to out-of-state companies. At the same time, it creates a problem for the taxing state in terms of the revenues that are lost because of the taxing state's failure to tax the interstate sale. Therefore, to insure that the local in-state business will not be subjected to a tax burden that does not reach the out-of-state business, a use tax is levied on the transactions that escape the sales tax. The use tax is applied at the same rate as the sales tax and is only enforced in connection with the sales tax. This can reasonably insure that resident business will not be placed at a competitive disadvantage. Applying this to the example, the purchaser would be subjected to a use tax in State X, making the tax cost of the property sale equal whether purchased from the Zeus Company or Poseidon Company.

Both the sales and use tax burden are passed on to the consumer, but it is the vendor who generally has the responsibility for collecting and remitting the tax to the state. The vendor becomes the fiduciary for the state. If the vendor neglects to collect the tax, the tax may become his own liability.

JURISDICTIONAL STANDARDS

Issues Involved

Throughout the first chapters on income taxation, there were two significant concepts that reappeared in many of the cases discussed. The first was the question of "nexus," or does an interstate business have sufficient local activity within a state to fall within the grasp of the state's taxing authority? If this question were answered in the affirmative, the second potential problem area was encountered. What equitable method could be used for determining the amount of the income tax? More specifically, how valid were the apportionment factors if they were used, and how reasonable was the division between allocable nonbusiness and apportionable business income?

These areas have provided much of the input for state and Federal court decisions. The legal dilemmas concerning sales and use taxation strongly parallel these conflicts. The question of nexus is not unique to income taxation. One of the primary considerations facing a company engaged in interstate commerce is whether its selling methods or business operations have sufficient contact within a particular state to require it to collect a use tax. The primary consideration is whether the taxing state is placing a constitutionally fair burden on that portion of interstate commerce to which it bears a special relation. There must be some local incident that is sufficient to bring the transaction within the state's taxing power.[8] In some instances, the requirement for use tax collections will violate the Constitution by placing an undue burden on interstate commerce. All the cases presented in this section deal with "nexus" for both sales and use taxes. Although the facts and circumstances of each case are unique, the amount of nexus in each case is always a question of degree. The issue of nexus can be summarized as follows, "Numerous contacts or presence in the taxing jurisdiction will satisfy nexus for a local sales tax. A small degree of contact or presence will satisfy nexus for a local use tax. If no local contact or presence is evident, then nexus is not apparent and neither a sales nor a use tax will be imposed.[9]

The second issue centers around the nature of the tax and the items to be taxed. Basically, there is little problem concerning the nature of the tax when a sales or use tax can easily be computed as a fixed percentage of the dollar value of the taxable transaction. The tax is usually quoted as a separate figure and added on to the seller's price. It is the definition of property subject to taxation that provides most of the variance between the states. There are some transactions that are simply not subject to a sales or use tax. These so-called "exempted" transactions are discussed in the next section of this chapter.

When a Vendor Is Required to Collect a Sales Tax

The requirement for the collection of a sales tax from intrastate activity is dictated by the satisfaction of a nexus requirement and a determination of where the goods are delivered or where title to the goods passes.

[8]*National Bellas Hess, Inc.* v. *Department of Revenue* 386 U.S. 753 (1967).
[9]Multistate Sales and Use Taxation p. 12.

Generally, a transaction will be subject to a sales tax if it is made by a vendor having business operations within the state and if the product sold is received, transferred, or delivered within the state. For example, Public Corporation has a branch office and warehouse in State K. On its first day of operations for the current fiscal year, two sales were made. For the first sale, the goods were to be picked up by the purchaser from Public's warehouse. For the second sale, the goods were to be shipped and delivered from a warehouse located in a neighboring state. Both of these sales are subject to State K's sales tax, since the goods were received or delivered in the state and Public has sufficient nexus as evidenced by the branch office and warehouse.

It is also possible for a state to levy a sales tax on a transaction where title to the merchandise passes within the state rather than requiring delivery of the merchandise within the state. Once again, sufficient nexus must exist. The importance of a use tax can also be illustrated here. Suppose, for example, that a corporation is doing business in State X which requires sales tax collections when the title to the goods passes in State X. In a neighboring State Y, sales taxes are required to be collected when goods are delivered in that state. It would appear that this company could escape the obligation of sales tax collections by purchasing all goods and receiving title in State Y and taking delivery of these goods in State X.[10] This is where the use tax would take over in State X to avoid lost revenues and to close the loophole.

A state will not be able to abuse its privilege to require sales tax collections if, for example, goods are merely being delivered within the state. A company must be conducting its operations or doing business within the state so as to satisfy the nexus requirement. The U.S. Supreme Court has ruled in the case of *McLeod* v. *J. E. Dilworth* 322 U.S. 327 (1944) that if there is no nexus a sales tax placed on sales of goods delivered in-state would be in violation of the U.S. Constitution.

Besides illustrating the circumstances that would prevent a state from enforcing sales tax collections, the *McLeod* v. *J. E. Dilworth* case also illustrated the close connection between sales and use taxes. Although the imposition of a sales tax in this case was denied by the Supreme Court, the imposition of a use tax would have been constitutional. The facts of this case are as follows.

J. E. Dilworth Company was a Tennessee corporation that sold machinery and mill supplies. The company's home office was located in Memphis. Dilworth Company was not qualified to do business in Arkansas and had no place of business in that state. The only contact Dilworth had with the residents of Arkansas was by means of traveling salesmen, and the traveling salesmen were all Tennessee residents. All solicitation for orders by the salesmen were taken, subject to acceptance and approval by the

---

[10]Multistate Sales & Use Taxation, p. 14.

Tennessee office, and all the goods were shipped from Tennessee. Title to the property passed on the delivery to the common carrier in Tennessee. The state of Arkansas held J. E. Dilworth liable for sales tax collections on these sales. Although the Supreme Court of Arkansas ruled in favor of the state, the U.S. Supreme Court reversed the decision on the basis that such a requirement would be in violation of the Commerce Clause.

Among other items, the Court specifically distinguished sales and use taxes, noting the fact that each tax must be justified on different constitutional grounds. The sales tax Arkansas sought to collect was clearly a tax on interstate commerce. Sufficient nexus within the state did not exist. The Court stated, "Though sales and use taxes may secure the same revenues and serve complementary purposes, they are, as we have indicated, taxes on different transactions and for different opportunities afforded by a state."

This leads into the question of what types of transactions trigger the requisite for use tax collection. The U.S. Supreme Court has faced this issue in several cases that have helped to establish jurisdictional rules. It is necessary for an interstate business to be familiar with these standards.

When a Vendor Is Required to Collect a Use Tax

The nexus guidelines for the collection of use taxes are more restrictive, as will be illustrated by this discussion of important U.S. Supreme Court decisions. These cases have determined when a corporation will be required to collect a use tax. Once it is determined that a vendor has sufficient nexus in a state, the corporation will register to act as an agent of the state to collect use tax, file the appropriate forms, and remit the tax collections to the state. Organizing these administrative functions and maintaining sufficient records of all transactions may not be overly burdensome for a corporation dealing with only a few states. Corporations with activities that encompass many states have a greater burden. Since each state will want to insure that all revenues are being collected, it is imperative for a business to evaluate its own operations in light of the following cases. A determination can then be made about whether a business' activities are sufficient to require it to collect a use tax.

Nelson v. *Sears Roebuck and Company 312 U.S. 359 (1941) and Nelson* v. *Montgomery Ward and Company 312 U.S. 373 (1941)*

Sears Roebuck and *Montgomery Ward* are two of the earlier cases dealing with the collection of use taxes. In both of these cases, the companies had a place of business in the taxing state of Iowa. Each company believed that its sales not originating from Iowa should not be subject to Iowa use tax collections.

Sears Roebuck and Company was a foreign corporation with retail outlets in Iowa. Sales made to Iowa residents originating from these stores included a sales tax that was remitted to the state. Sears did not feel it was required of them to collect a use tax on sales from mail orders sent by Iowa buyers to out-of-state locations. The Sears' argument was based on the belief that since these orders were shipped from the out-of-state locations and delivered by mail or by common carrier, there was insufficient nexus in Iowa. The U.S. Supreme Court affirmed the Iowa Supreme Court decision and held that the mail order business was subject to use tax collection because sufficient nexus was established by Sears' retail business operations in the state.

The circumstances in the *Montgomery Ward* case were very similar to the *Sears* case. The major distinction lies in the fact that in addition to its branch operations in Iowa, Montgomery Ward sent advertisements to Iowa residents notifying them that they could order products through the mail from out-of-state outlets. The Supreme Court also held Montgomery Ward responsible for the collection of use taxes on these sales, even though the sales originated in another state. Montgomery Ward's in-state solicitation, along with its branch operations, provided sufficient nexus to require the company to collect use taxes on products sold to Iowa users.

General Trading Company v. State Tax Commission 322 U.S. 335 (1944)

Sufficient nexus within a state has been deemed to exist when a company has a "place of business" within the state. Exactly what constitutes having a place of business for use tax purposes was illustrated in the *General Trading Company* case.

The General Trading Company was a Minnesota corporation that was not qualified to do business in the state of Iowa. There were no offices or warehouses maintained in the state. The company's only activity within that state was the solicitation or orders through traveling salesmen. Orders received by these salesmen were taken subject to approval at offices in Minnesota. The Iowa use tax law stated that every retailer maintaining a place of business in Iowa must collect this tax from Iowa purchasers. Although in the *Sears* and *Montgomery Ward* cases a physical business locale existed in Iowa, the General Trading Company had no localized place of business. The state Tax Commissioner and the Iowa Supreme Court held the company liable for use tax collections.

The U.S. Supreme Court affirmed the decision of the Iowa Supreme Court. A tax imposed on goods shipped from Minnesota to Iowa by means of common carrier or mail did not place a burden on interstate commerce. The nature of General Trading Company's operations provided a sufficient link to subject the company to the collection of a use tax.

The U.S. Supreme Court stated, " . . . the mere fact that property is used for interstate commerce or has come into an owner's possession as a result of interstate commerce does not diminish the protection which he may draw from a state to the upkeep of which he may be asked to bear his fair share." In effect, this case decided that the activities of a traveling salesman within a state are equivalent to a "place of business" for purposes of use tax collections.

The *General Trading* and *J. E. Dilworth* cases were decided together by the U.S. Supreme Court, because the circumstances surrounding the operations of the two companies were almost identical. The distinction drawn was that in Dilworth the issue was the collection of a sales tax, whereas in General Trading it was the collection of a use tax.

Scripto, Incorporated v. *Carson et al. 362 U.S. 207 (1959)*

Scripto v. *Carson* was another important case that helped to establish ground rules for determining when a state could require a seller to collect use tax. The guidelines set by the *General Trading Company* case were stretched even further with the result of this decision. The pertinent facts are as follows.

Scripto, Incorporated, operated an advertising specialty division called Adgif in Atlanta, Georgia. Adgif sold mechanical writing instruments used for advertising purposes. Various types of printed material could be placed on the instruments. Adgif did not have a place of business, an office, or a regular employee located within the state of Florida. Furthermore, it did not maintain a merchandise inventory in Florida nor did it have a bank account within the state. Rather than using its own traveling salesmen, Adgif contracted independent brokers or jobbers to solicit sales in Florida. Orders received for products were then sent to the Atlanta office for acceptance or rejection. Settlement of accounts was thus between the buyer and Adgif. The state of Florida levied a $5150.66 assessment on Scripto for failure to collect a use tax on those products sold and used within the state. The issue, once again, was the question of nexus. Scripto believed that the requirement of the Florida statute to collect a use tax placed an undue burden on interstate commerce. The U.S. Supreme Court, however, upheld the assessment.

The rationale of the Court was based on two basic issues. First, the fact that nonemployees were used rather than regular employees traveling throughout the state was considered to have no significance. As stated by the Court, "The formal shift in the contractual tagging of a salesman as 'independent' neither results in changing his local function of solicitation nor bears upon its effectiveness in securing a substantial flow of goods into Florida." The *General Trading* case established that in-state sales solicitors can be considered equivalent to having a "place of business" in the state. Continuing along this line of reasoning, the Court concluded that a state solicitor need not be a full-time employee so long as the solicitor represents the seller.

Second, "minimum connections" necessary within the state were actually found to be more than sufficient because the jobbers conducted continuous solicitation in Florida. The only aspect of the sales transaction not incurring in Florida was the acceptance of the sales order. The tax was therefore found to be nondiscriminatory because it was levied on the use and enjoyment of property purchased by Florida residents that had become a part of the mass of property in the state. The actual burden of the tax was placed on the purchaser of the product who used it within Florida. Scripto would only be liable for this tax when it failed to collect it from the ultimate consumer.

The *Scripto* decision is undoubtedly important because of its impact on nexus for use tax collection. It is also interesting when considered from a historic point of view. In Chapter 4, the background activities leading up to the creation of the Multistate Tax Compact dealt with the extensive taxation study conducted by Congress. After the study was completed by the Special Subcommittee on State Taxation of Interstate Commerce, various interstate taxation bills were introduced, beginning with House Report 11798. It was the *Scripto* decision that prompted Congress to extend its study of state taxation to cover all aspects of interstate commerce, including sales and use taxation.

National Bellas Hess, Incorporated v. *Department of Revenue 386 U.S. 753 (1967)*

At this point, it may appear as though the slightest activity within a state will trigger the requirement for use tax collection. Starting with the *Sears Roebuck* and *Montgomery Ward* cases and continuing through *General Trading* and *Scripto,* the U.S. Supreme Court has endorsed the states' right to require use tax collection. The *National Bellas Hess* case is an important exception to this trend. The type of contact a business is permitted in a state without requiring use tax collection was illustrated by this case.

National Bellas Hess was a mail order house, its principal place of business being located in Kansas City, Missouri. It was not licensed to do business in Illinois and, accordingly, did not maintain an office, warehouse, or any place of business within the state nor did it solicit orders by means of salesmen. Furthermore, it had no telephone listing in the state and had done no advertising on television, radio, or newspaper. National Bellas Hess did have contacts in the state through a catalog it mailed to its customers twice a year. The catalog was also sent to other customers throughout the country. In addition, flyers were occasionally mailed to past and potential customers. All orders for merchandise were mailed to National Bellas Hess for acceptance at its headquarters in Missouri. Goods were then delivered to the customers, using either mail or common carriers.

The Illinois Department of Revenue considered National Bellas Hess to be a retailer soliciting orders in the state and therefore subject to regulations for use tax collection. National Bellas Hess argued that Illinois was creating an unconstitutional burden on interstate commerce and therefore was not subject to the requirement for use tax collection. The U.S. Supreme Court reversed the Illinois Supreme Court decision and ruled that Illinois could not require a foreign mail order company such as National Bellas Hess to collect and remit Illinois use tax on sales made to Illinois residents. The critical factors were, first, the company's only activities in the state were the solicitation of orders through catalogs and flyers and, second, deliveries were made using the mail or common carrier. The U.S. Supreme Court distinguished the earlier cases (*Sears* and *Montgomery Ward*) involving a mail order seller with retail outlets, solicitors, and property within a state from a seller such as National Bellas Hess that did no more than communicate to its customers in the state by mail, followed by delivery of the goods by mail or common carrier. Comparatively, the activities of National Bellas Hess were strictly interstate and to subject them to Illinois use taxes would constitute a violation of the Commerce Clause.

Several years later, the Illinois Supreme Court narrowed the effect of the *National Bellas Hess* decision in *Readers Digest v. Department of Revenue 44 ILL 2d 354 (1970)*. In this case, *Readers Digest* was held to be liable for use tax collections on its mail order sales into the state of Illinois because it had a subsidiary located within the state. Even though the activities of the subsidiary had no relation to the product being taxed, the company's presence in the state was sufficient to make the parent company liable for use tax collection.

Miller Brothers v. Maryland 347 U.S. 340 (1953)

The *Miller Brothers* case is also representative of when a vendor will not be required to collect a use tax. Insufficient nexus was shown to exist between the state of Maryland and the taxpayer where some of the taxpayer's sales "spilled over" into Maryland.

Miller Brothers was a Delaware vendor whose business was located in Delaware. All sales were made at this store, no orders being accepted by mail or telephone. Advertisements for the store that appeared in Delaware newspapers and on Delaware radio stations also reached some of the nearby residents in Maryland. Consequently, Maryland residents went to Miller Brothers in Delaware to make purchases. The customers would take their purchases with them or have them delivered by common carrier or occasionally by the store delivery truck. When a customer came to the store, there was no easy means for detecting whether they were Maryland residents. Former customers from both states did however receive some sales notices. The state of Maryland considered these contacts to be sufficient to require Miller Brothers to collect use taxes for the state, even though only a nominal amount was involved for the several years in question. Miller Brothers appealed and the U.S. Supreme Court backed its position that there was a lack of nexus within the state.

National Geographic Society v. *California Board of Equalization 51 L Ed 2d 631 (1977)*

The *National Geographic* decision is the most recent Supreme Court case to provide a standard for use tax collection. The case concerns the National Geographic Society, a nonprofit educational corporation.

The National Geographic Society published a magazine entitled *National Geographic* and operated a mail order business from the District of Columbia for the sale of various types of personal property. The Society had activities in the state of California that consisted of two offices which solicited advertising for the magazine. These offices performed no activities related to the operation of the mail order business, yet the California Supreme Court associated the sales office with the mail order business and concluded that this provided sufficient nexus between the taxpayer and the state to constitutionally uphold the collection of a use tax. The position taken by the Society was based on the fact the its contacts with customers in California were related only to its mail order business which relied on common carriers or the mail. The two offices located in the state were not connected to the mail order business, and it was therefore argued that the guidelines of the *National Bellas Hess* case should be followed.

The U.S. Supreme Court affirmed the California Supreme Court decision, holding that use tax collections will be required when an out-of-state seller has offices in the state where it conducts its business, even though the offices are not used or related to its selling activities. The Court did clarify that this does not imply that the "slightest presence" rule advocated by the California Supreme Court was sufficient to subject the seller to use tax collection requirements. The facts and circumstances of each case must be reviewed, and the facts here indicated a sufficient link between National Geographic's activities and the state.

Highlights of All the Leading Cases

The necessity for a link between a foreign business and taxing state has been illustrated in the description of the preceding court cases. Exhibit 7.1 is designed to present a chronological summarization of these cases.

Practical Considerations

Based on the discussion of these court cases it becomes apparent that any business which makes sales into a state imposing a use tax must be aware of the state's laws and regulations. A periodic review of each company's

Exhibit 7.1

Case — Year	Significant Holdings by the U.S. Supreme Court
Sears Roebuck and *Montgomery Ward*, 1941	Mail order sellers with retail outlets in a state provide sufficient nexus with the state. The sales subject to use tax collections need not originate through these outlets.
General Trading Company, 1944	A company employing one or more salesmen to solicit orders in a state will be subject to use tax collections in the state. The salesmen do not have to work full time to meet this test.
Miller Brothers, 1954	"Spillover" sales into a state without sufficient solicitation is not enough activity to subject a vendor to use tax collection.
Scripto, 1960	A company with an independent broker serving as a conduit for orders taken out of state will be subject to use tax collection.
National Bellas Hess, 1967	A company is not required to collect a use tax when it has only two contacts with a state by mailing catalogs and flyers and by using the mail or common carrier to send customers the ordered goods.
National Geographic, 1977	A company will be required to collect a use tax if it maintains offices in the state from which it conducts activities, even though the offices bear no relation to its selling activities.

situation should be made because of potential changes in both the corporation's activities and the state's jurisdictional position. Concern over use tax collections have been increasing recently because of the following reasons[11]:

1 States are taking more aggressive positions in enforcing their laws, particularly when it can also further support their own revenue needs. For example, during an audit of a company, if it is discovered that a tax has not properly been added to a sales invoice, many states will send a questionnaire to the vendor concerning its activities in the state.

[11]Richard J. Krol, "Current Approaches to Doing Business for Sales and Use Tax Nexus Purposes," 50 *Journal of Taxation* (May 1979), p. 308.

2 There may be a greater number of these audits in the future being
   conducted by the Multistate Tax Commission, particularly since the
   U.S. Supreme Court's sanctioning of the Multistate Tax Compact.[12]

3 In most states, a fiduciary relationship exists, whereby the vendor will
   be responsible for ultimate payment of the tax if the vendor fails to
   collect the tax from the proper customer. Although these vendors could
   ultimately look back to their customers for reimbursement, it may not
   be practical if only small amounts are due from many sources. The
   costs of recollecting may exceed the actual tax liability. Furthermore,
   many vendors may not even consider to collect the tax at a later date
   because of the company's customer relation policies.

4 As with many other state taxes, the cumulative effect of noncompliance
   with a state's collection procedures can have a significant dollar impact
   on a business. The statute of limitations does not begin to run until a
   return has been filed with the state. Therefore, even if a company fails
   to collect and remit taxes because it believes it does not have sufficient
   nexus within a state, the state can look back to when nexus first
   occurred and seek payments from that point in time.

Therefore, because many questions can exist about when an occasional
activity within a state will provide the necessary link or satisfy a state's
nexus requirements, the activities of each business must be analyzed.
Exhibit 7.2 highlights some of the activities a business might have within a
state and considers the potential use tax consequences.[13]

EXEMPTION POLICIES

Reasons for Exemption

Corporations are parties to various types of transactions throughout each
business year. Each transaction may or may not be subject to a sales or use
tax. If a corporation were to purchase 100 shares of stock, the purchase
price would consist of the fair market value of the stock and usually a
broker's commission. No sales tax would be paid. Similarly, if this same
corporation were to invest in land, no additional sales tax would be added
on to the purchase price of the land. Yet, if a purchase order for office
supplies were to be sent to a supplier, a sales tax must be added on to the
retail price of the goods. When an order for machinery or equipment is
made, depending on the state in which the corporation is located, a sales

---

[12]See Chapter 4 of this book for a discussion of the Multistate Tax Compact and the case of
U.S. Steel v. *Multistate Tax Commission* 54 L Ed 2d 682 (1978).
[13]Krol, "Current Approaches to Doing Business for Sales and Use Tax Nexus Purposes"
pp. 309–311.

Exhibit 7.2

Connection or Link with a State	Tax Considerations
1. Making deliveries of merchandise into the state	In determining whether a company will be subject to a state's use tax requirements, two factors must be considered: **(a)** The frequency of the deliveries, **(b)** The manner in which the deliveries are made. Occasional deliveries by common carrier or even using a company's vehicle should not subject a company to tax use collections.[a] Deliveries made on a regular basis but by common carrier should also not subject a company to use tax collections.[b] However, if a company makes regular deliveries using its own vehicles, sufficient nexus may be considered to be established.[c]
2. Drop shipments into a state	A *drop shipment* is a shipment made by the seller to someone other than the purchaser. For example, X sells goods to Y but is told by Y to deliver the goods to Z. X sends its bill to Y and receives payment from Y. Y then sends its bill to Z and receives payment from Z. In this example, a tax may have to be collected, depending on the method of delivery into a state and the manner in which a state views its tax. The state can view its tax as a tax on transactions occurring within the state, or the state might focus its tax on the party delivering the goods into the state. In these later cases, most states do not mention whether the method of delivery considered by itself would have any effect on a company's responsibility to collect taxes.
3. Over-the-counter sales	To be required to collect a tax on over-the-counter sales, the use of the goods in the taxing state must be known to the seller from the seller's own actions. For example, if a company sells its goods over the counter to an out-of-state customer and then delivers the goods into the taxing state, the company will be required to collect the tax if there is sufficient nexus within the state. In other words, the use of the goods in the taxing state cannot merely be based on a seller's knowledge, it must be based on the seller's

Exhibit 7.2 *(continued)*

Connection or Link with a State	Tax Considerations
	actions, such as the actual sending or delivery of goods into the state.[d] If the state in which the property is to be used cannot claim jurisdiction over the seller, the over-the-counter sale cannot be directly reached. However, there may be an informal collection agreement between neighboring states to solve the problem of border retailers.
4. Sales-related personnel sent into a state	Sending any sales-related personnel into a state may or may not be considered sufficient nexus to subject a seller to collect taxes, depending on a state's law and regulations. Since most states do not specifically speak to the activities of repairmen or service representatives, it is necessary to consider a state's definition of "doing business." If doing business is defined by the state in very narrow terms, there will most likely not be any basis for requiring use tax collections. If doing business is defined in broad terms and the state can demonstrate that the presence of these personnel within its borders allows the continuance of a contractual relationship between the buyer and seller, then use tax collections could be required.
5. Nonsales personnel within a state	Nonsales personnel of a company — such as individuals on training programs or purchasing agents who are within a state for a short period of time — would not subject the company to registration as a vendor within the state. These company personnel can conduct limited activities within a state because the "slightest presence" test is not a sufficient test for determining whether nexus exists.[e] A more definite link or connection to the state would be required.
6. Independent contractors	The presence of independent contractors within a state to solicit sales will create sufficient nexus with a taxing state.[f]
	If an out-of-state vendor merely wanted to conduct a mail order business with customers in a state and not have any obligations to collect use taxes, the vendor may find it

Exhibit 7.2 *(continued)*

Connection or Link with a State	Tax Considerations
	possible to do so by changing the status of its independent contractor in the state. By properly planning the business activities, the company can convert the status of an independent contractor to that of a customer of the company. In these cases, the company is no longer doing business with its own agent in the state but with a customer acting on his own behalf.[g] However, in these circumstances, the customer would become responsible for sales tax collections in the state.
7. Collection and credit activities in a state	There have been no state or Supreme Court decisions involving the issue of whether collection activities alone would subject a company to use tax collections. It seems doubtful that such activities would trigger collection responsibilities. If a company found it necessary to perform collection activities within a state whose state law did not specifically cover this activity, the use of an independent agency to perform these services should be considered. If a state's law specifically mentions this type of activity, there are no constitutional restrictions preventing a state from requiring the company to register as an agent, provided the activity were performed on a regular basis.
8. Advertising	It is possible that the use of a local advertising media in a state could be sufficient to create nexus in that jurisdiction. Therefore, if local advertising is necessary and a company wanted to avoid use tax collections, a company should consider only using the U.S. Postal Service or the telephone. Furthermore, it is recommended that there be no other types of contacts with the state. When a company's only contact with a state is advertising through the use of the national media as well as catalogs and flyers, use tax collections are not required.[h]
9. Qualification in the state	Qualification to do business within a state may require that a company file income tax returns in that state. It does not require a

Exhibit 7.2 *(continued)*

Connection or Link with a State	Tax Considerations
	company to register as a collector of use taxes if no activities are being carried on.
10. Ownership of real property in the state	If real property were used for any type of business purpose in the state, a state could require the collection of use taxes.[i] If the property were merely acquired and being held only for possible future expansion, it should not be considered a sufficient connection with the state. However, if a company wanted to avoid any possible problems in this area, the company might find it worthwhile to consider the acquisition and holding of real property in a state by using a separate subsidiary company. Any potential Federal or state income tax consequences would also have to be evaluated.
11. Ownership of work in process in a state	Work in process in a state is similar to maintaining real property used in a business. Therefore, if a state's law specifically covers this topic, sufficient nexus could be created. If a state's law does not cover this area, an argument could be made that the existence of work in process inventory does not constitute doing business in a state. Therefore, no nexus with the state has been created.
12. Ownership of finished goods in a state	When a company maintains a finished inventory of goods in a state and makes sales to customers in the state from goods located outside the state, the company will be required to collect a use tax.[j] If sales are made to customers in a state from the finished goods also located in the state, it is the state's sales tax that would be collected, since the activity is strictly intrastate.
13. Maintaining consigned goods in a state	It is possible for a state to consider the consignment of goods sufficient contact in the state to create nexus. However, other states may specifically exclude consigned property from the definition of when a company is engaged in business in the state.[k] For those states where consigned goods creates sufficient nexus, a company must account

Exhibit 7.2 *(continued)*

Connection or Link with a State	Tax Considerations
	for the use taxes on all of its sales into the state, including mail order sales that would not have been subject to the tax were it not for the consigned goods being held in the state.

[a]*Miller Brothers Company* v. *Maryland* 347 U.S. 340 (1953).
[b]*National Bellas Hess, Incorporated* v. *Department of Revenue* 386 U.S. 753 (1967).
[c]For example, see Massachusetts' Sales Tax Law, Chapter 64.H, Section 1(5).
[d]*American Oil Company* v. *Neill* 380 U.S. 451 (1965).
[e]*National Geographic Society* v. *California Board of Equalization* 51 L Ed 2d 631 (1977).
[f]*Scripto, Incorporated* v. *Carson et al.* 362 U.S. 207 (1959).
[g]*Alabama* v. *McFadden-Bartell Corporation* 194 So. 2d 543 (1967).
[h]*National Bellas Hess, Incorporated* v. *Department of Revenue* 386 U.S. 753 (1967).
[i]*National Geographic Society* v. *California Board of Equalization.*
[j]*National Geographic Society* v. *California Board of Equalization.*
[k]For example, see Massachusetts Law Section 64H, Section 1(4)(d).

tax may or may not be paid. Why are only some transactions taxed when other sales are considered immune from this additional burden?

Throughout the history of our country's tax laws, the problem of an all-encompassing tax levy has been a difficult matter to deal with. Whether in the interest of the public, economic gain, or administrative realities, exceptions to laws are quite common. The IRC is laden with terminology such as "except for" or "excluding" certain transactions. The sales and use tax laws are no different. The exemptions for sales and use taxes vary between the states, and this creates compliance problems for the interstate business.

The Ultimate Consumer—Bearer of the Tax

The general belief that sales taxes are to be paid by the ultimate consumer of a product has formed the basis of an important exemption existing in all states. All property purchased for resale is exempt from sales or use tax. The goods in question can either be purchased in their present form to be resold to the ultimate consumer or combined with other goods to become a part of a new product.

If sales taxes had to be paid on each ingredient of a final product, the ultimate consumer would end up paying higher prices to absorb the additional taxes of the producers, in addition to carrying the burden of the sales or use tax itself. Suppose, for example, that Company X, which is engaged in the manufacture and sale of bookshelves and decorative wall units, purchases the two basic materials, lumber and hardware, used for their products. Company X purchases the lumber and hardware from various distributors, depending on the quality and quantity to be used. If Company X had to pay a sales tax on these purchases, the taxes paid would become an additional cost to be reflected in the eventual retail price of the bookshelves or wall units. Furthermore, if the vendor of the lumber or hardware had to pay sales or use tax when purchasing the goods, this tax would also be passed on to Company X and, finally, to the customers of Company X. It is easy to see why items held for resale are exempt from the sales tax. Not having this exemption would be contrary to the original intent of the tax.

Sales to Selected Parties

Exemption policies are also guided by the nature of the buyer. Typically, these exemptions deal with sales to governmental bodies or to exempt organizations. Every state is precluded from taxing sales to the U.S. government. In addition, some states exempt sales when the state itself is the purchaser, and sometimes this exemption is extended to local or municipal governing bodies. Finally, exempt organizations, whether organized for educational or religious purposes, are also included in this special class of purchasers. Exemptions of this nature are granted as a matter of public interest.

Isolated Sales

In some states, "isolated," "casual," or "occasional" sales are also exempt from sales and use tax. Although some states have expressly exempted sales of this kind,[14] it is important to analyze a state's statutory provisions and interpretations. In a few states where there are no express provisions exempting the "occasional" sale, the courts have provided for such exemptions through their interpretations of the state's statute. Interpretations of a "business," "activity," or "retail sale" within a state have been determined so as to exclude any isolated, casual, or occasional sales.[15]

Nature of the Transaction

The predominant business activity will vary from state to state. Consequently, the exemption policies for goods and services purchased in each state will also vary. It is important to keep in mind that these tax exemption policies, like all tax laws, influence and are influenced by the business climate and other conditions.

[14]*Commonwealth ex rel. Luckett* v. *Revday Industries, Incorporated* 432 S.W. 2d 819 (1968).
[15]*State* v. *Bay Towing & Dredging Company* 90 So. 2d 743 (1956); *Glass-Tite Industries, Incorporated* v. *State Board of Equalization* 266 Cal. App. 2d 691, 72 Cal. Rptr. 244 (1968); *Main Aviation Corporation* v. *Johnson* 196 A.2d 748 (1964).

The following list illustrates transactions that are either not subject to taxation or exempted from taxation. This list is not all inclusive, it is merely a sample to show the variety of exemptions that exist.

EXEMPT AND NONTAXABLE TRANSACTIONS

1 Sales for resale.
2 Sales of tangible personal property that becomes a component or ingredient of an article to be resold.
3 Sales to religious, or charitable organizations.
4 Temporary storage (production unit fabricated in one state and used in another).
5 Sales directly to U.S. government.
6 Sales to the state and its political subdivisions.
7 Sales to private nonprofit educational institutions.
8 Sales to consumers who pay tax direct to state.
9 Sales of fuel used in creating gas, power, steam, or electricity for resale.
10 Sales of fuel for domestic heating.
11 Sales in interstate commerce.
12 Sales of fuels and supplies for vessels engaged in foreign and interstate commerce.
13 Air and/or water pollution control facilities, including chemicals for operation.
14 Rental of tangible personal property to wholesalers or jobbers who rerent to their customers.
15 Manufacturing or processing machinery or equipment.

A Case in Point—Why Some States Exempt Sales of Machinery

The taxation or exemption of sales and transfers of machinery will be used as an example to illustrate some of the considerations that could influence a state to alter its exemption policies. Machinery is an interesting category because of the way it was and is being handled by the states. At one time, very few states exempted these sales. Now some 25 states exempt or partically exempt these sales. (See *All State Handbook,* Prentice-Hall, 1978, paragraph 254). The most recent state to adopt this exemption was Illinois. There are three basic reasons why exemptions are given to sales of machinery. First, a tax on machinery would be equivalent to a tax on investment, thereby discouraging corporate expansion. Second, the tax discriminates between certain types of industries. Third, it is hard to determine who bears the ultimate burden of the tax.[16]

[16]State and Local Sales Tax, p. 24.

Industrial expansion occurs when the economic climate is conducive and permissive of additional investments. New businesses, or companies expanding their present operations, will be faced with substantial expenditures for machinery. The Federal government encourages investments through the mechanism of the investment credit.[17] When a state imposes a tax on such transactions, it is possible that the burden of this additional charge, if large enough, will discourage efforts by a corporation to make new investments. The additional amounts paid for these taxes will have to be recovered by a corporation to get a high enough return on its capital. Whereas the state may benefit from larger revenues in the short run by collecting taxes on machinery, the picture in the long run may not be as bright because of the potential effects of a lower economic growth rate. Less investment by manufacturing concerns can mean smaller incomes for employees and a reduced rate of growth for jobs.[18]

Capital-intense industries will be hit with the sales tax on machinery more than labor-intense industries simply because of the nature of the enterprises. This will increase the cost of capital goods over the cost of service-oriented products. For example, "If the tax on machinery is treated like other costs, it will eventually account for a slight price increase for capital intensive goods. Such price increases are likely to exceed somewhat the amount attributable to the tax alone because distributors and retailers apply percentage markups to the intermediate prices that include the tax element. These price differentials between goods produced with taxed machinery and others are magnified at each succeeding level of distribution. As a result, some goods are taxed more heavily than others, in a pattern devoid of conscious policy."[19]

Finally, there is no way to determine who bears the ultimate burden of the tax on machinery. As previously stated one of the reasons for exemption is to maintain the original intent behind the tax. Only the ultimate consumer should pay the tax. When machinery is taxed, the charge is shifted to various parties within and out of the state, making it difficult to pinpoint who specifically is paying the tax. For example, "When machinery is subjected to tax, prices of some commodities are likely to reflect a larger tax element than those of others, and prices of manufactured goods as a group will include a heavier tax share than those of services. Furthermore, some manufactured products are exported to out-of-state buyers while others are sold to residents. In these circumstances, estimates of who bears the ultimate burden becomes little more than crude guesses—in contrast to the informed guesses we can make about who pays tax on consumer goods."[20]

On the other side, the states that do tax machinery have the potential to

[17]Section 38 IRC 1954.
[18]State and Local Sales Tax, p. 25.
[19]State and Local Sales Tax, p. 25.
[20]State and Local Sales Tax, p. 25.

receive rather larger amounts of revenue. When a state is predominately capital oriented, it is possible that the additional tax will not affect any corporate decisions concerning whether an expansion should be made or a new business should be started. It is taken for granted that investments in machinery will be made. The corporations could consider the sales tax as a necessary expense of doing business. In addition, it is possible that some administrative problems can be avoided by the states by not exempting this item.

Exemption Certificates

General

Whereas all states having sales and use taxes allow exemptions, the risk associated with the acceptance of claimed exemptions can be very substantial. It is important to remember that the state places a burden on the seller to collect the appropriate tax. The burden of collection extends to proving that all sales for which a tax was not collected fall into some exempt or nontaxable category. For some sellers, this may not be too great a burden. For example, a retailer has virtually no exempt sales, because none could qualify for exemption. All the retailer's customers would be the ultimate consumer of the property. This seller attaches tax to every sale and remits it to the state. Collection becomes a routine business task. Likewise, a manufacturer who sells all his products to distributors who then resells to retailers would not have a substantial burden. All this manufacturer's sales would fall into the "resale" exemption, and this seller would not attach a tax to any of his sales. However, if he has registered for sales and use taxes with the particular state, he would have the burden of showing that the sales were exempt. He would do this by having on file exemption certificates from customers in the form described later. These exemption certificates are the evidence required by the state to justify not collecting tax from the customer.

The greatest burden of collecting sales and use taxes falls on the seller who has a variety of products that are being sold to both consumers and exempt customers. For example, assume a steel manufacturer sells to distributors, manufacturers, and to contractors (consumers). Careful administration of sales and use tax collection is necessary so that this seller fulfills his obligation to the state. A breakdown in this administration could result in the manufacturer being liable to the state for the tax that should have been collected from the customer.

Form of Exemption Certificate

VALIDITY

The proof requirements of the states can take different forms. Generally, if the following are included, the burden of proof will have been met.

1   State registration number of the buyer.

2   Description and exempt purpose of the property purchased.

3   The signature of the buyer or of an authorized representative of the buyer.

The presence of these elements may not conclusively meet the burden placed on the seller. The seller must exercise care to determine that the property being sold is of a type normally sold to that customer for that customer's exempt use. As an illustration, assume that the same steel manufacturer receives an exemption certificate for structural steel from a manufacturer who normally buys coiled steel to be manufactured into a given product, say, steel drums. The seller must recognize this anomaly at the time of sale, and if he has reason to believe that the structural steel is to be consumed by the manufacturer, for instance, in a plant expansion, the exemption certificate must be disregarded. This places an undue burden on the seller in the opinion of many sellers. These sellers argue that with the thousands of customers a company may have, it is virtually impossible to be thoroughly acquainted with each to the extent that border line distinctions between normal exempt purchases and extraordinary taxable purchases can be made. The better and more practical practice advocated by such sellers is the "good faith" approach. This rule would relieve the seller of collection responsibility if he accepts an exemption certificate in good faith, provided the certificate is valid in all other respects.

The reason for the states' reluctance to follow such a concept is obvious. It is much less costly from an administrative viewpoint to place the burden on the seller. If the seller fails for any reason, the state can force collection through such seller. It would be much more difficult to chase a multitude of buyers to determine taxability.

FORM OF CERTIFICATES

Unit Certificate   An exemption certificate may be given by a purchaser for the purpose of making a single purchase exempt. The certificate, in addition to the three requirements for validity, would be identified with the purchase order or shipment. It may be in the form of a separate document, or it may be encompassed into the purchase order itself. It is valid only for that particular purchase.

Blanket Certificate   To avoid the necessity of completing an exemption certificate for every purchase, the states allow a single certificate to cover all similar exempt purchases. Thus if the steel manufacturer had frequent sales of steel coils to a manufacturer of steel drums, a blanket certificate would suffice indefinitely to meet the burden of proving the exempt nature of the sale. Caution is again necessary by the steel manufacturer to detect a variance.

For example, the drum manufacturer may one day want to make a taxable purchase. In this case, he would notify the steel manufacturer that tax should be charged on this particular purchase. Commonly, this notification would be reflected on the customer's purchase order. It is incumbent on the seller to recognize such notification, since this takes precedence over the blanket exemption certificate.

Uniform Exemption Certificate

Exemption certificate requirements vary among the states in terms of format. Some do not have a single form. Rather, various forms have been devised for use in particular situations. The use of different forms adds to the difficulty of administering the collection of tax by sellers.

The MTC has proposed a uniform sales and use tax certificate form which is reproduced on Exhibit 7.3. The form eliminates the necessity of more than one document for a particular state. For ease of handling, the form can be reprinted on index cards, which facilitates filing.

The states that have accepted this form are indicated on the reverse side of the form. Note that the seller is cautioned about his requirement to exercise care concerning whether the property being sold is of such a nature that it would normally be exempt for the reason stated in the certificate.

Importance of Exemption Certificates

FOR THE SELLER

It has already been stated that the burden is on the seller to establish exemption. If he fails in this burden, the seller will find that the tax will be assessed against him in most states. Although the tax is assessed and collected from the seller, this does not mean that the seller cannot then bill the tax to the customer. The difficulty with this is that some customers may no longer be in business, or for some reason they may no longer be readily reachable. Also, assessment against the seller usually includes interest from the time the tax should have been paid to the state, and many states are prone to charge penalties for failure to collect tax. Attempts to pass interest and penalty charges to the customer would be strongly resisted.

FOR THE PURCHASER

The payment of taxes to an authorized collection agent of the state is a cost of doing business and cannot be circumvented by the purchaser. However, a taxpayer is obligated to pay only that which it is legally required to pay. Therefore, the purchaser of taxable property must be alert to allowable exemptions. Failure of recognition of the exemption, coupled with the resulting failure to execute a valid exemption certificate to the seller, would result in tax being charged where none was appropriate. The seller, as

UNIFORM SALES & USE TAX CERTIFICATE FORM

SALES TAX EXEMPTION CERTIFICATE
MULTI-JURISDICTION

(See reverse side for instructions)

Issued to (Seller)   Address

I certify that _____ is engaged as a registered
                                                 ___ Wholesaler

                                                 ___ Retailer
               _____
               Street Address or P.O. Box No.   ___ Manufacturer

                                                 ___ Lessor (*See note on reverse side.)
               _____
               City   State   Zip Code
                                                 ___ Other (Specify): _____ and
                                                 ___

               _____

is registered with the below listed states and cities within which your firm would deliver
purchases to us and that any such purchases are for wholesale, resale, ingredients or
components of a new product to be resold, leased, or rented in the normal course of our
business. We are in the business of wholesaling, retailing, manufacturing, leasing (renting)
the following: _____

_____

City or State   State Registration or ID No.   City or State   State Registration or ID No.

City or State   State Registration or ID No.   City or State   State Registration or ID No.

City or State   State Registration or ID No.   City or State   State Registration or ID No.

I further certify that if any property so purchased tax-free is used or consumed by the firm
as to make it subject to a Sales or Use Tax we will pay the tax due direct to the proper taxing authority when state law so provides or inform the seller for added tax billing. This
certificate shall be part of each order which we may hereafter give to you, unless otherwise
specified, and shall be valid until canceled by us in writing or revoked by the city or
state.

General description of products to be purchased from the seller:

_____

Under penalties of perjury, I swear or affirm that the information on ths form is true and
correct as to every material matter.

Authorized Signature (Owner, Partner, or Corporate Officer)   Title   Date

---

Exhibit 7.3

previously noted, has a strong burden to collect tax, and this leads to his
inclination to charge tax on the presumption that all sales are taxable. It is
the buyer's responsibility to claim his exemption. For example, a common
exemption granted to manufacturers is for new pollution control facilities.
An unawareness of this exemption would add a costly premium to this type
expenditure.

Registration

In practical terms to the seller, a sales tax can be thought of as the tax
charged on intrastate sales, and a use tax can be thought of as the tax

(Reverse Side)

TO OUR CUSTOMERS:

In order to comply with the majority of state and local sales tax law requirements, it is necessary that we have in our files a properly executed exemption certificate from all of our customers who claim sales tax exemption. If we do not have this certificate, we are obligated to collect the tax for the state in which the property is delivered.

If you are entitled to sales tax exemption, please complete the certificate and send it to us at your earliest convenience. If you purchase tax-free for a reason for which this form does not provide, please send us your special certificate or statement.

This form of certificate has been determined to be acceptable to the following states as of January 31, 1974:

Alabama	Maryland	South Carolina
Alaska	Michigan	South Dakota
Arizona	Minnesota	Tennessee
Arkansas	Missouri	Texas
District of Columbia	Nevada	Utah
Georgia	New Mexico	Vermont
Idaho	North Dakota	Virginia
Illinois	Oklahoma	Washington
Iowa	Pennsylvania	Wisconsin
Maine	Rhode Island	Wyoming

NOTE: Arizona law provides that a seller will be held liable for sales tax due on any sales with respect to which an exemption certificate is found to be invalid, for whatever reason.

Illinois, Iowa, and South Dakota do not have an exemption on sales of property for subsequent lease or rental.

CAUTION TO SELLER: In order for the certificate to be accepted in good faith by the seller, the seller must exercise care that the property being sold is of a type normally sold wholesale, resold, leased, rented, or utilized as an ingredient or component part of a product manufactured by the buyer in the usual course of his business. A seller failing to exercise due care could be held liable for the sales tax due in some states or cities.

Misuse of this certificate by the seller, lessor, buyer, lessee, or the representative thereof may be punishable by fine, imprisonment, or loss of right to issue certificates in some states or cities.

Exhibit 7.3 *(continued)*

charged to customers on interstate sales. To illustrate this, assume an interstate seller operates as follows.

Manufacturing Plant and Warehouse	Dallas, Texas
Sales offices	Kansas City, Missouri
	Rockford, Illinois
Other states in which customers are located	Michigan
	Indiana
	Ohio

All orders are accepted in Dallas and shipped from there. All sales are of a character to be subject to the sales and use taxes of the states where sold.

This seller is faced with collection responsibility with respect to Texas, Missouri, and Illinois as a result of having business locations in those states. The seller's activities will have led to his having registered with these states. Assume that the taxes that the seller will be remitting are the sales tax collections for Texas and the use tax collections of Missouri and Illinois. For Indiana, Michigan, and Ohio, the seller may have collection responsibility if he comes up to the jurisdictional standards established by the previously discussed court cases. This determination is very important to the interstate seller, also as previously discussed.

While the ultimate determination of jurisdiction will depend on the rules set forth in the various court decisions, a generalization about the overall jurisdictional standards has been made by the MTC.[21] These standards are shown next. A vendor is required to pay or collect and remit the tax imposed by this act if within this state he directly or by agent or other representatives engages in the following:

1 Has or utilizes an office, distribution house, warehouse, service enterprise, or other place of business.
2 Maintains a stock of goods.
3 Regularly solicits orders whether such orders are accepted in this state, unless the activity in this state consists solely of advertising or of solicitation by direct mail.
4 Regularly engages in the delivery of property in this state other than by common carrier or U.S. mail.
5 Regularly engages in any activity in connection with the leasing or servicing of property located within this state.

In any event, the seller needs to closely monitor his activities in these states to conclusively be able to prove lack of jurisdiction. If the nexus boundary has been broached, there may be a matter of back liability to be settled with the state. If the state detects jurisdiction and forces registration, it will very likely hold the seller liable for payment of tax of previous periods that he should have collected from in-state customers.

COMPLIANCE AND ADMINISTRATION

By the Corporation

It has been mentioned several times throughout this chapter that the consumer is to be the ultimate bearer of a sales or use tax. It is the vendor, however, who must serve in a fiduciary capacity to collect the tax from the buyer and remit it to the state. There are times though when a consumer will pay a state directly, particularly if large sums of money are involved. But since it is more common for vendors to collect the taxes, the compliance and administration problems of corporations are discussed in terms of these vendors.

[21] Seventh Annual Report MTC, Appendix D.

The compliance problems for the corporations being considered here include both the largest and the smallest organizations. Compliance by the smaller corporation often tends to be more burdensome and demanding, so the additional recordkeeping required by the states is often inadequate or at times nonexistent. Generally, the larger corporations will comply more strictly to sales and use tax regulations because of tight controls exerted from both internal and external forces. Specific government agencies often demand various financial reports, and internal and external auditors require certain information to be generated from within the corporate accounting system. Meeting the requirements of reporting the voluminous financial and nonfinancial statistical information to government agencies, auditors, stockholders, and management lessens the burden of compliance with sales and use tax regulations. Furthermore, qualified, trained personnel are employed by larger corporations to question and analyze and finally produce the required data.

A reasonable estimate of the salaries attributable to work done on sales and use tax data, along with the additional expense of tracing documentation for audits, can be computed, based on the results of time studies. In addition to these costs are the potential uncollected sales and use taxes that must be absorbed and any further expenses involved in an audit. Some states allow vendors to keep a small percentage of the collections as compensation for this additional work. For many vendors, these collection allowances will adequately cover compliance costs.

By the States

One of the reasons sales and use taxes were so appealing to the states was the ease of administration. Although the states could have turned to each individual purchaser for these taxes, collectibility has been facilitated with the use of vendors as agents of the state. There are many thousands of vendors throughout the country who are required to engage in tax collections. States maintain control over these businesses by requiring each company to register with the state, thereby receiving an identification or registration number. These companies must then file a periodic return, usually monthly, and report all sales, even if there is no tax to be remitted. Those enterprises with large dollar collections are required to make prepayments or estimated payments of these taxes in a manner similar to the filing of quarterly estimated payments for Federal income tax purposes.

If all corporations strictly complied with the legal requirements of each state, the role of the state auditor would be simplified. A large cost of administering these taxes is due to the costs of the audits, partially because there is some subjectiveness involved in evaluating the circumstances in many cases. Also, for the small businesses, the auditors may have to reconstruct data or help the taxpayer establish better controls over its accounting system. There is still no way to patrol every dollar of tax being collected or to insure that taxes collected are actually remitted to the state.

Despite these difficulties, these taxes are relatively inexpensive for the state to administer.

Audits

The additional burden the seller/collector of sales and use taxes endures is that of being regularly audited by enforcement agencies of the states. These audits have two main thrusts. One is to uncover deficiencies in the sellers' operations that lead to failure to charge tax. The other is to examine the taxpayers' purchases to verify that all tax due has been paid on property acquired for taxable use. Each of these thrusts is discussed in general terms.

Audit of Sales

DETAILED AUDIT

The audit approach in the examination of sales transactions is to review the customer invoices of transactions involving in-state buyers. Those transactions that involved exempt sales may be questioned, and support for the exempt status may be requested to the auditor. Evidence in the form of an exemption certificate should suffice, unless it appears the product sold is not of the type that would normally be within the exemption.

Usually, no matter how tight the administration of sales and use tax collections may be, some deficiency can be detected on audit. Some examples of these deficiencies and the remedy, if any, are as follows.

1　Exemption certificates are not on file to support sales classified as exempt.
　Remedy—The taxpayer ordinarily will be permitted to contact the customer and obtain an exemption certificate.
2　Sales appear to be outside the scope of the exemption certificate.
　Remedy—The customer may be contracted to determine the use by the customer. Evidence of exempt use will satisfy the auditor regarding the exempt nature of the sale.
3　Incorrect rate charged. This can easily occur during a rate change in a state or through inadvertently referring to the wrong state rate when attaching the tax.
　Remedy—Correction to customer billing or determine if customer has made payment to the state.
4　Omission of tax on taxable sales. Omissions usually are a result of loose administration or outright clerical errors.
　Remedy—Correction to customer billing or determine if customer has made payment to the state.

The sum of such errors and deficiencies at the conclusion of the audit is a tentative assessment against the seller/collector.

The seller still has an opportunity to reduce the assessment during the audit. Those errors that were a result of failure to charge the customer at all or charging the wrong rate may be removed from the assessment by contacting the customer to see if the tax, or additional tax, due on the material purchased was recognized by the customer and paid to the state. If so, the state, when presented with evidence from the customer that the tax was paid, will not again assess the tax against the seller.

When a deficiency has been paid, the seller is permitted to bill the customer for tax that should have been billed during the audit period and use the funds to offset the payment to the state. As previously mentioned, the seller is liable for any interest or penalty attached to the assessment.

TEXT AUDIT

Most sales and use tax audits cover a span of three or four years. In this period, an interstate seller may have many thousands of invoices to be examined. Further, the file copies of these invoices are not usually arranged by state. To do a detailed audit for the entire period would necessitate looking at every invoice to find the in-state sales and then auditing these invoices for exceptions. To circumvent this need, the auditor and the seller will tentatively agree to a sampling of selected months. The objective of this is to determine an error percentage which will then be projected on the presumption that the test period results are representative of the entire audit period. The advantage of this to the auditor is that it simply reduces the necessary work to a fraction of that required for a detailed audit.

The advantage to the seller is also related to the time element. That is, the time required for completion can be greatly shortened. However, the test audit is for the convenience of the seller only. It should not be agreed to prior to the completion of the audit, at which time the seller can judge whether the results appear to be representative. If the results seem clearly nonrepresentative, then the seller should insist on a detailed audit. In some states, test audits are permitted by law, in which case the seller would have no choice about the use of a test method.

The disadvantage of a test audit is that the deficiency cannot be billed to customers. For example, assume the audit reveals an invoice for $1000 to Customer M in the test month where tax in the amount of $50 should have been collected. Further, assume that the $1000 invoice as 0.001 of all the sales within the exempt classification examined in the test month. If the total exempt sales for the audit period is $10,000,000, the deficiency is $500 ($10,000 × .05). The seller may regard this as reasonable and express a willingness to accept an assessment based on the audit sample. The seller will realize though that only $50 can be billed to Customer M to offset the $500 assessment. The $450 remainder represents similar invoices to unknown customers.

In a test audit, the seller must be cautious about whether the sample is planned to produce a result representative of the entire audit period. Once the exceptions are noted by the auditor for the test month, it is extremely important for even the smallest exception to be cleared, since all the final exceptions will be projected. Exceptions in the test period can be cleared in the same manner as those in a detailed audit.

Audit of Purchases

The second audit thrust is to verify that the taxpayer, in this case the consumer, has paid tax on all the taxable property it has purchased. When the taxpayer buys taxable property, it will be faced with the collection of tax by the seller, if the seller is registered with the state. In this event, the seller will charge tax unless the taxpayer claims exemption and supports the claim with the proper exemption certificate. If the taxpayer erroneously claims exemption, a tax deficiency exists that could be detected on audit.

Deficiencies arise for many reasons. For example, the taxpayer may in good faith issue an exemption certificate for a purchase it regards as exempt. Controversy can arise here between the state and the taxpayer regarding the interpretation of the exemption. This type of controversy is typical among those states that allow an exemption for machinery and equipment used in manufacturing and narrows the scope to "direct" use. Interpretative problems then arise about whether conveyor systems, fork lift trucks, and so on, are within the exemption.

If the taxpayer buys taxable property from a seller who is not registered, the tax will not be collected by such seller. This could occur when purchasing from any seller who has insufficient nexus with the taxing state. The taxpayer in this situation should recognize such and maintain administrative procedures to "accrue" the tax. That is, an accounting entry will be generated charging expense and setting up a tax liability to the state. This liability will be paid when the taxpayer files its sales and use tax returns for the period. The procedure established must provide an appropriate audit trail. That is, the auditor must be able to trace the tax accrual from the invoice into the liability account and be able to subsequently trace the liability into the return reflecting payment to the state.

In an audit of purchases, the examiner will be concerned with property that would ordinarily be of a taxable nature. Rather than examine all invoices that have been paid by the taxpayer, the examination will be limited to those invoices charged to accounts where one would expect taxable purchases to be charged. Examples of these accounts are fixed depreciable property, repair and maintenance accounts, and supplies. Accounts such as "purchases," that is, purchases of raw materials for further manufacture, would not be examined because it would be expected that all charges to this account would be exempt under the resale exemption.

Having determined which accounts to examine, the auditor can proceed to review entries to these accounts. In every accounting system, an entry into a specific account is referenced to a source document. The auditor will work back from the account to the source document and from the source document be able to tell the nature of the charge and whether it represents a taxable purchase. The source document, which will be an invoice from the seller, will also indicate whether tax was charged.

DETAILED AUDIT

The approach on a detailed audit of purchases is the same procedure as that for sales invoices, except in this instance the auditor will be reviewing invoices representing purchases. The first step in an audit of this type will be to determine the accounts to be examined and then decide to what extent the entries will be examined. In a large business, the number of entries into an account will be extremely large. Furthermore, retrieving the source document from the files of invoices is a very time-consuming chore. A complete detailed audit of any expense account is not practical. For this reason, some cutoff in the number of entries is made to limit the scope of the audit. This limitation on the number of entries to be examined may take the form of looking at those entries that exceed a specified dollar amount. The tedious task of tracing entries to source documents and retrieving those documents then begins.

Once the source documents have been retrieved and reviewed, exceptions will be recorded for the entire audit period and summarized into a total assessment. The remedy for the reduction of the auditor's determination often focuses on whether the material is exempt. An example of this was given in the discussion of the audit of sales, concerning the applicability of an exemption for machinery and equipment. Also, disagreement could readily occur with respect to whether material is part of a manufactured product, thus exempt under resale provisions, or whether the material is merely a consumable supply, not part of the manufactured product.

Whereas it is uncommon for a complete detailed audit to be conducted with respect to expense accounts for a large company, it is not uncommon for such an audit to occur with respect to fixed depreciable assets. Charges to fixed asset accounts are not so frequent as those to expense accounts, and it is not impractical to do a complete review of all the source documents to these accounts.

Fixed depreciable asset accounts carry forward in the balance sheet from year to year. The changes to these accounts can be noted from one year to the next, and the source documents that account for increases can be retrieved and reviewed. From the viewpoint of the auditor, it is important to review all depreciable property acquisitions for the simple reason that this type of property is often high in cost, and failure to pay tax would result in a substantial loss of revenue to the state. Furthermore, the combination of large cost and irregular frequency make it impractical to audit on a test basis.

In terms of expense accounts, a complete detailed audit is virtually impossible. The term "detailed audit" with respect to expense accounts merely means that some kind of review is made of selected expense accounts for the entire audit period.

In the review of source documents, the auditor may discover purchases that are taxable where no tax was charged. The applicable tax in this instance will be assessed by the auditor. There is an interplay here between the seller and the buyer. The seller may later be assessed on the same invoice when his sales invoices are examined. The seller can escape assessment in this instance by obtaining verification from the buyer that tax was paid on audit to the state.

In other situations where tax was not charged, the taxpayer may have accrued the tax and paid it to the state. This serves to satisfy the liability to the state the same as if it were paid to the seller/collector. Again, there is an interplay between buyer and seller. When the seller is audited and the same invoice comes to light, the seller may become liable for the tax again. This duplicative payment can be avoided by the seller if he obtains verification that the tax has been paid by the buyer. The liability to the state will have been satisfied in this instance by the assessment against the buyer.

TEXT AUDIT

Because of the normally large number of entries into accounts—such as repairs, maintenance, supplies, and the like—an audit based on a sampling of entries is usually advisable. The objective of the sample is to determine a deficiency for a given period that will be representative of the entire audit period.

The audit procedure will be to examine entries into the selected account for the month or months deemed appropriate. It is important for the taxpayer to closely examine the exceptions and determine that the amounts deemed taxable by the auditor are truly taxable and, if taxable, that tax has not been accrued and paid. The result of the test determines a deficiency for the entire audit; this means that any taxable invoice will be increased by some multiple to project it over the audit period.

In light of this discussion, consider this example in which an auditor from State M wants to examine all purchases of the "maintenance and repair materials" account for a three-year period. Recognizing the impossibility of such a task, the auditor proposes to audit on a test basis. The scope of the audit is limited to a review of the source documents for one month, with the understanding that the result for the test month will be projected over the audit period by multiplying such result by 36.

The result of the test audit, as shown by the auditor's workpapers, is a deficiency of $1000, determined from his finding that 50 invoices were for taxable purchases where no tax has been paid. The total liability is then projected as $1000 \times 36 = \$36,000$. In reviewing the audit workpapers, the taxpayer discovers that tax was accrued on five of the invoices, tax was paid to the vendor on two of the purchases, and three of the invoices represent nontaxable purchases. In total, these reduce the $1000 test-month deficiency to $750 and the three-year assessment to $27,000 ($750 \times 36$).

CHAPTER EIGHT

Gross Receipts Taxes

OBSERVATIONS FROM THE REPORT OF THE SPECIAL SUBCOMMITTEE ON STATE TAXATION OF INTERSTATE COMMERCE[1]

The nature and extent of the gross receipts tax is best described in the Special Subcommittee's report. Pertinent provisions are restated in this chapter, along with selected exhibits. It should be remembered that from the time the report was published up to the present changes may have occurred within any particular state tax therein described. However, changes that have occurred do not detract from the usefulness of a review of the date compiled for the report. Although particular changes may have evolved, the general nature of this tax remains the same.

General Characteristics

Although taxes based on the price of goods and services are probably the most widely used of state levies, most of these taxes are sales taxes. Only a few impose a tax of general applicability on the gross receipts of a business. These taxes are to be distinguished from retail sales taxes because they are not consumer taxes in the sense that the businesses on which they are imposed do not customarily separately state and collect the tax from purchasers at the retail level. Some of the states also use a retail sales tax, but each has developed a somewhat different relation between the two forms of taxes. The economic significance of the distinction between the sales tax and the gross receipts tax is that businesses subject to the latter type of tax treat it as part of their general costs not identified with any particular sales and are thus faced with the task of avoiding the absorption of the tax from profits. Furthermore, those businesses able to shift all or part of the tax forward in higher prices will, unlike businesses collecting the sales tax, reflect the gross receipts tax in prices of goods sold in states other than the taxing state.

Since gross receipts taxes are of several varieties, it may be helpful to mention the general characteristics of each type. The "business or occupa-

[1]Vol. 3, Part V, June 30, 1965.

tion" taxes imposed by Washington and West Virginia are most typically gross receipts taxes. They are broad-based levies, with few exemptions, on the privilege of engaging in various business activities within the state and are considered to be primarily imposed in place of an income tax. Being broadly based and imposed on numerous business functions, they tend to be multistage taxes in the sense that the taxes are imposed at more than one level in the production and distribution process. Both states rely heavily on these taxes as revenue producers.

The Alaska tax is a rather rudimentary gross receipts tax. A number of businesses are exempt, with the reasons being because they are subject to other business taxes, they are favored, or they desire to avoid multistage taxation. The result is largely a single-stage tax at the retail level. The rate structure, graduated according to total receipts, is the same for nearly all businesses covered. For those businesses subject to the tax, the rates are sufficiently high to make the tax a significant cost of operation.

Unlike the other gross receipts taxes that are on the privilege of doing business, the Indian tax is on the privilege of earning gross income. In spite of this difference in the subject of tax, the Indiana levy shared with the Washington and West Virginia taxes' similar breadth of coverage, similar multistage features, and a similar rate of differentiation policy. The different privileges subject to the Indiana tax, however, did result in a few variations from the other taxes. For example, the Indiana levy showed a greater inclusiveness; that is, business taxpayers included in their tax base such nonbusiness receipts as those from the sale of capital assets or from the sale of treasury stock. The reorganization of Indiana's tax structure in 1963, in which a corporate and personal income tax and a sales and use tax were enacted, reduced the coverage of the gross receipts tax without, however, altering its basic feature as a tax on the privilege of earning gross income. The removal of most of the broad classes of taxpayers has resulted in a tax imposed primarily on corporations whose liability under the gross receipts tax exceeds their liability under the net income tax. As such, the importance of the gross receipts tax as a revenue producer has been diminished, whereas the unusualness of its function has been heightened.

A somewhat ambiguous position is occupied by the taxes imposed by Hawaii and Mississippi. The tax in each state, as imposed on retailers, was considered with the sales taxes. Since the tax is separately stated and collected from the purchaser at the retail level, these taxes are not distinguishable from other sales taxes and present similar problems. As imposed at the wholesale level, although a separate statement is also customary in both states, these taxes are considered here because their multistage characteristic implies a further shift forward of the tax. The business buyer from whom the tax is collected on a wholesale purchase does not when reselling his purchase customarily separately state and collect the tax paid by him. Thus the tax is also, in effect, a tax on retailers collected by wholesalers, and the retailer is faced with the same kind of problem of avoiding the absorption of the tax as is the business subjected to the other taxes classified as gross receipts taxes. Hawaii also imposes its tax on all other levels in the production and distribution process, but the tax imposed on the privilege of production and manufacturing is not customarily separately stated and collected and is thus of no less a gross receipts character than the other taxes considered.

Nature of the Tax

One of the attractive features of gross receipts taxes, both to those who pay them and to those who administer them, is the simplicity of their application. Not only are there fewer problems for the taxpayer than are posed by the income tax or the sales tax, but also those problems that appear similar to ones in the income tax or sales tax are usually more easily resolved. For the prospective gross receipts taxpayer, the main issues are these: Is he a taxable person; if he is, into what taxing category or categories does he or his transactions fit, and, finally, how much of his gross receipts are taxable?

The first problem has two aspects: whether there is jurisdiction over the person and whether the person is exempt under the provisions of the tax. As seen later the significance of the former question is largely dependent on the issue of the constitutional power of the state to tax the person's receipts.

With a few exceptions, gross receipts taxes are taxes on all persons exercising the privilege of engaging in business activities other than those specifically exempted. One of the exceptions is the Indiana tax that is on the privilege of earning gross income and is primarily restricted to corporations. The Delaware taxes are, of course, limited to manufacturers and the four or five specified categories of merchants. Otherwise, the breadth of the taxes depends on the extent of the exemptions and varies from the rather narrow Alaska tax to the very broad tax levied by West Virginia.

Exemptions are of several general kinds. First, businesses taxed under other business privilege taxes, whether based on gross receipts or on some other measure, are normally exempted. Businesses in this category are usually regarded as appropriate subjects for special taxation and regulation. Some examples are banks, insurance companies, and utilities, although by no means is there uniformity.

A second group of exemptions consists of those businesses whose preservation and expansion the state favors as a matter of policy. Farming, for example, is taxed only in Hawaii.

The final category of exemptions is somewhat different from the others and involves the reduction of the number of times transactions involving the same goods are taxed.

Development

The same economic conditions of the 1930s that accelerated the adoption of state corporate income taxes and brought sales taxation to quick maturity also played a part in the development of the smaller group of gross receipts taxes. The inadequacy of the property tax to meet growing state revenue needs, particularly in the depression era of the 1930s, led the states to turn to such types of what was considered the "sales tax" form of taxation as "retail sales or consumer taxes," "general sales or turnover taxes," "gross income taxes," and "gross receipts taxes."

Several states, however, experimented with the gross receipts tax as a boost to their lagging tax structures. Exhibit 8.1 shows the dates of adoption of the present gross receipts taxes.

The development of gross receipts taxation stems back only in part to the revenue needs of the states in the early 1920s and 1930s. Some gross receipts taxes have their roots in the nineteenth-century property taxes on merchants and manufacturers and flat sum occupational license taxes. The taxes imposed by Delaware, Louisiana, and Alaska are part of this development. The adoption of the present Alaska tax in 1949 involved a consolidation of separate occupational license taxes dating from 1899 and was not a new development nor was the Louisiana tax adopted in 1934 a new tax. The Delaware tax on mechants was originally imposed in 1852 and used the cost value of stocks on hand until 1871 when the tax base was changed to cost of purchases.

Criticism

The use of the gross receipts tax has generally been defended on the grounds that it is a very efficient, reliable way to tax business. The simplicity of this tax's basis makes it easy to comply with and easy to administer, and the tax can even be imposed in place of several taxes,

Exhibit 8.1

State	Year
Delaware	
Merchants' License Tax	1871
Manufacturers' License Tax	1913
West Virginia	1921
Mississippi	1930
Indiana	1933
Washington	1933
Louisiana	1934
Hawaii	1935
Alaska	1949

producing a high yield with low rates because of its broad base. In addition, in times of recession it assures the state a more stable source of revenue than does the income tax. The gross receipts tax may accomplish the objective of business taxation more nearly than does the income tax by requiring all businesses that benefit from governmental services to contribute to the support of those services.

However, gross receipts taxation has had many critics. The primary criticism has been that the burden of the gross receipts tax falls indiscriminately and unfairly. It is conceded that it is part of the theory of gross receipts taxation that the burden should so fall but that the tax burden is tolerable only when the rates are very low. Since, with a few exceptions, the rates are not very low, it is contended that the tax is economically oppressive.

The argument runs as follows. Although in many instances the tax can be wholly shifted by the business paying it in higher prices or in lower wages or costs of materials, very often it must be partially or completely absorbed. Whether the tax can be passed on depends on the elasticity of demand for the individual company's product and other market conditions. That it is often absorbed to varying extents is well accepted. For these businesses, the tax absorbed can considerably reduce profits. For example, a fairly profitable firm netting $5 for every $100 in receipts and paying a tax of 1/2 of 1 percent will have its net profits, before income taxes are paid, reduced by 10 percent by the gross receipts tax. But relatively, it is even worse for the business with a low profit or a loss.

The gross receipts tax does more harm, it is contended, than driving some marginal enterprises out of business. It favors the large and established concerns and thus inhibits competition. For example, the smaller company tends to be less able to weather the impact of the gross receipts tax during its lean years than the large company, and before the smaller company has had a chance to regain a profitable position it may be out of business.

Another way that the larger company has an advantage over the smaller one is through its greater ability to integrate several stages of production and distribution and thus pay one tax on the final sale of a product, whereas the nonintegrated firm handles a product for which a tax may have been paid at each stage. The large integrated firm is thus given an advantage over its small, nonintegrated competitors. A third drawback is that the entry of new businesses is hindered by the heavy impact of gross receipts taxation, since new businesses typically have lower profit margins and also would tend to be in a less favorable competitive position to shift the tax.

Aside from these general defects, one major inequity usually stressed by critics of gross receipts taxation is that no account is taken of the variations from one business group to another in the ratio of profits to gross receipts. For example, wholesalers of a certain type of goods may typically have a small profit margin but a rapid turnover, whereas manufacturers of certain articles may have a slow turnover but large profit margins. These are not variations resulting from inefficient operation of particular businesses but represent basic differences in the way business groups operate, and these differences extend to very fine breakdowns in the type of business group. Within each of these groups there is the further variation based on size of receipts, with the larger companies typically having greater profit margins. Thus the argument runs that this is a tax which on its face purports to lay an even burden but which in actuality lays a very uneven one. As such the gross receipts tax is inequitable and unsound. The unevenness of the impact of the gross receipts tax when rates are other than very low is probably the one most severely criticized feature of the tax and one to be reckoned with in appraising the likelihood of any widespread acceptance of the tax.

Another aspect of gross receipts taxation that has aroused criticism is the effect of the tax on the economy. As mentioned earlier, veritically integrated firms enjoy the advantage of being able to sell a product with fewer taxes being reflected in the final price. It is claimed, therefore, that gross receipts taxation encourages integration of businesses, with a consequent untoward effect on competition in general. Where there is no integration and a tax is paid at each stage in the production and distribution process and the tax is passed on, the consequent pyramiding of the price is criticized. The point of this criticism is that the size of the tax burden is larger than is apparent from adding the rates for each imposition, since the tax is included in the cost to which each seller's markup percentage is applied.

Appendix G contains data developed by the special subcommittee on state taxation of Interstate Commerce.

LEADING DECISIONS

The limitation of the rights of the states to impose gross receipts taxes has been defined in numerous state cases as well as in U.S. Supreme Court decisions. Leading cases are herein described to present a picture of the jurisdictional rules.

J. D. Adams Manufacturing Company v. Storen et al. 304 U.S. 307 (1938)

Adams Manufacturing was an Indiana corporation with its home office and principal operations in the state. Most of the company's sales were to customers outside Indiana. Sales of manufactured products were shipped from Indiana pursuant to orders forwarded from out of state and accepted at the home office.

Pertinent to the decision on the issue of whether the Indiana tax applied to the receipts from sales to customers outside Indiana was the question of the exact nature of the tax itself. The Court accepted the Indiana Attorney General's definition that the tax was a privilege tax on the receipt of gross income, thus a tax on gross receipts from commerce.

The problem the U.S. Supreme Court had with this definition was that . . . "the tax includes in its measure, without apportionment, receipts derived from activities in interstate commerce; and that the exaction is of such a character that if lawful it may in substance be laid to the fullest extent by states in which the goods are sold as well as those in which they are manufactured. Interstate commerce would thus be subjected to the risk of a double tax burden to which interstate commerce is not exposed and which the commerce clause forbids."

The Indiana Supreme Court, in sustaining the tax, had relied strongly on *American Manufacturing Company* v. *St. Louis* 250 U.S. 459. The U.S. Supreme Court distinguished this case from *Adams* by noting that in *American Manufacturing Company* the nature of the tax was a *license tax, measured by gross receipts* for the privilege of manufacturing and in no way was laid on that taxpayer's sales or on the income from such sales. The Court therefore concluded: "So long as the sales price of the goods sold in interstate commerce induces compensation for a purely intrastate activity (the manufacture of the goods sold) it may be reached for local taxation by a tax on the privilege of manufacturing, measured by the value of the goods manufactured." It was because the Indiana tax reduced indiscriminately and without apportionment the gross compensation for both interstate commerce and intrastate activities that it failed in terms of the interstate sales. Thus the sales originating in Indiana and terminating in other states were not subject to the tax.

Western Live Stock et al. v. Bureau of Revenue et al. 303 U.S. 250 (1938)

The taxpayer in this case published a monthly trade journal in New Mexico where its only place of business was located. The journal was circulated within New Mexico and in other states to paid subscribers. Shipment was made by mail or other means of transportation. The journal contained advertisements, some of which were obtained from the solicitation of out-of-state advertisers. The out-of-state advertisers shipped advertising cuts, mats, information, and copy to the taxpayer publisher. After the advertisements appeared in the journal, payment was due the taxpayer from the advertisers.

The tax levied by New Mexico was a privilege tax on those engaged in specified businesses and was on gross receipts. The issue in this case was whether this tax applied to the gross receipts from out-of-state advertisers. Western Live Stock contended its out-of-state receipts were not subject to the New Mexico tax because the contracts with these out-of-state advertisers involved negotiations across state lines and because the magazine was distributed to points outside New Mexico. It believed a tax on these receipts was a burden on interstate commerce.

The U.S. Supreme Court, in affirming the state supreme court, concluded that the multiple tax possibility raised by the taxpayer was too remote. The tax was not applied to the receipts from subscriptions circulated interstate. Further, there was no possibility of multiple taxation, since no other state could tax the same receipts.

Thus the tax was properly imposed, with no violation of the Commerce Clause. All the events on which the tax was conditioned—preparation, printing, publication of the advertising matter, and the receipt of payments—occurred in New Mexico, and the tax struck a balance with the concept that an interstate business must pay its way.

Norton Company v. Department of Revenue 340 U.S. 534 (1951)

Norton Company was a Massachusetts corporation that manufactured and sold abrasive machines and supplies. It had a branch office and a warehouse located in Illinois from which it made local retail sales and utilized as a means of forwarding orders to its home office. The retail outlet was also used as a distribution point. Orders were shipped by carload lot to this outlet where the shipments were then broken down and forwarded in their original package to customers.

Norton also made sales in Illinois through a second channel. It received orders directly from Illinois customers, accepted these orders in Massachusetts, and made shipments from Massachusetts to Illinois without utilizing the Illinois retail outlet.

The tax concerned was the Illinois Retailer Occupation Tax (ROT) that was a tax upon persons engaged in the business of selling tangible personal property at retail in this state. The base for computation of the tax was gross receipts. The Illinois Supreme Court ruled that Illinois could impose the tax on all sales of the taxpayer, regardless of where the orders were accepted and which warehouse filled the order. The presence of the local retail outlet was deemed to attribute all income derived from Illinois sales to that outlet and render it all taxable. The U.S. Supreme Court decision was that the second category of sales was not subject to tax because the particular transactions were dissociated from the local business and were interstate in nature.

The Court viewed the ROT as a gross receipts tax, which in concept it is. Actually, Illinois was prevented from imposing a sales tax by its constitution, and the ROT was merely a device to circumvent this restriction. In practice, the ROT is more akin to a sales tax than a gross receipts tax.

At the time of the *Norton* case, Illinois did not have a use tax. Norton's activities would undoubtedly have subjected it to the requirement for collection of Illinois use tax had it been in effect. Today, Norton would be required to collect Illinois use tax from its customers, thereby eliminating the controversy under present law. However, there remains the question of Municipal Retailers Occupation Tax (MROT). This tax too would be viewed as gross receipts tax, and there is no complementary Municipal Use Tax. Thus the advantage of the Norton-type operation exists today but only to the extent of MROT. (For an analogy, see Chapter 7's discussion of sales and use taxes for the implication of a sales tax imposed in a state without a complimentary use tax.)

The important rule established in this case is that shipments in interstate commerce terminating in a gross receipts state may be nontaxable if a dissociation with in-state activities can be shown. The burden is on the taxpayer to show that the sales are unrelated to in-state activity.

General Motors Corporation v. State of Washington 377 U.S. 436 (1964)

In this case, the Washington Supreme Court dealt with the same question as the Illinois Supreme Court in the *Norton* case about whether shipments from out of state terminating in Washington were subject to the Washington gross receipts tax. The Washington business and occupation tax statute imposed the tax on the privilege of engaging in business activities.

General Motors was a Delaware corporation qualified to do business in Washington. The company's principal business activity was the manufacture and sale of automobiles, trucks, and other vehicles. The company also sold various parts and accessories. The business activity of the General Motors Corporation (GMC) being taxed in Washington was the wholesale sales activity of its parts division. GMC maintained warehouses in Seattle, Washington, and Portland, Oregon, from which shipments of parts and accessories were made to Washington customers (retail dealers). The sales to Washington customers from Seattle, Washington, were not contested, GMC having paid tax on these receipts. Sales to Washington customers shipped from the warehouse in Portland were contested under the Due Process and Commerce clauses.

The Due Process defense was dispatched by the U.S. Supreme Court with the finding that GMC had failed to show a dissociation with the sales in question, as was shown with Norton. On the contrary, the activities of GMC were shown to consist of extensive promotional and service efforts pervading virtually every aspect of the retail dealers' operations. The activities conducted by field organization representatives were intimately associated with the dealers on matters of accounting, business operations, sales and service techniques, inventories of parts and accessories, showrooms, service facilities, and used car operations. Less tangible involve-

ment included substantial advertising by various media. Although not
directly participating in retail sales, there was no question that these
activities increased retail sales, thus increasing wholesale sales of GMC. A
showing of disassociation, in the opinion of the Court, was not accomplished. The activities provided sufficient nexus on which to base the
tax, and Washington was taxing only that activity which took place within
its orders, which was within the requirements of the Due Process Clause.

The principal argument with respect to the Commerce Clause defense
was that assessment failed the multiple burden test. GMC contended that
discrimination against interstate commerce would occur if it were required
to pay a tax in another state, say, a tax on manufacturing as done by St.
Louis. That is, St. Louis imposes a license tax measured by the receipts
from goods manufactured in St. Louis no matter where shipped. The Court
concluded that GMC had not demonstrated what definite burden, in a
constitutional sense, the St. Louis tax places on the interstate shipments.
(Cf. *International Harvester Company* v. *Evatt* 329 U.S. 416, 421–423.)

In form, the GMC activities were not greatly different from Norton.
Both cases involved in-state sales outlets with other sales being made from
out of state under similar circumstances. However, in GMC, when inquiry
was directed to the amount and effect of the activities related to the
interstate sales element, form could not prevail in the Court's opinion.

Standard Pressed Steel Company v. State of Washington Department of Revenue 42 L Ed 2d 719 (1975)

This case is an extension of *General Motors* regarding the determination of
nexus. Nexus, in turn, determines the taxability of interstate sales terminating in Washington.

Standard Pressed Steel Company maintained a single employee whose
main function was to service Standard's principal customer in Washington:
the Boeing Company. The employee operated from his home. He consulted
with Boeing regarding anticipated needs and requirements for aerospace
fasteners. He also followed up any difficulties concerning the use of the
product, being assisted in this by a group of engineers who visited the
customer about three days every six weeks. The resident engineer arranged
for these meetings. All orders were sent directly out of state to Standard
for acceptance, and shipment was made to Washington by common carrier.

Standard argued the Due Process defense on the ground that in-state
activities were so thin and inconsequential that there was no reasonable
relation between the tax and the benefits and protection conferred by the
state. The U.S. Supreme Court was unimpressed with this argument,
viewing it as verging on the frivolous in light of Standard having a full-time
employee in the state making possible the realization and continuance of
valuable contractual relations.

Standard relied a great deal on *Norton* with regard to its Commerce Clause defense. Here the Court emphasized that the question in *Norton* was one of nexus, with the burden placed on the taxpayer to make a showing of dissociation between in-state activity and interstate sales.

The Supreme Court upheld the tax because the tax was on the gross receipts from sales made to a local consumer, all of which was intrastate.

Mueller Brass Company v. Gross Income Tax Division 265 NE 2d 704 (1971) Indiana S. Ct.

In this litigation it is useful to start with the result of the case and then examine the circumstances.

Territory	Products	Taxation
Northern	Standard	Exempt
Indiana	Industrial	Exempt
Southern	Standard	Taxable
Indiana	Industrial	Taxable
	House accounts	Exempt

Mueller Brass Company, a manufacturer of nonferrous metal products, did all its manufacturing outside Indiana. The company's "standard" products were sold primarily to plumbing and refrigeration wholesalers and manufacturers. Its "industrial products" were custom manufactured according to customer specification.

The southern two-thirds of the state of Indiana was included within the responsibility of the Indianapolis sales office. This office consisted of a sales manager and staff. This staff performed all contacts with customers, although all orders were forwarded out of state for acceptance and shipment. The Indianapolis office was not involved with customers in the northern third of Indiana, these customers being serviced from out-of-state offices, again with orders accepted out of state and shipment being made from out of state.

The conclusions of the court were based on the fact that sufficient nexus existed in the state with respect to sales in the southern two-thirds of Indiana (except the house accounts that were related to the home office in Michigan). Mueller Brass Company had localized itself in Indiana to a substantial degree. It had gained the advantage of a local business and could not therefore also claim the immunity of interstate commerce. The nexus requirement of the Due Process Clause was met. All other sales made within the state were dissassociated from in-state activities and were outside the realm of the Indiana Gross Income Tax in keeping with the rule of *Norton Company*.

Complete Auto Transits, Incorporated v. Brady, Chairman, Mississippi State Tax Commission 430 U.S. 274 (1977)

The taxpayer provided intrastate transport of assembled vehicles shipped from out of state to Jackson, Mississippi. The vehicles were transported to in-state dealers. The tax involved was a privilege tax for engaging in business within the state. Specifically, "upon every person operating a pipeline, railroad, airplane, bus, truck, or any other transportation business for the transportation of persons or property for compensation or hire between points within this state, there is hereby levied, assessed, and shall be collected, a tax equal to five per cent (5%) of the gross income of such business . . ." according to the Mississippi Code, Section 10109 (2) as amended. (The statute is now Section 27-65-19 (2) of the 1972 code. It was amended August 1, 1972, to exclude the transportation of property.)

The taxpayer relied primarily on the rule of law established in *Spector Motor*[2] that a tax on the "privilege" of engaging in an activity in the state may not be applied to an activity that is part of interstate commerce. The U.S. Supreme Court regarded this rule to be out of touch with economic reality. It reasoned that such a rule reflects an underlying philosophy that interstate commerce should enjoy a sort of "free trade" immunity from state taxation. The better philosophy is to be found in cases such as *Western Live Stock* v. *Bureau of Revenue* and *General Motors Corporation* v. *Washington* and *Northwestern Cement Company* v. *Minnesota*. These cases illustrate that the Commerce Clause will not be violated when the tax (1) is applied to an activity with a substantial nexus with the taxing state, (2) is fairly apportioned, (3) does not discriminate against interstate commerce, and (4) is fairly related to the services provided by the state. Thus the longstanding *Spector Motor* rule was overruled.[3]

Summary

The important considerations of gross receipts taxes are these:

1 Gross receipts taxes are usually imposed on the seller and not collected from the buyer.
2 The rule that the seller may avoid the gross receipts tax by showing a disassociation between certain in-state activity and sales transactions is valid, but the burden of showing dissociation is on the taxpayer.
3 Interstate sales having a destination in the taxing state are taxable, given sufficient nexus.

---

[2]*Spector Motor Service* v. *O'Connor* 340 U.S. 602 (1951).
[3]However, see *Colonial Pipeline Company* v. *Traigle* 421 U.S. 100 (1975), where doubt had already been cast on the reliability of the *Spector* rule.

4   Interstate sales originating in the taxing state will nearly always be exempt, since the threat of multiple taxation would otherwise exist.

5   Intrastate sales are taxable.

CONTRASTING GROSS RECEIPTS TAXES WITH SALES AND USE TAXES

Generally, a gross receipts tax is imposed on the seller for the privilege of engaging in one or another activity. The tax base can be measured by the sales price of tangible property, real and personal; intangible property; services; and other forms of gross income.

Sales and use taxes, on the other hand, are imposed on the buyer of tangible personal property for the privilege of buying, in the case of a sales tax, or for the privilege of using such property in the case of a use tax. The tax base is derived from the sales price. Sales and use taxes are collected from the customer at the time the transaction is completed and paid over to the state by the seller.

The jurisdictional standard for use tax collection is very stringent, although falling short of the "slightest presence" rule advocated by the California Supreme Court in *National Geographic*.[4] The jurisdictional rule for gross receipts tax is not as stringent. It is still possible to avoid tax under the *Norton* rule by showing disassociation. (Note that it is easier for a court to find jurisdiction for use tax, since the seller has only the collection function to perform. Finding jurisdiction for gross receipts tax is equivalent to imposing an additional tax burden for the seller, such as in the case of an income tax.) The burden of showing disassociation should not be regarded as unsubstantial in view of the *Standard Pressed Steel* decision.

OUTLINE OF A GROSS RECEIPTS TAX—THE WASHINGTON BUSINESS AND OCCUPATION TAX

A brief study outline of the Washington gross income tax provides better understanding of the nature and operation of such a levy. The Washington tax is a major revenue source for the state. It is additional to the sales and use tax in effect in that state, but the state does not have a tax based on income.

The tax is on the privilege of engaging in certain types of business activity. The rates established depend on the class of activity and vary

[4]*National Geographic Society* v. *California Board of Equalization* 51 L Ed 2d 631 (1977).

between different taxpayers. Typical rates applicable to the interstate taxpayer making sales to Washington customers are as follows:

Retailing and wholesaling	0.0044
Perishable meat processors	0.0033
Harvesting timber	0.0065
Manufacturing seafood products	0.00125

These statutory rates are subject to a 6 percent surtax for the period June 1977 through June 1979.

The business activities taxed and the rates are described next. The rates shown include the 6 percent surtax. Thus the rate for wholesalers of 0.004664 consists of the permanent rate of 0.0044 and a 6 percent surtax of 0.000264. The classifications shown here are those required to be shown on the business and occupation tax return. These do not include all classifications subject to the tax that are detailed in the statute.

Extracting for Hire or Processing for Hire

Persons taxable under this classification are those providing labor and mechanical services under contract to those engaged in the business of extraction or manufacturing. The tax is 0.004664 applied to gross income.

Manufacturing Wheat into Flour or Manufacturing Raw Seafood Products

Washington manufacturers are taxable on the gross sales of these products to customers outside Washington. The tax rate is 0.001325. (Sales of similar products to customers in Washington would be taxable under the "Wholesaling" or "Retailing" classification.)

Travel Agent Commissions

Commission gross income is taxable at 0.00265.

Splitting or Processing Dried Peas

Gross income is taxable at 0.00265.

Slaughtering, Breaking, Processing Perishable Meat—Wholesale

All persons are taxable under this classification who are engaged in such business activities or making sales at wholesale either in this state or in interstate commerce. Persons performing such activities for hire for other than consumers are also taxable under this classification. Gross income is taxable at a rate of 0.003498.

Manufacturing—Aluminum

Gross income from the value of the products manufactured is taxable at a rate of 0.00424.

Printing and Publishing—Processing for Hire

Gross income from the commercial printing or publishing of newspapers, magazines, and periodicals is taxable at a rate of 0.004664.

Manufacturing—Fresh Fruit and Vegetable Products

The value of products processed by canning, preserving, freezing, or dehydrating is taxable at a rate of 0.00318.

Manufacturing ᵃ(Other)

The gross income from products manufactured is taxable at a rate of 0.004664.

Wholesaling—Wheat, Oats, Corn, Barley, and Dry Peas

Gross income is taxable at a rate of 0.000106.

Wholesaling—Cigarettes

Cigarettes sold by manufacturers from warehouses in Washington at wholesale are taxable at 0.0018656.

Wholesaling Functions

The value of articles of tangible personal property transferred from a warehouse to a retail location in Washington where no change of ownership or title occurs is taxable at 0.004664.

Wholesaling (Other)

Gross receipts are taxable at 0.004664.

Private Cold Storage Warehouse

Gross income is taxable at 0.004664.

ᵃNote that the manufacturing categories are with respect to products manufactured in Washington and shipped out of state. Products manufactured in Washington and sold in Washington would be subject to either the retail or wholesale category of tax. The rates are the same.

Radio and TV Broadcasting

Gross income (excluding network, national, and regional advertising) is taxable at 0.004664.

Publicly Owned Road Construction

Gross income from contracts for the construction, improvement, or repair of streets and roads on land owned by cities, counties, or the Federal government is taxable at 0.004664.

Government Contracting

Gross income from constructing, repairing, decorating, or improving buildings or structures for the Federal government or for county or city housing authorities is taxable at 0.004664.

Service and Other Business Activities

Taxpayers in this classification include every business except those specifically exempted. Gross income is taxable at 0.0106.

Retailing

Gross proceeds of sales are taxable at a rate of 0.004664.

Business and Occupation Tax Exemptions and Deductions

The law allows certain exemptions and deductions under the business and occupation tax classifications. Those of general application are the following:

1 Persons whose volume of business under all classifications is less than $300 during a month. If the amount is $300 or more, no volume exemption is allowed.
2 Persons whose business activities are taxable under the public utility act.
3 Persons engaged in the business of commercial farming on owned or leased land, except when products are sold at retail. No exemption from tax is allowed on the production and sale of Christmas trees, whether harvested from unimproved land or grown on cultivated farm land.
4 Persons whose contests or meets are licensed by the State Athletic Commission or by the State Horse Racing Commission.
5 Person in respect to employment in the capacity of employee or servant.

6 Amounts derived by persons engaged in the production and sale of hatching eggs or poultry for use in the production for sale of poultry or poultry products.

7 Gross proceeds of sales of real estate (but commissions and interest are taxable).

8 Certain accommodation sales. (For example, a sale to another party at no markup to enable the other party to meet the needs of a customer.)

9 Under the wholesaling functions, tax in respect to transfers of property purchased from a wholesaler who has paid a business and occupation tax to the state upon the same articles.

10 Cash discounts taken by purchasers.

11 Credit losses (bad debts) sustained.

12 Federal and state taxes included in the selling price of motor vehicle fuel.

13 Compensation for the receiving, washing, sorting, and packing of fresh horticultural products and the materials and supplies used therein when performed for a commercial farmer.

14 Compensation for services rendered to patients by hospitals operated by a governmental instrumentality, by hospitals operated as nonprofit corporations or by nursing homes, and by homes for unwed mothers operated as religious or charitable organizations.

15 Amounts derived by certain interstate and foreign business activities. (See the later discussion on jurisdictional standards.)

16 Under certain conditions the tax will not apply to charges to a county or city for labor and services in the mining, sorting, crushing, screening, washing, hauling, and stockpiling of sand, gravel, and rock for public road construction or repair.

17 Certain deductions are permitted to financial institutions for interest on residential first mortgages and government obligations.

18 Fees and charges paid to a political subdivision for services provided by another political subdivision of the kind falling under the Service and Other Activities classification.

Jurisdictional Standards

The distinctions between taxable and nontaxable transactions are made in Rule 193 of the Washington Department of Revenue. Part A of Rule 193 deals with sales of goods originating in Washington made to persons in other states. If a retail or wholesale sale is made where delivery is to a purchaser in Washington, the sale is taxable even though the customer intends to remove the property to another state for use or resale. Delivery occurs in Washington, even though the customer picks up the merchandise and takes it out of state. If a retail or wholesale sale is made with delivery to the customer outside Washington the transaction is not taxable. Delivery outside Washington may be made by the seller's transportation equipment or by common carrier.

Part B of Rule 193 (presented subsequently) deals with interstate sales delivered to customers in Washington—that is, sales originating outside Washington and terminating in Washington. The standards laid down here are consistent with the decisions in *Standard Pressed Steel, General Motors,* and *Norton.*

Part B—Rule 193

Retailing and wholesaling sales to persons in Washington are taxable when the property is shipped from outside Washington to a customer in the state and the seller carries on or has carried on local activity which is significantly associated with the seller's ability to establish and maintain a market in Washington for such sales. If a person carries on significant activity in the state and conducts no other business in Washington except the business of making sales, the burden of establishing that the instate activities are not significantly associated with the Washington sales rests with the seller. The characterization or nature of the activity performed in Washington is immaterial so long as it is significantly associated in any way with the seller's ability to establish and maintain a market for its products in Washington. The essential question is whether the instate services enable the seller to make the sales.

(The following activities are given as examples of activities which would provide sufficient nexus for application of the business and occupation tax.)

1. The seller's branch office, local outlet, or other place of business in Washington is utilized in any way, such as in receiving the order, franchise, or credit investigation, or distribution of the goods.

2. The order for the goods is given in this state to an agent or other representative connected with the seller's branch office, local outlet, or other place of business.

3. The order for the goods is solicited in this state by an agent or other representative of the seller.

4. The delivery of the goods is made by a local outlet or from a local stock of goods of the seller in this state.

5. Where an out-of-state seller, either directly or by an agent or other representative, performs significant services in relation to establishment and maintenance of sales into the state, the business tax is applicable, even though (a) the seller may not have formal sales offices in Washington or (b) the agent or representative may not be formally characterized as a salesman.

6. Where an out-of-state seller either directly or by an agent or other representative in this state installs its products in this state as a condition

of the sales, the installation services shall be deemed significant services for establishing and maintaining a market in this state for such installed products and the gross proceeds from the sale and installation are subject to business tax.

The rule goes further to state that under the foregoing principles, sales transactions in which the property is shipped directly from a point outside the state to the purchaser in this state are exempt only if there is and there has been no participation whatsoever in this state, the seller's branch office, local outlet, or other local place of business, or by an agent or other representative of the seller. A franchise or credit investigation of a prospective purchaser and/or recommendation or approval by a local office on which subsequent transactions are based is such a utilization of the local office as to render such subsequent transactions taxable.

Bibliography

Barrett, Thomas J., "Multistate Sales and Use Taxation," *Journal of Corporate Taxation,* Vol. 3, No. 1, Spring 1976, pp. 5–27.

Britton, Floyd E., "Taxation without Representation Modernized," *Taxes,* August 1960, pp. 628–649.

Cappetta, Fredrick P., "The Joint Audit Program of the Multistate Tax Commission," Address presented at the 33rd Annual Institute on Federal Taxation of the New York University School of Continuing Education, November 11, 1974. Reproduced in the Seventh Annual Report, Multistate Tax Commission, June 30, 1974, pp. 52–63.

Commerce Clearing House Publications, *Michigan Single Business Tax Division Releases,* Single Business Tax Bulletin, 1978.

Commerce Clearing House Publications, *Michigan Tax Reports,* No. 240, June 27, 1977.

Commerce Clearing House Publications, Single Business Tax Questions and Answers, Michigan State Tax Reporter, Vol. 1, September 15, 1975, Vol. 2, October 20, 1975; Vol. 3, Vol. 4, April 21, 1976; Vol. 5, June 15, 1976; Vol. 6, August 23, 1976; Vol. 7, October 22, 1976; Vol. 11, March 24, 1978; Vol. 12, August 10, 1978.

Dexter, W. D., "The Business vs. Nonbusiness Distinction under UDITPA," *Urban Lawyer,* Vol. 10, No. 2, Spring 1978.

Goodman, Sidney D., "Michigan's Single Business Tax," *Tax Executive,* Vol. 28, No. 3, April 1976, pp. 213–221.

Hansen, Gary J., "Business vs. Nonbusiness Income of Large Multinational Corporations under UDITPA," *Taxes,* June 1979, pp. 366–373.

Harris, "Interstate Apportionment of Business Income," *American Economic Revue,* Vol. 49, No. 399, 1959.

Harris, "Economic Aspects of Interstate Apportionment of Business Income," *Taxes,* Vol. 37, 1950.

Hearings on State Taxation of Interstate Commerce before the Senate Select Committee on Small Business, 86th Congress, First Session, 1959.

Hearings before the Special Subcommittee on State Taxation of Interstate Commerce of the House Committee on the Judiciary, 89th Congress, Second Session, Series 14, 1966.

Hellerstein, Jerome R., "An Academician's View of State Taxation of Interstate Commerce," *Tax Law Review,* Vol. 16, No. 2, January 1961, pp. 159–176.

Hellerstein, Jerome R., "The Unitary Business Principle and Multicorporate Enterprises: An Examination of the Major Controversies," *Tax Executive,* Vol. 27, No. 4, July 1975, pp. 313–327.

Hellerstein, Jerome R., "Allocation and Nexus in State Taxation of Interstate Businesses," *Tax Law Review,* Vol. 20, No. 2, January 1965, pp. 259–283.

Hellerstein, Jerome R., "Recent Developments in State Tax Apportionment and the Circumscription of Unitary Business," *National Tax Journal*, Vol. 21, 1968, pp. 487–503.

House Report 2158, 90th Congress, First Session, 1967.

House Report 7906, 91st Congress, First Session, 1969.

House Report 669, 95th Congress, First Session, 1977.

Indiana Department of Revenue, *Statement and Related Information in Support of the Withdrawal of the State of Indiana from Membership in the Multistate Tax Compact*, Indiana, March 1977.

Indiana Department of Revenue, State of Indiana, *Survey on the Uniformity of State Tax Laws*, Indiana, February 1977.

Industry Statement, Hearings on State Taxation of Interstate Commerce, Mondale Subcommittee of Senate Finance Committee, 93rd Congress, First Congress, September 18, 1973.

"Interstate Taxation Bill Goes to House Floor," *Taxes*, July 1969, pp. 400–410.

Keesling, Frank, "A Current Look at the Combined Report and Uniformity in Allocation Practices," *Journal of Taxation*, Vol. 42, 1975, p. 106.

Keesling, Frank M., "The Combined Report and Uniformity in Allocation Practices," Address delivered in 1974 at the Annual Meeting of the Multistate Tax Commission, Denver, Colorado, reproduced in the Seventh Annual Report, Multistate Tax Commission, June 30, 1974, pp. 33–44.

Keesling, Frank M., and Warren, John S., "California's Uniform Division of Income for Tax Purposes Act," Part I and Part II, *UCLA Law Review*, Vol. 15:156 and 15:655, 1967, 1968, pp. 156–175 and 655–677.

Keesling, Warren, "The Unitary Concept in the Allocation of Income," *Hastings Law Journal*, Vol. 12, 1960, pp. 42–60.

Krol, Richard, "Minimizing the Corporate Interstate Tax Burden," *AICPA Continuing Education Program*.

Krol, Richard, "Taxpayers Balking at Submitting to Audits of Multistate Tax Commission," *Journal of Taxation*, December 1975.

Krol, Richard J., "Current Approaches to Doing Business for Sales and Use Tax Nexus Purposes," *Journal of Taxation*, Vol. 50, No. 5, May 1979, pp. 308–311.

LaVelle, Wilbur F., "What Constitutes a Unitary Business," *University of Southern California Law Center Tax Institute*, 1973, pp. 239–250.

Livingston, Carlyle O., and Hepler, Michael I., "The Multistate Business Taxation Jungle: Will Congress Take Remedial Action?" *Tax Advisor*, July 1974.

McKim, Samuel J., III, "Michigan Single Business Tax Seen as a VAT," *Tax Executive*, Vol. 29, No. 1, October 1976, pp. 25–84.

Miller, Peter, "State Income Taxation of Multiple Corporations and Multiple Businesses," *Taxes*, February 1971, pp. 102–121.

Multistate Tax Commission, Seventh Annual Report, for the Fiscal Year Ending June 30, 1974.

Multistate Tax Commission Adds to the Interstate Tax Confusion, Notification from the Committee on State Taxation, Council of State Chambers of Commerce, September 20, 1971.

National Tax Association, *Interim Report of Committee on Interstate Allocation of Business Income, Proceeding of National Tax Association*, 1958.

National Tax Association, *Proceedings of National Tax Association*, 1939.

National Tax Association, *Second Preliminary Report of the Committee on Tax Status and Allocation, Proceedings of National Tax Association,* 1950.

Nemeth, S. C., Jr., and Agee, H. O., Jr., "State Taxation of Multistate Business: Resolution or Stalemate?," *Taxes,* Vol. 48, April 1970, pp. 237–252.

Peters, James H., "Revised Multistate Tax Commission Regs Define 'Business' and 'Nonbusiness' Income," *Journal of Taxation,* February 1974, pp. 122–126.

Peters, James H., "The Distinction between Business Income and Nonbusiness Income," *Law Center Institute, University of California 25th Tax Institute,* Vol. 25, p. 251.

Pierce, William J., "The Uniform Division of Income for State Tax Purposes," *Taxes,* October 1957, p. 747.

Report on State Taxation of Interstate Commerce, House Report 565, 89th Congress, First Session, 1965.

Report on State Taxation of Interstate Commerce, House Report 1480, 88th Congress, Second Session, Vols. 1 and 2, 1964.

Report on State Taxation of Interstate Commerce, House Report 952, 89th Congress, First Session, 1965.

Rudolph, E. George, "State Taxation of Interstate Business: The Unitary Business Concept and Affiliated Corporated Groups," *Tax Law Review,* Vol. 25, No. 2, January 1970, pp. 171–210.

Sanden, B. Kenneth, "VAT: What, How, Where," *Tax Advisor,* March 1973, pp. 150–157.

Smith, Dan Throop, "When-If-We Have the VAT," *Harvard Business Review,* January–February 1973, pp. 6–24.

State Taxation of Income Derived from Interstate Commerce, Senate Report No. 658, 86th Congress, First Session, 1959.

State Taxation of Interstate Commerce, Senate Report No. 453, 86th Congress, First Session, 1959.

Studenski and Glasser, "New Threat in State Business Taxation," *Harvard Business Review,* Vol. 36, 1958.

Tax Foundation, *State and Local Sales Tax,* New York.

Taxation of Business with Multistate Operations H.R. 11798, Comments of Honorable Fred L. Cox, Director, Interstate Tax Affairs, Georgia Department of Revenue, before the House of Representatives, Committee of the Judiciary, Special Subcommittee on State Taxation of Interstate Commerce, Washington, D.C., Thursday, March 10, 1966.

Young, J. Nelson, "The Single Factor Sales Formula and the Moorman Manufacturing Company Decision—A Backward Step in the Apportionment of Income of Interstate Business," *Taxes,* Vol. 56, No. 11, November 1978, p. 657.

Multistate Tax Commission Apportionment Regulations Adopted under Article IV of the Multistate Tax Compact

General—The regulations numerical references are to Article IV of the Multistate Tax Compact and its subsections.

Prologue—These Regulations are intended to set forth rules concerning the application of the apportionment and allocation provisions of Article IV of the Multistate Tax Compact. The apportionment rules set forth in these Regulations are applicable to any taxpayer having business income, regardless of whether or not it has nonbusiness income, and the allocation rules set forth in these Regulations are applicable to any taxpayer having nonbusiness income, regardless of whether or not it has business income.

The only exceptions to these allocation and apportionment rules contained in these Regulations are those set forth in Regulation IV.18. pursuant to the authority of Article IV.18. of the Compact.

These Regulations are not intended to modify existing rules concerning jurisdictional standards.

1. (a) Business and Nonbusiness Income Defined—Article IV. 1. (a) defines "business income" as income arising from transactions and activities in the regular course of the taxpayer's trade or business and includes income from tangible and intangible property if the acquisition, management, and disposition of the property constitute integral parts of the taxpayer's regular trade or business operations. In essence, all income which arises from the conduct of trade or business operations of a taxpayer is business income. For purposes of administration of Article IV, the income of the taxpayer is business income unless clearly classifiable as nonbusiness income.

Nonbusiness income means all income other than business income.

The classification of income by the labels occasionally used, such as manufacturing income, compensation for services, sales income, interest, dividends, rents, royalties, gains, operating income, nonoperating income, etc., is of no aid in determining whether income is business or nonbusiness income. Income of any type or class and from any source is business income if it arises from transactions and activity occurring in the regular course of a trade or business. Accordingly, the critical element in determining whether income is "business income" or "nonbusiness income" is the identification of the transactions and activity which are the elements of a particular trade or business. In general all transactions and activities of the taxpayer which are dependent upon or contribute to the operations of the taxpayer's economic enterprise as a whole constitute the taxpayer's trade or business and will be transactions and activity arising in the regular course of, and will constitute integral parts of, a trade or business. (See Regulation IV.1.(c). for more specific examples of the classification of income as business or nonbusiness income; see Regulations IV.1.(b) and IV.2.(b)(2) for further explanation of what constitutes a trade or business.)

1.   (b).   Two or More Businesses of a Single Taxpayer—A taxpayer may have more than one "trade or business." In such cases, it is necessary to determine the business income attributable to each separate trade or business. The income of each business is then apportioned by an apportionment formula which takes into consideration the instate and outstate factors which relate to the trade or business the income of which is being apportioned.

Example: The taxpayer is a conglomerate with three operating divisions. One division is engaged in manufacturing aerospace items for the federal government. Another division is engaged in growing tobacco products. The third division produces and distributes motion pictures for theaters and television. Each division operates independently; there is no strong central management. Each division operates in this state as well as in other states. In this case, it is fair to conclude that the taxpayer is engaged in three separate "trades or businesses." Accordingly, the amount of business income attributable to the taxpayer's trade or business activities in this state is determined by applying an appropriate apportionment formula to the business income of each business.

The determination of whether the activities of the taxpayer constitute a single trade or business or more than one trade or business will turn on the facts in each case. In general, the activities of the taxpayer will be considered a single business if there is evidence to indicate that the segments under consideration are integrated with, dependent upon, or contribute to each other and the operations of the taxpayer as a whole. The following factors are considered to be good indicia of a single trade or business, and the presence of any of these factors creates a strong presumption that the activities of the taxpayer constitute a single trade or business:

(1) **Same type of business.** A taxpayer is generally engaged in a single trade or business when all of its activities are in the same general line. For example, a taxpayer which operates a chain of retail grocery stores will almost always be engaged in a single trade or business.

(2) **Steps in a vertical process.** A taxpayer is almost always engaged in a single trade or business when its various divisions or segments are engaged in different steps in a large, vertically structured enterprise. For example, a taxpayer which explores for and mines copper ores; concentrates, smelts, and refines the copper ores; and fabricates the refined copper into consumer products is engaged in a single trade or business, regardless of the fact that the various steps in the process are operated substantially independently of each other with only general supervision from the taxpayer's executive offices.

(3) **Strong centralized management.** A taxpayer which might otherwise be considered as engaged in more than one trade or business is properly considered as engaged in one trade or business when there is a strong central management, coupled with the existence of centralized departments for such functions as financing, advertising, research, or purchasing. Thus, some conglomerates may properly be considered as engaged in only one trade or business when the central executive officers are normally involved in the operations of the various divisions and there are centralized offices which perform for the divisions the normal matters which a truly independent business would perform for itself, such as accounting, personnel, insurance, legal, purchasing, advertising, or financing.

1. (c). Business and Nonbusiness Income: Application of Definitions—The following are rules and examples for determining whether particular income is business or nonbusiness income. (The examples used throughout these regulations are illustrative only and do not purport to set forth all pertinent facts.)

(1) **Rents from real and tangible personal property**—Rental income from real and tangible property is business income if the property with respect to which the rental income was received is used in the taxpayer's trade or business or is incidental and therefore is includable in the property factor under Regulation IV.10.

Example (i): The taxpayer operates a multistate car rental business. The income from car rentals is business income.

Example (ii): The taxpayer is engaged in the heavy construction business in which it uses equipment such as cranes, tractors, and earth-moving vehicles. The taxpayer makes short-term leases of the equipment when particular pieces of equipment are not needed on any particular project. The rental income is business income.

Example (iii): The taxpayer operates a multistate chain of men's clothing stores. The taxpayer purchases a five-story office building for use in connection with its trade or business. It uses the street floor as one of its retail stores and the second and third floors for its general corporate headquarters. The remaining two floors are leased to others. The rental of the two floors is incidental to the operation of the taxpayer's trade or business. The rental income is business income.

Example (iv): The taxpayer operates a multistate chain of grocery stores. It purchases as an investment an office building in another state with surplus funds and leases the entire building to others. The net rental income is not business income of the grocery store trade or business. Therefore, the net rental income is nonbusiness income.

Example (v): The taxpayer operates a multistate chain of men's clothing stores. The taxpayer invests in a 20-story office building and uses the street floor as one of its retail stores and the second floor for its general corporate headquarters. The remaining 18 floors are leased to others. The rental of the eighteen floors is not incidental to but rather is separate from the operation of the taxpayer's trade or business. The net rental income is not business income of the clothing store trade or business. Therefore, the net rental income is nonbusiness income.

Example (vi): The taxpayer constructed a plant for use in its multistate manufacturing business and 20 years later the plant was closed and put up for sale. The plant was rented for a temporary period from the time it was closed by the taxpayer until it was sold 18 months later. The rental income is business income and the gain on the sale of the plant is business income.

Example (vii): The taxpayer operates a multistate chain of grocery stores. It owned an office building which it occupied as its corporate headquarters. Because of inadequate space, taxpayer acquired a new and larger building elsewhere for its corporate headquarters. The old building was rented to an investment company under a five-year lease. Upon expiration of the lease, taxpayer sold the building at a gain (or loss). The net rental income received over the lease period is nonbusiness income and the gain (or loss) on the sale of the building is nonbusiness income.

(2) **Gains or losses from sales of assets.** Gain or loss from the sale, exchange or other disposition of real or tangible or intangible personal property constitutes business income if the property while owned by the taxpayer was used in the taxpayer's trade or business. However, if such property was utilized for the production of nonbusiness income or otherwise was removed from the property factor before its sale, exchange, or other disposition, the gain or loss will constitute nonbusiness income. See Regulation IV.10.

Example (i): In conducting its multistate manufacturing business, the taxpayer systematically replaces automobiles, machines, and other equipment used in the business. The gains or losses resulting from those sales constitute business income.

Example (ii): The taxpayer constructed a plant for use in its multistate manufacturing business and 20 years later sold the property at a gain while it was in operation by the taxpayer. The gain is business income.

Example (iii): Same as (ii) except that the plant was closed and put up for sale but was not in fact sold until a buyer was found 18 months later. The gain is business income.

Example (iv): Same as (ii) except that the plant was rented while being held for sale. The rental income is business income and the gain on the sale of the palnt is business income.

Example (v): The taxpayer operates a multistate chain of grocery stores. It owned an office building which it occupied as its corporate headquarters. Because of inadequate space, taxpayer acquired a new and larger building elsewhere for its corporate headquarters. The old building was rented to an unrelated investment company under a five-year lease. Upon expiration of the lease, taxpayer sold the building at a gain (or loss). The gain (or loss) on the sale is nonbusiness income and the rental income received over the lease period is nonbusiness income.

(3) **Interest.** Interest income is business income where the intangible with respect to which the interest was received arises out of or was created in the regular course of the taxpayer's trade or business operations or where the purpose for acquiring and holding the intangible is related to or incidental to such trade or business operations.

Example (i): The taxpayer operates a multistate chain of department stores, selling for cash and on credit. Service charges, interest, or time-price differentials and the like are received with respect to installment sales and revolving charge accounts. These amounts are business income.

Example (ii): The taxpayer conducts a multistate manufacturing business. During the year the taxpayer receives a federal income tax refund and collects a judgment against a debtor of the business. Both the tax refund and the judgment bore interest. The interest income is business income.

Example (iii): The taxpayer is engaged in a multistate manufacturing and wholesaling business. In connection with that business, the taxpayer maintains special accounts to cover such items as workmen's compensation claims, rain and storm damage, machinery replacement, etc. The monies in those accounts are invested at interest. Similarly, the taxpayer temporarily invests funds intended for payment of federal, state, and local tax obligations. The interest income is business income.

Example (iv): The taxpayer is engaged in a multistate money order and traveler's checks business. In addition to the fees received in connection with the sale of the money orders and traveler's checks, the taxpayer earns interest income by the investment of the funds pending their redemption. The interest income is business income.

Example (v): The taxpayer is engaged in a multistate manufacturing and selling business. The taxpayer usually has working capital and extra cash totaling $200,000 which it regularly invests in short-term interest bearing securities. The interest income is business income.

Example (vi): In January the taxpayer sold all the stock of a subsidiary for $20,000,000. The funds are placed in an interest-bearing account pending a decision by management as to how the funds are to be utilized. The interest income is nonbusiness income.

(4) **Dividends.** Dividends are business income where the stock with respect to which the dividends are received arises out of or was acquired in the regular course of the taxpayer's trade or business operations or where the purpose for acquiring and holding the stock is related to or incidental to such trade or business operations.

Example (i): The taxpayer operates a multistate chain of stock brokerage houses. During the year the taxpayer receives dividends on stock it owns. The dividends are business income.

Example (ii): The taxpayer is engaged in a multistate manufacturing and wholesaling business. In connection with that business the taxpayer maintains special accounts to cover such items as workmen's compensation claims, etc. A portion of the monies in those accounts is invested in interest-bearing bonds. The remainder is invested in various common stocks listed on national stock exchanges. Both the interest income and any dividends are business income.

Example (iii): The taxpayer and several unrelated corporations own all of the stock of a corporation whose business operations consist solely of acquiring and processing materials for delivery to the corporate owners. The taxpayer acquired the stock in order to obtain a source of supply of materials used in its manufacturing business. The dividends are business income.

Example (iv): The taxpayer is engaged in a multistate heavy construction business. Much of its construction work is performed for agencies of the federal government and various state governments. Under state and federal laws applicable to contracts for these agencies, a contractor must have adequate bonding capacity, as measured by the ratio of its current assets (cash and marketable securities) to current liabilities. In order to maintain an adequate bonding capacity the taxpayer holds various stocks and interest-bearing securities. Both the interest income and any dividends received are business income.

Example (v): The taxpayer receives dividends from the stock of its subsidiary or affiliate which acts as the marketing agency for products manufactured by the taxpayer. The dividends are business income.

Example (vi): The taxpayer is engaged in a multistate glass manufacturing business. It also holds a portfolio of stock and interest-bearing securities, the acquisition and holding of which are unrelated to the manufacturing business. The dividends and interest income received are nonbusiness income.

(5) **Patent and copyright royalties.** Patent and copyright royalties are business income where the patent or copyright with respect to which the royalties were received arises out of or was created in the regular course of the taxpayer's trade or business operations or where the purpose for acquiring and holding the patent or copyright is related to or incidental to such trade or business operations.

Example (i): The taxpayer is engaged in the multistate business of manufacturing and selling industrial chemicals. In connection with that business the taxpayer obtained patents on certain of its products. The taxpayer licensed the production of the chemicals in foreign countries, in return for which the taxpayer receives royalties. The royalties received by the taxpayer are business income.

Example (ii): The taxpayer is engaged in the music publishing business and holds copyrights on numerous songs. The taxpayer acquires the assets of a smaller publishing company, including music copyrights. These acquired copyrights are thereafter used by the taxpayer in its business. Any royalties received on these copyrights are business income.

Example (iii): Same as example (ii), except that the acquired company also held the patent on a type of phonograph needle. The taxpayer does not manufacture or sell phonographs or phonograph equipment. Any royalties received on the patent would be nonbusiness income.

1. (d). **Proration of Deductions**—In most cases an allowable deduction of a taxpayer will be applicable only to the business income arising from a particular trade or business or to a particular item of nonbusiness income. In some cases an allowable deduction may be applicable to the business incomes of more than one trade or business and/or to several items of nonbusiness income. In such cases the deduction shall be prorated among such trades or businesses and such items of nonbusiness income in a manner which fairly distribute the deduction among the classes of income to which it is applicable.

In filing returns with this state, if the taxpayer departs from or modifies the manner of prorating any such deduction used in returns for prior years, the taxpayer shall disclose in the return for the current year the nature and extent of the modification.

If the returns or reports filed by a taxpayer with all states to which the taxpayer reports under Article IV of this Compact or the Uniform Division of Income for Tax Purposes Act are not uniform in the application or proration of any deduction, the taxpayer shall disclose in its return to this state the nature and extent of the variance.

2. (a). **Definitions**—(1) "Taxpayer" means [each state should insert the definition in Article II.3. or the definition in its own tax laws].

(2) "Apportionment" refers to the division of business income between states by the use of a formula containing apportionment factors.

(3) "Allocation" refers to the assignment of nonbusiness income to a particular state.

(4) "Business activity" refers to the transactions and activity occurring in the regular course of a particular trade or business of a taxpayer.

2. (b)(1). Application of Article IV: Apportionment—If the business activity in respect to any trade or business of a taxpayer occurs both within and without this state, and if by reason of such business activity the taxpayer is taxable in another state, the portion of the net income (or net loss) arising from such trade or business which is derived from sources within this state shall be determined by apportionment in accordance with Article IV.9. to IV.17.

2. (b)(2). Application of Article IV: Combined Report—If a particular trade or business is carried on by a taxpayer and one or more affiliated corporations, nothing in Article IV or in these regulations shall preclude the use of a "combined report" whereby the entire business income of such trade or business is apportioned in accordance with Article IV.9. to IV.17.

2. (b)(3). Application of Article IV: Allocation—Any taxpayer subject to the taxing jurisdiction of this state shall allocate all of its nonbusiness income or loss within or without this state in accordance with Article IV.4. to IV.8.

2. (c). Consistency and Uniformity in Reporting—In filing returns with this state, if the taxpayer departs from or modifies the manner in which income has been classified as business income or nonbusiness income in returns for prior years, the taxpayer shall disclose in the return for the current year the nature and extent of the modification.

If the returns or reports filed by a taxpayer for all states to which the taxpayer reports under Article IV of this Compact or the Uniform Division of Income for Tax Purposes Act are not uniform in the classification of income as business or nonbusiness income, the taxpayer shall disclose in its return to this state the nature and extent of the variance.

3. (a). Taxable in Another State: In General—Under Article IV.2. the taxpayer is subject to the allocation and apportionment provisions of Article IV if it has income from business activity that is taxable both within and without this state. A taxpayer's income from business activity is taxable without this state if such taxpayer, by reason of such business activity (i.e., the transactions and activity occurring in the regular course of a particular trade or business), is taxable in another state within the meaning of Article IV.3. A taxpayer is taxable within another state if it meets either one of two tests: (1) If by reason of business activity in another state the taxpayer is subject to one of the types of taxes specified in Article IV.3.(1), namely: A net income tax, a franchise tax measured by net income, a franchise tax for the privilege of doing business, or a corporate stock tax: or (2) If by reason of such business activity another state has jurisdiction to subject the taxpayer to a net income tax, regardless of whether or not the state imposes such a tax on the taxpayer.

A taxpayer is not taxable in another state with respect to a particular trade or business merely because the taxpayer conducts activities in such other state pertaining to the production of nonbusiness income or business activities relating to a separate trade or business.

3. (b). Taxable in Another state: When a Taxpayer is "Subject to" a Tax under Article IV.3.(1)—(1) A taxpayer is "subject to" one of the taxes specified in Article IV.3.(1), if it carries on business activities in such state and such state imposes such a tax thereon. Any taxpayer which asserts that it is subject to one of the taxes specified in Article IV.3. (1) in another state shall furnish to the [tax administrator] of this state upon his request evidence to support such assertion. The [tax administrator] of this state may request that such evidence include proof that the taxpayer has filed the requisite tax return in such other state and has paid any taxes imposed under the law of such other state; the taxpayer's failure to produce such proof may be taken into account in determining whether the taxpayer in fact is subject to one of the taxes specified in Article IV.3.(1) in such other state.

If the taxpayer voluntarily files and pays one or more of such taxes when not required to do so by the laws of that state or pays a minimal fee for qualification, organization, or for the privilege of doing business in that state, but

(a)   does not actually engage in business activities in that state, or

(b)   does actually engage in some business activity, not sufficient for nexus, and the minimum tax bears no relation to the taxpayer's business activities within such state, the taxpayer is not "subject to" one of the taxes specified within the meaning of Article IV.3.(1).

Example: State A has a corporation franchise tax measured by net income, for the privilege of doing business in that state. Corporation X files a return and pays the $50 minimum tax, although it carries on no business activities in State A. Corporation X is not "taxable" in State A.

(2)   **The concept of taxability** in another state is based upon the premise that every state in which the taxpayer is engaged in business activities may impose an income tax even though every state does not do so. In states which do not, other types of taxes may be imposed as a substitute for an income tax. Therefore, only those taxes enumerated in Article IV.3.(1) which may be considered as basically revenue raising rather than regula-

tory measures shall be considered in determining whether the taxpayer is "subject to" one of the taxes specified in Article IV.3.(1) in another state.

Example (i): State A requires all nonresident corporations which qualify or register in State A to pay to the Secretary of State an annual license fee or tax for the privilege of doing business in the state regardless of whether the privilege is in fact exercised. The amount paid is determined according to the total authorized capital stock of the corporation; the rates are progressively higher by bracketed amounts. The statute sets a minimum fee of $50 and a maximum fee of $500. Failure to pay the tax bars a corporation from utilizing the state courts for enforcement of its rights. State A also imposes a corporation income tax. Nonresident Corporation X is qualified in State A and pays the required fee to the Secretary of State but does not carry on any business activity in State A (although it may utilize the courts of State A). Corporation X is not "taxable in" State A.

Example (ii): Same facts as Example (i) except that Corporation X is subject to and pays the corporation income tax. Payment is prima facie evidence that Corporation X is "subject to" the net income tax of State A and is "taxable" in State A.

Example (iii): State B requires all nonresident corporations qualified or registered in State B to pay to the Secretary of State an annual permit fee or tax for doing business in the state. The base of the fee or tax is the sum of (1) outstanding capital stock, and (2) surplus and undivided profits. The fee or tax base attributable to State B is determined by a three-factor apportionment formula. Nonresident Corporation X which operates a plant in State B, pays the required fee or tax to the Secretary of State. Corporation X is "taxable in" State B.

Example (iv): State A has a corporation franchise tax measured by net income for the privilege of doing business in that state. Corporation X files a return based upon its business activities in the state but the amount of computed liability is less than the minimum tax. Corporation X pays the minimum tax. Corporation X is subject to State A's corporation franchise tax.

3. (c). Taxable in Another State; When a State has Jurisdiction to Subject a Taxpayer to a Net Income Tax—The second test, that in Article IV.3.(2), applies if the taxpayer's business activity is sufficient to give the state jurisdiction to impose a net income tax by reason of such business activity under the Constitution and statutes of the United States. Jurisdiction to tax is not present where the state is prohibited from imposing the tax by reason of the provisions of Public Law 86-272, 15 U.S.C.A. §§ 381-385. In the case of any "state" as defined in Article IV.1(h), other than a state of the United States or political subdivision of such state, the determination of whether such "state" has jurisdiction to subject the taxpayer to a net income tax shall be made as though the jurisdictional standards applicable to a state of the United States applied in that "state." If jurisdiction is otherwise present, such "state" is not considered as without jurisdiction by reason of the provisions of a treaty between that state and the United States.

Example: Corporation X is actively engaged in manufacturing farm equipment in State A and in foreign country B. Both State A and foreign country B impose a net income tax but foreign country B exempts corporations engaged in manufacturing farm equipment. Corporation X is subject to the jurisdiction of State A and foreign country B.

9. Apportionment Formula—All business income of each trade or business of the taxpayer shall be apportioned to this state by use of the apportionment formula set forth in Article IV.9. The elements of the apportionment formula are the property factor (see Regulation IV.10.), the payroll factor (see Regulation IV.13.) and the sales factor (see Regulation IV.15.) of the trade or business of the taxpayer.

10. (a). Property Factor: In General—The property factor of the apportionment formula for each trade or business of the taxpayer shall include all real and tangible personal property owned or rented by the taxpayer and used during the tax period in the regular course of such trade or business. The term "real and tangible personal property" includes land, buildings, machinery, stocks of goods, equipment, and other real and tangible personal property but does not include coin or currency. Property used in connection with the production of nonbusiness income shall be excluded from the property factor. Property used both in the regular course of taxpayer's trade or business and in the production of nonbusiness income shall be included in the factor only to the extent the property is used in the regular course of taxpayer's trade or business. The method of determining that portion of the value to be included in the factor will depend upon the facts of each case. The property factor shall include the average value of property includable in the factor. See Reg. IV.12.

10. (b). Property Factor: Property Used for the Production of Business Income—Property shall be included in the property factor if it is actually used or is available for or capable of being used during the tax period in the regular course of the trade or business of the taxpayer. Property held as reserves or standby facilities or property held as a reserve source of materials shall be included in the factor. For example, a plant temporarily idle or raw material reserves not currently being processed are includable in the factor. Property or equipment under construction during the tax period, (except inventoriable goods in process) shall be excluded from the factor until such property is actually used in the regular course of the trade or business of the taxpayer. If the property is partially used in the regular course of the trade or business of the taxpayer while under construction, the value of the property to the extent used shall be included in the property factor. Property used in the regular course of the trade or business of the taxpayer shall remain in the property factor until its permanent withdrawal is established by an identifiable event such as its conversion to the production of nonbusiness income, its sale, or the lapse of an extended period of time (normally, five years) during which the property is held for sale.

Example (i): Taxpayer closed its manufacturing plant in State X and held such property for sale. The property remained vacant until its sale one year later. The value of the manufacturing plant is included in the property factor until the plant is sold.

Example (ii): Same as above except that the property was rented until the plant was sold. The plant is included in the property factor until the plant is sold.

Example (iii): Taxpayer closed its manufacturing plant and leased the building under a five-year lease. The plant is included in the property factor until the commencement of the lease.

Example (iv): The taxpayer operates a chain of retail grocery stores. Taxpayer closed Store A, which was then remodeled into three small retail stores such as a dress shop, dry cleaning, and barber shop, which were leased to unrelated parties. The property is removed from the property factor on the date the remodeling of Store A commenced.

10. (c). Property Factor: Consistency in Reporting—In filing returns with this state, if the taxpayer departs from or modifies the manner of valuing property, or of excluding or including property in the property factor, used in returns for prior years, the taxpayer shall disclose in the return for the current year the nature and extent of the modification.

If the returns or reports filed by the taxpayer with all states to which the taxpayer reports under Article IV of this Compact or the Uniform Division of Income for Tax Purposes Act are not uniform in the valuation of property and in the exclusion or inclusion of property in the property factor, the taxpayer shall disclose in its return to this state the nature and extent of the variance.

10. (d). Property Factor: Numerator—The numerator of the property factor shall include the average value of the real and tangible personal property owned or rented by the taxpayer and used in this state during the tax period in the regular course of the trade or business of the taxpayer. Property in transit between locations of the taxpayer to which it belongs shall be considered to be at the destination for purposes of the property factor. Property in transit between a buyer and seller which is included by a taxpayer in the denominator of its property factor in accordance with its regular accounting practices shall be included in the numerator according to the state of destination. The value of mobile or movable property such as construction equipment, trucks, or leased electronic equipment which are located within and without this state during the tax period shall be determined for purposes of the numerator of the factor on the basis of total time within the state during the tax period. An automobile assigned to a traveling employee shall be included in the numerator of the factor of the state to which the employee's compensation is assigned under the payroll factor or in the numerator of the state in which the automobile is licensed.

11. (a). Property Factor; Valuation of Owned Property—Property owned by the taxpayer shall be valued at its original cost. As a general rule "original cost" is deemed to be the basis of the property for federal income tax purposes (prior to any federal adjustments) at the time of acquisition by the taxpayer and adjusted by subsequent capital additions or improvements thereto and partial disposition thereof, by reason of sale, exchange, abandonment, etc.

Example (i): The taxpayer acquired a factory building in this state at a cost of $500,000 and 18 months later expended $100,000 for major remodeling of the building. Taxpayer files its return for the current taxable year on the calendar-year basis. Depreciation deduction in the amount of $22,000 was claimed on the building for its return for the current taxable year. The value of the building includable in the numerator and denominator of the property factor is $600,000 as the depreciation deduction is not taken into account in determining the value of the building for purposes of the factor.

Example (ii): During the current taxable year, X Corporation merges into Y Corporation in a tax-free reorganization under the Internal Revenue Code. At the time of the merger, X Corporation owns a factory which X built five years earlier at a cost of $1,000,000. X has been depreciating the factory at the rate of two per cent per year, and its basis in X's hands at the time of the merger is $900,000. Since the property is acquired by Y in a transaction in which, under the Internal Revenue Code, its basis in Y's hands is the same as its basis in X's, Y includes the property in Y's property factor at X's original cost, without adjustment for depreciation; i.e., $1,000,000.

Example (iii): Corporation Y acquires the assets of Corporation X in a liquidation by which Y is entitled to use its stock cost as the basis of the X assets under § 334(b)(2) of the 1954 Internal Revenue Code (i.e., stock possessing 80 per cent control is purchased and liquidated within two years). Under these circumstances, Y's cost of the assets is the purchase price of the X stock, prorated over the X assets.

If original cost of property is unascertainable, the property is included in the factor at its fair market value as of the date of acquisition by the taxpayer.

(2) Inventory of stock of goods shall be included in the factor in accordance with the valuation method used for federal income tax purposes.

(3) Property acquired by gift or inheritance shall be included in the factor at its basis for determining depreciation for federal income tax purposes.

11. (b). Property Factor; Valuation of Rented Property—(1) Property rented by the taxpayer is valued at eight times the net annual rental rate. The net annual rental rate for any item of rented property is the annual rental rate paid by the taxpayer for such property, less the aggregate annual subrental rates paid by subtenants of the taxpayer. (See Reg. IV.18.(a) for special rules where the use of such net annual rental rate produces a negative or clearly inaccurate value or where property is used by the taxpayer at no charge or rented at a nominal rental rate.)

Subrents are not deducted when the subrents constitute business income because the property which produces the subrents is used in the regular course of a trade or business of the taxpayer when it is producing such income. Accordingly there is no reduction in its value.

Example (i): The taxpayer receives subrents from a bakery concession in a food market operated by the taxpayer. Since the subrents are business income they are not deducted from rent paid by the taxpayer for the food market.

Example (ii): The taxpayer rents a 5-story office building primarily for use in its multistate business, uses three floors for its offices and subleases two floors to various other businesses and persons such as professional people, shops and the like. The rental of the two floors is incidental to the operation of the taxpayer's trade or business. Since the subrents are business income they are not deducted from the rent paid by the taxpayer.

Example (iii): The taxpayer rents a 20-story office building and uses the lower two stories for its general corporation headquarters. The remaining 18 floors are subleased to others. The rental of the eighteen floors is not incidental to but rather is separate from the operation of the taxpayer's trade or business. Since the subrents are nonbusiness income they are to be deducted from the rent paid by the taxpayer.

(2) "Annual rental rate" is the amount paid as rental for property for a 12-month period (i.e., the amount of the annual rent). Where property is rented for less than a 12-month period, the rent paid for the actual period of rental shall constitute the "annual rental rate" for the tax period. However, where a taxpayer has rented property for a term of 12 or more months and the current tax period covers a period of less than 12 months (due, for example, to a reorganization or change of acccounting period), the rent paid for the short tax period shall be annualized. If the rental term is for less than 12 months, the rent shall not be annualized beyond its term. Rent shall not be annualized because of the uncertain duration when the rental term is on a month to month basis.

Example (i): Taxpayer A which ordinarily files its returns based on a calendar year is merged into Taxpayer B on April 30. The net rent paid under a lease with 5 years remaining is $2,500 a month. The rent for the tax period January 1 to April 30 is $10,000. After the rent is annualized the net rent is $30,000 ($2,500 × 12).

Example (ii): Same facts as in Example (i) except that the lease would have terminated on August 31. In this case the annualized net rent is $20,000 ($2,500 × 8).

(3) "Annual rent" is the actual sum of money or other consideration payable, directly or indirectly, by the taxpayer or for its benefit for the use of the property and includes:

(A) Any amount payable for the use of real or tangible personal property, or any part thereof, whether designated as a fixed sum of money or as a percentage of sales, profits, or otherwise.

Example: A taxpayer, pursuant to the terms of a lease, pays a lessor $1,000 per month as a base rental and at the end of the year pays the lessor one per cent of its gross sales of $400,000. The annual rent is $16,000 ($12,000 plus one per cent of $400,000 or $4,000).

(B) Any amount payable as additional rent or in lieu of rents, such as interest, taxes, insurance, repairs or any other items which are required to be paid by the terms of the lease or other arrangement, not including amounts paid as service charges, such as utilities, janitor services, etc. If a payment includes rent and other charges unsegregated, the amount of rent shall be determined by consideration of the relative values of the rent and other items.

Example (i): A taxpayer, pursuant to the terms of a lease, pays the lessor $12,000 a year rent plus taxes in the amount of $2,000 and interest on a mortgage in the amount of $1,000. The annual rent is $15,000.

Example (ii): A taxpayer stores part of its inventory in a public warehouse. The total charge for the year was $1,000 of which $700 was for the use of storage space and $300 for inventory insurance, handling and shipping charges, and C.O.D. collections. The annual rent is $700.

"Annual rent" does not include incidental day-to-day expenses such as hotel or motel accommodations, daily rental of automobiles, etc.

(4) Leasehold improvements shall, for the purposes of the property factor, be treated as property owned by the taxpayer regardless of whether the taxpayer is entitled to remove the improvements or the improvements revert to the lessor upon expiration of the lease. Hence, the original cost of leasehold improvements shall be included in the factor.

12. Property Factor; Averaging Property Values—As a general rule the average value of property owned by the taxpayer shall be determined by averaging the values at the beginning and ending of the tax period. However, the [tax administrator] may require or allow averaging by monthly values if such method of averaging is required to properly reflect the average value of the taxpayer's property for the tax period.

Averaging by monthly values will generally be applied if substantial fluctuations in the values of the property exist during the tax period or where property is acquired after the beginning of the tax period or disposed of before the end of the tax period.

Example: The monthly value of the taxpayer's property was as follows:

January	$ 2,000	July	$ 15,000
February	2,000	August	17,000
March	3,000	September	23,000
April	3,500	October	25,000
May	4,500	November	13,000
June	10,000	December	2,000
	$25,000		$ 95,000
		TOTAL	$120,000

The average value of the taxpayer's property includable in the property factor for the income year is determined as follows:

$$12,000 \div 12 = \$10,000$$

Averaging with respect to rented property is achieved automatically by the method of determining the net annual rental rate of such property as set forth in Reg. IV. 11. (b).

13. (a). Payroll Factor; in General—(1) The payroll factor of the apportionment formula for each trade or business of the taxpayer shall include the total amount paid by the taxpayer in the regular course of its trade or business for compensation during the tax period.

(2) The total amount "paid" to employees is determined upon the basis of the taxpayer's accounting method. If the taxpayer has adopted the accrual method of accounting, all compensation properly accrued shall be deemed to have been paid. Notwithstanding the taxpayer's method of accounting, at the election of the taxpayer, compensation paid to employees may be included in the payroll factor by use of the cash method if the taxpayer is required to report such compensation under such method for unemployment compensation purposes.

The compensation of any employee on account of activities which are connected with the production of nonbusiness income shall be excluded from the factor.

Example (i): The taxpayer uses some of its employees in the construction of a storage building which, upon completion, is used in the regular course of taxpayer's trade or business. The wages paid to those employees are treated as a capital expenditure by the taxpayer. The amount of such wages is included in the payroll factor.

Example (ii): The taxpayer owns various securities which it holds as an investment separate and apart from its trade or business. The management of the taxpayer's investment portfolio is the only duty of Mr. X, an employee. The salary paid to Mr. X is excluded from the payroll factor.

(3) The term "compensation" means wages, salaries, commissions, and any other form of remuneration paid to employees for personal services. Payments made to an independent contractor or any other person not properly classifiable as an employee are excluded. Only amounts paid directly to employees are included in the payroll factor. Amounts considered paid directly include the value of board, rent, housing, lodging, and other benefits or services furnished to employees by the taxpayer in return for personal services provided that such amounts constitute income to the recipient under the federal Internal Revenue Code. In the case of employees not subject to the federal Internal Revenue Code, e.g., those employed in foreign countries, the determination of whether such benefits or services would constitute income to the employees shall be made as though such employees were subject to the federal Internal Revenue Code.

(4) The term "employee" means (A) any officer of a corporation, or (B) any individual who, under the usual common-law rules applicable in determining the employer-employee relationship, has the status of an employee. Generally, a person will be considered to be an employee if he is included by the taxpayer as an employee for purposes of the payroll taxes imposed by the Federal Insurance Contributions Act; except that, since certain individuals are included within the term "employees" in the Federal Insurance Contributions Act who would not be employees under the usual common-law rules, it may be established that a person who is included as an employee for purposes of the Federal Insurance Contributions Act is not an employee for purposes of this regulation.

(5) In filing returns with this state, if the taxpayer departs from or modifies the treatment of compensation paid used in returns for prior years, the taxpayer shall disclose in the return for the current year the nature and extent of the modification.

If the returns or reports filed by the taxpayer with all states to which the taxpayer reports under Article IV of this Compact or the Uniform Division of Income for Tax Purposes Act are not uniform in the treatment of compensation paid, the taxpayer shall disclose in its return to this state the nature and extent of the variance.

13.   (b).   Payroll Factor: Denominator—The denominator of the payroll factor is the total compensation paid everywhere during the tax period. Accordingly, if compensation paid to employees whose services are performed entirely in a state where the taxpayer is immune from taxation, for example, by Public Law 86-272, is included in the denominator of the payroll factor.

Example: A taxpayer has employees in its state of legal domicile (State A) and is taxable in State B. In addition the taxpayer has other employees whose services are performed entirely in State C where the taxpayer is immune from taxation by Public Law 86-272. As to these latter employees, the compensation will be assigned to State C where their services are performed (i.e., included in the denominator—but not the numerator—of the payroll factor) even though the taxpayer is not taxable in State C.

13. (c). Payroll Factor: Numerator—The numerator of the payroll factor is the total amount paid in this state during the tax period by the taxpayer for compensation. The tests in Article IV.14. to be applied in determining whether compensation is paid in this state are derived from the Model Unemployment Compensation Act. Accordingly, if compensation paid to employees is included in the payroll factor by use of the cash method of accounting or if the taxpayer is required to report such compensation under such method for unemployment compensation purposes, it shall be presumed that the total wages reported by the taxpayer to this state for unemployment compensation purposes constitutes compensation paid in this state except for compensation excluded under Regulation IV.13.(a) to IV.14. The presumption may be overcome by satisfactory evidence that an employee's compensation is not properly reportable to this state for unemployment compensation purposes.

14. Payroll Factor: Compensation Paid in this State—Compensation is paid in this state if any one of the following tests, applied consecutively, are met:

(1) The employee's service is performed entirely within the state.

(2) The employee's service is performed both within and without the state, but the service performed without the state is incidental to the employee's service within the state. The word "incidental" means any service which is temporary or transitory in nature, or which is rendered in connection with an isolated transaction.

(3) If the employee's services are performed both within and without this state, the employee's compensation will be attributed to this state:

(A) if the employee's base of operations is in this state; or

(B) if there is no base of operations in any state in which some part of the service is performed, but the place from which the service is directed or controlled is in this state; or

(C) if the base of operations or the place from which the service is directed or controlled is not in any state in which some part of the service is performed but the employee's residence is in this state.

The term "base of operations" is the place of more or less permanent nature from which the employee starts his work and to which he customarily returns in order to receive instructions from the taxpayer or communications from his customers or other persons or to replenish stock or other materials, repair equipment, or perform any other functions necessary to the exercise of his trade or profession at some other point or points. The term "place from which the service is directed or controlled" refers to the place from which the power to direct or control is exercised by the taxpayer.

15. (a). Sales Factor: In General—(1) Article IV.1.(g) defines the term "sales" to mean all gross receipts of the taxpayer not allocated under paragraphs (5) through (8) of Article IV. Thus, for the purposes of the sales factor of the apportionment formula for each trade or business of the taxpayer, the term "sales" means all gross receipts derived by the taxpayer from transactions and activity in the regular course of such trade or business. The following are rules for determining "sales" in various situations:

(A)   In the case of a taxpayer engaged in manufacturing and selling or purchasing and reselling goods or products, "sales" includes all gross receipts from the sales of such goods or products (or other property of a kind which would properly be included in the inventory of the taxpayer if on hand at the close of the tax period) held by the taxpayer primarily for sale to customers in the ordinary course of its trade or business. Gross receipts for this purpose means gross sales, less returns and allowances, and includes all interest income, service charges, carrying charges, or time-price differential charges incidental to such sales. Federal and state excise taxes (including sales taxes) shall be included as part of such receipts if such taxes are passed on to the buyer or included as part of the selling price of the product.

(B)   In the case of cost plus fixed fee contracts, such as the operation of a government-owned plant for a fee, "sales" include the entire reimbursed cost, plus the fee.

(C)   In the case of a taxpayer engaged in providing services, such as the operation of an advertising agency, or the performance of equipment service contracts, research and development contracts, "sales" includes the gross receipts from the performance of such services including fees, commissions, and similar items.

(D)   In the case of a taxpayer engaged in renting real or tangible property, "sales" includes the gross receipts from the rental, lease, or licensing the use of the property.

(E)   In the case of a taxpayer engaged in the sale, assignment, or licensing of intangible personal property such as patents and copyrights, "sales" includes the gross receipts therefrom.

(F)   If a taxpayer derives receipts from the sale of equipment used in its business, such receipts constitute "sales." For example, a truck express company owns a fleet of trucks and sells its trucks under a regular replacement program. The gross receipts from the sales of the trucks are included in the sales factor.

(2)   In some cases certain gross receipts should be disregarded in determining the sales factor in order that the apportionment formula will operate fairly to apportion to this state the income of the taxpayer's trade or business. See Regulation IV.18(b).

(3)   In filing returns with this state, if the taxpayer departs from or modifies the basis for excluding or including gross receipts in the sales factor used in returns for prior years, the taxpayer shall disclose in the return for the current year the nature and extent of the modification.

If the returns or reports filed by the taxpayer with all states to which the taxpayer reports under Article IV of this Compact or the Uniform Division of Income for Tax Purposes Act are not uniform in the inclusion or exclusion of gross receipts, the taxpayer shall disclose in its return to this state the nature and extent of the variance.

15.   (b).   Sales Factor: Denominator—The denominator of the sales factor shall include the total gross receipts derived by the taxpayer from transactions and activity in the regular course of its trade or business, except receipts excluded under Regulation IV.18.(b).

15.   (c).   Sales Factor; Numerator—The numerator of the sales factor shall include the gross receipts attributable to this state and derived by the taxpayer from transactions and activity in the regular course of its trade or business. All interest income, service charges, carrying charges, or time-price differential charges incidental to such gross receipts shall be included regardless of the place where the accounting records are maintained or the location of the contract or other evidence of indebtedness.

16.   (a).   Sales Factor; Sales of Tangible Personal Property in this State—(1) Gross receipts from the sales of tangible personal property (except sales to the United States Government; see Reg. IV. 16. (b)) are in this state:

(A)   if the property is delivered or shipped to a purchaser within this state regardless of the f.o.b. point or other conditions of sale; or

(B)   if the property is shipped from an office, store, warehouse, factory, or other place of storage in this state and the taxpayer is not taxable in the state of the purchaser.

(2)   Property shall be deemed to be delivered or shipped to a purchaser within this state if the recipient is located in this state, even though the property is ordered from outside this state.

Example: The taxpayer, with inventory in State A, sold $100,000 of its products to a purchaser having branch stores in several states including this state. The order for the purchase was placed by the purchaser's central purchasing department located in State B. $25,000 of the purchase order was shipped directly to purchaser's branch store in this state. The branch store in this state is the "purchaser within this state" with respect to $25,000 of the taxpayer's sales.

(3) Property is delivered or shipped to a purchaser within this state if the shipment terminates in this state, even though the property is subsequently transferred by the purchaser to another state.

Example: The taxpayer makes a sale to a purchaser who maintains a central warehouse in this state at which all merchandise purchases are received. The purchaser reships the goods to its branch stores in other states for sale. All of taxpayer's products shipped to the purchaser's warehouse in this state is property "delivered or shipped to a purchaser within this state."

(4) The term "purchaser within this state" shall include the ultimate recipient of the property if the taxpayer in this state, at the designation of the purchaser, delivers to or has the property shipped to the ultimate recipient within this state.

Example: A taxpayer in this state sold merchandise to a purchaser in State A. Taxpayer directed the manufacturer or supplier of the merchandise in State B to ship the merchandise to the purchaser's customer in this state pursuant to purchaser's instructions. The sale by the taxpayer is "in this state."

(5) When property being shipped by a seller from the state of origin to a consignee in another state is diverted while enroute to a purchaser in this state, the sales are in this state.

Example: The taxpayer, a produce grower in State A, begins shipment of perishable produce to the purchaser's place of business in State B. While enroute the produce is diverted to the purchaser's place of business in this state in which state the taxpayer is subject to tax. The sale by the taxpayer is attributed to this state.

(6) If the taxpayer is not taxable in the state of the purchaser, the sale is attributed to this state if the property is shipped from an office, store, warehouse, factory, or other place of storage in this state.

Example: The taxpayer has its head office and factory in State A. It maintains a branch office and inventory in this state. Taxpayer's only activity in State B is the solicitation of orders by a resident salesman. All orders by the State B salesman are sent to the branch office in this state for approval and are filled by shipment from the inventory in this state. Since taxpayer is immune under Public Law 86-272 from tax in State B, all sales of merchandise to purchasers in State B are attributed to this state, the state from which the merchandise was shipped.

(7) If a taxpayer whose salesman operates from an office located in this state makes a sale to a purchaser in another state in which the taxpayer is not taxable and the property is shipped directly by a third party to the purchaser, the following rules apply:

(A)   If the taxpayer is taxable in the state from which the third party ships the property, then the sale is in such state.

(B)   If the taxpayer is not taxable in the state from which the property is shipped, then the sale is in this state.

Example: The taxpayer in this state sold merchandise to a purchaser in State A. Taxpayer is not taxable in State A. Upon direction of the taxpayer, the merchandise was shipped directly to the purchaser by the manufacturer in State B. If the taxpayer is taxable in State B, the sale is in State B. If the taxpayer is not taxable in State B, the sale is in this state.

16.   (b).   Sales Factor; Sales of Tangible Personal Property; To United States Government in this State—(1) Gross receipts from the sales of tangible personal property to the United States Government are in this state if the property is shipped from an office, store, warehouse, factory, or other place of storage in this state. For the purposes of this regulation, only sales for which the United States Government makes direct payment to the seller pursuant to the terms of a contract constitute sales to the United States Government. Thus, as a general rule, sales by a subcontractor to the prime contractor, the party to the contract with the United States Government, do not constitute sales to the United States Government.

Example (i): A taxpayer contracts with General Services Administration to deliver X number of trucks which were paid for by the United States Government. The sale is a sale to the United States Government.

Example (ii): The taxpayer as a subcontractor to a prime contractor with the National Aeronautics and Space Administration contracts to build a component of a rocket for $1,000,000. The sale by the subcontractor to the prime contractor is not a sale to the United States Government.

17.   Sales Factor: Sales Other than Sales of Tangible Personal Property in this State—(1) In General. Article IV. 17. provides for the inclusion in the numerator of the sales factor of gross receipts from transactions other than sales of tangible personal property (including transactions with the United States Government); under this section gross receipts are attributed to this state if the income producing activity which gave rise to the receipts is performed wholly within this state. Also, gross receipts are attributed to this state if, with respect to a particular item of income, the income producing activity is performed within and without this state but the greater proportion of the income producing activity is performed in this state, based on costs of performance.

(2)   Income producing activity; defined. The term "income producing activity" applies to each separate item of income and means the transactions and activity directly engaged in by the taxpayer in the regular course of its trade or business for the ultimate purpose of obtaining gains or profit. Such activity does not include transactions and activities performed on behalf of a taxpayer, such as those conducted on its behalf by an inde-

pendent contractor. Accordingly, the income producing activity includes but is not limited to the following:

(A)   The rendering of personal services by employees or the utilization of tangible and intangible property by the taxpayer in performing a service.

(B)   The sale, rental, leasing, or licensing or other use of real property.

(C)   The rental, leasing, licensing, or other use of tangible personal property.

(D)   The sale, licensing, or other use of intangible personal property.

The mere holding of intangible personal property is not, of itself, an income producing activity.

(3)   Costs of performance; defined. The term "costs of performance" means direct costs determined in a manner consistent with generally accepted accounting principles and in accordance with accepted conditions or practices in the trade or business of the taxpayer.

(4)   Application. (A) In General. Receipts (other than from sales of tangible personal property) in respect to a particular income producing activity are in this state if:

(a)   the income producing activity is performed wholly within this state; or

(b)   the income producing activity is performed both in and outside this state and a greater proportion of the income producing activity is performed in this state than in any other state, based on costs of performance.

(B)   Special rules. The following are special rules for determining when receipts from the income producing activities described below are in this state:

(a)   Gross receipts from the sale, lease, rental, or licensing of real property are in this state if the real property is located in this state.

(b)   Gross receipts from the rental, lease, or licensing of tangible personal property are in this state if the property is located in this state. The rental, lease, licensing, or other use of tangible personal property in this state is a separate income producing activity from the rental lease, licensing or other use of the same property while located in another state; consequently, if property is within and without this state during the rental, lease, or licensing period, gross receipts attributable to this state shall be measured by the ratio which the time the property was physically present or was used in this state bears to the total time or use of the property everywhere during such period.

Example: Taxpayer is the owner of 10 railroad cars. During the year, the total of the days each railroad car was present in this state was 50 days. The receipts attributable to the use of each of the railroad cars in this state are a separate item of income and shall be determined as follows:

$$\frac{(10 \times 50 =)\ 500}{3650} \times \text{Total Receipts} = \text{Receipts Attributable to this State}$$

(c) Gross receipts for the performance of personal services are attributable to this state to the extent such services are performed in this state. If services relating to a single item of income are performed partly within and partly without this state, the gross receipts for the performance of such services shall be attributable to this state only if a greater portion of the services were performed in this state, based on costs of performance. Usually where services are performed partly within and partly without this state the services performed in each state will constitute a separate income producing activity; in such case the gross receipts for the performance of services attributable to this state shall be measured by the ratio which the time spent in performing such services in this state bears to the total time spent in performing such services everywhere. Time spent in performing services includes the amount of time expended in the performance of a contract or other obligation which gives rise to such gross receipts. Personal service not directly connected with the performance of the contract or other obligation, as for example, time expended in negotiating the contract, is excluded from the computations.

Example (i): Taxpayer, a road show, gave theatrical performances at various locations in State X and in this state during the tax period. All gross receipts from performances given in this state are attributed to this state.

Example (ii): The taxpayer, a public opinion survey corporation, conducted a poll by its employees in State X and in this state for the sum of $9,000. The project required 600 man hours to obtain the basic data and prepare the survey report. Two hundred of the 600 man hours were expended in this state. The receipts attributable to this state are $3,000.

$$\frac{(200 \text{ man hours} \times \$9,000)}{600 \text{ man hours}}$$

18. (a). Special Rules—In General—Article IV.18. provides that if the allocation and apportionment provisions of Article IV do not fairly represent the extent of the taxpayer's business activity in this state, the taxpayer may petition for or the tax administrator may require, in respect to all or any part of the taxpayer's business activity, if reasonable:

(1)   Separate accounting;

(2)   The exclusion of any one or more of the factors;

(3)   The inclusion of one or more additional factors which will fairly represent the taxpayer's business activity in this state; or

(4)   The employment of any other method to effectuate an equitable allocation and apportionment of the taxpayer's income.

Article IV.18. permits a departure from the allocation and apportionment provisions of Article IV only in limited and specific cases. Article

IV.18. may be invoked only in specific cases where unusual fact situations (which ordinarily will be unique and nonrecurring) produce incongruous results under the apportionment and allocation provisions contained in Article IV.

In the case of certain industries such as air transportation, rail transportation, ship transportation, trucking, television, radio, motion pictures, various types of professional athletics, and so forth, the foregoing regulations in respect to the apportionment formula do not set forth appropriate procedures for determining the apportionment factors. Nothing in Article IV.18. or in this Regulation IV.18. shall preclude [the tax administrator] from establishing appropriate procedures under Article IV.10. to 17. for determining the apportionment factors for each such industry, but such procedures shall be applied uniformly.

18. (b). Special Rules—Property Factor—The following special rules are established in respect to the property factor of the apportionment formula:

(1) If the subrents taken into account in determining the net annual rental rate under Regulation IV.11.(b) produce a negative or clearly inaccurate value for any item of property, another method which will properly reflect the value of rented property may be required by the [tax administrator] or requested by the taxpayer.

In no case however shall such value be less than an amount which bears the same ratio to the annual rental rate paid by the taxpayer for such property as the fair market value of that portion of the property used by the taxpayer bears to the total fair market value of the rented property.

Example: The taxpayer rents a 10-story building at an annual rental rate of $1,000,000. Taxpayer occupies two stores and sublets eight stores for $1,000,000 a year. The net annaul rental rate of the taxpayer must not be less than two-tenths of the taxpayer's annual rental rate for the entire year, or $200,000.

(2) If property owned by others is used by the taxpayer at no charge or rented by the taxpayer for a nominal rate, the net annual rental rate for such property shall be determined on the basis of a reasonable market rental rate for such property.

18. (c). Special Rules—Sales Factor—The following special rules are established in respect to the sales factor of the apportionment formula:

(1) Where substantial amounts of gross receipts arise from an incidental or occasional sale of a fixed asset used in the regular course of the taxpayer's trade or business, such gross receipts shall be excluded from the sales factor. For example, gross receipts from the sale of a factory or plant will be excluded.

(2)   Insubstantial amounts of gross receipts arising from incidental or occasional transactions or activities may be excluded from the sales factor unless such exclusion would materially affect the amount of income apportioned to this state. For example, the taxpayer ordinarily may include or exclude from the sales factor gross receipts from such transactions as the sale of office furniture, business automobiles, etc.

(3)   Where the income producing activity in respect to business income from tangible personal property can be readily identified, such income is included in the denominator of the sales factor and, if the income producing activity occurs in this state, in the numerator of the sales factor as well. For example, usually the income producing activity can be readily identified in respect to interest income received on deferred payments on sales of tangible property (Regulation IV.15.(a).(1) (A)) and income from the sale, licensing, or other use of intangible personal property (Regulation IV.17.(1) (D)).

Where business income from intangible property cannot be attributed to any particular income producing activity of the taxpayer, such income cannot be assigned to the numerator of the sales factor for any state and shall be excluded from the denominator of the sales factor. For example, where business income in the form of dividends received on stock, royalties received on patents or copyrights, or interest received on bonds, debentures, or government securities results from the mere holding of the intangible personal property by the taxpayer, such dividends and interest shall be excluded from the denominator of the sales factor.

Comprehensive Example —Computation of the California Tax for a Unitary Company

Listed on the following pages are data for the Helen Corporation and its affiliated companies, the Ulysses Corporation, the Achilles Corporation, and the Paris Corporation. This information is to be used in computing the California franchise tax for the taxable year ended December 31, 1979. For purposes of identifying this affiliated group on the California combined tax return, we will refer to these corporations collectively as Helen Corporation and its combined unitary affiliates.

There are three basic steps in this problem which are necessary in order to compute the 1979 California franchise tax. The first step is the computation of the factor information, the second is the computation of a combined profit and loss statement, and the third is the conversion of this combined net income to unitary income subject to apportionment.

Form 1120

Department of the Treasury
Internal Revenue Service

U.S. Corporation Income Tax Return

For calendar year 1979 or other taxable year beginning
1979, ending _____ 19___

1979

Check if a—
A Consolidated return ☐
B Personal Holding Co. ☐
C Business Code No. (See Page 8 of instructions)

Use IRS label. Otherwise please print or type.

Name **Paris Corporation**

Number and street **910 South Third Street**

City or town, State, and ZIP code **San Francisco, California 94101**

D Employer identification number (see instruction W) **36-8165381**

E Date incorporated **August 18, 1948**

F Enter total assets (see instruction X) $ _____

Gross Income

1 (a) Gross receipts or sales $ .... (b) Less returns and allowances $ .... Balance ▶	1(c)	732,262
2 **Less:** Cost of goods sold (Schedule A) and/or operations (attach schedule)	2	543,732
3 Gross profit	3	188,530
4 Dividends (Schedule C)	4	483
5 Interest on obligations of the United States and U.S. instrumentalities	5	–
6 Other interest	6	365
7 Gross rents	7	–
8 Gross royalties	8	150
9 (a) Capital gain net income (attach separate Schedule D)	9(a)	1,141
(b) Net gain or (loss) from Form 4797, line 11, Part II (attach Form 4797)	9(b)	(273)
10 Other income (see instructions—attach schedule)	10	2,576
11 TOTAL income—Add lines 3 through 10	11	192,972

Deductions

12 Compensation of officers (Schedule E)	12	1,259
13 (a) Salaries and wages .... 13(b) Less WIN and jobs credit(s) .... Balance ▶	13(c)	31,615
14 Repairs (see instructions)	14	33,588
15 Bad debts (Schedule F if reserve method is used)	15	1,105
16 Rents	16	5,047
17 Taxes	17	10,920
18 Interest	18	24,737
19 Contributions (not over 5% of line 30 adjusted per instructions—attach schedule)	19	–
20 Amortization (attach schedule)	20	900
21 Depreciation from Form 4562 (attach Form 4562) ...., less depreciation claimed in Schedule A and elsewhere on return ...., Balance ▶	21	56,992
22 Depletion	22	–
23 Advertising	23	1,812
24 Pension, profit-sharing, etc. plans (see instructions) (enter number of plans ▶ ....)	24	11,840
25 Employee benefit programs (see instructions)	25	3,099
26 Other deductions (attach schedule)	26	47,552
27 TOTAL deductions—Add lines 12 through 26	27	230,466
28 Taxable income before net operating loss deduction and special deductions (subtract line 27 from line 11)	28	(37,494)
29 **Less:** (a) Net operating loss deduction (see instructions—attach schedule) . 29(a)		
(b) Special deductions (Schedule I) . . . . 29(b)	29	
30 Taxable income (subtract line 29 from line 28)	30	(37,494)

Tax

31 TOTAL TAX (Schedule J)	31	–
32 Credits: (a) Overpayment from 1978 allowed as a credit		
(b) 1979 estimated tax payments		
(c) Less refund of 1979 estimated tax applied for on Form 4466 . (............)		
(d) Tax deposited: Form 7004 .... Form 7005 (attach) .... Total ▶		
(e) Credit from regulated investment companies (attach Form 2439)		
(f) Federal tax on special fuels and oils (attach Form 4136 or 4136-T)	32	
33 TAX DUE (subtract line 32 from line 31). See instruction G for depositary method of payment. (Check ▶ ☐ if Form 2220 is attached. See page 3 of instructions.) ▶ $	33	–
34 OVERPAYMENT (subtract line 31 from line 32)	34	–
35 Enter amount of line 34 you want: **Credited to 1980 estimated tax** ▶ .... Refunded ▶	35	–

Please Sign Here

Under penalties of perjury, I declare that I have examined this return, including accompanying schedules and statements, and to the best of my knowledge and belief, it is true, correct, and complete. Declaration of preparer (other than taxpayer) is based on all information of which preparer has any knowledge.

Signature of officer .... Date .... ▶ Title ....

Paid Preparer's Information

Preparer's signature and date ▶

Firm's name (or yours, if self-employed) and address ▶

Check if self-employed ▶ ☐

Preparer's social security no. ....

E.I. No. ▶

ZIP code ▶

U.S. Corporation Income Tax Return

For calendar year 1979 or other taxable year beginning
1979, ending _____ 19___

1979

Check if a—
A Consolidated return ☐
B Personal Holding Co. ☐
C Business Code No. (See Page 8 of instructions)

Use IRS label. Otherwise please print or type.

Name: Helen Corporation
Number and street: 3000 Lake Shore Drive
City or town, State, and ZIP code: Chicago, Illinois 60657

D Employer identification number (see instruction W)
36-3683823

E Date incorporated
June 30, 1954

F Enter total assets (see instruction X)
$

Gross Income

1 (a) Gross receipts or sales $ _____ (b) Less returns and allowances $ _____ Balance ▶	1(c)	
2 **Less:** Cost of goods sold (Schedule A) and/or operations (attach schedule)	2	
3 Gross profit	3	
4 Dividends (Schedule C)	4	1,000
5 Interest on obligations of the United States and U.S. instrumentalities	5	
6 Other interest	6	16,552
7 Gross rents	7	
8 Gross royalties	8	
9 (a) Capital gain net income (attach separate Schedule D)	9(a)	
(b) Net gain or (loss) from Form 4797, line 11, Part II (attach Form 4797)	9(b)	
10 Other income (see instructions—attach schedule)	10	
11 TOTAL income—Add lines 3 through 10	11	17,552

Deductions

12 Compensation of officers (Schedule E)	12	
13 (a) Salaries and wages _____ 13(b) Less WIN and jobs credit(s) _____ Balance ▶	13(c)	554
14 Repairs (see instructions)	14	
15 Bad debts (Schedule F if reserve method is used)	15	
16 Rents	16	
17 Taxes	17	258
18 Interest	18	10,099
19 Contributions (not over 5% of line 30 adjusted per instructions—attach schedule)	19	
20 Amortization (attach schedule)	20	
21 Depreciation from Form 4562 (attach Form 4562) _____, less depreciation claimed in Schedule A and elsewhere on return _____, Balance ▶	21	
22 Depletion	22	
23 Advertising	23	
24 Pension, profit-sharing, etc. plans (see instructions) (enter number of plans ▶ _____)	24	
25 Employee benefit programs (see instructions)	25	
26 Other deductions (attach schedule)	26	211
27 TOTAL deductions—Add lines 12 through 26	27	11,122
28 Taxable income before net operating loss deduction and special deductions (subtract line 27 from line 11)	28	6,430
29 **Less:** (a) Net operating loss deduction (see instructions—attach schedule) 29(a) _____		
(b) Special deductions (Schedule I) 29(b) _____	29	
30 Taxable income (subtract line 29 from line 28)	30	6,430

Tax

31 TOTAL TAX (Schedule J)	31	
32 **Credits:** (a) Overpayment from 1978 allowed as a credit _____		
(b) 1979 estimated tax payments _____		
(c) Less refund of 1979 estimated tax applied for on Form 4466 . (_____)		
(d) Tax deposited: Form 7004 _____ Form 7005 (attach) _____ Total ▶ _____		
(e) Credit from regulated investment companies (attach Form 2439) _____		
(f) Federal tax on special fuels and oils (attach Form 4136 or 4136–T) _____	32	
33 TAX DUE (subtract line 32 from line 31). See instruction G for depositary method of payment	33	
(Check ▶ ☐ if Form 2220 is attached. See page 3 of instructions.) ▶ $ _____		
34 OVERPAYMENT (subtract line 31 from line 32)	34	
35 Enter amount of line 34 you want: Credited to 1980 estimated tax ▶ _____ Refunded ▶	35	

Under penalties of perjury, I declare that I have examined this return, including accompanying schedules and statements, and to the best of my knowledge and belief, it is true, correct, and complete. Declaration of preparer (other than taxpayer) is based on all information of which preparer has any knowledge.

Please Sign Here

Signature of officer _____ Date _____ ▶ Title _____

Paid Preparer's Information

Preparer's signature and date ▶		Check if self-employed ▶ ☐	Preparer's social security no.
Firm's name (or yours, if self-employed) and address ▶		E.I. No. ▶	
		ZIP code ▶	

Form 1120

Department of the Treasury
Internal Revenue Service

U.S. Corporation Income Tax Return

For calendar year 1979 or other taxable year beginning
1979, ending _____ 19___

1979

Check if a—		
A Consolidated return ☐		
B Personal Holding Co. ☐		
C Business Code No. (See Page 8 of instructions)		

Use IRS label. Otherwise please print or type.

Name: Achilles Corporation

Number and street: 400 West Main Street

City or town, State, and ZIP code: Springfield, Illinois 62701

D Employer identification number (see instruction W)
37-3181154

E Date incorporated
January 22, 1934

F Enter total assets (see instruction X)
$

Gross Income

1 (a) Gross receipts or sales $ 143,222 (b) Less returns and allowances $ 1,454 Balance ▶	1(c)	141,768
2 **Less:** Cost of goods sold (Schedule A) and/or operations (attach schedule)	2	101,361
3 Gross profit	3	40,407
4 Dividends (Schedule C)	4	1,000
5 Interest on obligations of the United States and U.S. instrumentalities	5	
6 Other interest	6	
7 Gross rents	7	120
8 Gross royalties	8	109
9 (a) Capital gain net income (attach separate Schedule D)	9(a)	
(b) Net gain or (loss) from Form 4797, line 11, Part II (attach Form 4797)	9(b)	1
10 Other income (see instructions—attach schedule)	10	3
11 TOTAL income—Add lines 3 through 10	11	41,640

Deductions

12 Compensation of officers (Schedule E)	12	439
13 (a) Salaries and wages _____ 13(b) Less WIN and jobs credit(s) _____ Balance ▶	13(c)	3,600
14 Repairs (see instructions)	14	5,776
15 Bad debts (Schedule F if reserve method is used)	15	558
16 Rents	16	983
17 Taxes	17	3,850
18 Interest	18	3
19 Contributions (not over 5% of line 30 adjusted per instructions—attach schedule)	19	2
20 Amortization (attach schedule)	20	196
21 Depreciation from Form 4562 (attach Form 4562) _____, less depreciation claimed in Schedule A and elsewhere on return _____, Balance ▶	21	12,263
22 Depletion	22	–
23 Advertising	23	372
24 Pension, profit-sharing, etc. plans (see instructions) (enter number of plans ▶ _____)	24	541
25 Employee benefit programs (see instructions)	25	940
26 Other deductions (attach schedule)	26	2,432
27 TOTAL deductions—Add lines 12 through 26	27	31,955
28 Taxable income before net operating loss deduction and special deductions (subtract line 27 from line 11)	28	9,685
29 **Less:** (a) Net operating loss deduction (see instructions—attach schedule) 29(a) _____		
(b) Special deductions (Schedule I) 29(b) _____	29	
30 Taxable income (subtract line 29 from line 28)	30	9,685

Tax

31 TOTAL TAX (Schedule J)	31	
32 **Credits:** (a) Overpayment from 1978 allowed as a credit		
(b) 1979 estimated tax payments		
(c) Less refund of 1979 estimated tax applied for on Form 4466 . ( )		
(d) Tax deposited: Form 7004 _____ Form 7005 (attach) _____ Total ▶		
(e) Credit from regulated investment companies (attach Form 2439)		
(f) Federal tax on special fuels and oils (attach Form 4136 or 4136-T)	32	
33 TAX DUE (subtract line 32 from line 31). See instruction G for depositary method of payment .	33	–
(Check ▶ ☐ if Form 2220 is attached. See page 3 of instructions.) ▶ $ _____		
34 OVERPAYMENT (subtract line 31 from line 32)	34	–
35 Enter amount of line 34 you want: **Credited to 1980 estimated tax** ▶ _____ Refunded ▶	35	–

Under penalties of perjury, I declare that I have examined this return, including accompanying schedules and statements, and to the best of my knowledge and belief, it is true, correct, and complete. Declaration of preparer (other than taxpayer) is based on all information of which preparer has any knowledge.

Department of the Treasury
Internal Revenue Service

U.S. Corporation Income Tax Return

For calendar year 1979 or other taxable year beginning
1979, ending .... 19 ....

1979

Check if a—	Use IRS label. Otherwise please print or type.	Name **Ulysses Corporation**	D Employer identification number (see instruction W) **37-8625342**
A Consolidated return ☐			
B Personal Holding Co. ☐		Number and street **9100 South Green**	E Date incorporated **December 15, 1950**
C Business Code No. (See Page 8 of instructions)		City or town, State, and ZIP code **Dallas, Texas 75221**	F Enter total assets (see instruction X) $

Gross Income

1 (a) Gross receipts or sales $ 4,053,231 (b) Less returns and allowances $ None Balance ▶		1(c)	4,053,231
2 **Less:** Cost of goods sold (Schedule A) and/or operations (attach schedule)		2	2,386,571
3 Gross profit		3	1,666,660
4 Dividends (Schedule C)		4	5,000
5 Interest on obligations of the United States and U.S. instrumentalities		5	—
6 Other interest		6	96
7 Gross rents		7	488
8 Gross royalties		8	—
9 (a) Capital gain net income (attach separate Schedule D)		9(a)	46
(b) Net gain or (loss) from Form 4797, line 11, Part II (attach Form 4797)		9(b)	(8,112)
10 Other income (see instructions—attach schedule)		10	11,525
11 TOTAL income—Add lines 3 through 10		11	1,675,703

Deductions

12 Compensation of officers (Schedule E)		12	1,264
13 (a) Salaries and wages .... 13(b) Less WIN and jobs credit(s) .... Balance ▶		13(c)	—
14 Repairs (see instructions)		14	54,376
15 Bad debts (Schedule F if reserve method is used)		15	(95)
16 Rents		16	6,733
17 Taxes		17	141,019
18 Interest		18	3,106
19 Contributions (not over 5% of line 30 adjusted per instructions—attach schedule)		19	623
20 Amortization (attach schedule)		20	
21 Depreciation from Form 4562 (attach Form 4562) .... , less depreciation claimed in Schedule A and elsewhere on return .... , Balance ▶		21	88,998
22 Depletion		22	89,020
23 Advertising		23	
24 Pension, profit-sharing, etc. plans (see instructions) (enter number of plans ▶ ....)		24	16,896
25 Employee benefit programs (see instructions)		25	4,870
26 Other deductions (attach schedule)		26	507,003
27 TOTAL deductions—Add lines 12 through 26		27	913,813
28 Taxable income before net operating loss deduction and special deductions (subtract line 27 from line 11)		28	761,890
29 **Less:** (a) Net operating loss deduction (see instructions—attach schedule)	29(a)		
(b) Special deductions (Schedule I)	29(b)	29	5,000
30 Taxable income (subtract line 29 from line 28)		30	756,890

Tax

31 TOTAL TAX (Schedule J)		31	
32 Credits: (a) Overpayment from 1978 allowed as a credit			
(b) 1979 estimated tax payments			
(c) Less refund of 1979 estimated tax applied for on Form 4466 . ( )			
(d) Tax deposited: Form 7004 .... Form 7005 (attach) .... Total ▶			
(e) Credit from regulated investment companies (attach Form 2439)			
(f) Federal tax on special fuels and oils (attach Form 4136 or 4136-T)		32	
33 TAX DUE (subtract line 32 from line 31). See instruction G for depositary method of payment .		33	—
(Check ▶ ☐ if Form 2220 is attached. See page 3 of instructions.) ▶ $			
34 OVERPAYMENT (subtract line 31 from line 32)		34	—
35 Enter amount of line 34 you want: **Credited to 1980 estimated tax** ▶ .... Refunded ▶		35	—

Please Sign Here

Under penalties of perjury, I declare that I have examined this return, including accompanying schedules and statements, and to the best of my knowledge and belief, it is true, correct, and complete. Declaration of preparer (other than taxpayer) is based on all information of which preparer has any knowledge.

▶ .... Signature of officer .... Date .... ▶ Title

Paid Preparer's Information

Preparer's signature and date ▶	Check if self-employed ▶ ☐	Preparer's social security no.
Firm's name (or yours, if self-employed) and address ▶	E.I. No. ▶	
	ZIP code ▶	

Helen Corporation — Factor Information ($000)

Property — Average value of property, including rent expense × 8	
Illinois	$285,800
Payroll	
Illinois	$ 540
All other states	14
	$ 554

Achilles Corporation — Factor Information ($000)

Property — Average value of property, including rent expense × 8	
California	$ 1,042
Illinois	61,020
All other sources	74,521
	$136,583
Payroll	
California	$ 100
Illinois	14,662
All other states	16,312
	$ 31,074
Sales — By state of destination	
California	$ 19,475
Illinois	20,115
All other states	102,178
	$141,768

Paris Corporation — Factor Information ($000)

Property — Average value of property, including rent expense × 8	
California	$ 77,728
Illinois	10,760
All other states	1,033,372
	$1,121,860
Payroll	
California	$ 11,400
Illinois	4,100
All other states	96,235
	$ 111,735
Sales — By state of destination	
California	$ 118,250
Illinois	10,350
All other states	603,662
	$ 732,262

Ulysses Corporation — Factor Information ($000)

Property — Average value of property, including rent expense × 8	
California	$ 2,055
Illinois	133,706
All other states	845,069
	$ 980,830
Payroll	
California	$ 1,350
Illinois	30,615
All other states	70,170
	$ 102,135
Sales — By state of destination	
California	$ 134,345
Illinois	40,150
All other states	3,878,736
	$4,053,231

Helen Corporation And Its Combined Unitary Affiliates — Intercompany Transactions

	Amount	Received by	Paid by
Rent income	$ 350	Ulysses	Paris
Royalty income	50	Paris	Achilles
Other income	7,500	Ulysses	Paris
Details of Gains and Losses			
	Paris	Achilles	Ulysses
Basis of property sold	$ 500	$ 0	$13,000
Proceeds of sale	1,368	1.00	4,934
Gain/(Loss)	$ 868	$1.00	$(8,066)

Intercompany Dividends
Helen received $1,000 from Ulysses

1. Assume that all income is business income, except $14,027 interest income of Helen Corporation.
2. California receipts consist of sales of tangible property only.
3. Uysses Corporation has state modifications that increase its total taxable income $26,726.
4. The rent paid by Paris to Ulysses is reflected in the property factor of Paris.

Helen Corporation And Its Combined Unitary Affiliates —
Schedules of Intercompany Transactions ($000)

Purchaser	Seller		
	Paris Corporation	Achilles Corporation	Ulysses Corporation
Total Sales			
Paris Corporation	—	1,825	18,627
Achilles Corporation	25,075	—	—
Ulysses Corporation	12,029	—	—
Sales in California			
Paris Corporation	—	927	2,727
Achilles Corporation	6,721	—	—
Ulysses Corporation	2,079	—	—

Step I Preparation of the Combined Apportionment Formula

Complete the following schedule using the state factor information and the schedule of intercompany sales.

	Helen Corporation	Paris Corporation	Achilles Corporation	Ulysses Corporation	Combined
Property (owned or rented)					
California property	————	————	————	————	
Less: Intercompany rent		————			
Total property everywhere		————			————
California ratio	————	————	————	————	
Payroll					
California payroll	————	————	————	————	
Total payroll	————	————	————	————	
					————
California ratio	————	————	————	————	
Receipts					
California sales	————	————	————	————	
Less: Intercompany sales	————	————	————	————	
Net California sales	————	————	————	————	
Total receipts					
Sales					
Dividends					
Interest					
Rent					
Royalties					
Proceeds					
Other income	————	————	————	————	
Total					
Less: Intercompany sales					
Dividends					
Rent					
Royalties					
Other income	————	————	————	————	
Subtotal					
Less: Nonbusiness	————	————	————	————	————
California ratio	————	————	————	————	
Total average (÷ 3)					

Step II Combined Profit and Loss Statement

Complete the following schedule using the 1979 corporate tax returns and the schedules of intercompany transactions. To facilitate the computations, all amounts should be rounded to thousands of dollars.

	Helen Corporation	Paris Corporation	Achilles Corporation	Ulysses Corporation	Total before Eliminations	Eliminations	Combined
Sales	$	$	$	$	$	$	$
Cost of sales							
Gross profit							
Dividends							
Interest government							
Interest other							
Rents							
Royalties							
Net gain losses							
Other income							
Total income	$	$	$	$	$	$	$

	$	$	$	$	$	$
Compensation of officers						
Salaries and wages						
Repairs						
Bad debts						
Rents						
Taxes						
Interest						
Contributions						
Amortization						
Depreciation						
Depletion						
Advertising						
Pension and profit sharing						
Other employee benefits						
Other deductions						
Total deductions	$	$	$	$	$	$
Net income before state adjustments	$	$	$	$	$	$
Intercompany eliminations						

Step III Conversion of Net Income to Unitary Business Income Subject to Apportionment

	Helen Corporation	Paris Corporation	Achilles Corporation	Ulysses Corporation	Combined
Net income before state adjustment per Step II	$	$	$	$	$
Add					
Various state adjustments					
Deduct					
Effect on business income (nonapportionable)					
Combined unitary business income subject to apportionment					
X apportionment per cent computed in Step I					
Unitary income apportioned to California					
State tax @ 9 per cent					

1979
California Tax for
Helen Corporation and
its Combined Unitary
Affiliates

SOLUTION TO COMPREHENSIVE EXAMPLE OF COMBINED REPORT FOR HELEN CORPORATION AND ITS UNITARY AFFILIATES

Step I Preparation of the Combined Apportionment Formula

Complete the following schedule using the state factor information and the schedule of intercompany sales.

	Helen Corporation	Paris Corporation	Achilles Corporation	Ulysses Corporation	Combined
Property (owned or rented)					
California Property	0	77,728	1,042	2,055	
Less: Intercompany rent (350 × 8)		(2,800)			
Total property everywhere	285,800	1,119,060	136,583	980,830	2,522,273
California ratio	0	0.029707	0.000413	0.000814	
Payroll					
California payroll	0	11,400	100	1,350	
Total payroll	554	111,735	31,074	102,135	245,498
California ratio	0	0.046436	0.000407	0.005499	
Receipts					
California sales	0	118,250	19,475	134,345	
Less: Intercompany sales	0	8,800	927	2,727	
Net California sales	0	109,450	18,548	131,618	

Total Receipts					
Sales	0	732,262	141,768	4,053,231	
Dividends	1,000	483	1,000	5,000	
Interest	16,552	365		96	
Rent			120	488	
Royalties		150	109		
Proceeds		1,368	1	4,934	
Other income		2,576	3	11,525	
Total	17,552	737,204	143,001	4,075,274	
Less: Intercompany sales		(37,104)	(1,825)	(18,627)	
Dividends	(1,000)				
Rent				(350)	
Royalties			(50)		
Other income				(7,500)	
Subtotal	16,522	700,100	141,126	4,048,797	
Less:Nonbusiness	(14,027)				
	2,525	700,100	141,126	4,048,797	4,892,548
California ratio	0	0.022371	0.003791	0.026902	
Total	0	0.098514	0.004611	0.033215	
Average (÷3)	0	0.032838	0.001537	0.011072	

Step II Combined Profit and Loss Statement

Complete the following schedule using the 1979 corporate tax returns and the schedules of intercompany transactions. To facilitate the computations, all amounts should be rounded to thousands of dollars.

	Helen Corporation	Paris Corporation	Achilles Corporation	Ulysses Corporation	Total before Eliminations	Eliminations	Combined
Sales	$	$ 732,262	$ 141,768	$4,053,231	$4,927,261	$ 57,556	$4,869,705
Cost of Sales		543,732	101,361	2,386,571	3,031,664	$ 57,556	2,974,108
Gross profit		188,530	40,407	1,666,660	1,895,597		1,895,597
Dividends	1,000	483	1,000	5,000	7,483	1,000	6,483
Interest government							
Interest other	16,552	365		96	17,013		17,013
Rents			120	488	608	350	258
Royalties		150	109		259	50	209
Net gain losses		868	1	(8,066)	(7,197)		(7,197)
Other income		2,576	3	11,525	14,104	7,500	6,604
Total income	$ 17,552	$ 192,972	$ 41,640	$1,675,703	$1,927,867	$ 8,900	$1,918,967
Compensation of officers	$	$ 1,259	$ 439	$ 1,264	$ 2,962		$ 2,962
Salaries and wages	554	31,615	3,600		35,769		35,769
Repairs		33,588	5,776	54,376	93,740	350	93,390
Bad debts		1,105	558	(95)	1,568		1,568

Rents		5,047	983	6,733	12,763		12,763
Taxes	258	10,920	3,850	141,019	156,047		156,047
Interest	10,099	24,737	3	3,106	37,945	3,500	34,445
Contributions			2	623	625		625
Amortization		900	196		1,096		1,096
Depreciation		56,992	12,263	88,998	158,253		158,253
Depletion				89,020	89,020		89,020
Advertising		1,812	372		2,184		2,184
Pention and profit sharing		11,840	541	16,896	29,277		29,277
Other employee benefits		3,099	940	4,870	8,909		8,909
Other deductions	211	47,552	2,432	507,003	557,198	4,050	553,148
Total deductions	$ 11,122	$ 230,466	$ 31,955	$ 913,813	$1,187,356	$ 7,900	$1,179,456
Net income before state adjustments	$ 6,430	$ (37,494)	$ 9,685	$ 761,890	$ 740,511	$ 1,000	$ 739,511
	(1,000)	(50)	50	(7,850)		1,000	
		7,850					
Intercompany eliminations	5,430	(29,694)	9,735	754,040		1,000	739,511

Step III Conversion of Net Income to Unitary Business Income Subject to Apportionment

	Helen Corporation	Paris Corporation	Achilles Corporation	Ulysses Corporation	Combined
Net income before state adjustment per Step II	$5,430	$(29,694)	$9,735	$754,040	$739,511
Add					
Various state adjustments				26,726	26,726
Deduct					
Effect on business income (nonapportionable)	(14,027)				(14,027)
Combined unitary business income subject to apportionment					752,210
X apportionment per cent computed in Step I	0	0.032838	0.001537	0.011072	
Unitary income apportioned to California	0	24,701	1,156	8,328	
State tax @ 9 per cent	0	$ 2,223	$ 104	$ 750	$ 3,077

1979 California Tax for Helen Corporation and its Combined Unitary Affiliates

Multistate Tax Compact

Index

The Council of State Governments 1755 Massachusetts Avenue, N.W. Washington, D.C.   20036

ARTICLE I   PURPOSES

The purposes of this compact are to:

1. Facilitate proper determination of State and local tax of multi-state taxpayers, including the equitable apportionment of tax bases and settlement of apportionment disputes.
2. Promote uniformity or compatibility in significant components of tax systems.
3. Facilitate taxpayer convenience and compliance in the filing of tax returns and in other phases of tax administration.
4. Avoid duplicative taxation.

ARTICLE II   DEFINITIONS

As used in this compact:

1. "State" means a State of the United States, the District of Columbia, the Commonwealth of Puerto Rico, or any Territory or Possession of the United States.
2. "Subdivision" means any governmental unit or special district of a State.
3. "Taxpayer" means any corporation, partnership, firm, association, governmental unit or agency or person acting as a business entity in more than one State.
4. "Income tax" means a tax imposed on or measured by net income including any tax imposed on or measured by an amount arrived at by deducting expenses from gross income, one or more forms of which expenses are not specifically and directly related to particular transactions.
5. "Capital stock tax" means a tax measured in any way by the capital of a corporation considered in its entirety.
6. "Gross receipts tax" means a tax, other than a sales tax, which is imposed on or measured by the gross volume of business, in terms of gross receipts or in other terms, and in the determination of which no deduction is allowed which would constitute the tax an income tax.
7. "Sales tax" means a tax imposed with respect to the transfer for a consideration of ownership, possession or custody of tangible personal property or the rendering of services measured by the price of the tangible personal property transferred or services rendered and which is required by State or local law to be separately stated from the sales price by the seller, or which is customarily separately stated from the sales price, but does not include a tax imposed exclusively on the sale

of a specifically identified commodity or article or class of commodities or articles.

8. ''Use tax'' means a nonrecurring tax, other than a sales tax, which (a) is imposed on or with respect to the exercise or enjoyment of any right or power over tangible personal property incident to the owner-ship, possession or custody or that property or the leasing of that property from another including any consumption, keeping, retention, or other use of tangible personal property and (b) is complementary to a sales tax.

9. ''Tax'' means an income tax, capital stock tax, gross receipts tax, sales tax, use tax, and any other tax which has a multistate impact, except that the provisions of Articles III, IV, and V of this compact shall apply only to the taxes specifically designated therein and the provi-sions of Article IX of this compact shall apply only in respect to determinations pursuant to Article IV.

ARTICLE III   ELEMENTS OF INCOME TAX LAWS

Taxpayer Option, State and Local Taxes

1. Any taxpayer subject to an income tax whose income is subject to apportionment and allocation for tax purposes pursuant to the laws of a party State or pursuant to the laws of subdivisions in two or more party States may elect to apportion and allocate his income in the manner provided by the laws of such State or by the laws of such States and subdivisions without reference to this compact, or may elect to appor-tion and allocate in accordance with Article IV. This election for any tax year may be made in all party States or subdivisions thereof or in any one or more of the party States or subdivisions thereof without reference to the election made in the others. For the purposes of this paragraph, taxes imposed by subdivisions shall be considered sepa-rately from State taxes and the apportionment and allocation also may be applied to the entire tax base. In no instance wherein Article IV is employed for all subdivisions of a State may the sum of all apportion-ments and allocations to subdivisions within a State be greater than the apportionment and allocation that would be assignable to that State if the apportionment or allocation were being made with respect to a State income tax.

Taxpayer Option, Short Form

2. Each party State or any subdivision thereof which imposes an income tax shall provide by law that any taxpayer required to file a return, whose only activities within the taxing jurisdiction consist of sales and

do not include owning or renting real estate or tangible personal property, and whose dollar volume of gross sales made during the tax year within the State or subdivision, as the case may be, is not in excess of $100,000 may elect to report and pay any tax due on the basis of a percentage of such volume, and shall adopt rates which shall produce a tax which reasonably approximates the tax otherwise due. The Multistate Tax Commission, not more than once in five years, may adjust the $100,000 figure in order to reflect such changes as may occur in the real value of the dollar, and such adjusted figure, upon adoption by the Commission, shall replace the $100,000 figure specifically provided herein. Each party State and subdivision thereof may make the same election available to taxpayers additional to those specified in this paragraph.

Coverage

3. Nothing in this Article relates to the reporting or payment of any tax other than an income tax.

ARTICLE IV   DIVISION OF INCOME

1. As used in this Article, unless the context otherwise requires:
   (a) "Business income" means income arising from transactions and activity in the regular course of the taxpayer's trade or business and includes income from tangible and intangible property if the acquisition, management, and disposition of the property constitute integral parts of the taxpayer's regular trade or business operations.
   (b) "Commercial domicile" means the principal place from which the trade or business of the taxpayer is directed or managed.
   (c) "Compensation" means wages, salaries, commissions and any other form of remuneration paid to employees for personal services.
   (d) "Financial organization" means any bank, trust company, savings bank, industrial bank, land bank, safe deposit company, private banker, savings and loan association, credit union, cooperative bank, small loan company, sales finance company, investment company, or any type of insurance company.
   (e) "Nonbusiness income" means all income other than business income.
   (f) "Public utility" means any business entity (1) which owns or operates any plant, equipment, property, franchise, or license for the transmission of communications, transportation of goods or persons, except by pipe line, or the production, transmission,

sale, delivery, or furnishing of electricity, water or steam; and (2) whose rates of charges for goods or services have been established or approved by a Federal, State, or local government or governmental agency.

(g) "Sales" means all gross receipts of the taxpayer not allocated under paragraphs of this Article.

(h) "State" means any State of the United States, the District of Columbia, the Commonwealth of Puerto Rico, any Territory or Possession of the United States, and any foreign country or political subdivision thereof.

(i) "This State" means the State in which the relevant tax return is filed or, in the case of application of this Article to the apportionment and allocation of income for local tax purposes, the subdivision or local taxing district in which the relevant tax return is filed.

2. Any taxpayer having income from business activity which is taxable both within and without this State, other than activity as a financial organization or public utility or the rendering of purely personal services by an individual, shall allocate and apportion his net income as provided in this Article. If a taxpayer has income from business activity as a public utility but derives the greater percentage of his income from activities subject to this Article, the taxpayer may elect to allocate and apportion his entire net income as provided in this Article.

3. For purposes of allocation and apportionment of income under this Article, a taxpayer is taxable in another State if (1) in that State he is subject to a net income tax, a franchise tax measured by net income, a franchise tax for the privilege of doing business, or a corporate stock tax, or (2) that State has jurisdiction to subject the taxpayer to a net income tax regardless of whether, in fact, the State does or does not.

4. Rents and royalties from real or tangible personal property, capital gains, interest, dividends or patent or copyright royalties, to the extent that they constitute nonbusiness income, shall be allocated as provided in paragraphs 5 through 8 of this Article.

5. (a) Net rents and royalties from real property located in this State are allocable to this State.

(b) Net rents and royalties from tangible personal property are allocable to this State: (1) if and to the extent that the property is utilized in this State, or (2) in their entirety if the taxpayer's commercial domicile is in this State and the taxpayer is not organized under the laws of or taxable in the State in which the property is utilized.

(c) The extent of utilization of tangible personal property in a State is determined by multiplying the rents and royalties by a fraction, the numerator of which is the number of days of physical location of the property in the State during the rental or royalty period in the taxable year and the denominator of which is the number of days of physical location of the property everywhere during all rental or royalty periods in the taxable year. If the physical location of the property during the rental or royalty period is unknown or unascertainable by the taxpayer, tangible personal property is utilized in the State in which the property was located at the time the rental or royalty payer obtained possession.

6. (a) Capital gains and losses from sales of real property located in this State are allocable to this State.

   (b) Capital gains and losses from sales of tangible personal property are allocable to this State if (1) the property had a situs in this State at the time of the sale, or (2) the taxpayer's commercial domicile is in this State and the taxpayer is not taxable in the State in which the property had a situs.

   (c) Capital gains and losses from sales of intangible personal property are allocable to this State if the taxpayer's commercial domicile is in this State.

7. Interest and dividends are allocable to this State if the taxpayer's commercial domicile is in this State.

8. (a) Patent and copyright royalties are allocable to this State: (1) if and to the extent that the patent or copyright is utilized by the payer in this State, or (2) if and to the extent that the patent copyright is utilized by the payer in a State in which the taxpayer is not taxable and the taxpayer's commercial domicile is in this State.

   (b) A patent is utilized in a State to the extent that it is employed in production, fabrication, manufacturing, or other processing in the State or to the extent that a patented product is produced in this State. If the basis of receipts from patent royalties does not permit allocation to States or if the accounting procedures do not reflect States of utilization, the patent is utilized in the State in which the taxpayer's commercial domicile is located.

   (c) A copyright is utilized in a State to the extent that printing or other publication originates in the State. If the basis of receipts from copyright royalties does not permit allocation to States or if the accounting procedures do not reflect States of utilization, the copyright is utilized in the State in which the taxpayer's commercial domicile is located.

9. All business income shall be apportioned to this State by multiplying the income by a frction, the numerator of which is the property factor

plus the payroll factor pus the sales factor, and the denominator of which is three.

10. The property factor is a fraction, the numerator of which is the average value of the taxpayer's real and tangible personal property owned or rented and used in this State during the tax period and the denominator of which is the average value of all the taxpayer's real and tangible personal property owned or rented and used during the tax period.

11. Property owned by the taxpayer is valued at its original cost. Property rented by the taxpayer is valued at eight times the net annual rental rate. Net annual rental rate is the annual rental rate paid by the taxpayer less any annual rental rate received by the taxpayer from subrentals.

12. The average value of property shall be determined by averaging the values at the beginning and ending of the tax period but the tax administrator may require the averaging of monthly values during the tax period if reasonably required to reflect properly the average value of the taxpayer's property.

13. The payroll factor is a fraction, the numerator of which is the total amount paid in this State during the tax period by the taxpayer for compensation and the denominator of which is the total compensation paid everywhere during the tax period.

14. Compensation is paid in this State if:
    (a) the individual's service is performed entirely within the State;
    (b) the individual's service is performed both within and without the State, but the service performed without the State is incidental to the individual's service within the State; or
    (c) some of the service is performed in the State and (1) the base of operations or, if there is no base of operations, the place from which the service is directed or controlled is in the State, or (2) the base of operations or the place from which the service is directed or controlled is not in any State in which some part of the service is performed, but the individual's residence is in this State.

15. The sales factor is a fraction, the numerator of which is the total sales of the taxpayer in this State during the tax period, and the denominator of which is the total sales of the taxpayer everywhere during the tax period.

16. Sales of tangible personal property are in this State if:
    (a) the property is delivered or shipped to a purchaser, other than the United States Government, within this State regardless of the f.o.b. point or other conditions of the sale; or
    (b) the property is shipped from an office, store, warehouse, factory, or other place of storage in the State and (1) the purchaser is the

United States Government or (2) the taxpayer is not taxable in the State of the purchaser.

17. Sales, other than sales of tangible personal property, are in this State if:
    (a) the income-producing activity is performed in this State: or
    (b) the income-producing activity is performed both in and outside this State and a greater proportion of the income-producing activity is performed in this State than in any other State, based on costs of performance.

18. If the allocation and apportionment provisions of this Article do not fairly represent the extent of the taxpayer's business activity in this State, the taxpayer may petition for or the tax administrator may require, in respect to all or any part of the taxpayer's business activity, if reasonable:
    (a) separate accounting;
    (b) the exclusion of any one or more of the factors;
    (c) the inclusion of one or more additional factors which will fairly represent the taxpayer's business activity in this State; or
    (d) the employment of any other method to effectuate an equitable allocation and apportionment of the taxpayer's income.

ARTICLE V   ELEMENTS OF SALES AND USE TAX LAWS

Tax Credit

1. Each purchaser liable for a use tax on tangible personal property shall be entitled to full credit for the combined amount or amounts of legally imposed sales or use taxes paid by him with respect to the same property to another State and any subdivision thereof. The credit shall be applied first against the amount of any use tax due the State, and any unused portion of the credit shall then be applied against the amount of any use tax due a subdivision.

Exemption Certificates, Vendors May Rely

2. Whenever a vendor receives and accepts in good faith from a purchaser a resale or other exemption certificate or other written evidence of exemption authorized by the appropriate State or subdivision taxing authority, the vendor shall be relieved of liability for a sales or use tax with respect to the transaction.

ARTICLE VI   THE COMMISSION

Organization and Management

1. (a)   The Multistate Tax Commission is hereby established. It shall be composed of one "member" from each party State who shall be the head of the State agency charged with the administration of the types of taxes to which this compact applies. If there is more than one such agency the State shall provide by law for the selection of the Commission member from the heads of the relevant agencies. State law may provide that a member of the Commission be represented by an alternate but only if there is on file with the Commission written notification of the designation and identity of the alternate. The Attorney General of each party State or his designee, or other counsel if the laws of the party State specifically provide, shall be entitled to attend the meetings of the Commission, but shall not vote. Such Attorneys General, designees, or other counsel shall receive all notices of meetings required under paragraph 1(e) of this Article.

   (b)   Each party State shall provide by law for the selection of representatives from its subdivisions affected by this compact to consult with the Commission member from that State.

   (c)   Each member shall be entitled to one vote. The Commission shall not act unless a majority of the members are present, and no action shall be binding unless approved by a majority of the total number of members.

   (d)   The Commission shall adopt an official seal to be used as it may provide.

   (e)   The Commission shall hold an annual meeting and such other regular meetings as its bylaws may provide and such special meetings as its Executive Committee may determine. The Commission bylaws shall specify the dates of the annual and any other regular meetings, and shall provide for the giving of notice of annual, regular and special meetings. Notices of special meetings shall include the reasons therefor and an agenda of the items to be considered.

   (f)   The Commission shall elect annually, from among its members, a Chairman, a Vice Chairman and a Treasurer. The Commission shall appoint an Executive Director who shall serve at its pleasure, and it shall fix his duties and compensation. The Executive Director shall be Secretary of the Commission. The Commission shall make provision for the bonding of such of its officers and employees as it may deem appropriate.

   (g)   Irrespective of the civil service, personnel or other merit system laws of any party state, the Executive Director shall appoint or

discharge such personnel as may be necessary for the performance of the functions of the Commission and shall fix their
duties and compensation. The Commission bylaws shall provide
for personnel policies and programs.

(h) The Commission may borrow, accept or contract for the services
of personnel from any State, the United States, or any other
governmental entity.

(i) The Commission may accept for any of its purposes and functions
any and all donations and grants of money, equipment, supplies,
materials and services, conditional or otherwise, from any governmental entity, and may utilize and dispose of the same.

(j) The Commission may establish one or more offices for the transacting of its business.

(k) The Commission shall adopt bylaws for the conduct of its business. The Commission shall publish its bylaws in convenient form,
and shall file a copy of the bylaws and any amendments thereto
with the appropriate agency or officer in each of the party States.

(l) The Commission annually shall make to the Governor and legislature of each party State a report covering its activities for the
preceding year. Any donation or grant accepted by the Commission or services borrowed shall be reported in the annual report of
the Commission, and shall include the nature, amount and conditions, if any, of the donation, gift, grant or services borrowed and
the identity of the donor or lender. The Commission may make
additional reports as it may deem desirable.

Committees

2. (a) To assist in the conduct of its business when the full Commission
is not meeting, the Commission shall have an Executive Committee of seven members, including the Chairman, Vice Chairman,
Treasurer and four other members elected annually by the Commission. The Executive Committee, subject to the provisions of
this compact and consistent with the policies of the Commission,
shall function as provided in the bylaws of the Commission.

(b) The Commission may establish advisory and technical committees, membership on which may include private persons and
public officials, in furthering any of its activities. Such committees
may consider any matter of concern to the Commission, including
problems of special interest to any party State and problems
dealing with particular types of taxes.

(c) The Commission may establish such additional committees as its
bylaws may provide.

Powers

3. In addition to powers conferred elsewhere in this compact, the Commission shall have power to:
    (a) Study State and local tax systems and particular types of State and local taxes.
    (b) Develop and recommend proposals for an increase in uniformity or compatibility of State and local tax laws with a view toward encouraging the simplification and improvement of State and local tax law and administration.
    (c) Compile and publish information as in its judgment would assist the party States in implementation of the compact and taxpayers in complying with State and local tax laws.
    (d) Do all things necessary and incidental to the administration of its functions pursuant to this compact.

Finance

4. (a) The Commission shall submit to the Governor or designated officer or officers of each party State a budget of its estimated expenditures for such period as may be required by the laws of that State for presentation to the legislature thereof.
    (b) Each of the Commission's budgets of estimated expenditures shall contain specific recommendations of the amounts to be appropriated by each of the party States. The total amount of appropriations requested under any such budget shall be apportioned among the party States as follows: one-tenth in equal shares; and the remainder in proportion to the amount of revenue collected by each party State and its subdivisions from income taxes, capital stock taxes, gross receipts taxes, sales and use taxes. In determining such amounts, the Commission shall employ such available public sources of information as, in its judgment, present the most equitable and accurate comparisons among the party States. Each of the Commission's budgets of estimated expenditures and requests for appropriations shall indicate the sources used in obtaining information employed in applying the formula contained in this paragraph.
    (c) The Commission shall not pledge the credit of any party State. The Commission may meet any of its obligations in whole or in part with funds available to it under paragraph (1)(i) of this Article: provided that the Commission takes specific action setting aside such funds prior to incurring any obligation to be met in whole or in part in such manner. Except where the Commission makes use of funds available to it under paragraph 1(i), the

Commission shall not incur any obligation prior to the allotment of
funds by the party States adequate to meet the same.

(d) The Commission shall keep accurate accounts of all receipts and
disbursements. The receipts and disbursements of the Commission shall be subject to the audit and accounting procedures
established under its bylaws. All receipts and disbursements of
funds handled by the Commission shall be audited yearly by a
certified or licensed public accountant and the report of the audit
shall be included in and become part of the annual report of the
Commission.

(e) The accounts of the Commission shall be open at any reasonable
time for inspection by duly constituted officers of the party States
and by any persons authorized by the Commission.

(f) Nothing contained in this Article shall be construed to prevent
Commission compliance with laws relating to audit or inspection
of accounts by or on behalf of any government contributing to the
support of the Commission.

ARTICLE VII   UNIFORM REGULATIONS AND FORMS

1. Whenever any two or more party States, or subdivisions of party
States, have uniform or similar provisions of law relating to an income
tax, the Commission may adopt uniform regulations for any phase of
the administration of such law, including assertion of jurisdiction to
tax, or prescribing uniform tax forms. The Commission may also act
with respect to the provisions of Article IV of this compact.

2. Prior to the adoption of any regulation, the Commission shall:

(a) As provided in its bylaws, hold at least one public hearing on due
notice to all affected party States and subdivisions thereof and to
all taxpayers and other persons who have made timely request of
the Commission for advance notice of its regulation-making proceedings.

(b) Afford all affected party States and subdivisions and interested
persons an opportunity to submit relevant written data and views,
which shall be considered fully by the Commission.

3. The Commission shall submit any regulations adopted by it to the
appropriate officials of all party States and subdivisions to which they
might apply. Each such State and subdivision shall consider any such
regulation for adoption in accordance with its own laws and procedures.

ARTICLE VIII   INTERSTATE AUDITS

1. This Article shall be in force only in those party States that specifically provide therefor by statute.

2. Any party State or subdivision thereof desiring to make or participate in an audit of any accounts, books, papers, records or other documents may request the Commission to perform the audit on its behalf. In responding to the request, the Commission shall have access to and may examine, at any reasonable time, such accounts, books, papers, records, and other documents and any relevant property or stock of merchandise. The Commission may enter into agreements with party States or their subdivisions for assistance in performance of the audit. The Commission shall make charges, to be paid by the State or local government or governments for which it performs the service, for any audits performed by it in order to reimburse itself for the actual costs incurred in making the audit.

3. The Commission may require the attendance of any person within the State where it is conducting an audit or part thereof at a time and place fixed by it within such State for the purpose of giving testimony with respect to any account, book, paper, document, other record, property or stock of merchandise being examined in connection with the audit. If the person is not within the jurisdiction, he may be required to attend for such purpose at any time and place fixed by the Commission within the State of which he is a resident: provided that such State has adopted this Article.

4. The Commission may apply to any court having power to issue compulsory process for orders in aid of its powers and responsibilities pursuant to this Article and any and all such courts shall have jurisdiction to issue such orders. Failure of any person to obey any such order shall be punishable as contempt of the issuing court. If the party or subject matter on account of which the Commission seeks an order is within the jurisdiction of the court to which application is made, such application may be to a court in the State or subdivision on behalf of which the audit is being made or a court in the State in which the object of the order being sought is situated. The provisions of this paragraph apply only to courts in a State that has adopted this Article.

5. The Commission may decline to perform any audit requested if it finds that its available personnel or other resources are insufficient for the purpose or that, in the terms requested, the audit is impracticable of satisfactory performance. If the Commission, on the basis of its experience, has reason to believe that an audit of a particular taxpayer, either at a particular time or on a particular schedule, would be of interest to a number of party States or their subdivisions, it may offer to make the

audit or audits, the offer to be contingent on sufficient participation therein as determined by the Commission.

6. Information obtained by any audit pursuant to this Article shall be confidential and available only for tax purposes to party States, their subdivisions or the United States. Availability of information shall be in accordance with the laws of the States or subdivisions on whose account the Commission performs the audit, and only through the appropriate agencies or officers of such States or subdivisions. Nothing in this Article shall be construed to require any taxpayer to keep records for any period not otherwise required by law.

7. Other arrangements made or authorized pursuant to law for cooperative audit by or on behalf of the party States or any of their subdivisions are not superseded or invalidated by this Article.

8. In no event shall the Commission make any charge against a taxpayer for an audit.

9. As used in this Article, "tax," in addition to the meaning ascribed to it in Article II, means any tax or license fee imposed in whole or in part for revenue purposes.

ARTICLE IX   ARBITRATION

1. Whenever the Commission finds a need for settling disputes concerning apportionments and allocations by arbitration, it may adopt a regulation placing this Article in effect, notwithstanding the provisions of Article VII.

2. The Commission shall select and maintain an Arbitration Panel composed of officers and employees of State and local governments and private persons who shall be knowledgeable and experienced in matters of tax law and administration.

3. Whenever a taxpayer who has elected to employ Article IV, or whenever the laws of the party State or subdivision thereof are substantially identical with the relevant provisions of Article IV, the taxpayer, by written notice to the Commission and to each party State or subdivision thereof that would be affected, may secure arbitration of an apportionment or allocation, if he is dissatisfied with the final administrative determination of the tax agency of the State or subdivision with respect thereto on the ground that it would subject him to double or multiple taxation by two or more party States or subdivisions thereof. Each party State and subdivision thereof hereby consents to the arbitration as provided herein, and agrees to be bound thereby.

4. The Arbitration Board shall be composed of one person selected by the taxpayer, one by the agency or agencies involved, and one member of the Commission's Arbitration Panel. If the agencies involved are

unable to agree on the person to be selected by them, such person shall be selected by lot from the total membership of the Arbitration Panel. The two persons selected for the Board in the manner provided by the foregoing provisions of this paragraph shall jointly select the third member of the Board. If they are unable to agree on the selection, the third member shall be selected by lot from among the total membership of the Arbitration Panel. No member of a Board selected by lot shall be qualified to serve if he is an officer of employee or is otherwise affiliated with any party to the arbitration proceeding. Residence within the jurisdiction of a party to the arbitration proceeding shall not constitute affiliation within the meaning of this paragraph.

5. The Board may sit in any State or subdivision party to the proceeding, in the State of the taxpayer's incorporation, residence or domicile, in any State where the taxpayer does business, or in any place that it finds most appropriate for gaining access to evidence relevant to the matter before it.

6. The Board shall give due notice of the times and places of its hearings. The parties shall be entitled to be heard, to present evidence, and to examine and cross-examine witnesses. The Board shall act by majority vote.

7. The Board shall have power to administer oaths, take testimony, subpoena and require the attendance of witnesses and the production of accounts, books, papers, records, and other documents, and issue commissions to take testimony. Subpoenas may be signed by any member of the Board. In case of failure to obey a subpoena, and upon application by the Board, any judge of a court of competent jurisdiction of the State in which the Board is sitting or in which the person to whom the subpoena is directed may be found may make an order requiring compliance with the subpoena, and the court may punish failure to obey the order as a contempt. The provisions of this paragraph apply only in States that have adopted this Article.

8. Unless the parties otherwise agree the expenses and other costs of the arbitration shall be assessed and allocated among the parties by the Board in such manner as it may determine. The Commission shall fix a schedule of compensation for members of Arbitration Boards and of other allowable expenses and costs. No officer or employee of a State or local government who serves as a member of a Board shall be entitled to compensation therefor unless he is required on account of his service to forego the regular compensation attaching to his public employment, but any such Board member shall be entitled to expenses.

9. The Board shall determine the disputed apportionment or allocation and any matters necessary thereto. The determinations of the Board shall be final for purposes of making the apportionment or allocation, but for no other purpose.

10. The Board shall file with the Commission and with each tax agency represented in the proceeding: the determination of the Board; the Board's written statement of its reasons therefor; the record of the Board's proceedings; and any other documents required by the arbitration rules of the Commission to be filed.

11. The Commission shall publish the determinations of Boards together with the statements of the reasons therefor.

12. The Commission shall adopt and publish rules of procedure and practice and shall file a copy of such rules and of any amendment thereto with the appropriate agency or officer in each of the party States.

13. Nothing contained herin shall prevent at any time a written compromise of any matter of matters in dispute, if otherwise lawful, by the parties to the arbitration proceeding.

ARTICLE X   ENTRY INTO FORCE AND WITHDRAWAL

1. This compact shall enter into force when enacted into law by any seven States. Thereafter, this compact shall become effective as to any other State upon its enactment thereof. The Commission shall arrange for notification of all party States whenever there is a new enactment of the compact.

2. Any party State may withdraw from this compact by enacting a statute repealing the same. No withdrawal shall affect any liability already incurred by or chargeable to a party State prior to the time of such withdrawal.

3. No proceeding commenced before an Arbitration Board prior to the withdrawal of a State and to which the withdrawing State or any subdivision thereof is a party shall be discontinued or terminated by the withdrawal, nor shall the Board thereby lose jurisdiction over any of the parties to the proceeding necessary to make a binding determination therein.

ARTICLE XI   EFFECT ON OTHER LAWS AND JURISDICTION

Nothing in this compact shall be construed to:

(a) Affect the power of any State or subdivision thereof to fix rates of taxation, except that a party State shall be obligated to implement Article III 2 of this compact.

(b) Apply to any tax or fixed fee imposed for the registration of a motor vehicle or any tax on motor fuel, other than a sales tax: provided that the definition of "tax" in Article VIII 9 may apply for the purposes of that Article and the Commission's powers of study and recommendation pursuant to Article VI 3 may apply.

(c)   Withdraw or limit the jurisdiction of any State or local court or administrative officer of body with respect to any person, corporation or other entity or subject matter, except to the extent that such jurisdiction is expressly conferred by or pursuant to this compact upon another agency or body.

(d)   Supersede or limit the jurisdiction of any court of the United States.

ARTICLE XII   CONSTRUCTION AND SEVERABILITY

This compact shall be liberally construed so as to effectuate the purposes thereof. The provisions of this compact shall be severable and if any phrase, clause, sentence or provision of this compact is declared to be contrary to the constitution of any State or of the United States or the applicability thereof to any government, agency, person, or circumstance is held invalid, the validity of the remainder of this compact and the applicability thereof to any government, agency, person or circumstance shall not be affected thereby. If this compact shall be held contrary to the constitution of any State participating therein, the compact shall remain in full force and effect as to the remaining party States and in full force and effect as to the State affected as to all severable matters.

Report of Special Subcommittee on State Taxation Administrative Interpretation of Nexus Standards

In order to determine the interpretation given the statutes and case law by States themselves, the Subcommittee submitted a questionnaire to capital stock tax administrators. The questionnaire, which may be found in Appendix F was a modified version of the Income Tax Nexus Questionnaire which had previously been sent to the administrators of State income tax programs. Like the Income Tax Nexus Questionnaire, it was designed to determine whether activities such as maintenance of an office, storage of goods, solicitation of orders, and various kinds of employee activities are considered sufficient to create liability.

Since five States[1] impose capital stock taxes in the form of an alternative or additional base to their income taxes, the Capital Stock Tax Nexus Questionnaire was not sent to these States. Instead, their answers to the income tax questionnaire were treated as equally applicable to the capital stock tax. Also excluded from the coverage of the questionnaire were eight States[2] which impose capital stock taxes (as distinguished from flat fees or property bases) only on domestic corporations. Thus, the group consisted of a total of twenty-four States, all of which impose capital stock taxes on foreign corporations.[3]

The questionnaire was mailed in October, 1964, and responses were received over the next few months. These responses fell into two groups.

---

[1]Connecticut, Massachusetts, New Jersey, New York, and Rhode Island.
[2]Colorado, District of Columbia, Delaware, Maine, Maryland, Nebraska, New Hampshire, and Oregon.
[3]Alabama, Arkansas, Florida, Georgia, Idaho, Illinois, Iowa, Kansas, Kentucky, Louisiana, Michigan, Mississippi, Missouri, New Mexico, North Carolina, Ohio, Oklahoma, Pennsylvania, South Carolina, Tennessee, Texas, Virginia, Washington, and West Virginia.

One group of capital stock tax administrators responded to the questions in detail by providing an answer to each of the questions presented. This involved making a determination as to the effect of each of the activities described. A second group of administrators gave a generalized response to the entire questionnaire, indicating that their practice was to impose the tax only on those corporations which qualify to do business in the State.

In addition to the above responses, the Subcommittee also received a response from Michigan which fell into neither group. The administrator found the questions to be unanswerable in "Yes" and "No" terms. As a result he provided a lengthy legal analysis.

The detailed responses to the Capital Stock Tax Nexus Questionnaire are presented in chart 30-A. (Appendix E) Also included in the chart are responses to identical questions asked in the Income Tax Nexus Questionnaire sent to States which impose a capital stock tax as an alternative to their income tax.

Several conclusions are suggested by a review of the chart. First, there is substantial diversity in the circumstances which are considered sufficient to make a corporation taxable. Second, numerous activities which would appear to represent extremely weak degrees of localization are considered to be an adequate basis for jurisdiction in at least some of the States. Thus, with respect to these two characteristics, the conclusions which can be drawn about nexus under capital stock taxes are like those drawn about income tax nexus.

In addition, a comparison of the results of the Capital Stock Tax Questionnaire with those of the Income Tax Nexus Questionnaire leads to a third conclusion. As generally interpreted by the administrators, the jurisdictional reach of the capital stock taxes extends as far as that of the direct income taxes. Since capital stock taxes are predominantly of the franchise type, this suggests that, at least in theory, administrators of franchise tax laws do not consider themselves to be limited by the rule in the *Spector* case.

Some typical patterns of response which illustrate the basis for the above conclusions are as follows:

In only one of the situations listed in the chart do the States unanimously impose the tax. This is with respect to the in-State solicitation of orders which are filled from a stock of goods stored in-State in a private warehouse. In each of the other situations listed in the chart there is diversity of varying degrees. Even if the corporation does no more in the State than solicit orders—an activity traditionally viewed as exclusively interstate[4]—there are two States which take the position that the corporation is subject to their franchise-type tax. When solicitation is coupled with some other relatively minor local activity, such as the use of company cars

---

[4]*Cheney Bros Co. v. Massachusetts* 246 U.S. 147 (1918).

by salesmen, the number of States asserting jurisdiction increases with the diversity of views likewise increasing.

It is clear that these interpretations by the administrators cannot be anticipated from a reading of the statutes and case law. For example, the Kentucky statute defines taxability in terms of "owning property or doing business in this state," the Texas statute also uses the term "doing business" but does not use the term "owning property." The statutes of both States are cast in franchise tax form. In Kentucky a corporation can send salesmen into the State to solicit orders and can also use its own vehicles in the State to deliver its products without being considered to be taxable. In Texas even the mere solicitation of orders creates liability regardless of whether the corporation owns any property in the State.

In a number of States, the tax administrators clearly make no attempt to determine jurisdiction on the basis of any pattern of activity within the State. In nine States[5] which responded to the Capital Stock Tax Nexus Questionnaire without answering the individual questions, the administrators explained that the question for them was simply whether the company has qualified. It appears that most of these States make no attempt to police the activities of foreign corporations for the sake of compelling compliance with the tax laws. Instead the taxes are enforced indirectly through collateral sanctions such as criminal penalties for unlicensed activities, civil penalties denying access to the State courts, or the denial of eligibility to bid on State contracts.

The administrative considerations which cause a State to rely on collateral sanctions as the means of enforcing a revenue measure may vary somewhat from State to State. Some administrators may feel that the amount of revenue involved for their State does not warrant an active enforcement program; others may feel that collateral sanctions are sufficiently effective to assure compliance.

CONCLUSIONS

An analysis of the statutes, decisional law, and administrative interpretations would lead to the conclusion that the problem of nexus with respect to capital stock taxes is as troublesome for interstate commerce as are income tax and sales tax nexus problems. However, because a fairly large number of capital stock taxes are not actively enforced and are imposed only on corporations which qualify to do business in the taxing State, the problem is less troublesome in practice.

[5]Florida, Georgia, Idaho, Illinois, Kansas, New Mexico, Virginia, Washington, and West Virginia.

This does not mean that there is no basis for concern about the nexus problems in this area. Indeed, if viewed in terms of the prescribed law there are three factors which can cause nexus problems as severe as those in other areas. First, the laws defining taxability are extremely vague—the statutes are indefinite, there are usually no administrative regulations, and the case law is unsettled. Second, State assertions of jurisdiction, as interpreted by administrators, are often as broad and indefinite with respect to capital stock taxes as they are with respect to direct net-income taxes. Third, questions of taxability under capital stock taxes are often inseparable from questions involving the ability to sue in State courts and the right to bid on State contracts.

For the company which actually encounters nexus problems in the capital stock tax area, the overall picture appears to be hopelessly confused. Although in many States the tax laws are not actively enforced, the corporation usually has no way of knowing which States have active programs and which States do not. If the corporation attempts to make an enlightened decision as to whether it will assume liability for a particular capital stock tax, it will usually find little or no published guidance. If the actual amount of liability is minimal and it is of consequence to the corporation to be able to bid on State contracts or sue in the State courts, it may be expedient to pay the tax. If, on the other hand, the amount of liability is significant and the nature of the corporation's business is such that the collateral penalties for noncompliance are inconsequential, it may be expedient for the corporation to resolve its doubts in favor of disregarding the tax. Thus, the structure of the capital stock tax system itself suggests that rules of expediency and convenience, more than rules of legal logic, will operate to determine the circumstances in which the taxes are paid.

Report of Special Subcommittee on State Taxation

NEXUS STANDARDS FOR CAPITAL STOCK TAXES ON FOREIGN CORPORATIONS

Contacts with Taxing States	AL	AR	CT	IA	KY	LA
Corporation qualified to do business in the state but has no other contact	X	X	3	X		X
Corporation not qualified to do business in the state but owns —						
Patents licensed to manufacturers in the state			3			
Accounts receivable from customers in the state			3			
Nonproductive realty in the state			3		X	
Income-producing realty in the state	X		3	X	X	
Sales obtained through independent contractors with offices accepting orders in the state on corporation's behalf and —						
No other activities		X				X
Corporation qualified to do business in the state	X	X	3	X		X
Goods in the state consigned to customers	X	X			X	X
"Missionary men" creating demand for products	X	X		X		X
Salesmen regularly soliciting orders in the state (without authority to accept unless otherwise indicated) and —						
No other activities		X				
Corporation qualified to do business in the state	X	X	X	X		X

MA	MS	MO	NJ	NY	NC	OH	OK	PA	RI	SC	TN	TX
3	X	X	3	3	X	X	X	X	3	X	X	X
3			3	3					3	X9		X
3			3	3					3			
3	X		3	3		X	X		3	X		
3	X	X	3	3	X	X	X		3	X	X	X
												X
3	X	X	3	3	X	X	X	X	3	X	X	X
X	X	X	X			X	X	X	X	X	X	X
							X			X9		X
												X
	X	X	X		X	X	X	X	X	X	X	X

Contacts with Taxing States	AL	AR	CT	IA	KY	LA
Telephone answering service in the state with local directory listing		X				
Stock of goods in the state from which goods are delivered in the state by common carrier						
In public warehouse	X	X		X	X	X
In private warehouse	X	X	X	X	X	X
Sales office in the state						
With orders accepted outside the state	X	X	X	X	X	
With orders accepted in the state	X	X	X	X	X	X
Salesmen residing in the state using homes for maintaining records only	X	X		X		
C.O.D. shipments into the state						
Regularly	X	X				
Occasionally	X	X				
Security interest regularly retained in goods sold	X	X		X		
Credit investigations and collections made by salesmen						
Regularly	X	X		X		X
Occasionally	X	X		4		X
Cars in the state owned by corporation and used by salesmen						
Regularly	X	X				X
Occasionally	X	X				X
Delivery of goods into state in company-operated vehicles						
Regularly	X	X		X		X
Occasionally	X	X		5		X
Installation or assembly of corporation's products by salesmen						
Regularly	X	X	X	X	X	X
Occasionally	X	X	X	6	X	X
Acceptance by orders in the state by salesmen						
Regularly	X	X		X		X
Occasionally	X	X		X		X
Servicing or repairing of corporation's products by its employees at no additional charge						
Regularly	X	X	X	X7		X
Occasionally	X	X	X	X7		X
Rarely		X		X7		

MA	MS	MO	NJ	NY	NC	OH	OK	PA	RI	SC	TN	TX
												X
	X	X	X	X	X	X	X	X	X	X	X	X
X	X	X	X	X	X	X	X	X	X	X	X	X
			X						X	X	X	X
X	X	X	X		X				X	X	X	X
												X
												X
												X
X	X						X			X		X
X		X	X		X				X	X		X
X		X	X		X				X	X10		X
										X		X
										X		X
							X					X
												X
X	X	X	X	X	X	X	X		X	X	X	X
X	X	X	X			X	X		X	X		X
X	X	X			X				X	X		X
X	X	X							X	X		X
X	X	X	X	X	X			X	X	X		X
X	X	X	X					8	X	X		X
	X	X								X		X

X—Indicates activity considered by the state to be sufficient to require the filing of a return.

1—Results do not apply if realty is leased to the corporation.

2—The administrator indicates that answers are based largely on considerations of legal theory and that in practice only qualified foreign corporations are taxed.

3—This question was not included in the questionnaire sent to the state.

4—The answer depends on the investigation being an isolated circumstance and completed within 30 days.

5—The answer depends on the delivery being an isolated circumstance.

6—The answer depends on the installation being an isolated circumstance.

7—Unless the transaction is an isolated circumstance and all service is completed within 30 days, a return is required.

8—A return is required if the service is not of a skilled nature.

9—The administrator indicates that the answer is qualified.

10—The administrator indicates some uncertainty as to the administrative practice.

Nexus Questionnaire—
Capital Stock Tax

The purpose of this questionnaire is to obtain information from state tax administrators with regard to two aspects of state capital stock taxes: First, the circumstances under which a foreign corporation would be liable to file a capital stock tax return with the state; and second, the circumstances under which a domestic or foreign corporation that is liable to file such a return would be allowed by the state to exclude a portion of its total capital stock from its taxable base.

INSTRUCTIONS

This questionnaire applies only to the following tax, and your answers should be solely in terms of that tax.

The questions that follow concern various types of contact that a hypothetical corporation might have with your state and one other state.

In each question it is to be assumed that the corporation's only contacts with the two states are those which are specified. Unless otherwise stated, it is to be assumed that the corporation has no contact whatsoever with any other state.

The facts described in the questions are not to be considered as cumulative. Rather, each question should be answered only on the basis of its own particular facts.

The question "is the corporation required to file a return" should be answered "Yes" only if you consider that the described contact with your state is sufficient to require the corporation to file a capital stock tax return with your state.

The question "can the corporation apportion its base" should be answered "Yes" only if you consider that the described contact with the other state is sufficient to permit the corporation to exclude a portion of its total capital stock in computing the base that is subject to the capital stock tax of your state.

In the event that you have difficulty in answering "Yes" or "No" to any question, please give the best answer you can and state whatever reservations you may have on a supplemental sheet of paper.

An extra copy of the questionnaire is enclosed for your convenience.

QUESTIONS

1. A corporation is not incorporated in your state. It is qualified to do business in your state, but has no other contact whatsoever with your state. Is the corporation required to file a return?

Yes _____ No _____

2. A corporation which is not incorporated in your state owns real property located in your state. The corporation is not qualified to do business in your state.

Is the corporation required to file a return—

(a) if the real property is income producing but is held for investment purposes and is not used in any trade or business conducted by the corporation?

Yes _____ No _____

(b) would your answer to part (a) of this question be different if the real property is not income producing?

Yes _____ No _____

(c) if the real property is used by the corporation exclusively in interstate commerce?

Yes _____ No _____

3. Assuming that the real property is rented to the corporation rather than owned by it, would any of the answers to questions 2(a)-(c) be different?

Yes _____ No _____

If your answer is "Yes," which ones?

4. A corporation which is not incorporated in your state has its place of business, including a factory, warehouse, and sales office, in another state. The corporation's only contact with your state is the ownership of a substantial amount of accounts receivable for goods sold to retail merchants located and doing business exclusively within your state. The sales were negotiated and accepted entirely within the other state, and the goods were delivered to the merchants f.o.b. the corporation's warehouse in the other state.

Is the corporation required to file a return?

Yes _____ No _____

5. A corporation is not incorporated in your state. Its only contact with your state is the ownership of a patented process which it licenses to another, and which the licensee uses in manufacturing within your state.
Is the corporation required to file a return?

Yes _____ No _____

6. If your answer to either question 4 or question 5 is "No," is this because the particular intangible property is not, under the rules of your state, deemed to be present in your state?

Yes _____ No _____

7. A corporation which is not incorporated in your state has its place of business, including a factory, warehouse, and sales office, in another state. Its employee-salesmen regularly solicit orders in your state. They do not use company cars and are not authorized to accept orders. The corporation ships goods into your state by mail or common carrier. Its only income is from the sale of its products.
Is the corporation required to file a return—

(a) if it conducts no other activities in your state?

Yes _____ No _____

(b) if the corporation is qualified to do business in your state?

Yes _____ No _____

(c) if the corporation's name is listed in a telephone directory in your state and it uses a local telephone answering service there?

Yes _____ No _____

(d) if the corporation fills orders to be delivered in your state by common carrier from a stock of goods maintained in a public warehouse in your state?

Yes _____ No _____

(e) if the corporation fills orders to be delivered in your state by common carrier from a stock of goods maintained in a private warehouse inyour state operated by the corporation?

Yes _____ No _____

(f) if the corporation maintains a sales office in your state with all orders subject to acceptance outside your state?

Yes _____ No _____

(g) if the corporation maintains a sales office in your state at which orders are accepted?

Yes _____ No _____

(h) if the employee-salesmen are residents of your state and maintain sales records and files in their homes, but do not use their homes as offices in any other respect?

Yes _____ No _____

(i) if goods are regularly shipped into your state c.o.d.?

Yes _____ No _____

(j) if goods are occasionally shipped into your state c.o.d.?

Yes _____ No _____

(k) if goods shipped to purchasers in your state are regularly sold subject to contracts of conditional sale or chattel mortgates?

Yes _____ No _____

(l) if the employee-salesmen regularly conduct credit investigations of customers and make collections in your state?

Yes _____ No _____

(m) if the employee-salesmen occasionally conduct credit investigations of customers and make collections in your state?

Yes _____ No _____

(n) if the employee-salesmen regularly use cars owned by the corporation?

Yes _____ No _____

(o) if the employee-salesmen occasionally use cars owned by the corporation?

Yes _____ No _____

(p) if the corporation regularly delivers goods into your state in company operated vehicles?

Yes _____ No _____

(q) if the corporation occasionally delivers goods into your state in company operated vehicles?

Yes _____ No _____

(r) if the corporation's employees regularly install or assemble its products in your state?

Yes _____ No _____

(s) if the corporation's employees occasionally install or assemble its products in your state?

Yes _____ No _____

(t) if the employee-salesmen regularly accept orders in your state?

Yes _____   No _____

(u) if the employee-salesmen occasionally accept orders in your state?

Yes _____   No _____

(v) if, as part of its sales agreements and without additional charge to its customers, the corporation's employees regularly service or repair its products in your state?

Yes _____   No _____

(w) if, as part of its sales agreements and without additional charge to its customers, the corporation's employees occasionally service or repair its products in your state?

Yes _____   No _____

(x) if, as part of its sales agreements and without charge to its customers, the corporation's employees in rare instances service or repair its products in your state?

Yes _____   No _____

8. A corporation which is not incorporated in your state has its place of business, including factory, warehouse, and sales office, in another state. It makes sales in your state through independent contractors who maintain offices in your state, and who accept orders in your state on behalf of the corporation. The corporation regularly ships goods into your state by mail or common carrier. The corporation's only income is from the sale of its products.

Is the corporation required to file a return—

Yes _____   No _____

(a) if it conducts no other activities in your state?

Yes _____   No _____

(b) if it is qualified to do business in your state?

Yes _____   No _____

(c) if it owns goods in your state on consignment to its customers?

Yes _____   No _____

(d) if the corporation sends into your state "missionary men" or "detail men" whose duties do not include the solicitation of orders, but are limited to creating a demand for the corporation's products?

Yes _____   No _____

9. A corporation which is not incorporated in your state owns real property located in another state. The corporation is not incorporated in the other state.

On the return which it files with your state, can the corporation apportion its base—

(a) if the real property is income producing but is held for investment purposes and is not used in any trade or business conducted by the corporation?

Yes _____ No _____

(b) would your answer to part (a) of this question be different if the real property is not income producing?

Yes _____ No _____

(c) if the real property is used by the corporation exclusively in interstate commerce?

Yes _____ No _____

10. Assuming that the real property is rented to the corporation rather than owned by it would any of the answers to question 9(a)-(c) be different?

Yes _____ No _____

If the answer is "Yes," which ones?

11. A corporation which is not incorporated in your state has its place of business including factory, warehouse and sales office in your state. The corporation owns a substantial amount of accounts receivable for goods sold to retail merchants located and doing business exclusively within another state. The sales were negotiated and accepted entirely within your state and the goods were delivered to the merchants f.o.b. the corporation's warehouse in your state. The corporation is not incorporated in the other state, and has no other contacts there.

On the return which it files with your State, can the corporation apportion its base?

Yes _____ No _____

12. A corporation is not incorporated in your state. It owns a patented process which it licenses to another, and which the licensee uses in manufacturing in another state. The corporation is not incorporated in the other state, and has no other contacts there.

On the return which it files with your state, can the corporation apportion its base?

Yes _____ No _____

13. If your answer to either question 11 or 12 is "No," is this because the particular intangible property is not under the rules of your state deemed to be present in the other state?

Yes _____ No _____

14. A corporation which is not incorporated in your state has its place of business, including a factory, warehouse, and sales office in your state. Its employee-salesmen regularly solicit orders in another state. They do not use company cars and are not authorized to accept orders. The corporation ships goods into the other state by mail or common carrier. Its only income is from the sales of its products.

On the return which it files with your state, can the corporation apportion its base—

(a) if it conducts no other activities in the other state?

Yes _____ No _____

(b) if the corporation is qualified to do business in the other state?

Yes _____ No _____

(c) if the corporation's name is listed in a telephone directory in the other state and it uses a local telephone answering there?

Yes _____ No _____

(d) if the corporation fills orders to be delivered in the other state by common carrier from a stock of goods maintained in a public warehouse in the other state?

Yes _____ No _____

(e) if the corporation fills orders to be delivered in the other state by common carrier from a stock of goods maintained in a private warehouse in the other state operated by the corporation?

Yes _____ No _____

(f) if the corporation maintains a sales office in the other state with all orders subject to acceptance outside the other state?

Yes _____ No _____

(g) if the corporation maintains a sales office in the other state at which orders are accepted?

Yes _____ No _____

(h) if the employee-salesmen are residents of the other state and maintain sales records and files in their homes, but do not use their homes as offices in any other respects?

Yes _____ No _____

(i) if goods are regularly shipped into the other state c.o.d.?

Yes _____ No _____

(j)   if goods are occasionally shipped into the other state c.o.d.?

Yes _____   No _____

(k)   if goods shipped to purchasers in the other state are regularly sold subject to contracts of conditional sale or chattel mortgages?

Yes _____   No _____

(l)   if the employee-salesmen regularly conduct credit investigations of customers and make collections in the other state?

Yes _____   No _____

(m) if the employee-salesmen occasionally conduct credit investigations of customers and make collections in the other state?

Yes _____   No _____

(n)   if the employee-salesmen regularly use cars owned by the corporation?

Yes _____   No _____

(o)   if the employee-salesmen occasionally use cars owned by the corporation?

Yes _____   No _____

(p)   if the corporation regularly delivers goods into the other state in company operated vehicles?

Yes _____   No _____

(q)   if the corporation occasionally delivers goods into the other state in company operated vehicles?

Yes _____   No _____

(r)   if the corporation's employees regularly install or assemble its products in the other state?

Yes _____   No _____

(s)   if the corporation's employees occasionally install or assemble its products in the other state?

Yes _____   No _____

(t)   if the employee-salesmen regularly accept orders in the other state?

Yes _____   No _____

(u)   if the employee-salesmen occasionally accept orders in the other state?

Yes _____   No _____

(v) if, as part of its sales agreements and without additional charge to its customers, the corporation's employees regularly service or repair its products in the other state?

Yes _____ No _____

(w) if, as part of its sales agreements and without additional charge to its customers, the corporation's employees occasionally service or repair its products in the other state?

Yes _____ No _____

(x) if, as part of its sales agreements and without charge to its customers, the corporation's employees in rare instances service or repair its products in the other state?

15. A corporation which is not incorporated in your state has its place of business, including factory, warehouse, and sales office in your state. It makes sales in another state through independent contractors who maintain offices in the other state, and who accept orders there on behalf of the corporation. The corporation regularly ships goods into the other state by mail or common carrier. The corporation is not incorporated in the other state. The corporation's only income is from the sale of its products.

On the return which it files with your state, can the corporation apportion its base—

(a) if it conducts no other activities in the other state?

Yes _____ No _____

(b) if it is qualified to do business in the other state?

Yes _____ No _____

(c) if it owns goods in the other state on consignment to its customers?

Yes _____ No _____

(d) if the corporation sends into the other state "missionary men" or "detail men" whose duties do not include the solicitation of orders, but are limited to creating a demand for the corporation's products?

Yes _____ No _____

16. Would any of the answers to questions 9 through 15 be different if the corporation *is* incorporated in your state?

Yes _____ No _____

If your answer to this question is "Yes", please indicate by an "X" in the appropriate column below whether the particular answers in question 9 through 15 would be the same or different.

Question Number	Answer Same	Answer Different
9 (a)	_____	_____
(b)	_____	_____
(c)	_____	_____
10	_____	_____
11	_____	_____
12	_____	_____
13	_____	_____
14 (a)	_____	_____
(b)	_____	_____
(c)	_____	_____
(d)	_____	_____
(e)	_____	_____
(f)	_____	_____
(g)	_____	_____
(h)	_____	_____
(i)	_____	_____
(j)	_____	_____
(k)	_____	_____
(l)	_____	_____
(m)	_____	_____
(n)	_____	_____
(o)	_____	_____
(p)	_____	_____
(q)	_____	_____
(r)	_____	_____
(s)	_____	_____
(t)	_____	_____
(u)	_____	_____
(v)	_____	_____
(w)	_____	_____
(x)	_____	_____
15 (a)	_____	_____
(b)	_____	_____
(c)	_____	_____
(d)	_____	_____

Charts and Tables

Table 35-6 Local Gross Receipts Tax Rates as of December 31, 1964
Twenty-two selected cities

Cities by State	Manufacturers	Wholesalers	Retailers
Alabama			
Birmingham	0.075%, $60 minimum	0.075% if over $100,000, $100 fixed fee[c]	Same
California			
Los Angeles	(a)	0.065% [65¢ per $1,000], $13 minimum	0.08% [80¢ per $1,000], $12 minimum
Florida			
Tampa	(a)	0.03% [30¢ per $1,000], $10 minimum	0.1% if over $3000 [$1 per $1,000], $10 fixed fee
Kentucky			
Convington	0.05%, $25 minimum	0.06%, $35 minimum	0.2%, $25 minimum
Lousiana			
New Orleans	(a)	0.025% to 0.1%, 21 brackets, $25 minimum, $6,000 maximum	0.08% to 0.2%, 26 brackets, $5 minimum, $6,000 maximum
Missouri			
Kansas City	0.085% [85¢ per $1,000]	0.1% [$1 per $1,000], $15 minimum	Same
St. Louis	0.175% [$1.75 per $1,000], $8.75 minimum	Same	Same
Nevada			
Las Vegas	(a)	0.056% to 0.25%. if below $2,400,000, 24 brackets, $40 minimum; 0.33% if over $2,400,000	Same
New Jersey			
Trenton	(a)	0.06% to 0.15%, 22 brackets, $5 minimum, 0.1% if over $1,000,000 [$10¢ per $1,0000]	Same
New Mexico			
Albuquerque	0.01%, $5 minimum	0.025%, $5 minimum	0.1%, $5 minimum
New York			
New York City	0.4% if over $10,000	Same	Same

	Rates vary with type of manufacturing activity		
North Carolina Charlotte		0.06% if over $50,000 [60¢ per $1,000], $75 fixed fee, $750 maximum	0.06% if over $5,000 [60¢ per $1,000], $15 fixed fee
Oregon Portland	0.14% if over $10,700, $15 fixed fee; if below $1,500, $2 fixed fee	Same	Same
Pennsylvania Philadelphia	0.3%	Same	Same
Pittsburgh	[a]	Not taxed	0.2%
South Carolina Columbia	0.05% [50¢ per $1,000], $50 minimum	Same	0.1% [$1 per $1,000], $20 minimum
Utah Provo	[a]	0.1% [$1 per $1,000], $12 minimum, $500 maximum	Same
Virginia Norfolk	0.0375% to 0.1%, 9 brackets, $50 minimum, $1,000 maximum	0.15%,[b] $50 fixed fee	0.35% if over $3,000, $35 fixed fee
Richmond	0.01% to 0.2%, 7 brackets, $20 minimum, $1,500 maximum	0.25%,[b] $30 fixed fee	0.38%, $30 fixed fee
Roanoke	[a]	0.33%,[b] $55 fixed fee	0.55%, $55 fixed fee
Washington Seattle	0.1%, $8 minimum	Same	Same
West Virginia Wheeling	0.19% [19¢ per $100], $5.50 minimum	0.09% [9¢ per $100], $5.50 minimum	0.23% [23¢ per $100], $5.50 minimum

Sources: (1) CCII State Tax Reporters; (2) correspondence with municipal leagues.

[a] Manufacturing activity generally does not appear to be taxed, although manufacturers may be taxed as wholesalers or retailers if they are not otherwise exempt.

[b] Based on cost of purchases.

[c] If gross receipts are less than $100,000 the tax is based on the value of stock, fixtures, and equipment.

[d] Alternative tax — 2 percent of net income over $750, plus $15 fixed fee.

[e] Alternative tax — 2 percent of sales, minus cost of goods and labor.

[f] Alternative tax — 3 percent of sales, minus cost of goods and labor.

Table 33-3 Rate Differentiation of Six Gross Receipts Taxes, 1964

	Number of Separate Rates	Range of Rates	Rates	Taxpayers or Taxable Event
Delaware	5	0.025% to 0.14%	$5 fixed fee, plus 0.025%	Manufacturers, processors
			$5 fixed fee, plus 0.14%	Retailers and wholesalers generally
			$10 fixed fee plus 0.14% merchandise cost	Branch stores, warehouses, and distributing depots of out-of-state businesses
			$5 fee credited against payment of 30¢ per $1,000 over $5,000	Certain produce dealers
			$200 fixed fee, plus 10¢ per $100	Vendors of damaged goods or goods of insolvents
Hawaii	3	0.5% to 3.5%	0.5%	Producers, manufacturers, wholesalers, blind persons
			1.5%	Insurance solicitors
			3.5%	All others
Indiana	2	0.5% to 2%	0.5%	Wholesale sales, retail merchants selling at retail, display advertising, dry cleaning and laundering, industrial processing or servicing for resellers
			2%	All others. Financial institutions, brokers, grain dealers, wholesale grocers
Mississippi	6	0.125% to 9%	0.125%	Wholesalers
			1%	Various sales to manufacturers and farmers
			2%	Contractors, retail sales of automobiles, aircraft, trucks, and truck-tractors
			3.5%	Retail sales, mining, miscellaneous service businesses, all others
			6%	Wholesale sales of illegal commodities
			9%	Retail sales of illegal commodities

State	No.	Rate range	Rate	Description
Washington	5	0.01% to 1%	0.01%	Wholesalers of wheat, oats, corn, and barley
			0.125%	Flour millers, seafood products manufacturers
			0.176%	Wholesale sales by manufacturer of cigarettes warehoused by him in the state
			0.44%	Extractors, manufacturers, wholesalers, retailers, printers and publishers, extractors and processors for hire, cold storage warehousemen, public road construction, certain insurance general agents
			1%	Services and other business activities
West Virginia	14	0.25% to 7.85%	0.25%	Wholesalers, processors of poultry and turkeys
			0.4%	Manufacturers
			0.5%	Retailers
			0.65%	Amusements
			1.05%	Industrial loan companies, small loan businesses, rentals or royalties from furnishing property for hire, services and miscellaneous businesses
			1.3%	Street, interurban, and electric railways
			1.35%	Coal producers
			2%	Timber producers, producers of quarried or mined limestone or sandstone
			2.6%	Contractors, miscellaneous public utilities, and natural resources producers
			3.9%	Natural gas companies, toll bridge companies, miscellaneous sales of electric light and power companies
			3.95%	Oil producers, blast furnace slag producers, producers of unquarried or mined sand, gravel, or other mineral products
			4%	Water companies
			5.2%	Electric light and power company sales for domestic purposes and commercial lighting
			7.85%	Producers of natural gas

Source: CCH State Tax Reporters

Table 33-2 Gross Receipts Tax Rates, Selected Years, 1934–1964

	Selected taxpayers	1934	1940	1950	1960	1964
Alaska	All[a]	Tax not in effect	Tax not in effect	$25 fee up to $20,000 0.5% on $20,000 to $100,000 0.25% over $100,000	No change	No change
Delaware	Manufacturers and processors	$5 fixed fee 0.02%	$5 fixed fee 0.025%	No change	No change	No change
	Retailers and wholesalers	$5 fixed fee 0.1% over $1,000	$5 fixed fee 0.1% over $5,000	$5 fixed fee 0.14%	No change	No change
	Branch stores, etc., of out-of-state businesses	$10 fixed fee 0.1% over $5,000	No change	$5 fixed fee 0.1% over $5,000	$10 fixed fee 0.14% over $5,000	No change
Hawaii	Manufacturers and producers	Tax not in effect	0.25%	1.5%	1%	0.5%
	Sugar and pineapple processors	Tax not in effect	1.25%	2.5%	No change	0.5%
	Wholesalers	Tax not in effect	0.25%	1%	1%	0.5%
Indiana	Wholesale sales	0.25%	No change	0.5%[b]	0.375%	0.5%
	Retail sales by "retailers"	1%	No change	0.625%[c]	0.375%	0.5%
	Retail sales by "nonretailers"	1%	No change	1.25%[b]	1.5%	2%

Louisiana	Wholesale merchants	$25 fee up to $50,000, with fees increasing to maximum of $6,000 over $10,000,000[d]	No change	No change	No change	No change
	Retail merchants	$5 fee up to $5,000, with fees increasing to $6,000 over $5,000,000[d]	No change	No change	No change	No change
Mississippi	Wholesale sales	0.195%	No change	No change	No change	No change
Washington	Extractors	0.3% to 1%	0.25%	No change	0.44%	No change
	Manufacturers	0.25%	No change	No change	0.44%	No change
	Wholesalers	0.2%	0.25%	No change	0.44%	No change
	Retailers	0.5%	0.25%	No change	0.44%	No change
	Producers of natural resources	1% to 6%	1.3% to 7.8%[e]	No change	1.35% to 7.85%	No change
West Virginia	Manufacturers	0.3%	0.39%[e]	No change	0.4%	No change
	Wholesalers	0.15%	0.195%[e]	No change	0.25%	No change
	Retailers	0.75%	0.5%	No change	No change	No change

Sources: (1) CCH State Tax Reporters; (2) Tax Research Foundation, Tax Systems of the World (5th ed., 1934), Tax Systems (8th ed., 1940); (3) State session laws.

[a]Except for banks, trust companies, and nonprofit electric and telephone membership cooperatives.
[b]Includes an additional 0.25% levied by the World War II Bonus Tax.
[c]Includes an additional 0.125% levied by the World War II Bonus Tax.
[d]Fees increase as range of gross receipts increases but are not progressive. Between the minimum and maximum fees the range of rates in percentages is 0.025% to 0.1% for wholesalers and 0.08% to 0.2% for retailers.
[e]Includes surtax of 30%.

Chart 34-A Nexus Standards for State Gross Receipts Taxes

Contacts with Taxing State	AK	IN	WA	WV
Sales obtained through independent contractors with offices accepting orders in the state on corporation's behalf				
Salesmen regularly soliciting orders in the state (without authority to accept unless otherwise indicated), goods being shipped into the state by mail or common carrier and —				
No other activities				
Collections made by salesmen			X	
Credit investigations made				
By salesmen				
By an independent contractor				
Acceptance of orders in the state by salesmen		X	X	
Salesmen residing in the state	X		X	
"Missionary men" creating demand for products				
Nonresident	X	X		
Office in the state	X	X		
Installation or assembly of corporation's products by its employees		1	X	X

Servicing or repairing of corporation's products at no additional charge				
By employees	X	X	X	
By employees out of office in the state	X	X	X	
By an independent contractor	X	X		
C.O.D. shipments into the state	X			
Delivery of goods into the state in company-operated vehicles	X	X	X	
Goods shipped in bulk, after orders are received, to a distributing facility in the state	X	X		
Security interest retained in goods sold				
Displaying goods at space leased occasionally and for short terms				
Goods in state consigned to customers				X
Stock of raw materials in the state used for the out-of-state manufacture of goods sent into the state	X			
Stock of goods in the state from which goods are delivered in the state by common carrier				
In public warehouse	X	X	X	
In private warehouse	X	X	X	
Sales office in the state				
With orders accepted outside the state	X	X		
With orders accepted in the state	X	X	X	
Goods sold from trucks with driver-salesmen	X	X	X	X

Source: State Gross Receipts Tax Questionnaire.

X — Indicates activity considered by the state to require the filing of a return.

1 — May or may not be sufficient, depending on specific circumstances.

Chart 34-B Includability of Receipts from Interstate Activities

Contacts with Taxing States	AK	IN	WA	WV
Sales obtained through independent contractors with offices accepting orders in the state on corporation's behalf				
Salesmen regularly soliciting orders in the state (without authority to accept unless otherwise indicated), goods being shipped into the state by mail or common carrier and —				
No other activities				
Collections made by salesmen		X	X	
Credit investigations made				
By salesmen	X			
By an independent contractor				
Acceptance of orders in the state by salesmen	X	X	X	
Salesmen residing in the state	X	1	X	
"Missionary men" creating demand for products				
Nonresident		X		
Resident	X	X		
Office in the state	X	X		
Installation or assembly of corporation's products by its employees	X	2	X	X
Servicing or repairing of corporation's products at no additional charge				
By employees	X	X	X	
By employees out of office in the state	X	X	X	
By an independent contractor	X	X		

Activity				
C.O.D. shipments into the state				
Delivery of goods into the state in company-operated vehicles				X
Goods shipped in bulk, after orders are received, to a distributing facility in the state			X	X
Security interest retained in goods sold				
Displaying goods at space leased occasionally and for short terms		X		X
Goods in state consigned to customers	X			
Stock of raw materials in the state used for the out-of-state manufacture of goods sent into the state				X
Stock of goods in the state from which goods are delivered in the state by common carrier				
In public warehouse	X	X	X	X
In private warehouse	X	X	X	X
Sales office in the state				
With orders accepted outside the state		X	X	X
With orders accepted in the state		X	X	X
Goods sold from trucks with driver-salesmen	X	X	X	X

Source: State Gross Receipts Tax Questionnaire.

X — Indicates activity considered by the state to require the filing of a return.

1 — May sometimes be sufficient.

2 — May or may not be sufficient, depending on specific circumstances.

Index